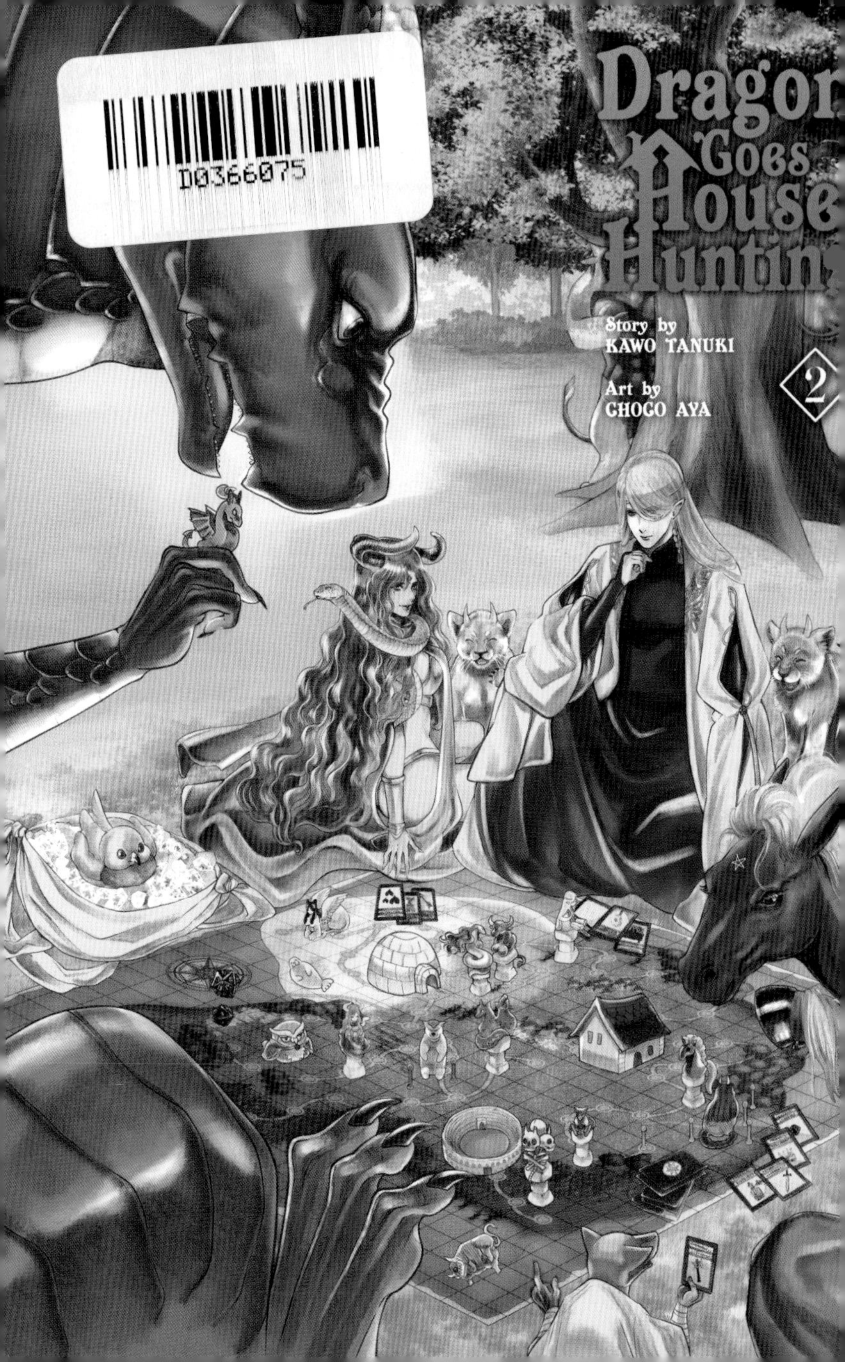
Dragon Goes House Hunting
Story by
KAWO TANUKI
Art by
CHOCO AYA
2

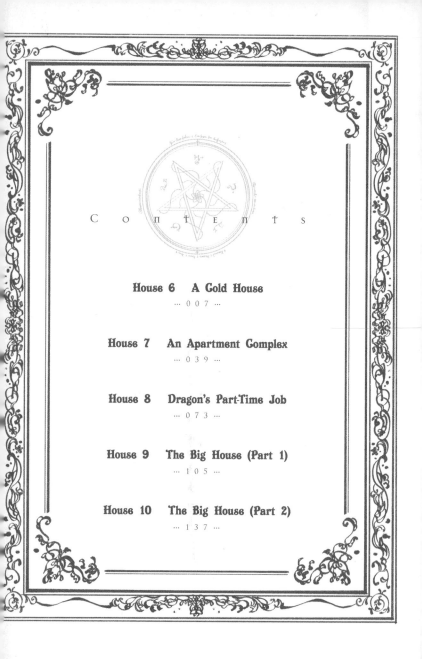

Contents

Dragon Goes House-Hunting

2

Story by
KAWO TANUKI

Art by
CHOCO AYA

STORY

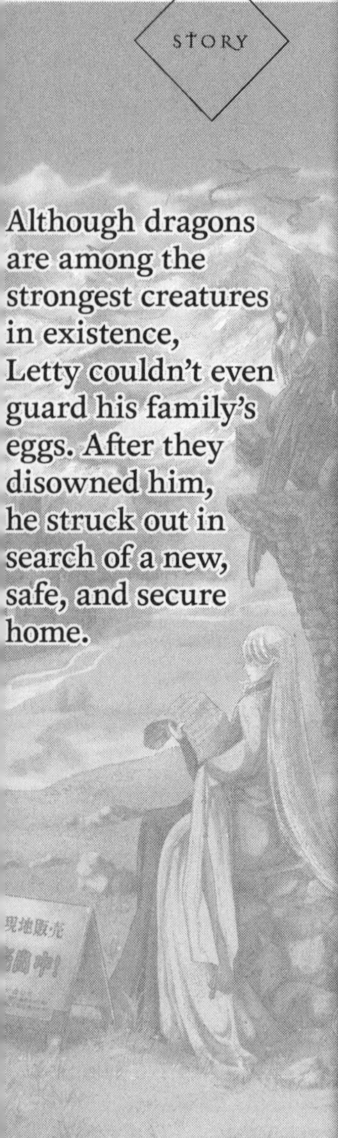

Although dragons are among the strongest creatures in existence, Letty couldn't even guard his family's eggs. After they disowned him, he struck out in search of a new, safe, and secure home.

CHARACTER

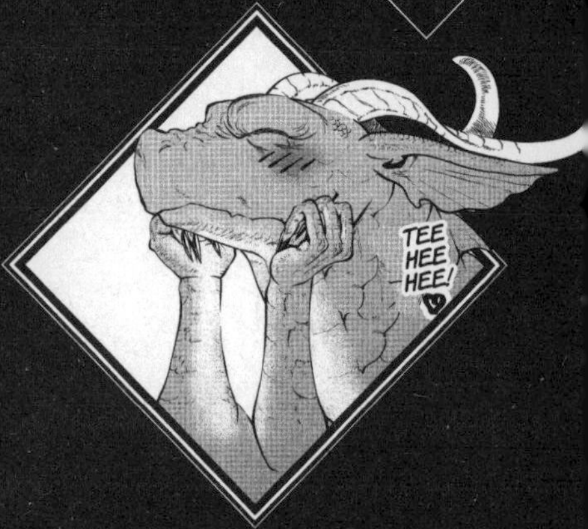
TEE HEE HEE!

Letty

A weak, cowardly dragon disowned by his family. In search of a dream home where even a weakling like him can live in peace and safety.

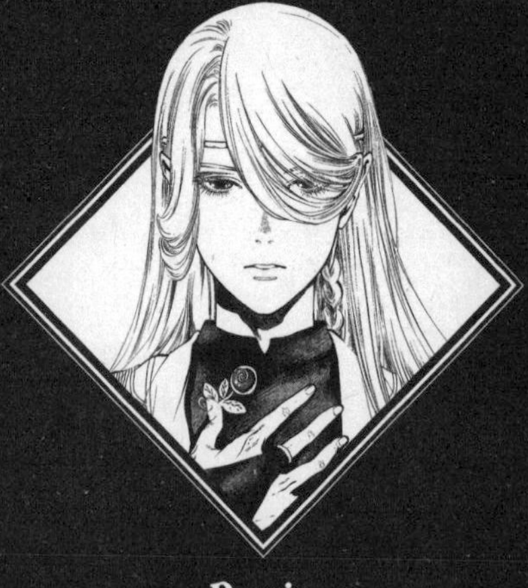

Dearia

A beautiful elven man who works in architecture and real estate. Saved Letty from the Yuusha and now helps him on his quest. Has a side gig as a demon lord.

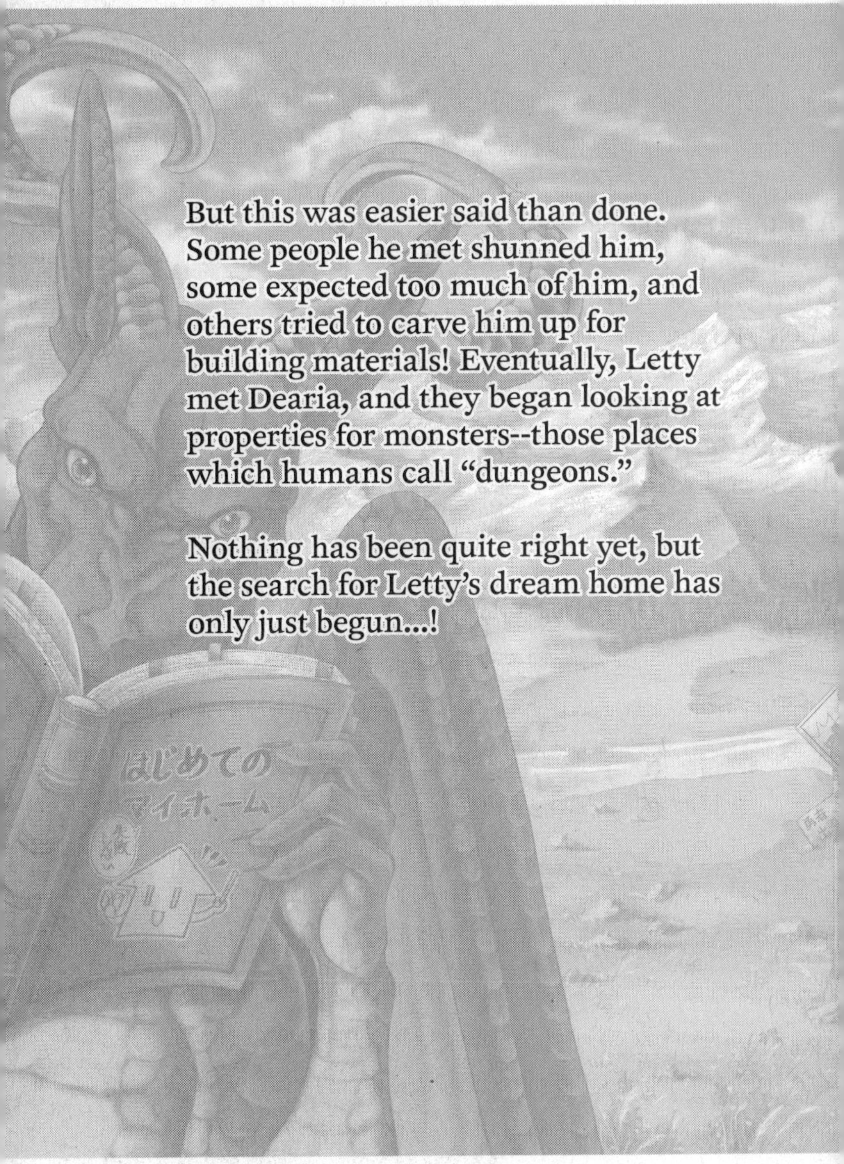
はじめての
マイホーム

But this was easier said than done. Some people he met shunned him, some expected too much of him, and others tried to carve him up for building materials! Eventually, Letty met Dearia, and they began looking at properties for monsters--those places which humans call "dungeons."

Nothing has been quite right yet, but the search for Letty's dream home has only just begun...!

Dragon Goes House-Hunting

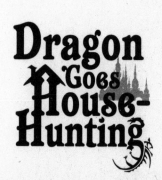

House 6: A Cold House

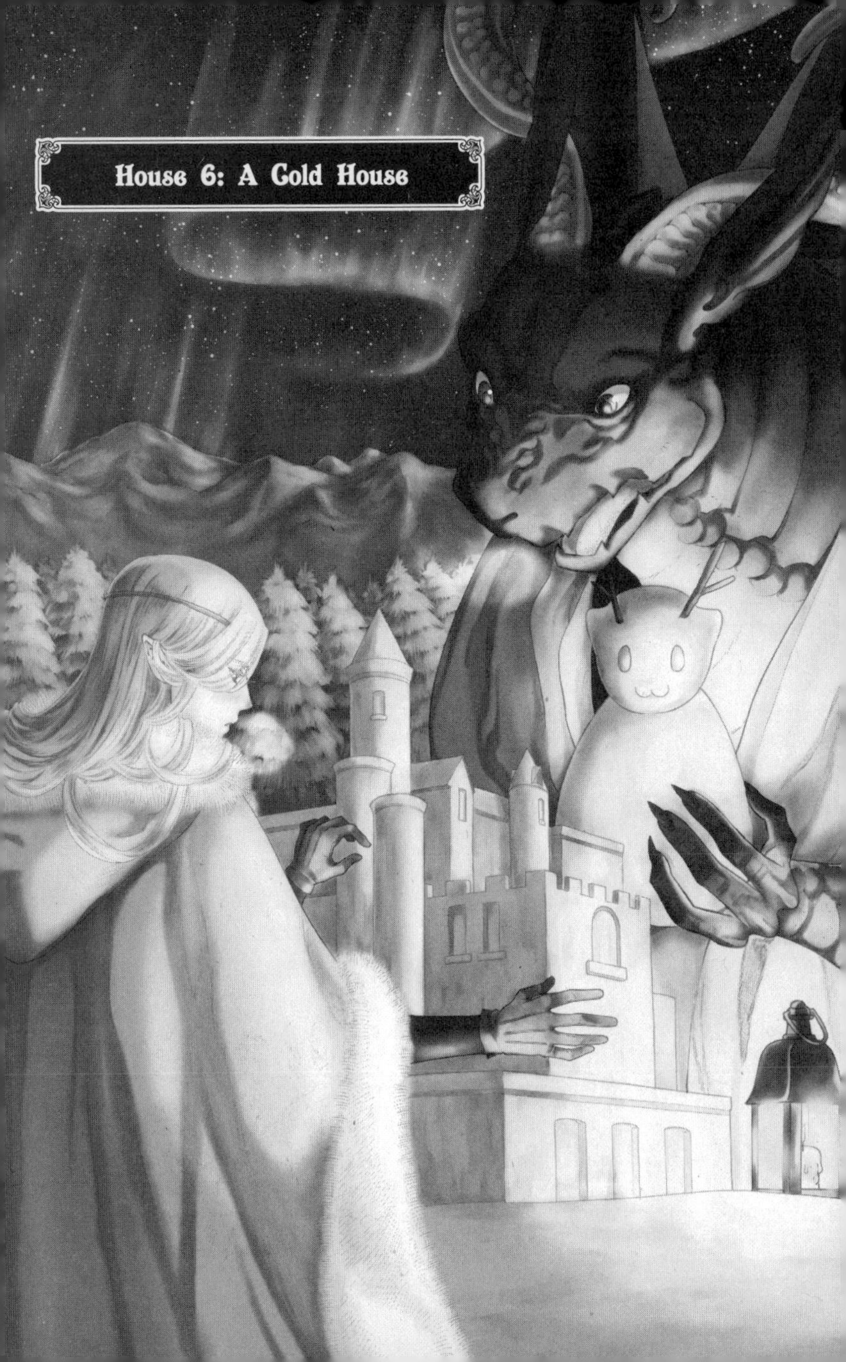

THIS IS THE RECEPTION HALL, AND THIS IS THE PARLOR...
OVER THERE ARE THE BACK STAIRS, AND IN THE BASEMENT IS THE EMPLOYEE HALL...
HE'S SO THOROUGH ...!

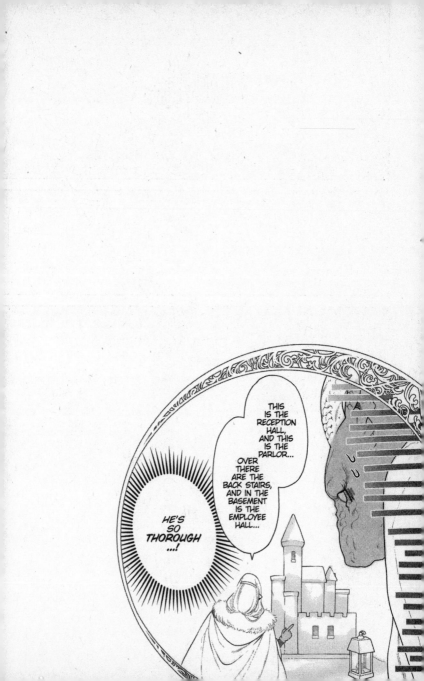

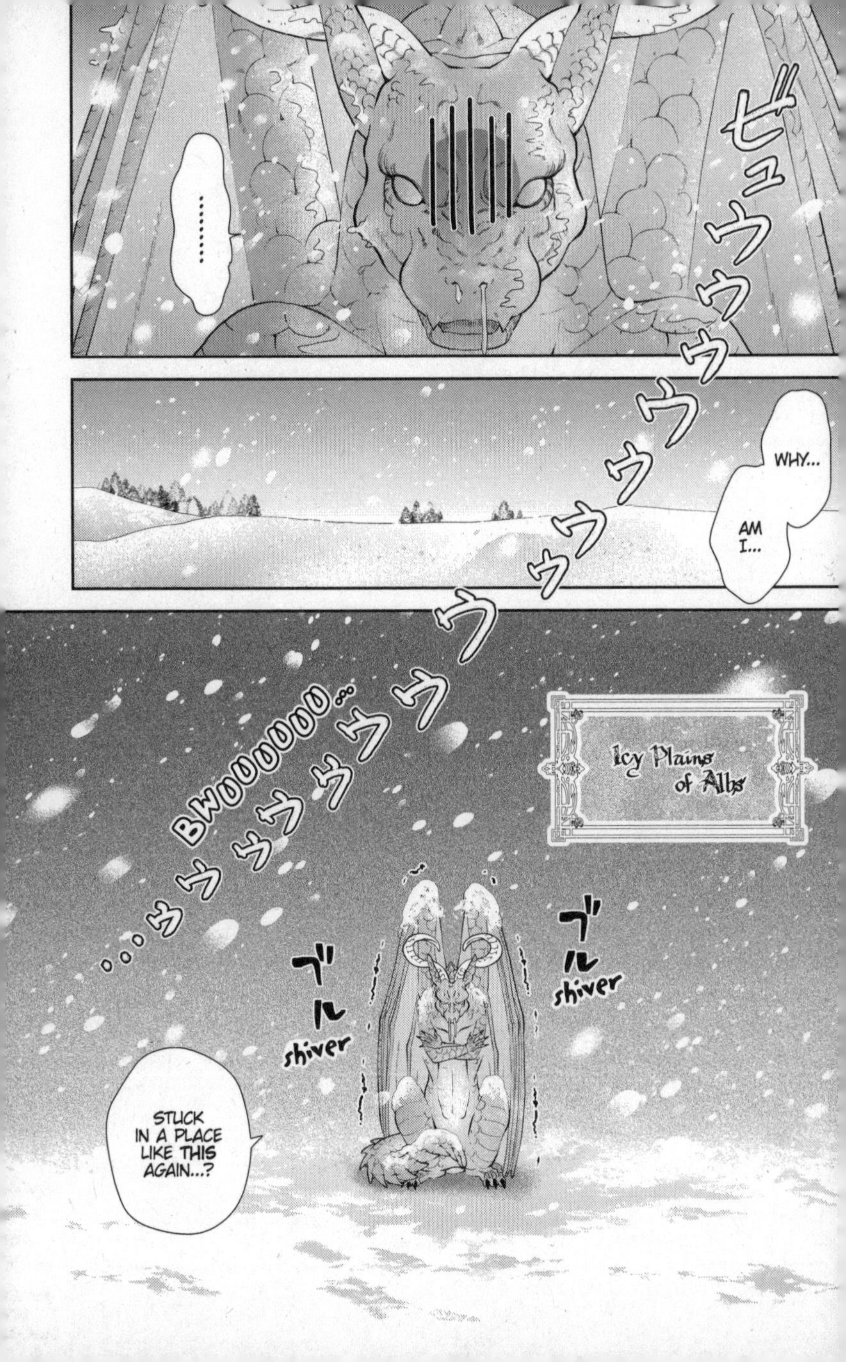
……
WHY... AM I...
ビュウウウウウウウウウウウウウウ…
Icy Plains of Albs
...BWOOOOOOO...
ブル shiver
ブル shiver
STUCK IN A PLACE LIKE THIS AGAIN...?

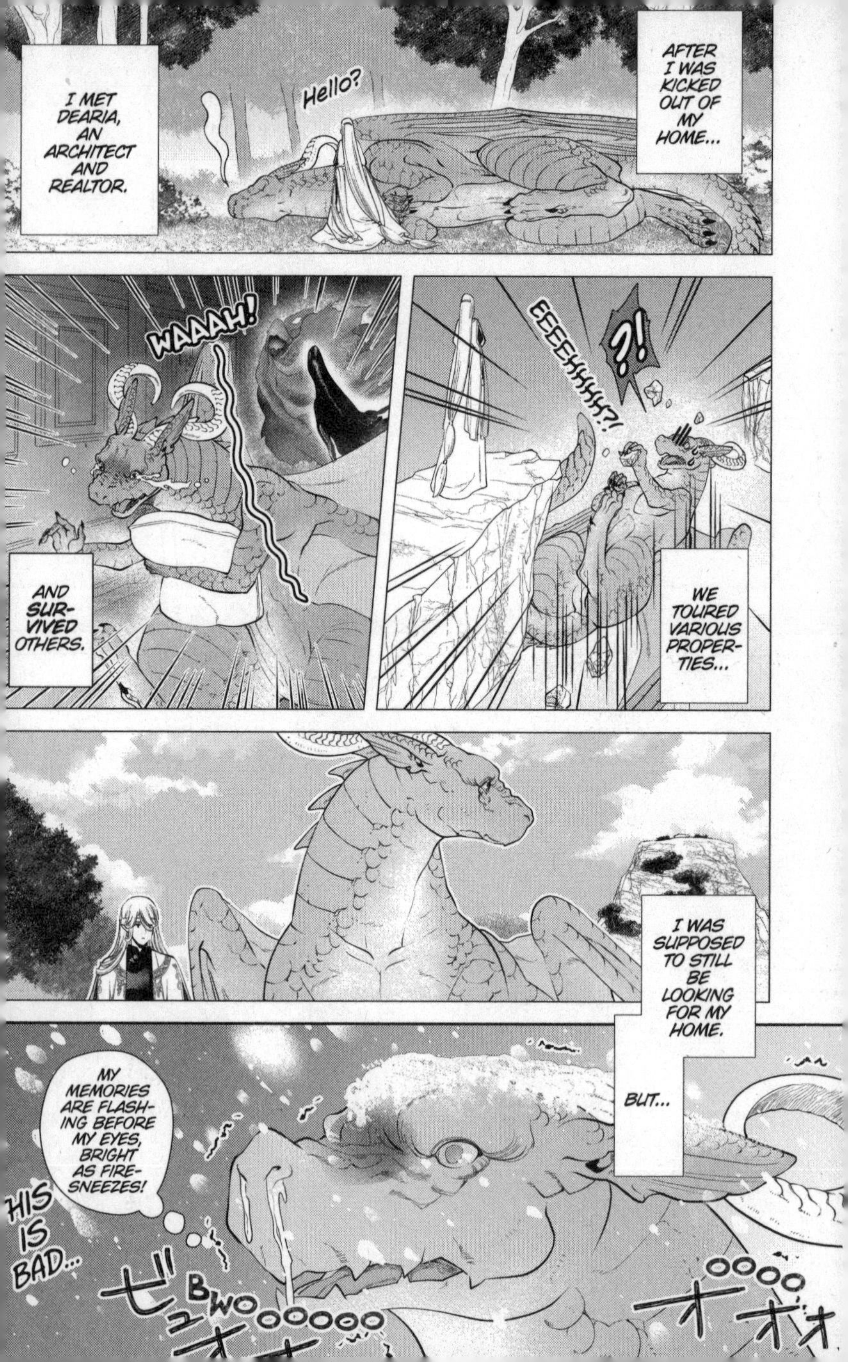
AFTER I WAS KICKED OUT OF MY HOME...
Hello?
I MET DEARIA, AN ARCHITECT AND REALTOR.
?!
EEEEHHHH?!
WE TOURED VARIOUS PROPERTIES...
WAAAH!
AND SURVIVED OTHERS.
I WAS SUPPOSED TO STILL BE LOOKING FOR MY HOME.
BUT...
MY MEMORIES ARE FLASHING BEFORE MY EYES, BRIGHT AS FIRE-SNEEZES!
HIS IS BAD...
BWOOOOOOOO
OOOOO

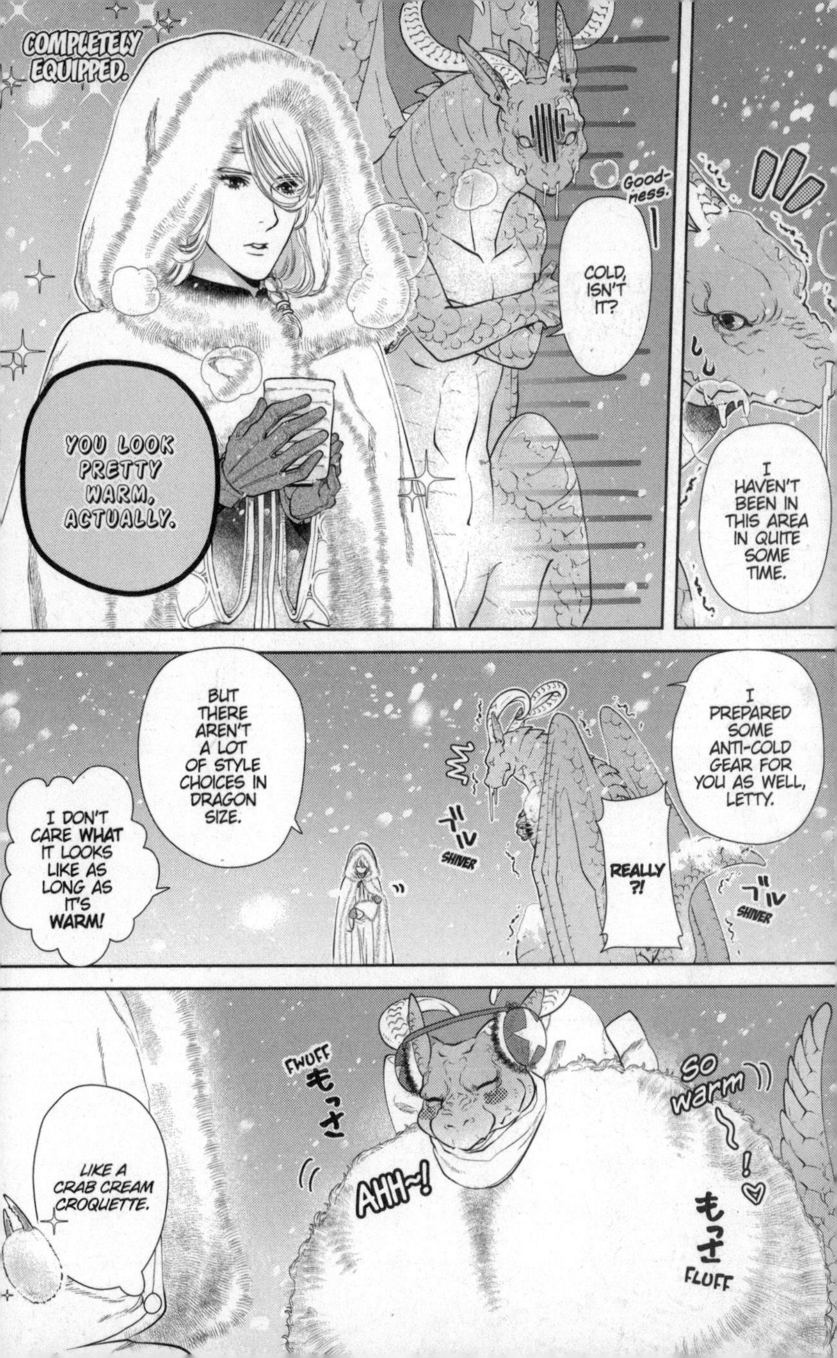
I HAVEN'T BEEN IN THIS AREA IN QUITE SOME TIME.
Good-ness.
COLD, ISN'T IT?
COMPLETELY EQUIPPED.
YOU LOOK PRETTY WARM, ACTUALLY.
I PREPARED SOME ANTI-COLD GEAR FOR YOU AS WELL, LETTY.
ブル SHIVER
REALLY?!
ブル SHIVER
BUT THERE AREN'T A LOT OF STYLE CHOICES IN DRAGON SIZE.
I DON'T CARE WHAT IT LOOKS LIKE AS LONG AS IT'S WARM!
So warm~!
もっさ FLUFF
AHH~!
FWUFF もっさ
LIKE A CRAB CREAM CROQUETTE.

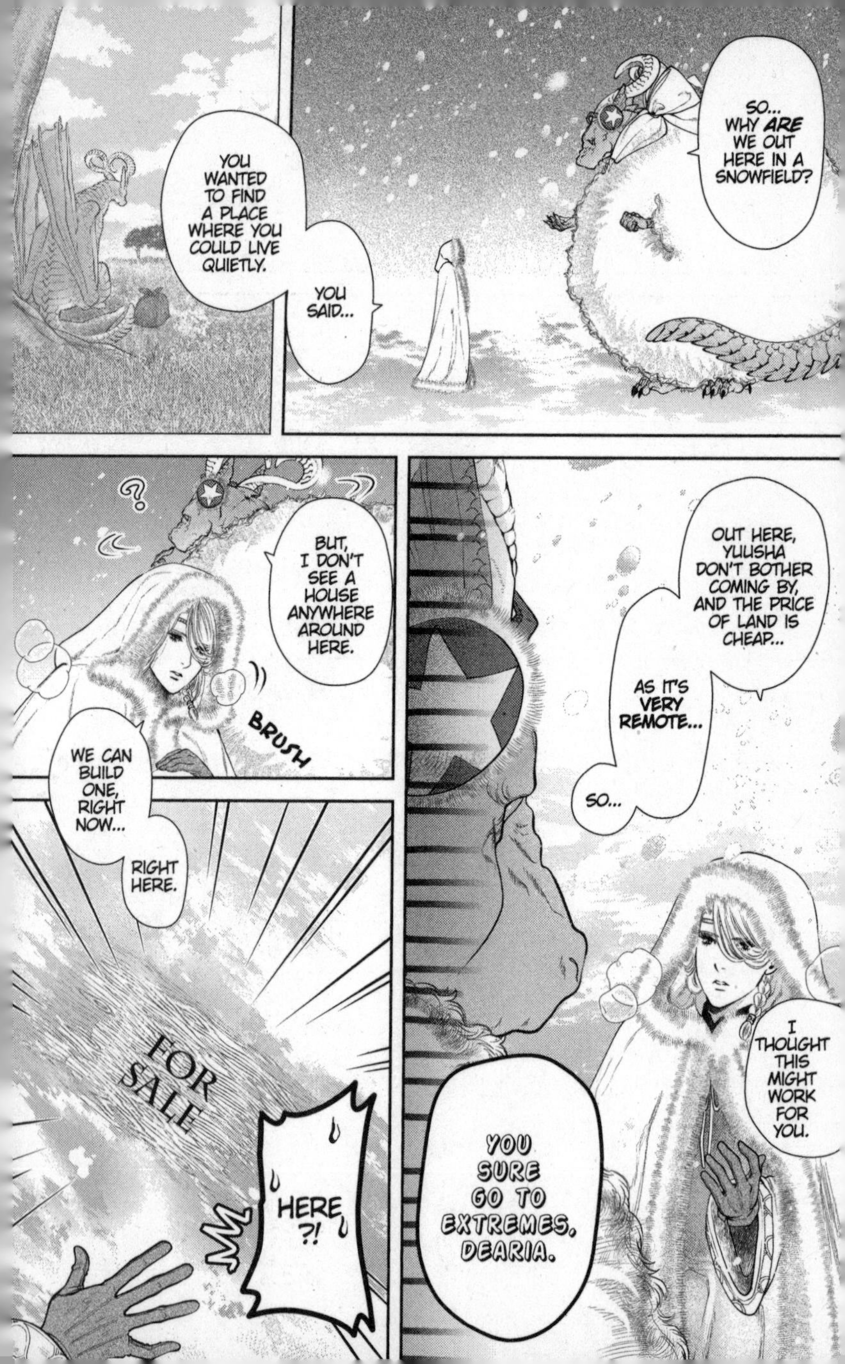

SO... WHY ARE WE OUT HERE IN A SNOWFIELD?
YOU SAID...
YOU WANTED TO FIND A PLACE WHERE YOU COULD LIVE QUIETLY.
OUT HERE, YUUSHA DON'T BOTHER COMING BY, AND THE PRICE OF LAND IS CHEAP...
AS IT'S VERY REMOTE...
SO...
I THOUGHT THIS MIGHT WORK FOR YOU.
YOU SURE GO TO EXTREMES, DEARIA.
?
BUT, I DON'T SEE A HOUSE ANYWHERE AROUND HERE.
BRUSH
WE CAN BUILD ONE, RIGHT NOW...
RIGHT HERE.
FOR SALE
HERE ?!

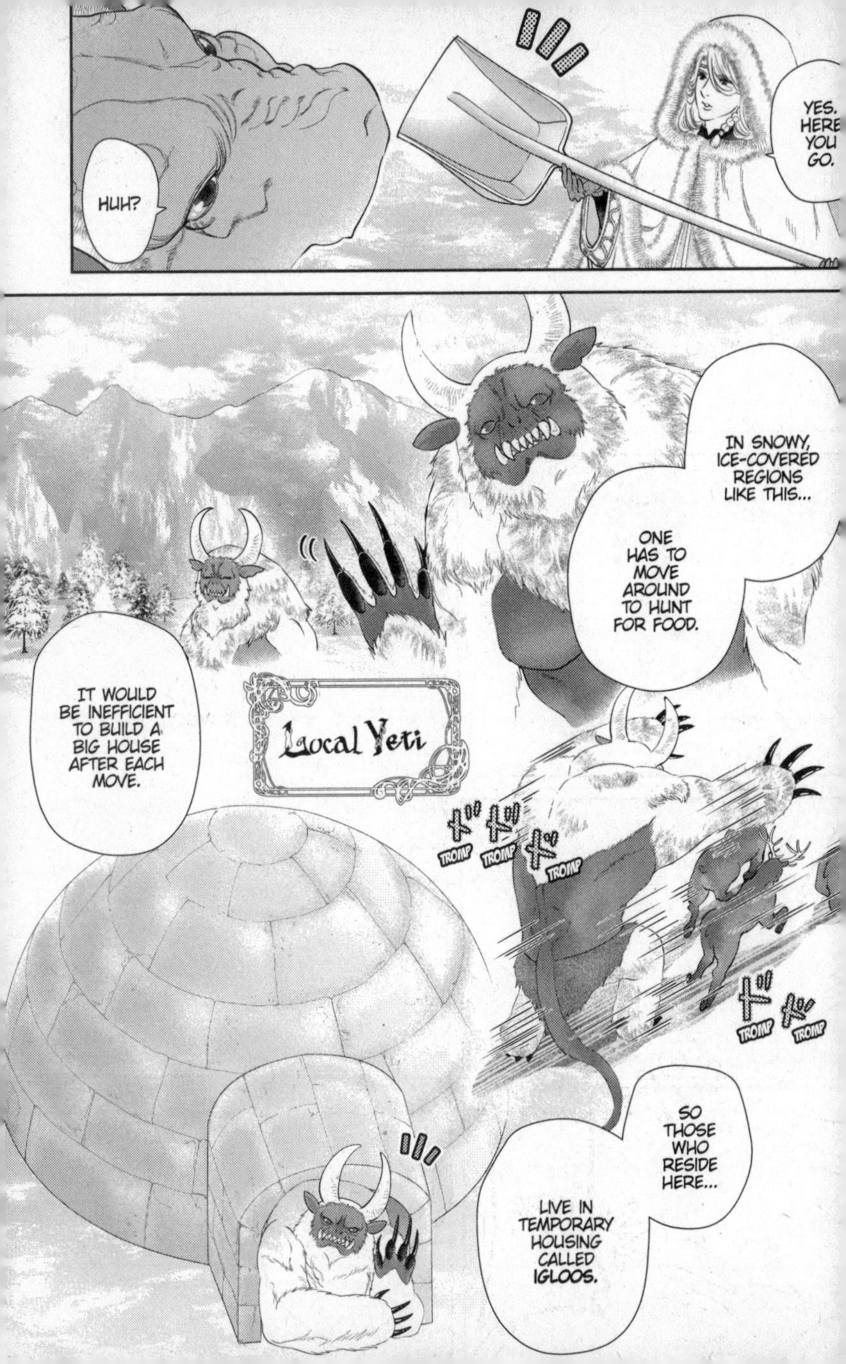
YES. HERE YOU GO.
HUH?
IN SNOWY, ICE-COVERED REGIONS LIKE THIS...
ONE HAS TO MOVE AROUND TO HUNT FOR FOOD.
IT WOULD BE INEFFICIENT TO BUILD A BIG HOUSE AFTER EACH MOVE.
Local Yeti
TROMP
TROMP
TROMP
TROMP
TROMP
SO THOSE WHO RESIDE HERE...
LIVE IN TEMPORARY HOUSING CALLED IGLOOS.

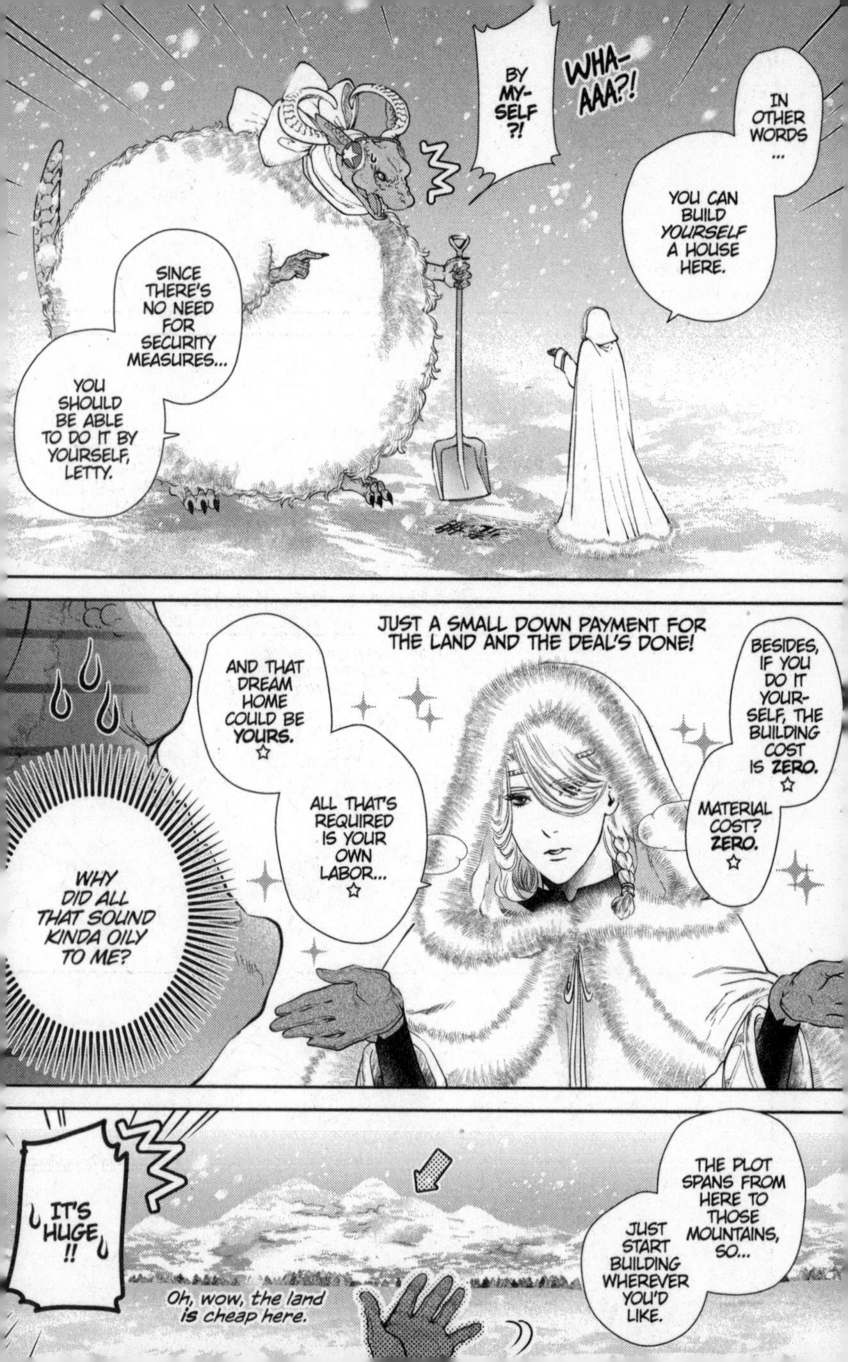

IN OTHER WORDS... YOU CAN BUILD YOURSELF A HOUSE HERE.
WHA-AAA?!
BY MY-SELF?!
SINCE THERE'S NO NEED FOR SECURITY MEASURES... YOU SHOULD BE ABLE TO DO IT BY YOURSELF, LETTY.
BESIDES, IF YOU DO IT YOURSELF, THE BUILDING COST IS ZERO. ☆
JUST A SMALL DOWN PAYMENT FOR THE LAND AND THE DEAL'S DONE!
MATERIAL COST? ZERO. ☆
AND THAT DREAM HOME COULD BE YOURS. ☆
ALL THAT'S REQUIRED IS YOUR OWN LABOR... ☆
WHY DID ALL THAT SOUND KINDA OILY TO ME?
THE PLOT SPANS FROM HERE TO THOSE MOUNTAINS, SO... JUST START BUILDING WHEREVER YOU'D LIKE.
IT'S HUGE!!
Oh, wow, the land is cheap here.

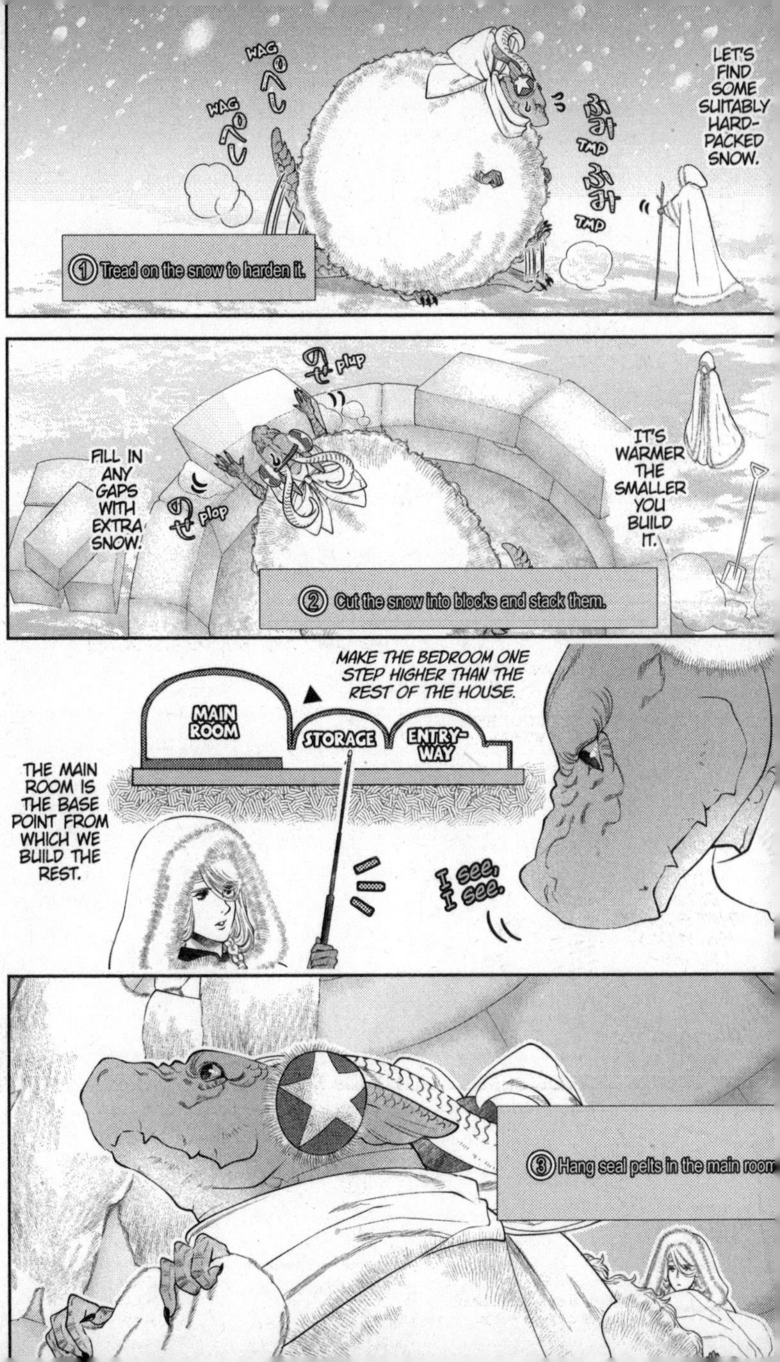
LET'S FIND SOME SUITABLY HARD-PACKED SNOW.
ふみ TMP
ふみ TMP
WAG
WAG
① Tread on the snow to harden it.
IT'S WARMER THE SMALLER YOU BUILD IT.
② Cut the snow into blocks and stack them.
plup
plop
FILL IN ANY GAPS WITH EXTRA SNOW.
I see, I see.
MAKE THE BEDROOM ONE STEP HIGHER THAN THE REST OF THE HOUSE.
MAIN ROOM
STORAGE
ENTRY-WAY
THE MAIN ROOM IS THE BASE POINT FROM WHICH WE BUILD THE REST.
③ Hang seal pelts in the main room

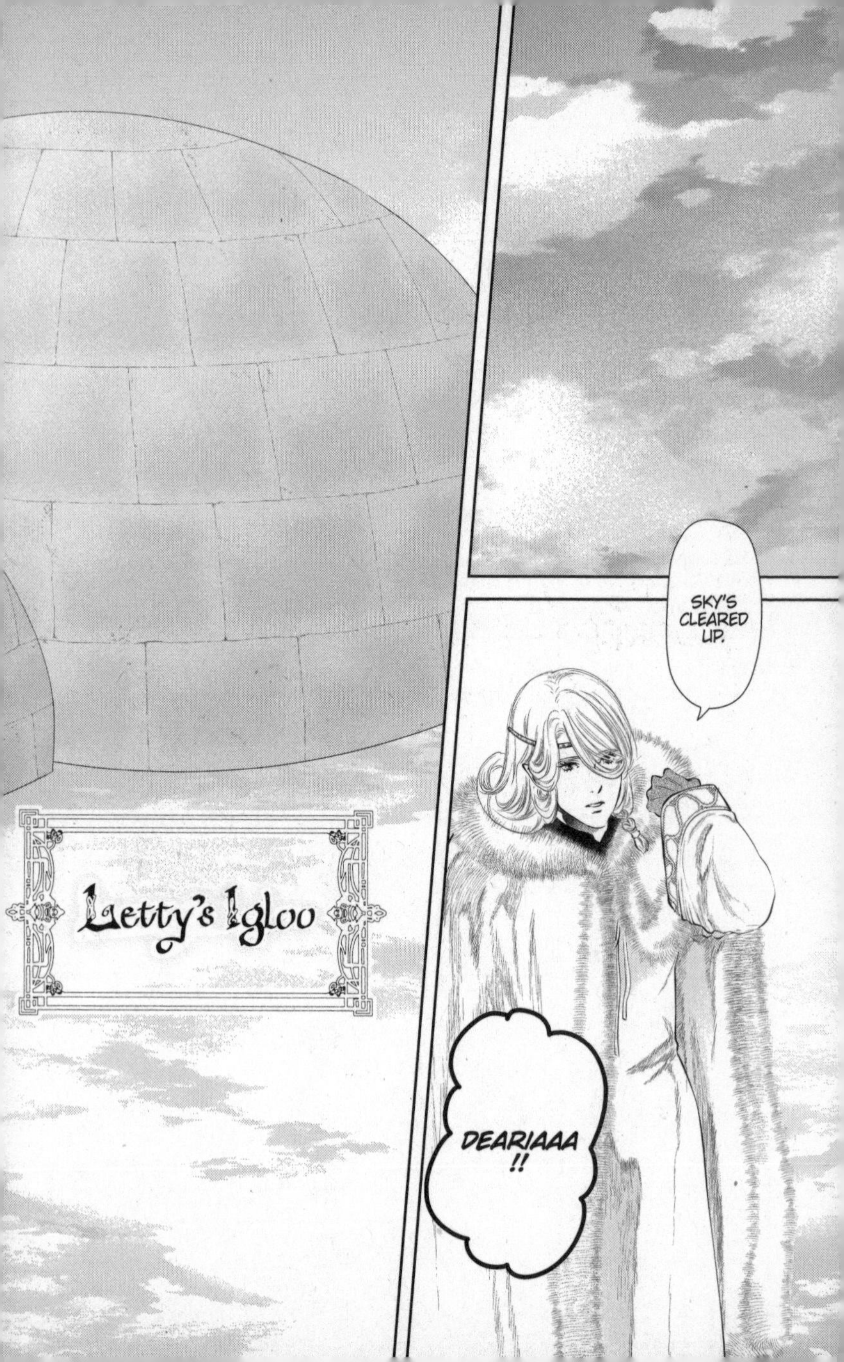
SKY'S CLEARED UP.
DEARIAAA !!
Letty's Igloo

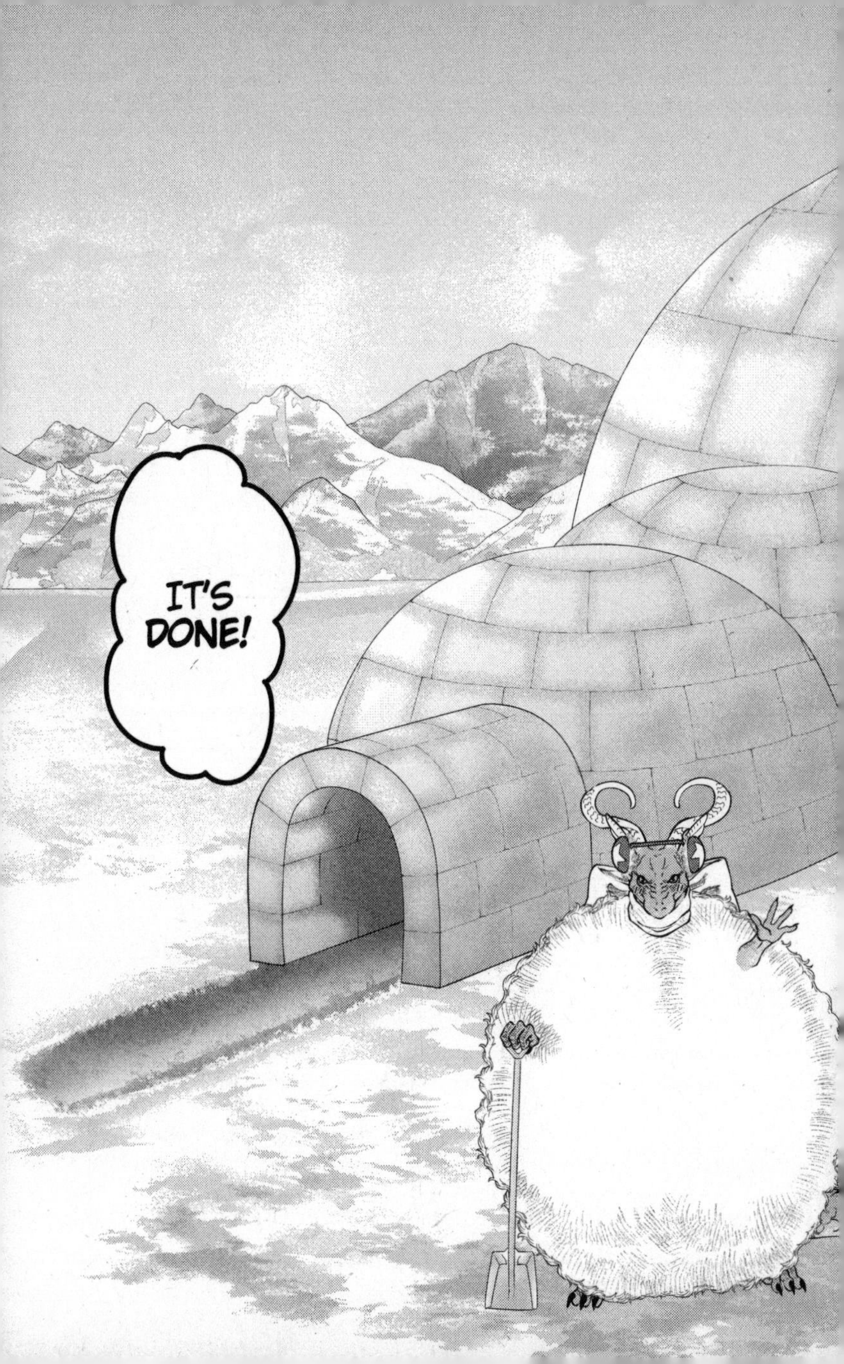
IT'S DONE!

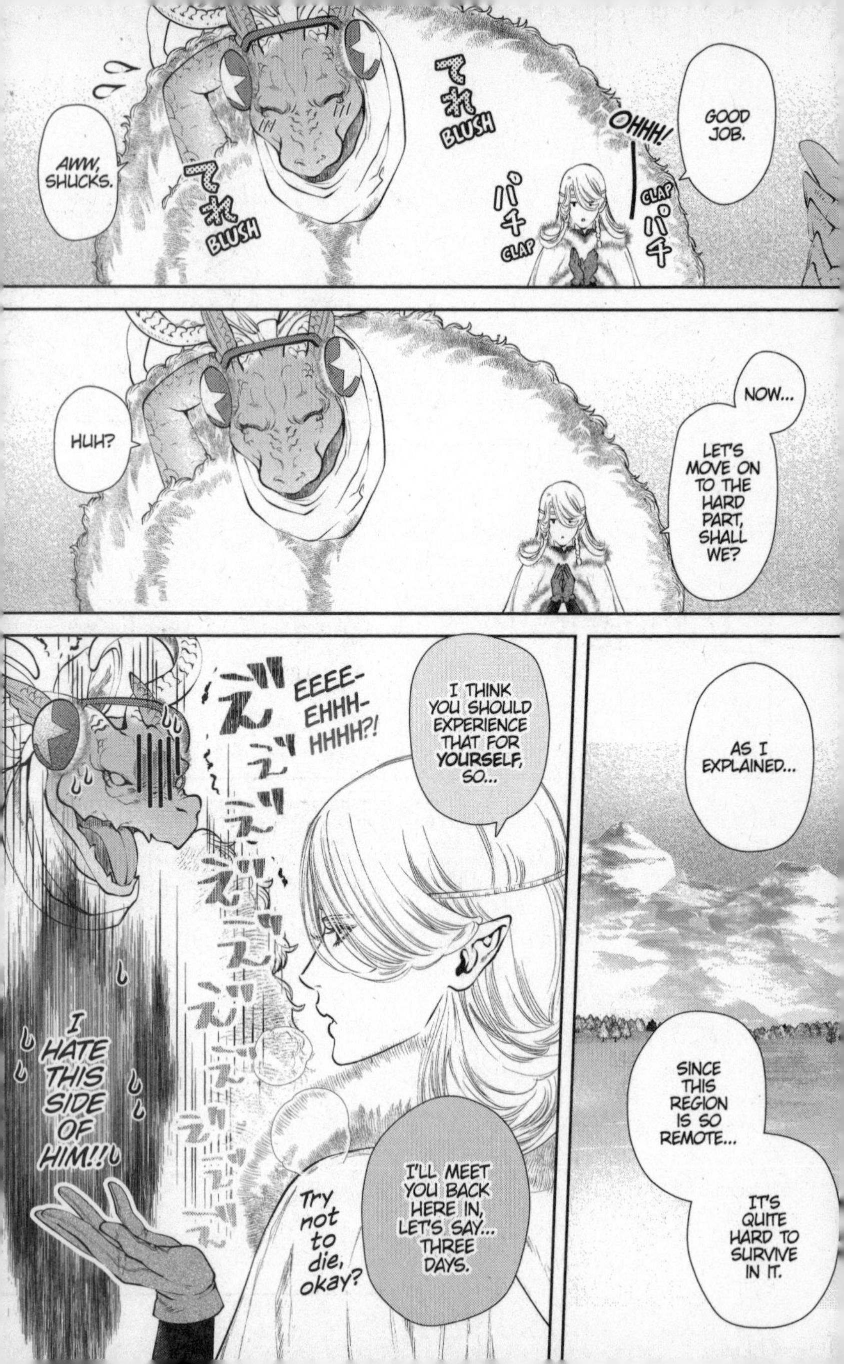
GOOD JOB.
OHHH!
CLAP パチ
パチ CLAP
てれ BLUSH
AWW, SHUCKS.
てれ BLUSH
NOW...
LET'S MOVE ON TO THE HARD PART, SHALL WE?
HUH?
AS I EXPLAINED...
SINCE THIS REGION IS SO REMOTE...
IT'S QUITE HARD TO SURVIVE IN IT.
I THINK YOU SHOULD EXPERIENCE THAT FOR YOURSELF, SO...
I'LL MEET YOU BACK HERE IN, LET'S SAY... THREE DAYS.
Try not to die, okay?
EEEE-EHHH-HHHH?!
I HATE THIS SIDE OF HIM!!

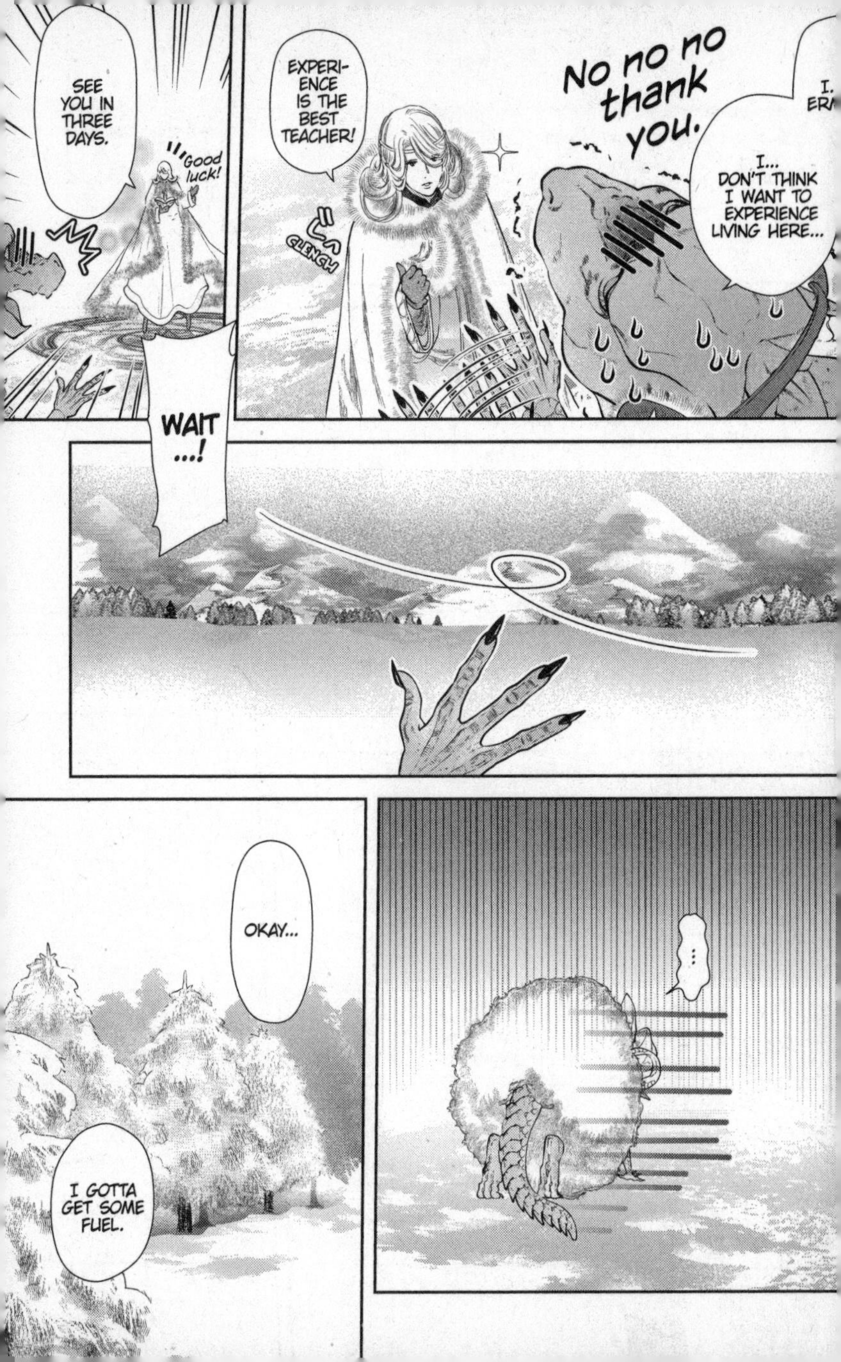
I... DON'T THINK I WANT TO EXPERIENCE LIVING HERE...
No no no thank you.
EXPERIENCE IS THE BEST TEACHER!
CLENCH
SEE YOU IN THREE DAYS.
Good luck!
WAIT...!
...
OKAY...
I GOTTA GET SOME FUEL.

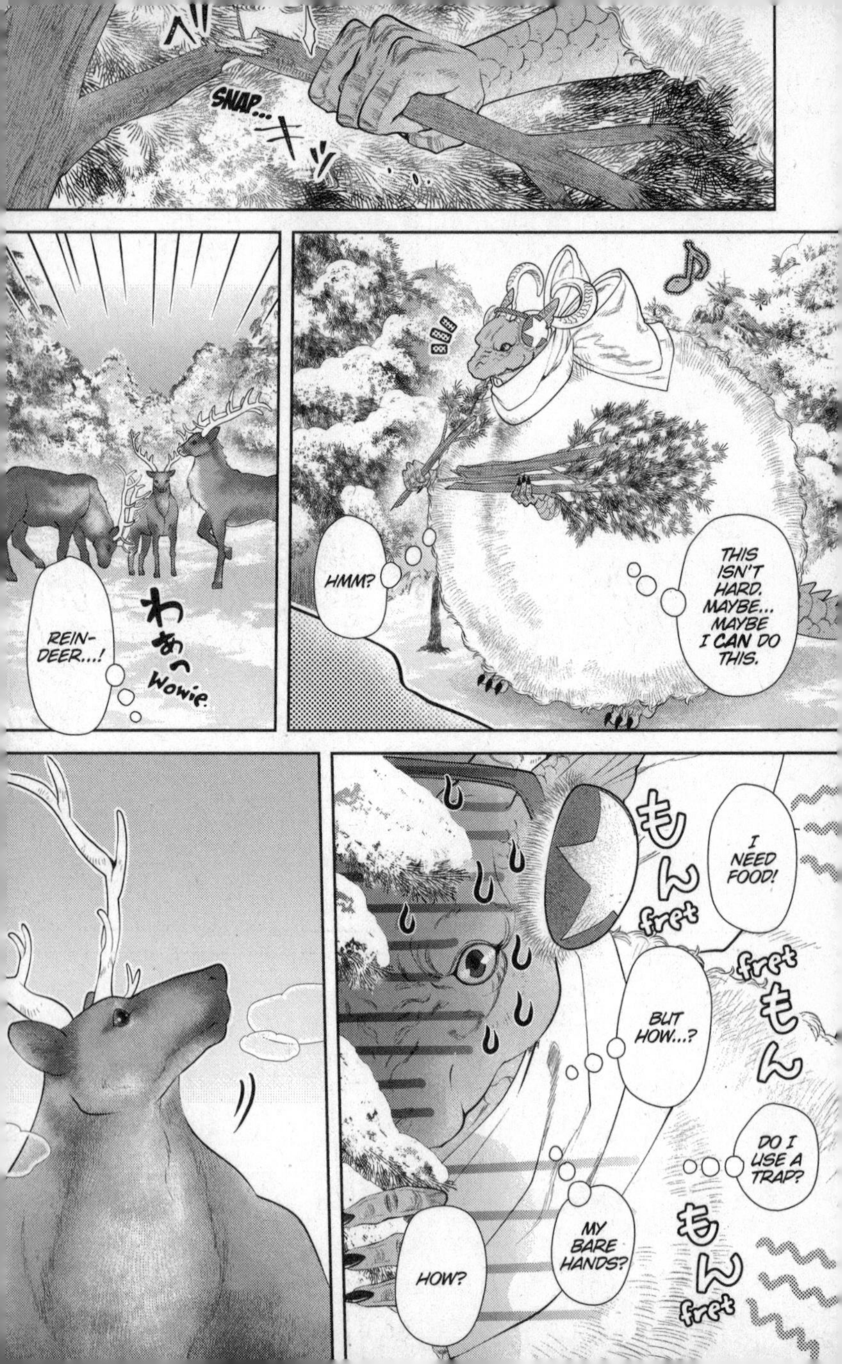
SNAP...
THIS ISN'T HARD. MAYBE... MAYBE I CAN DO THIS.
HMM?
REIN-DEER...!
わあ〜
Wowie.
I NEED FOOD!
もん
fret
fret
もん
BUT HOW...?
DO I USE A TRAP?
MY BARE HANDS?
もん
fret
HOW?

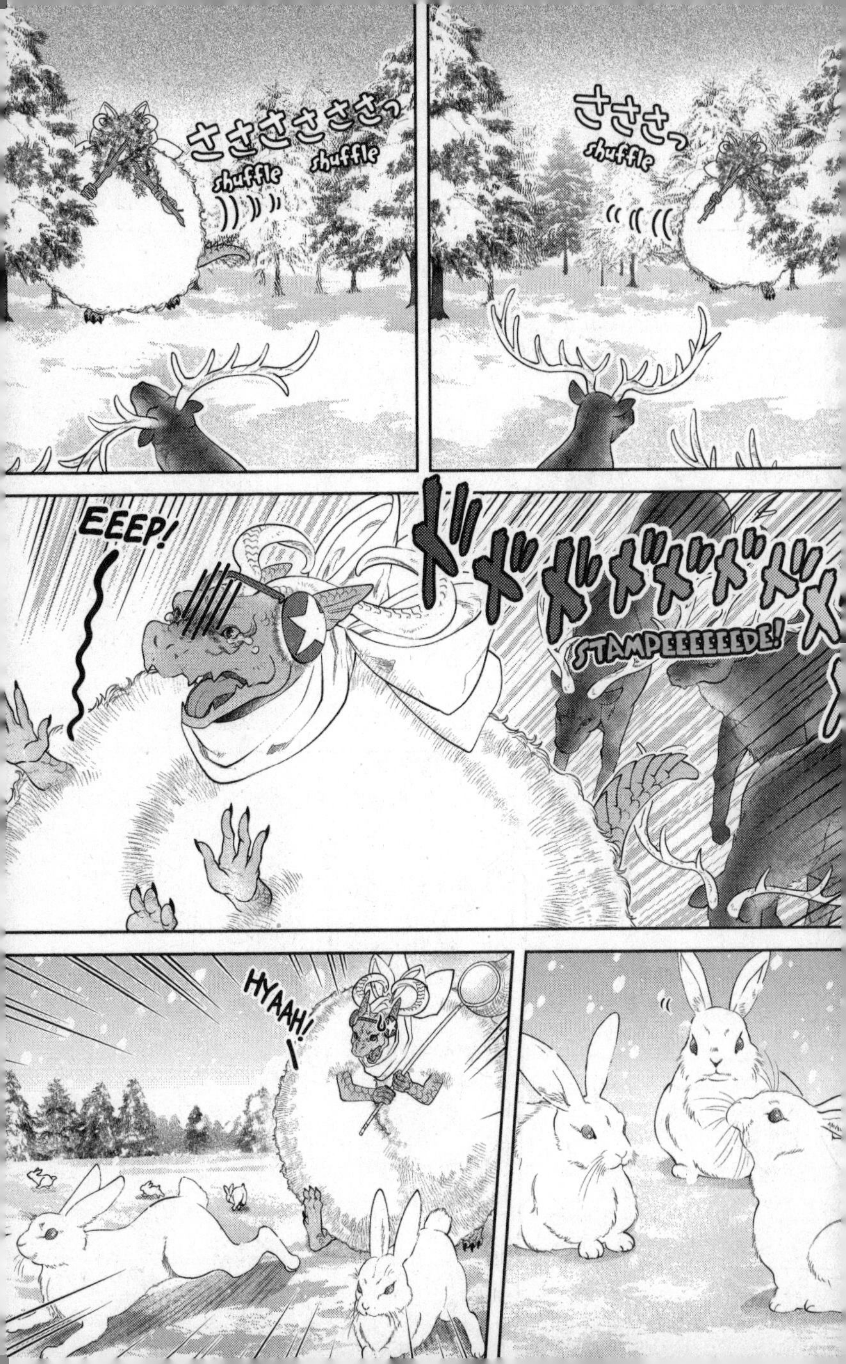
さささっ
shuffle
さささささっ
shuffle
shuffle
ドドドドドドド
STAMPEEEEEEDE!
EEEP!
HYAAAH!

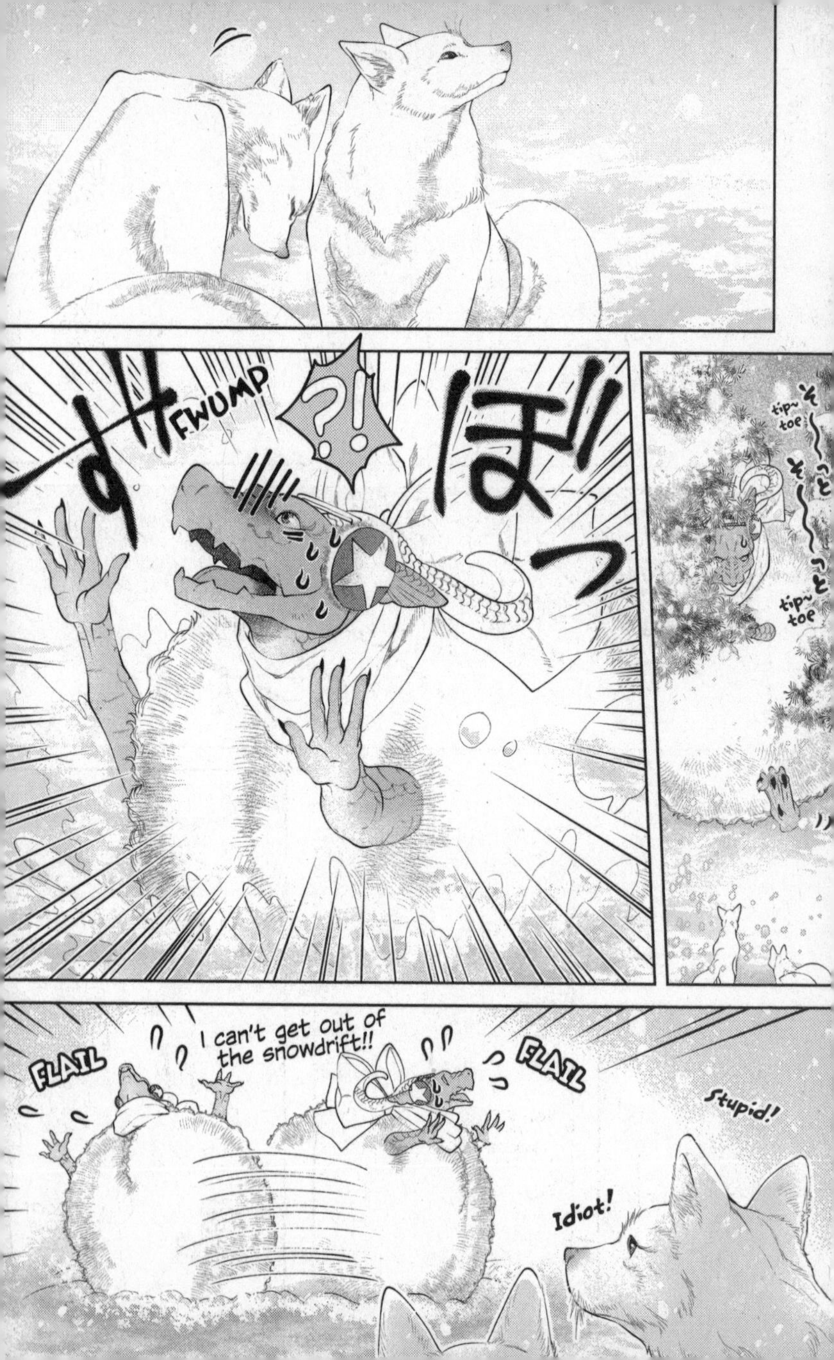
tip~ toe
そ~っと
そ~っと
tip~ toe
ずぼっ
FWUMP
?!
Stupid!
FLAIL
I can't get out of the snowdrift!!
FLAIL
Idiot!

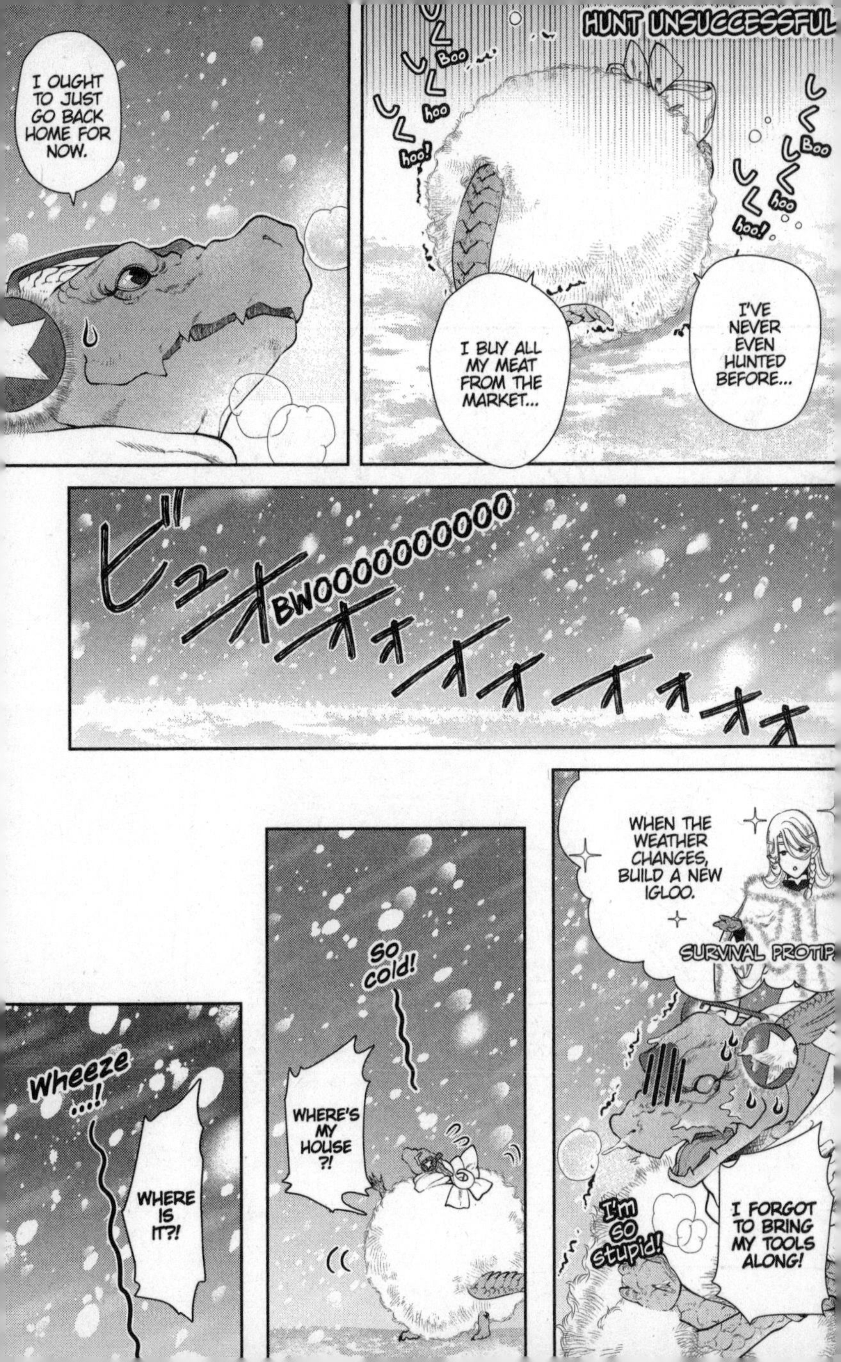

HUNT UNSUCCESSFUL
しくしく
Boohoo!
しくしく
Boohoo!
I'VE NEVER EVEN HUNTED BEFORE...
I BUY ALL MY MEAT FROM THE MARKET...
I OUGHT TO JUST GO BACK HOME FOR NOW.
ビュオオオオオオオオオ
BWOOOOOOOOOOOO
WHEN THE WEATHER CHANGES, BUILD A NEW IGLOO.
SURVIVAL PROTIP.
I FORGOT TO BRING MY TOOLS ALONG!
I'm so stupid!
So cold!
WHERE'S MY HOUSE?!
Wheeze...!
WHERE IS IT?!

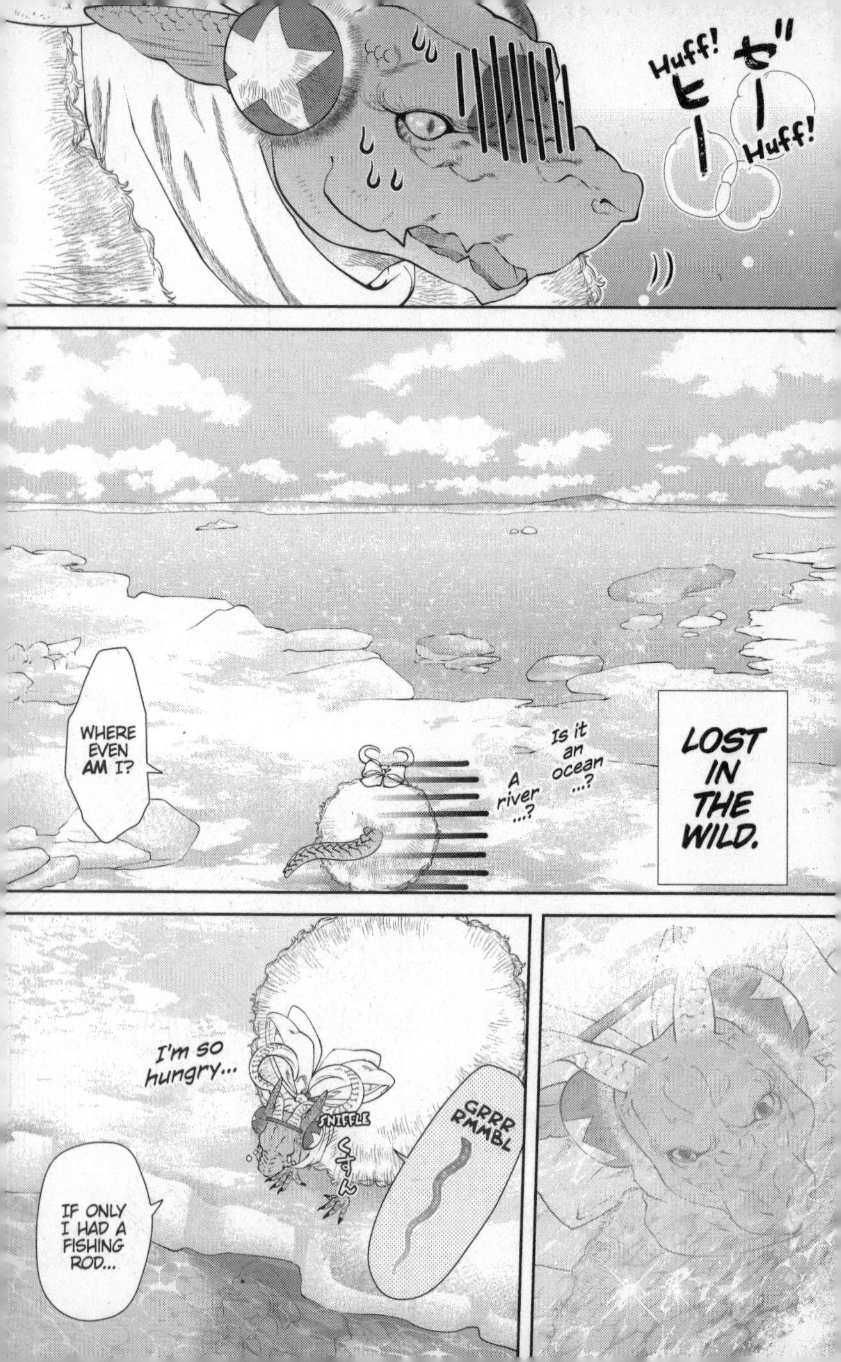
ゼー
Huff!
ヒー
Huff!
LOST IN THE WILD.
Is it an ocean ...?
A river ...?
WHERE EVEN AM I?
GRRR RMMBL
SNIFFLE
くすん
I'm so hungry...
IF ONLY I HAD A FISHING ROD...

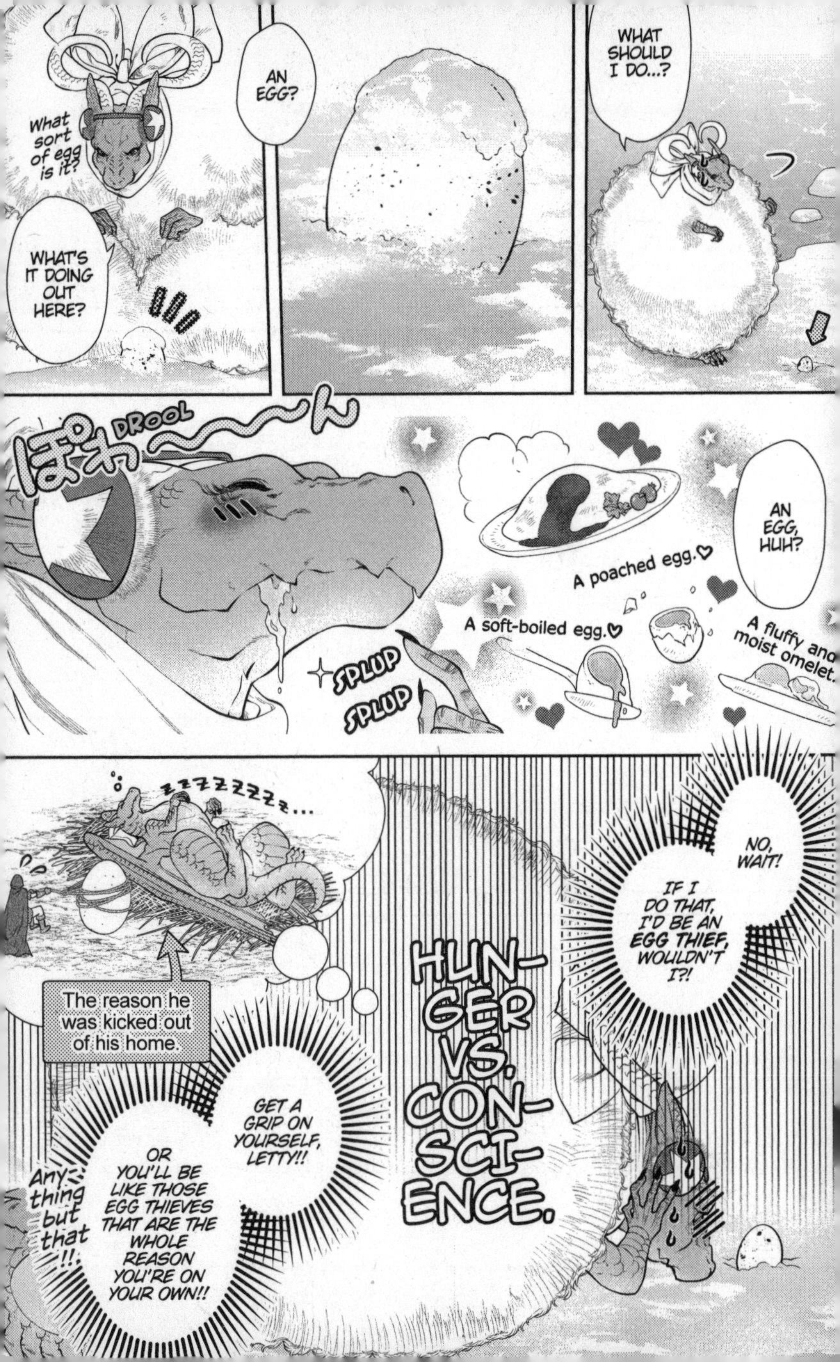
WHAT SHOULD I DO...?
AN EGG?
What sort of egg is it?
WHAT'S IT DOING OUT HERE?
AN EGG, HUH?
A poached egg.♡
A fluffy and moist omelet.
A soft-boiled egg.♡
SPLUP
SPLUP
ぽわ〜〜〜ん
DROOL
NO, WAIT!
IF I DO THAT, I'D BE AN EGG THIEF, WOULDN'T I?!
HUN-GER VS. CON-SCI-ENCE.
ZZZZZZZZZ...
The reason he was kicked out of his home.
GET A GRIP ON YOURSELF, LETTY!!
OR YOU'LL BE LIKE THOSE EGG THIEVES THAT ARE THE WHOLE REASON YOU'RE ON YOUR OWN!!
Any-thing but that!!

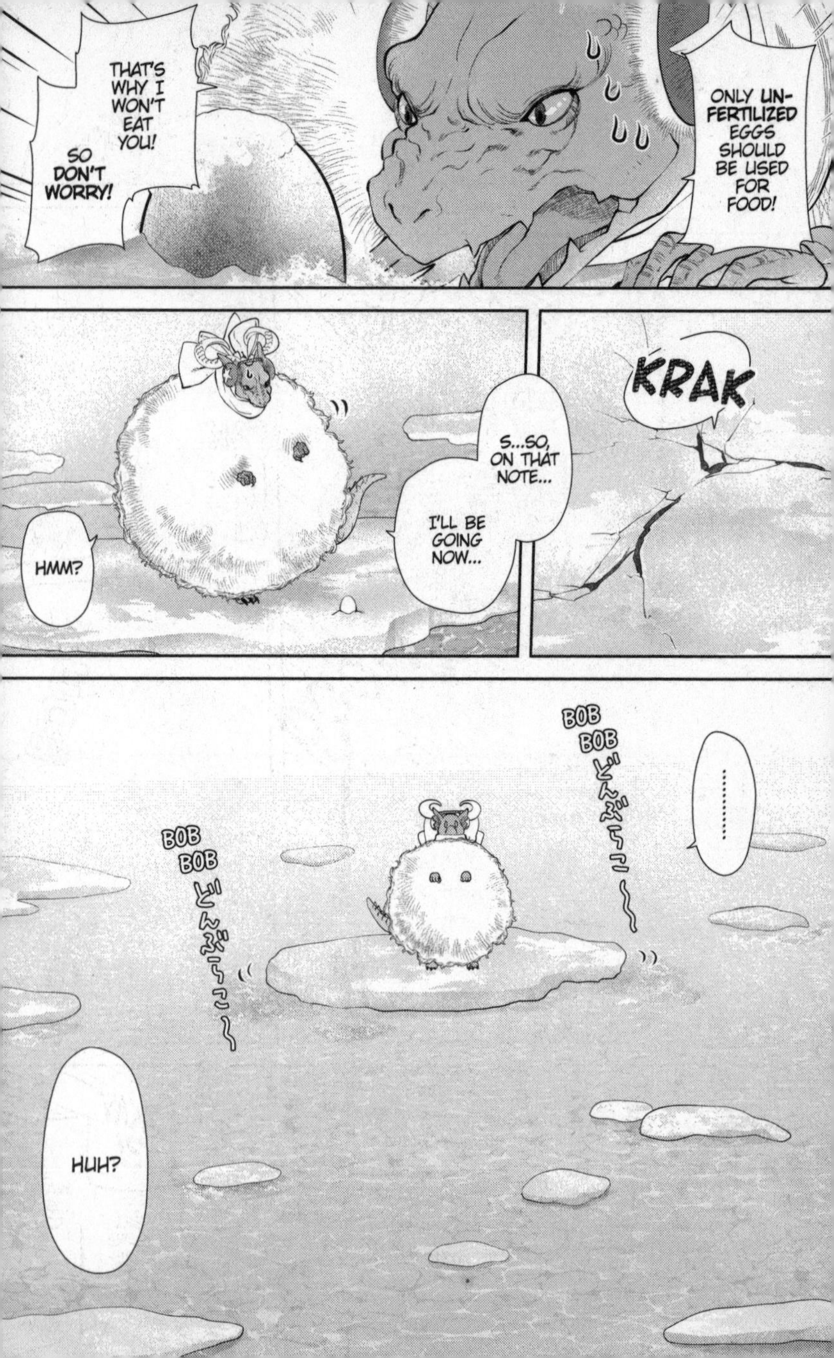

ONLY UN-FERTILIZED EGGS SHOULD BE USED FOR FOOD!
THAT'S WHY I WON'T EAT YOU!
SO DON'T WORRY!
KRAK
S...SO, ON THAT NOTE...
I'LL BE GOING NOW...
HMM?
......
BOB BOB どんぶらこ~
BOB BOB どんぶらこ~
HUH?

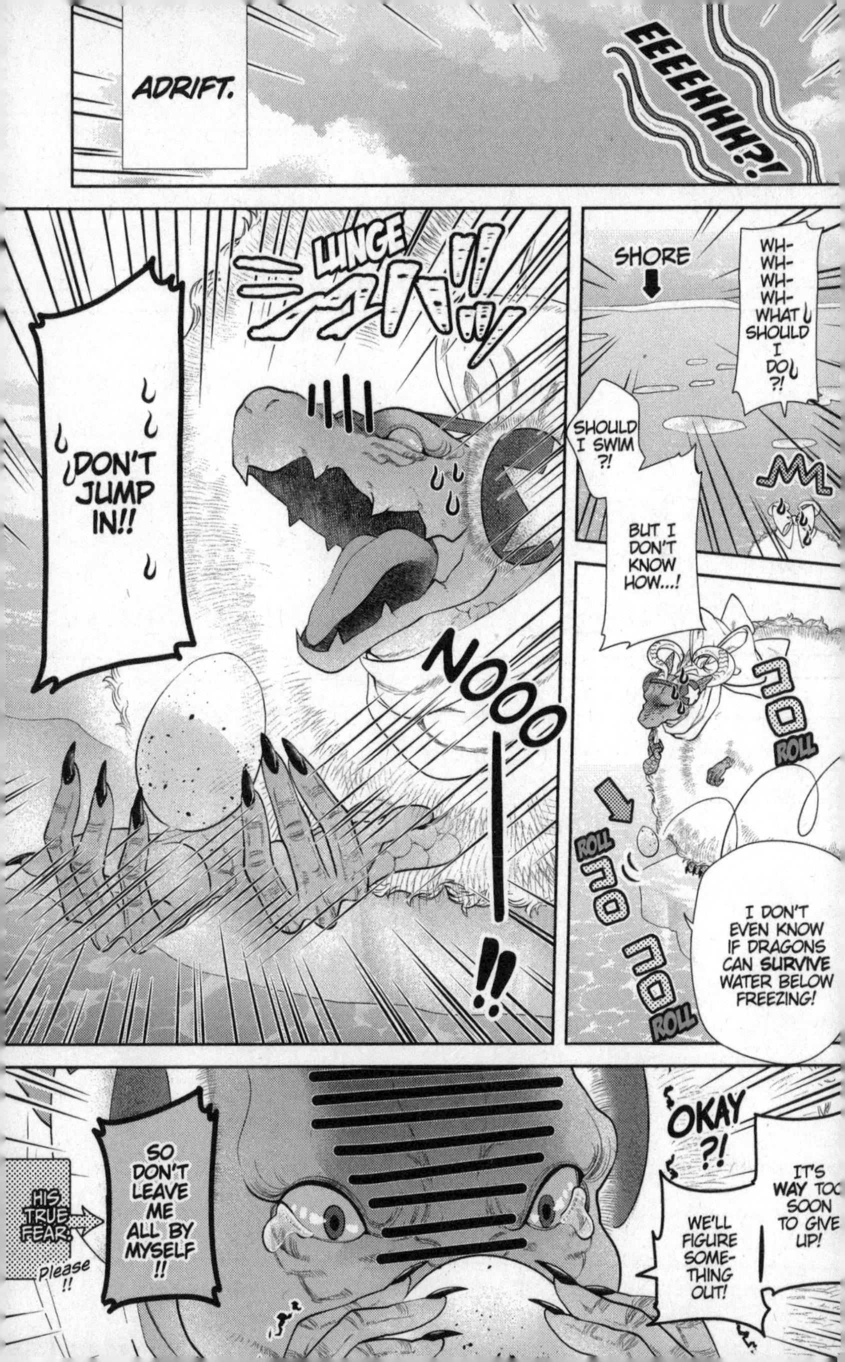
EEEEHHHH?!
ADRIFT.
SHORE
WH-WH-WH-WH-WHAT SHOULD I DO?!
SHOULD I SWIM?!
BUT I DON'T KNOW HOW...!
ROLL ROLL
ROLL ROLL
I DON'T EVEN KNOW IF DRAGONS CAN SURVIVE WATER BELOW FREEZING!
LUNGE
NOOOO—!!
DON'T JUMP IN!!
IT'S WAY TOO SOON TO GIVE UP!
OKAY?!
WE'LL FIGURE SOMETHING OUT!
SO DON'T LEAVE ME ALL BY MYSELF!!
HIS TRUE FEAR
please!!

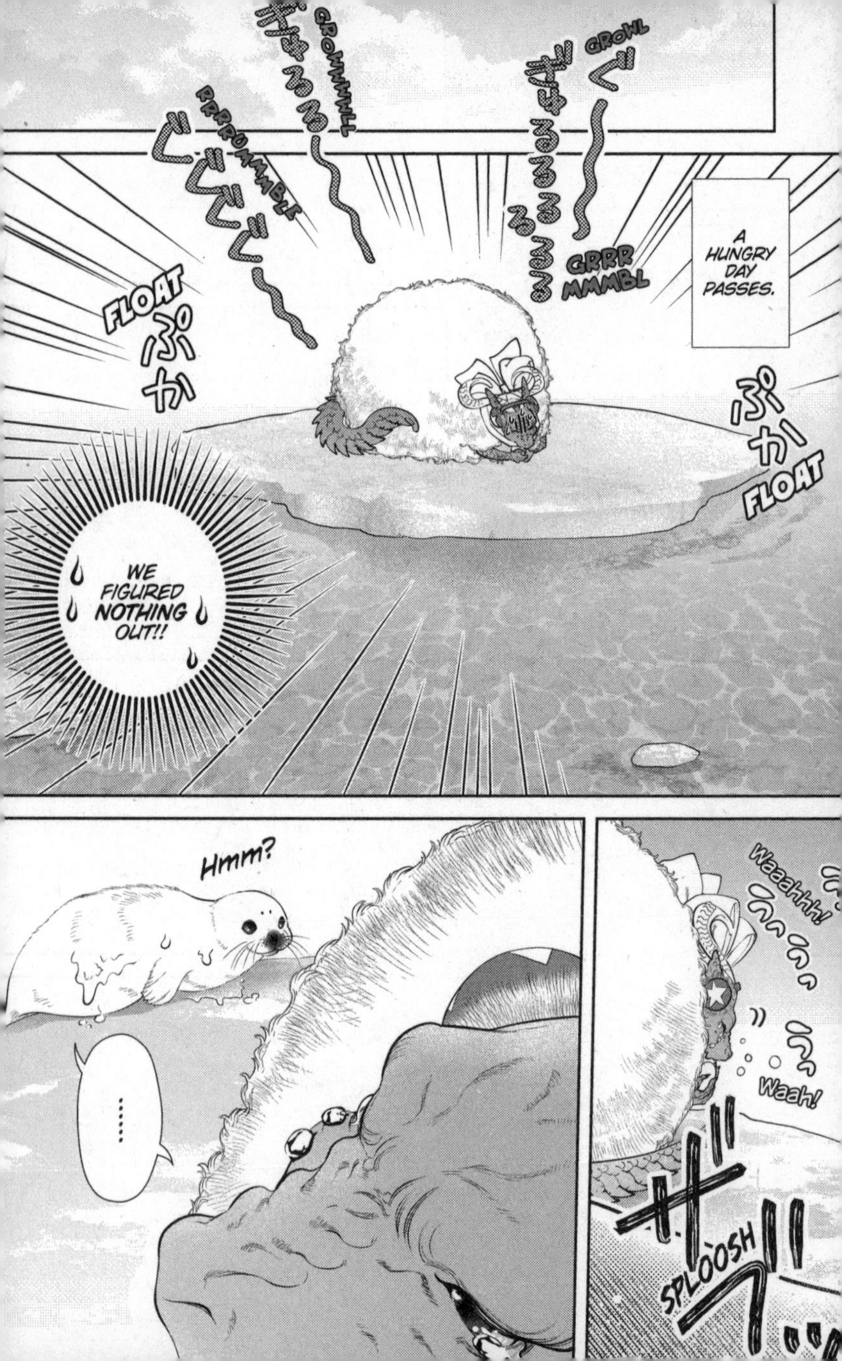
GROWL
ぐ〜
ぎゅるるるるる
GRRR MMMBL
GROWWWL
ぎゅるる〜
RRRRUMMMBLE
ごごごご〜
A HUNGRY DAY PASSES.
ぷか〜
FLOAT
FLOAT
ぷか
WE FIGURED NOTHING OUT!!
Waaahhh!
うぅぅぅ
Waah!
ザッ
SPLOOSH
Hmm?
……

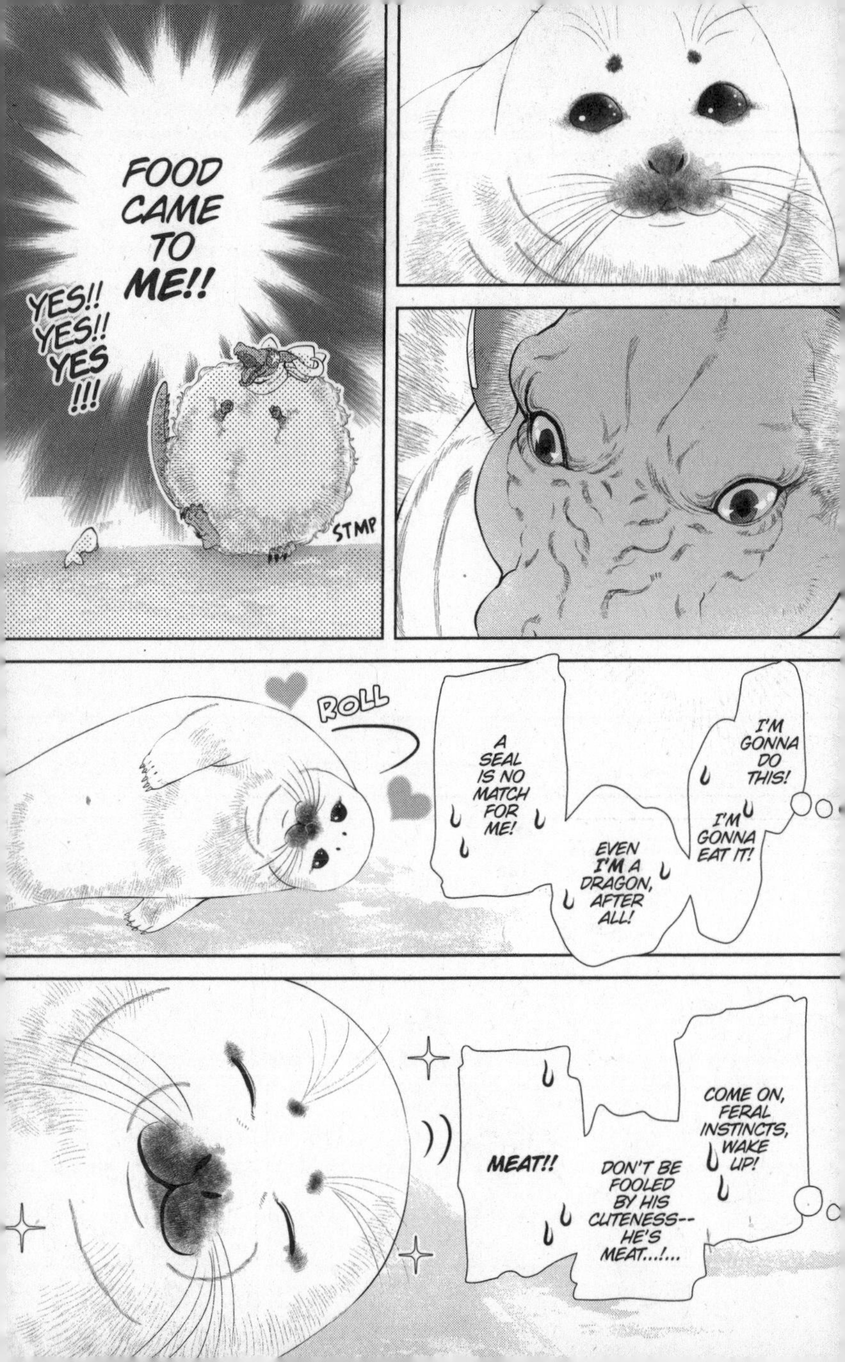
FOOD CAME TO ME!!
YES!! YES!! YES!!!
STMP
I'M GONNA DO THIS!
I'M GONNA EAT IT!
EVEN I'M A DRAGON, AFTER ALL!
A SEAL IS NO MATCH FOR ME!
ROLL
COME ON, FERAL INSTINCTS, WAKE UP!
DON'T BE FOOLED BY HIS CUTENESS-- HE'S MEAT...!...
MEAT!!

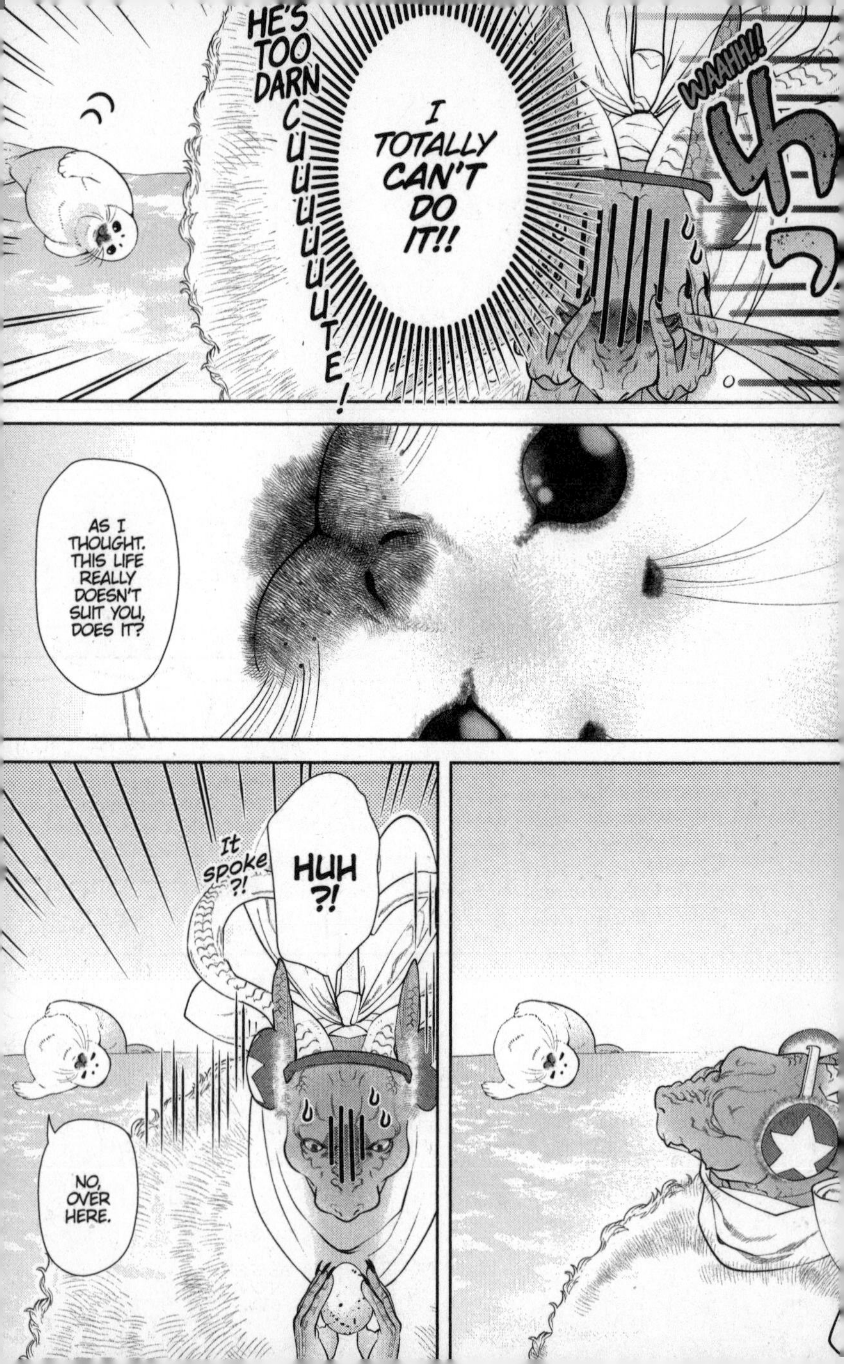
WAAHH!!
I TOTALLY CAN'T DO IT!!
HE'S TOO DARN CUUUUUUUUTE!
AS I THOUGHT. THIS LIFE REALLY DOESN'T SUIT YOU, DOES IT?
HUH?!
It spoke?!
NO, OVER HERE.

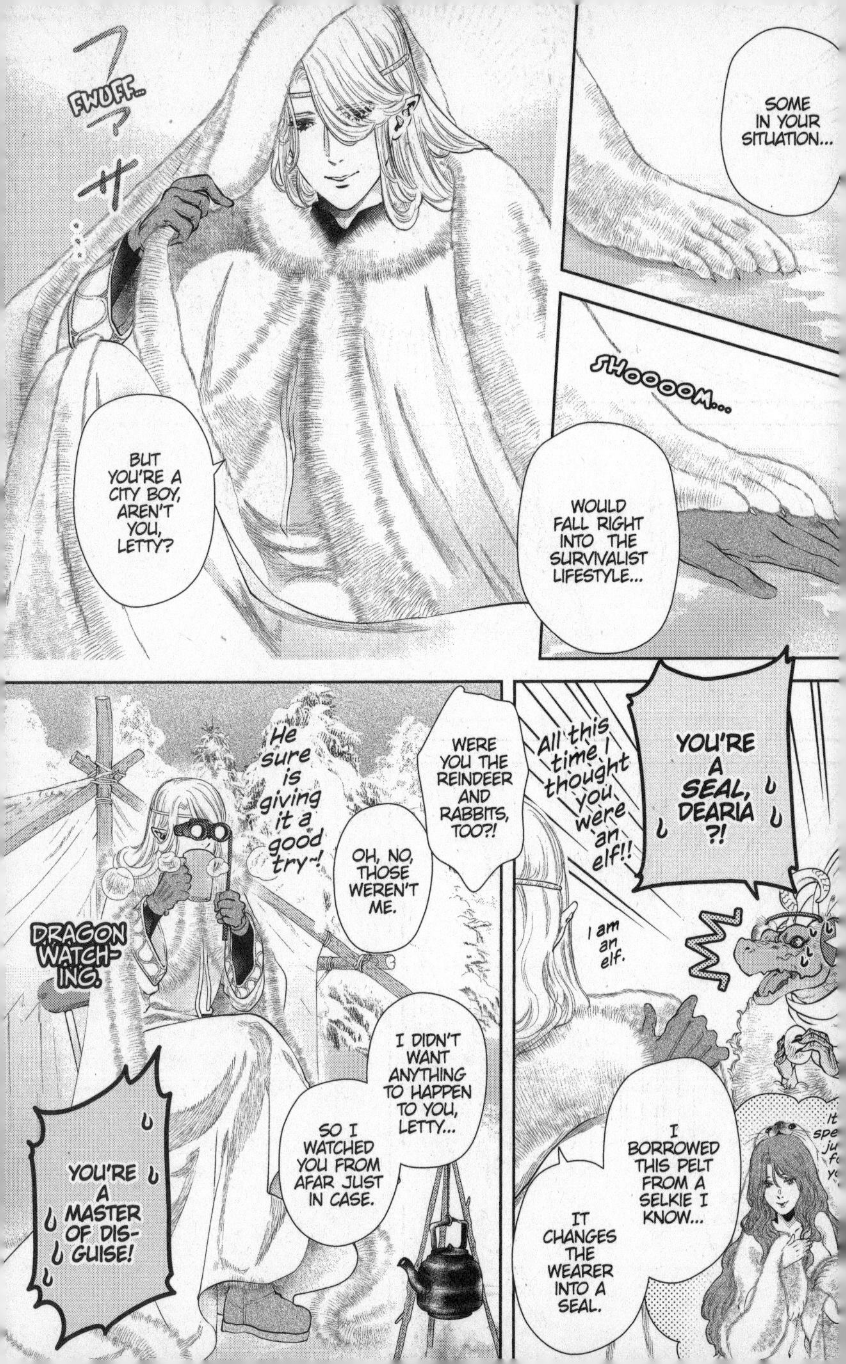

SOME IN YOUR SITUATION...
SHOOOOOM...
WOULD FALL RIGHT INTO THE SURVIVALIST LIFESTYLE...
FWUFF...
BUT YOU'RE A CITY BOY, AREN'T YOU, LETTY?
YOU'RE A SEAL, DEARIA?!
All this time I thought you were an elf!!
I am an elf.
I BORROWED THIS PELT FROM A SELKIE I KNOW...
IT CHANGES THE WEARER INTO A SEAL.
WERE YOU THE REINDEER AND RABBITS, TOO?!
He sure is giving it a good try~!
OH, NO, THOSE WEREN'T ME.
I DIDN'T WANT ANYTHING TO HAPPEN TO YOU, LETTY...
SO I WATCHED YOU FROM AFAR JUST IN CASE.
DRAGON WATCHING.
YOU'RE A MASTER OF DISGUISE!

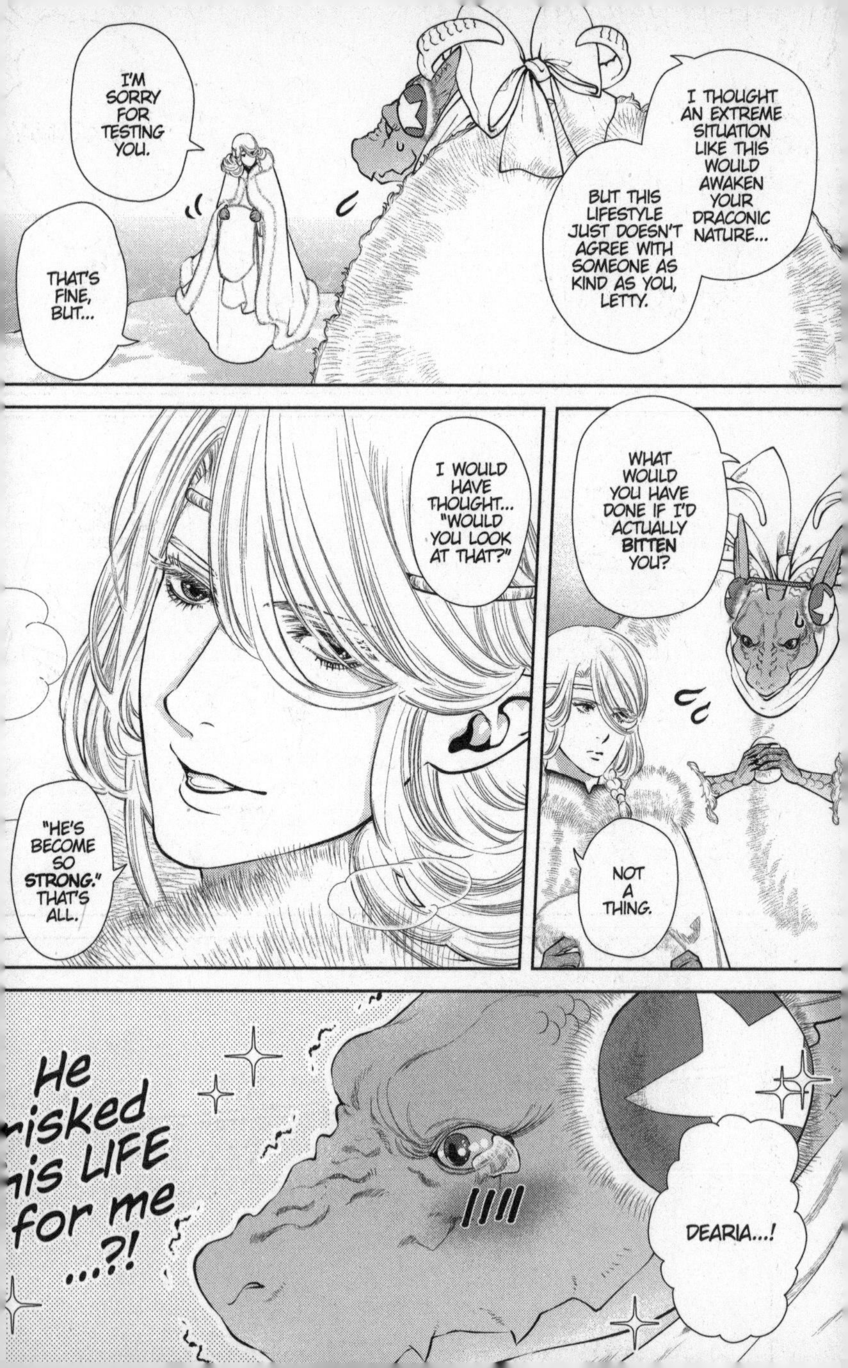
I THOUGHT AN EXTREME SITUATION LIKE THIS WOULD AWAKEN YOUR DRACONIC NATURE...
BUT THIS LIFESTYLE JUST DOESN'T AGREE WITH SOMEONE AS KIND AS YOU, LETTY.
I'M SORRY FOR TESTING YOU.
THAT'S FINE, BUT...
WHAT WOULD YOU HAVE DONE IF I'D ACTUALLY BITTEN YOU?
NOT A THING.
I WOULD HAVE THOUGHT... "WOULD YOU LOOK AT THAT?"
"HE'S BECOME SO STRONG." THAT'S ALL.
DEARIA...!
He risked his LIFE for me ...?!

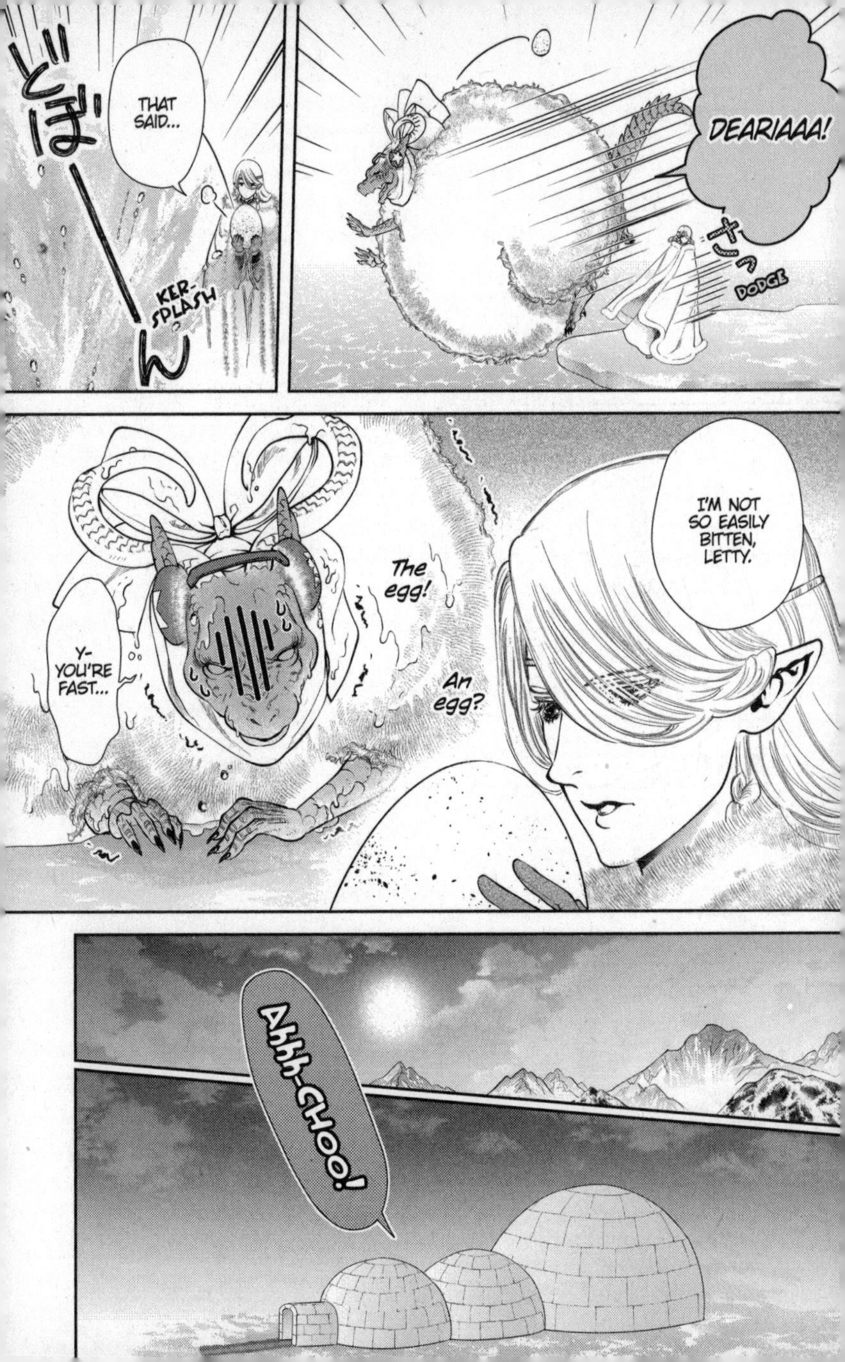
DEARIAAA!
さっ
DODGE
THAT SAID...
どぼーん
KER-SPLASH
I'M NOT SO EASILY BITTEN, LETTY.
The egg!
An egg?
Y-YOU'RE FAST...
Ahhh-CHOO!

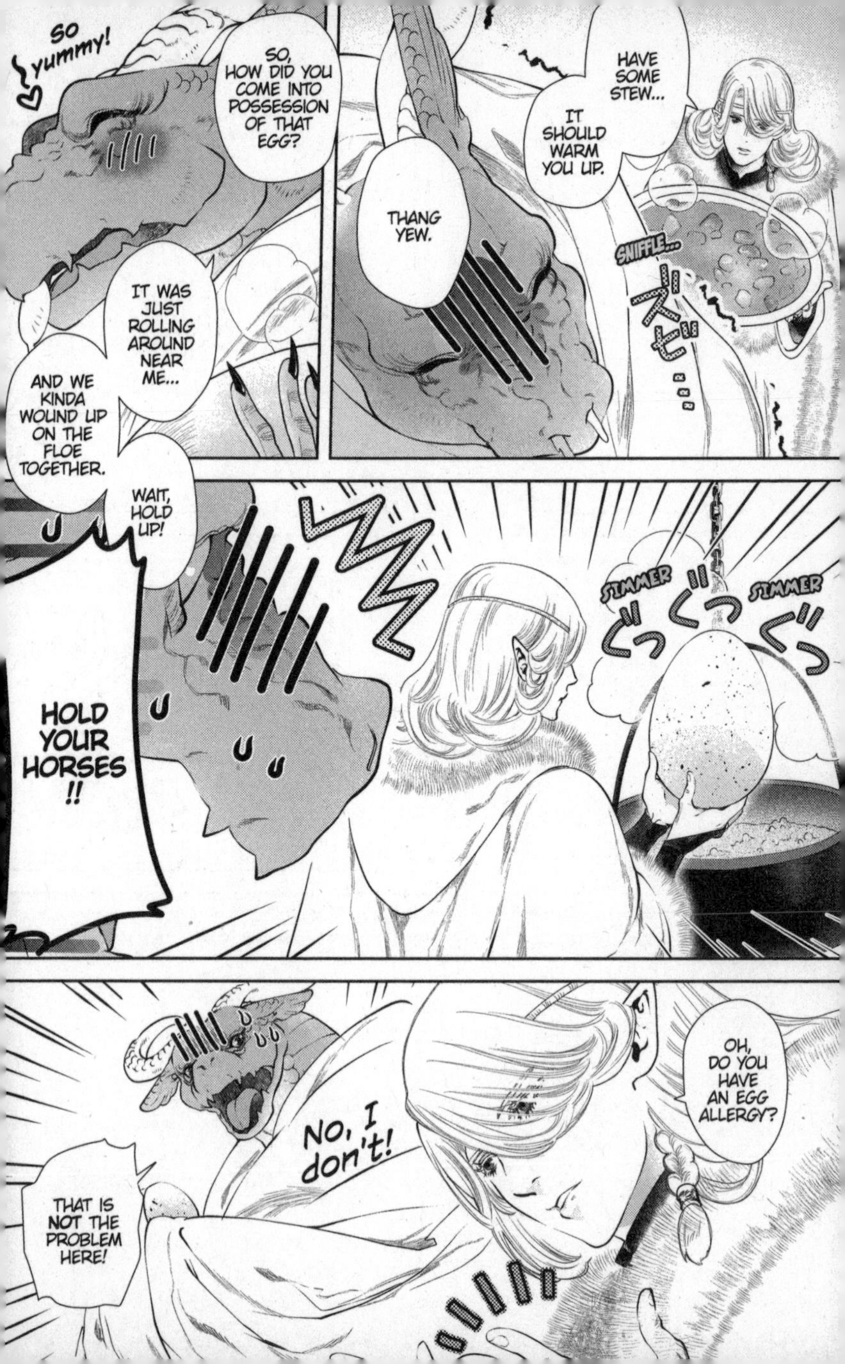
HAVE SOME STEW...
IT SHOULD WARM YOU UP.
SNIFFLE...
ズビ...
THANG YEW.
SO, HOW DID YOU COME INTO POSSESSION OF THAT EGG?
So yummy!
IT WAS JUST ROLLING AROUND NEAR ME...
AND WE KINDA WOUND UP ON THE FLOE TOGETHER.
SIMMER SIMMER
ぐつぐつ
WAIT, HOLD UP!
HOLD YOUR HORSES!!
OH, DO YOU HAVE AN EGG ALLERGY?
No, I don't!
THAT IS NOT THE PROBLEM HERE!

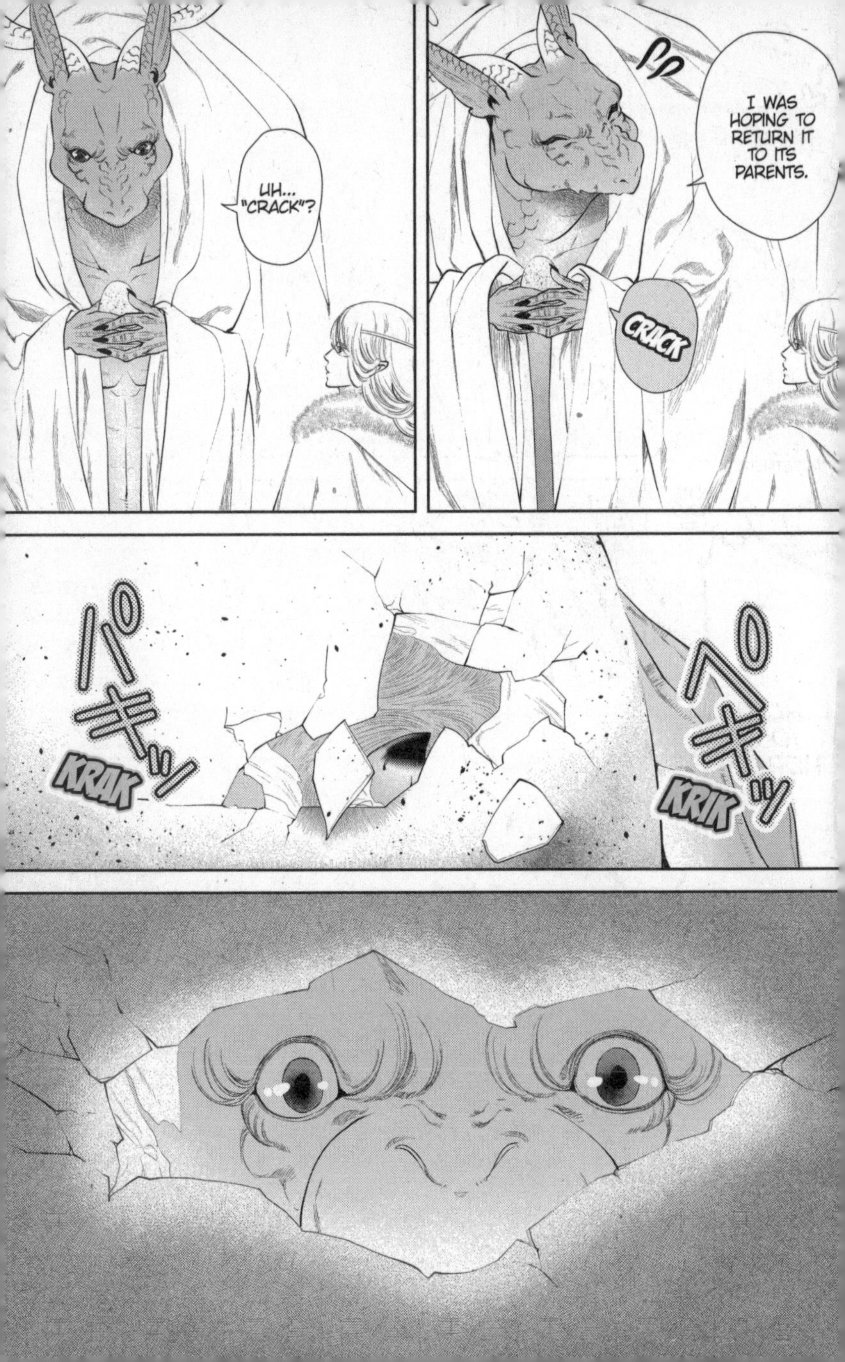
I WAS HOPING TO RETURN IT TO ITS PARENTS.
CRACK
UH... "CRACK"?
ペキッ
KRIK
パキッ
KRAK

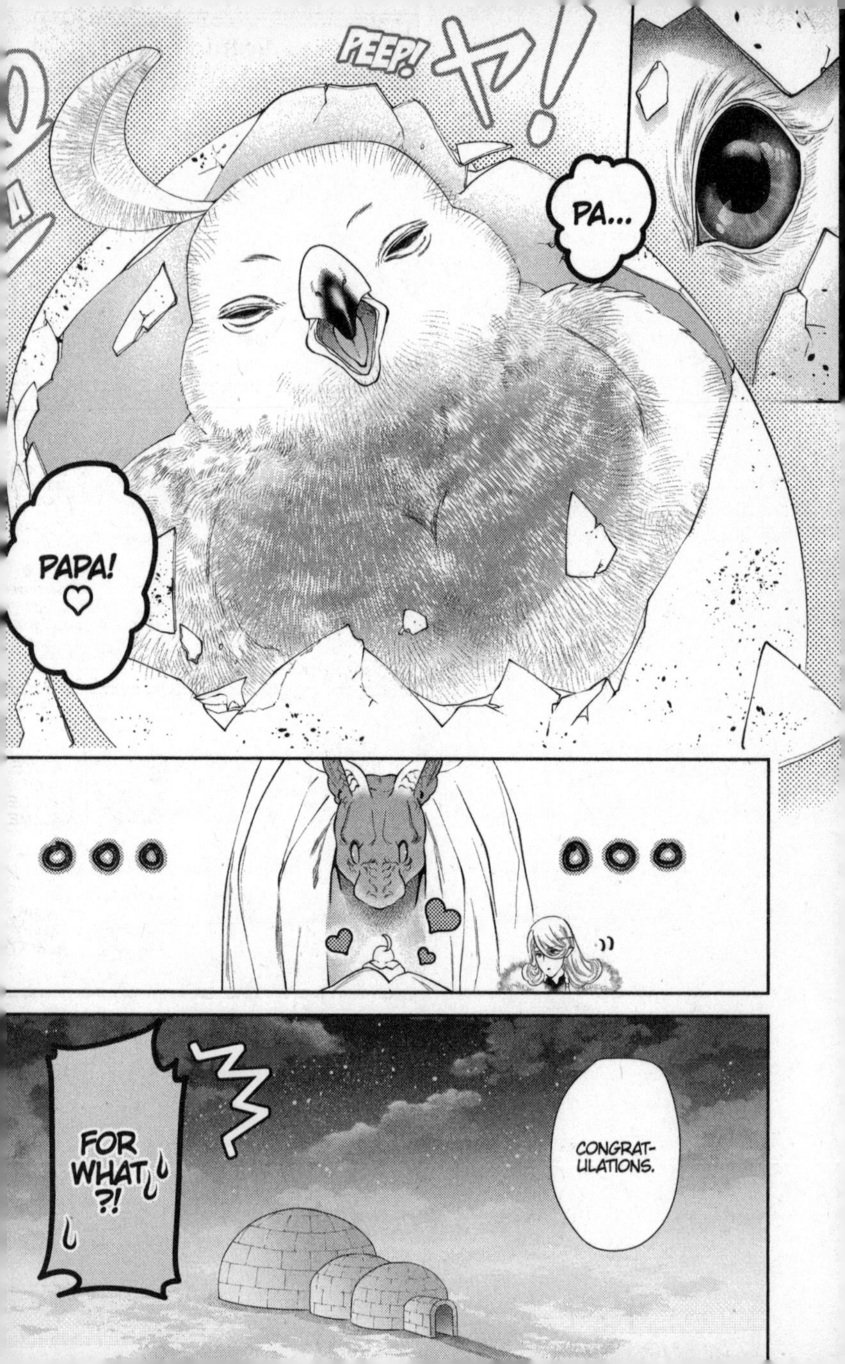
PEEP! ヤ!
PA...
PAPA! ♡
CONGRAT-ULATIONS.
FOR WHAT?!

Conflict

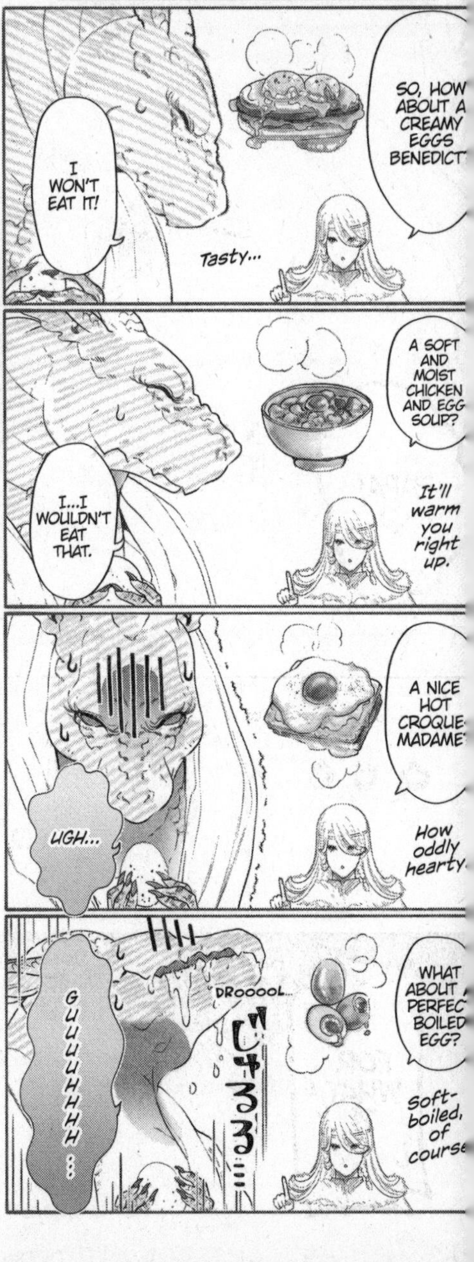
SO, HOW ABOUT A CREAMY EGGS BENEDICT
Tasty...
I WON'T EAT IT!
A SOFT AND MOIST CHICKEN AND EGG SOUP?
It'll warm you right up.
I...I WOULDN'T EAT THAT.
A NICE HOT CROQUE-MADAME
How oddly hearty
UGH...
WHAT ABOUT PERFEC BOILED EGG?
Soft-boiled, of course
DROOOOL...
じゅるる…
GUUUUHHHH...

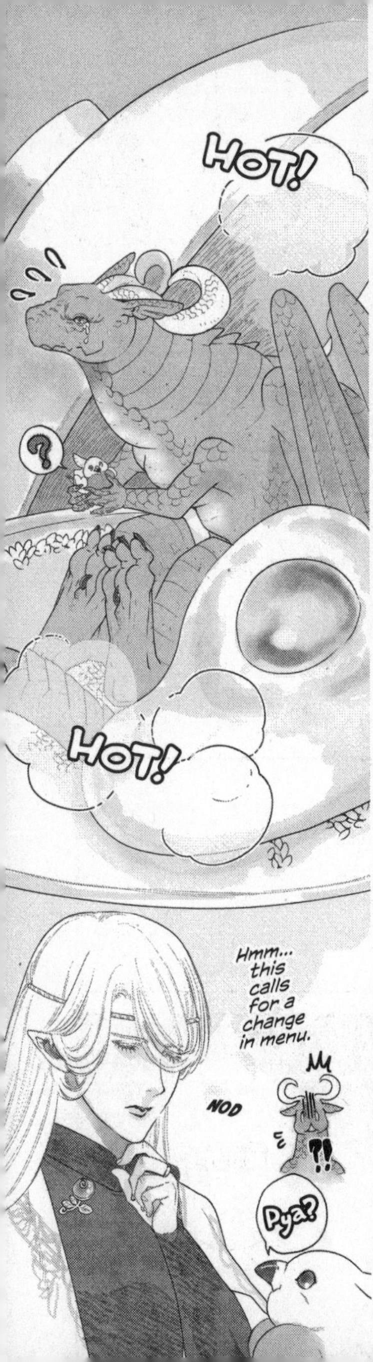
HOT!
?
HOT!
Hmm... this calls for a change in menu.
NOD
?!
Pya?

Dragon Goes House-Hunting

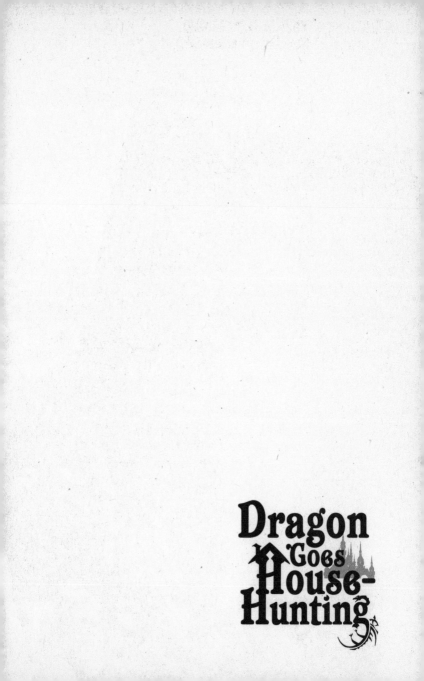

House 7: An Apartment Complex

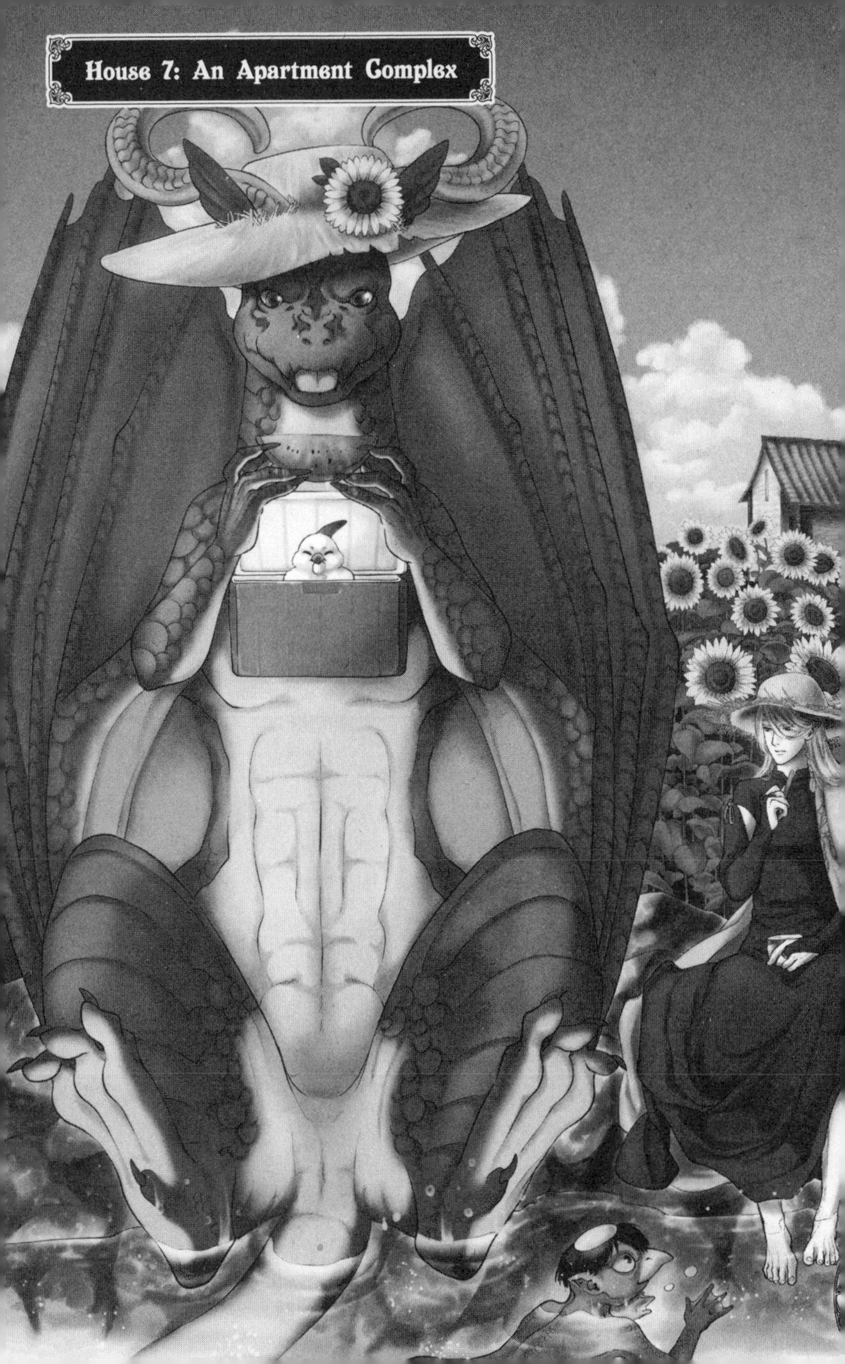

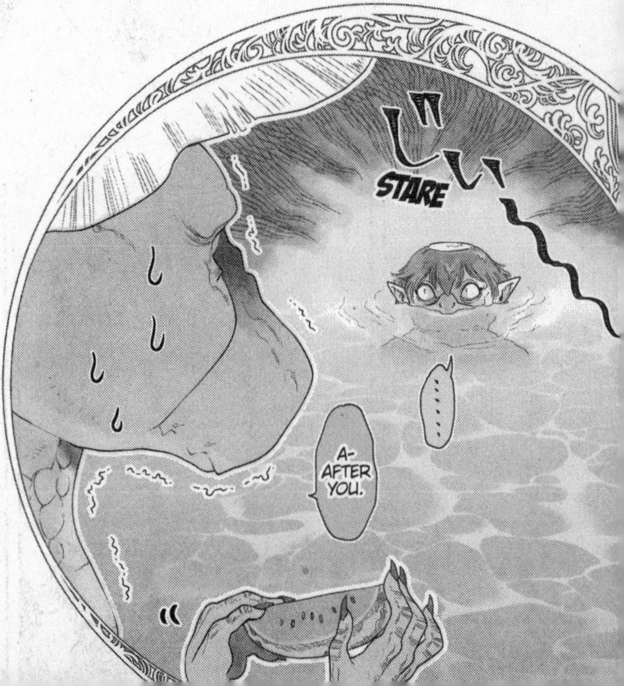
じぃーー
STARE
......
A-
AFTER
YOU.

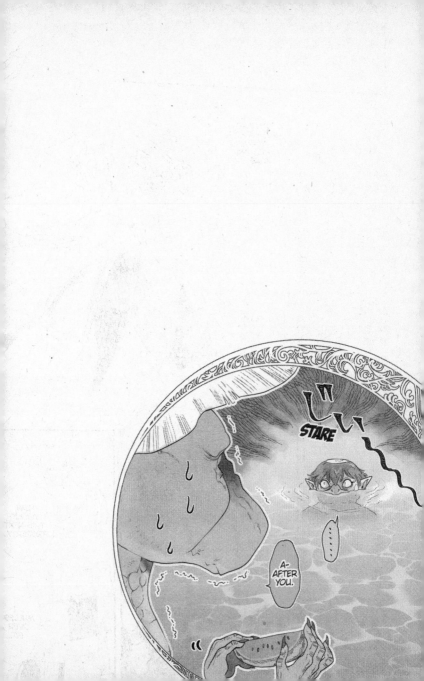

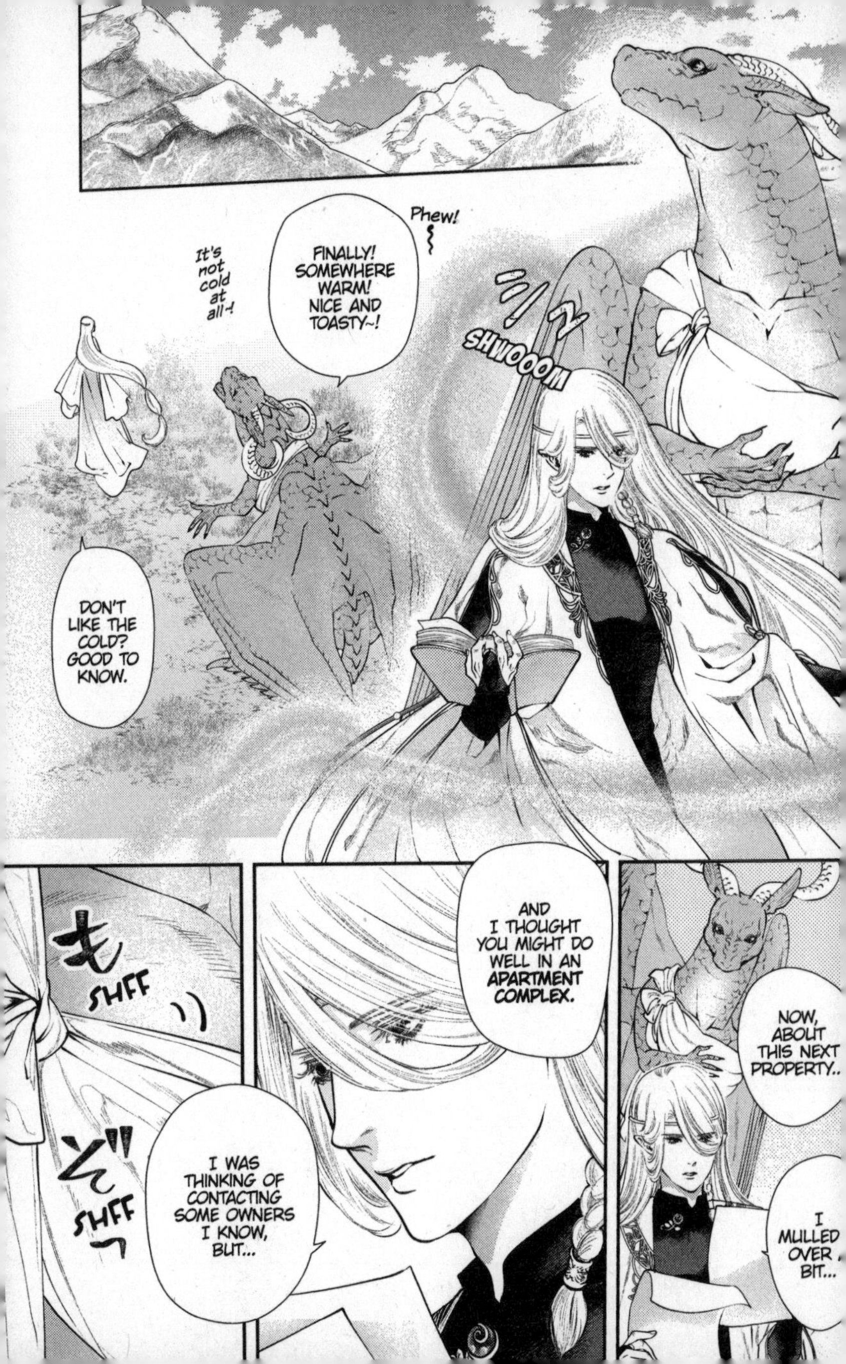
SHWOOOM
Phew!
FINALLY! SOMEWHERE WARM! NICE AND TOASTY~!
It's not cold at all~!
DON'T LIKE THE COLD? GOOD TO KNOW.
NOW, ABOUT THIS NEXT PROPERTY..
I MULLED OVER BIT...
AND I THOUGHT YOU MIGHT DO WELL IN AN APARTMENT COMPLEX.
I WAS THINKING OF CONTACTING SOME OWNERS I KNOW, BUT...
SHFF
SHFF

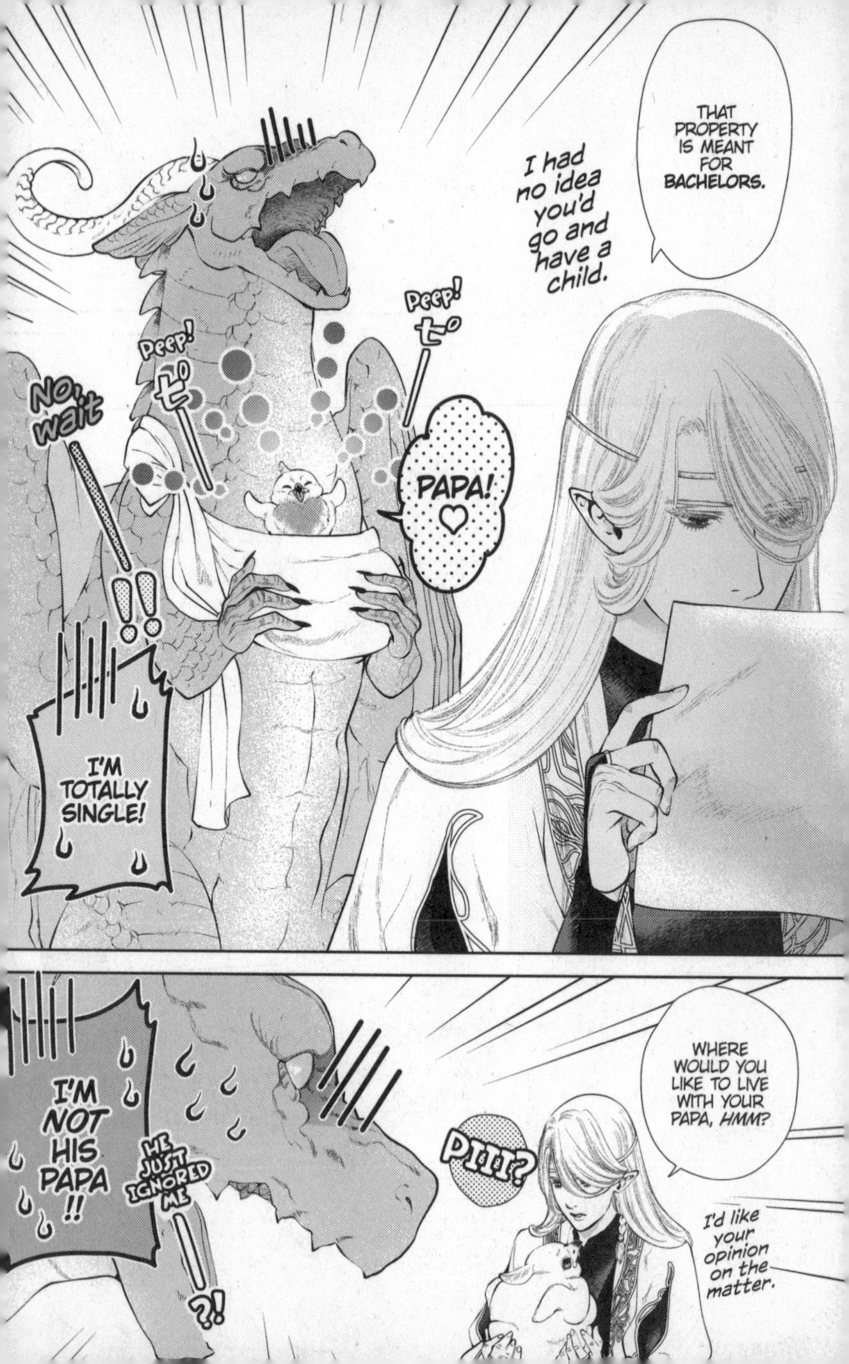
THAT PROPERTY IS MEANT FOR BACHELORS.
I had no idea you'd go and have a child.
Peep! ピ
PAPA! ♡
Peep! ピ
No, wait
!!
I'M TOTALLY SINGLE!
WHERE WOULD YOU LIKE TO LIVE WITH YOUR PAPA, *HMM?*
I'd like your opinion on the matter.
PIII?
HE JUST IGNORED ME
?!
I'M NOT HIS PAPA!!

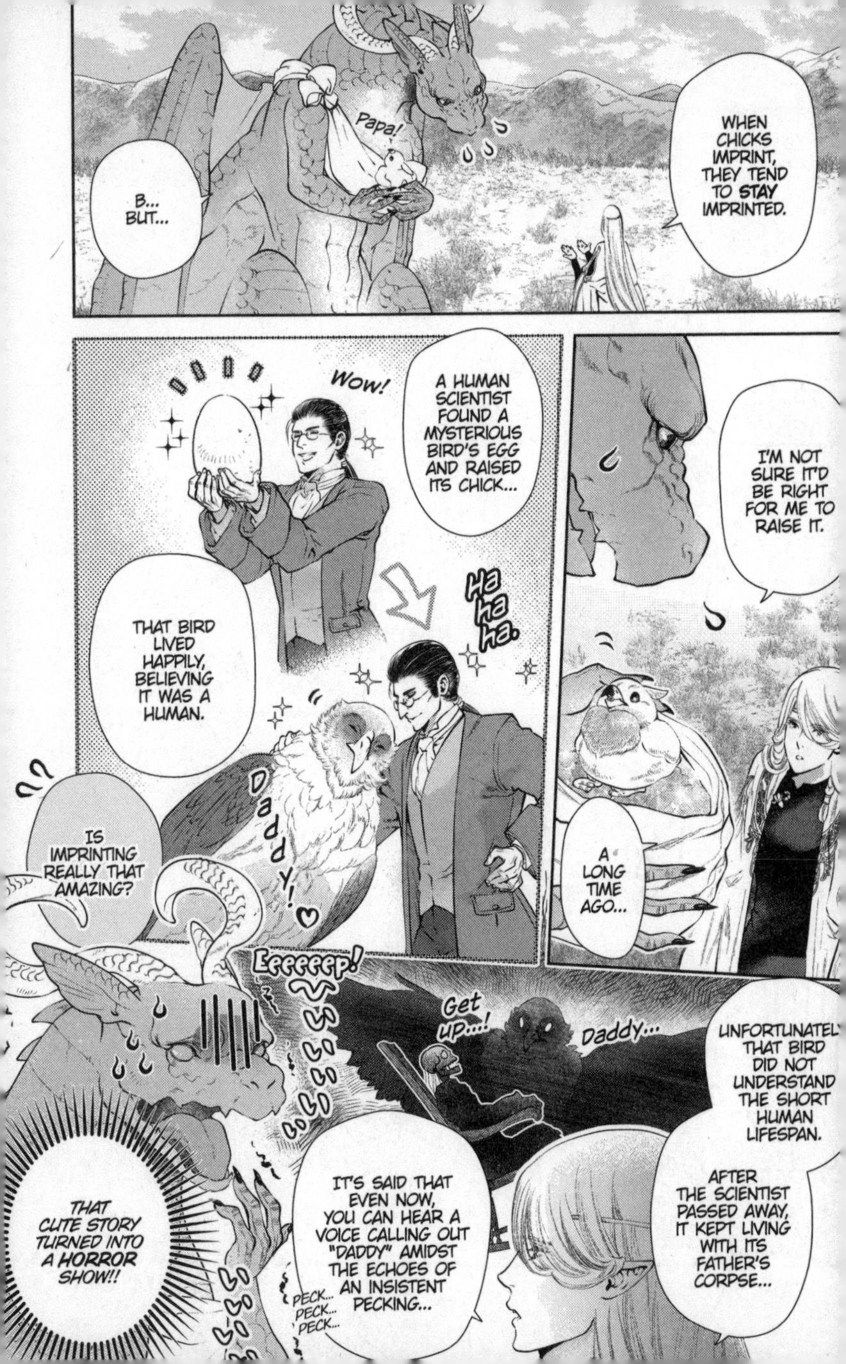
WHEN CHICKS IMPRINT, THEY TEND TO STAY IMPRINTED.
Papa!
B... BUT...
I'M NOT SURE IT'D BE RIGHT FOR ME TO RAISE IT.
A LONG TIME AGO...
A HUMAN SCIENTIST FOUND A MYSTERIOUS BIRD'S EGG AND RAISED ITS CHICK...
Wow!
Ha ha ha.
THAT BIRD LIVED HAPPILY, BELIEVING IT WAS A HUMAN.
Daddy!
IS IMPRINTING REALLY THAT AMAZING?
UNFORTUNATEL THAT BIRD DID NOT UNDERSTAND THE SHORT HUMAN LIFESPAN.
AFTER THE SCIENTIST PASSED AWAY, IT KEPT LIVING WITH ITS FATHER'S CORPSE...
Daddy...
Get up...!
Eeeeeep!
IT'S SAID THAT EVEN NOW, YOU CAN HEAR A VOICE CALLING OUT "DADDY" AMIDST THE ECHOES OF AN INSISTENT PECKING...
PECK... PECK... PECK...
THAT CUTE STORY TURNED INTO A HORROR SHOW!!

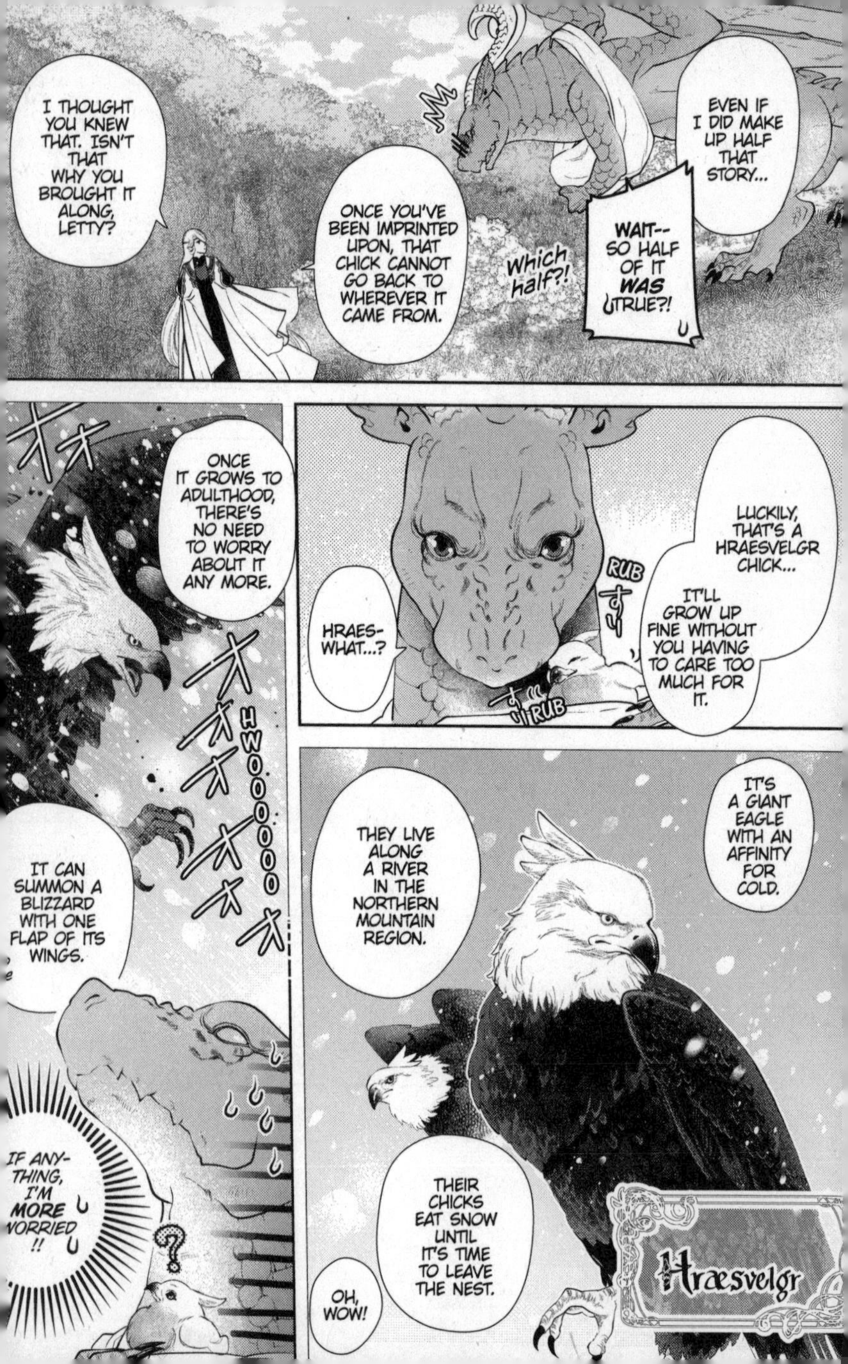
EVEN IF I DID MAKE UP HALF THAT STORY...
WAIT-- SO HALF OF IT **WAS** TRUE?!
Which half?!
ONCE YOU'VE BEEN IMPRINTED UPON, THAT CHICK CANNOT GO BACK TO WHEREVER IT CAME FROM.
I THOUGHT YOU KNEW THAT. ISN'T THAT WHY YOU BROUGHT IT ALONG, LETTY?
LUCKILY, THAT'S A HRAESVELGR CHICK...
IT'LL GROW UP FINE WITHOUT YOU HAVING TO CARE TOO MUCH FOR IT.
RUB すり
HRAES-WHAT...?
すり RUB
IT'S A GIANT EAGLE WITH AN AFFINITY FOR COLD.
THEY LIVE ALONG A RIVER IN THE NORTHERN MOUNTAIN REGION.
THEIR CHICKS EAT SNOW UNTIL IT'S TIME TO LEAVE THE NEST.
Hræsvelgr
OH, WOW!
ONCE IT GROWS TO ADULTHOOD, THERE'S NO NEED TO WORRY ABOUT IT ANY MORE.
HWOOOOOOOO
IT CAN SUMMON A BLIZZARD WITH ONE FLAP OF ITS WINGS.
IF ANYTHING, I'M **MORE** WORRIED!!

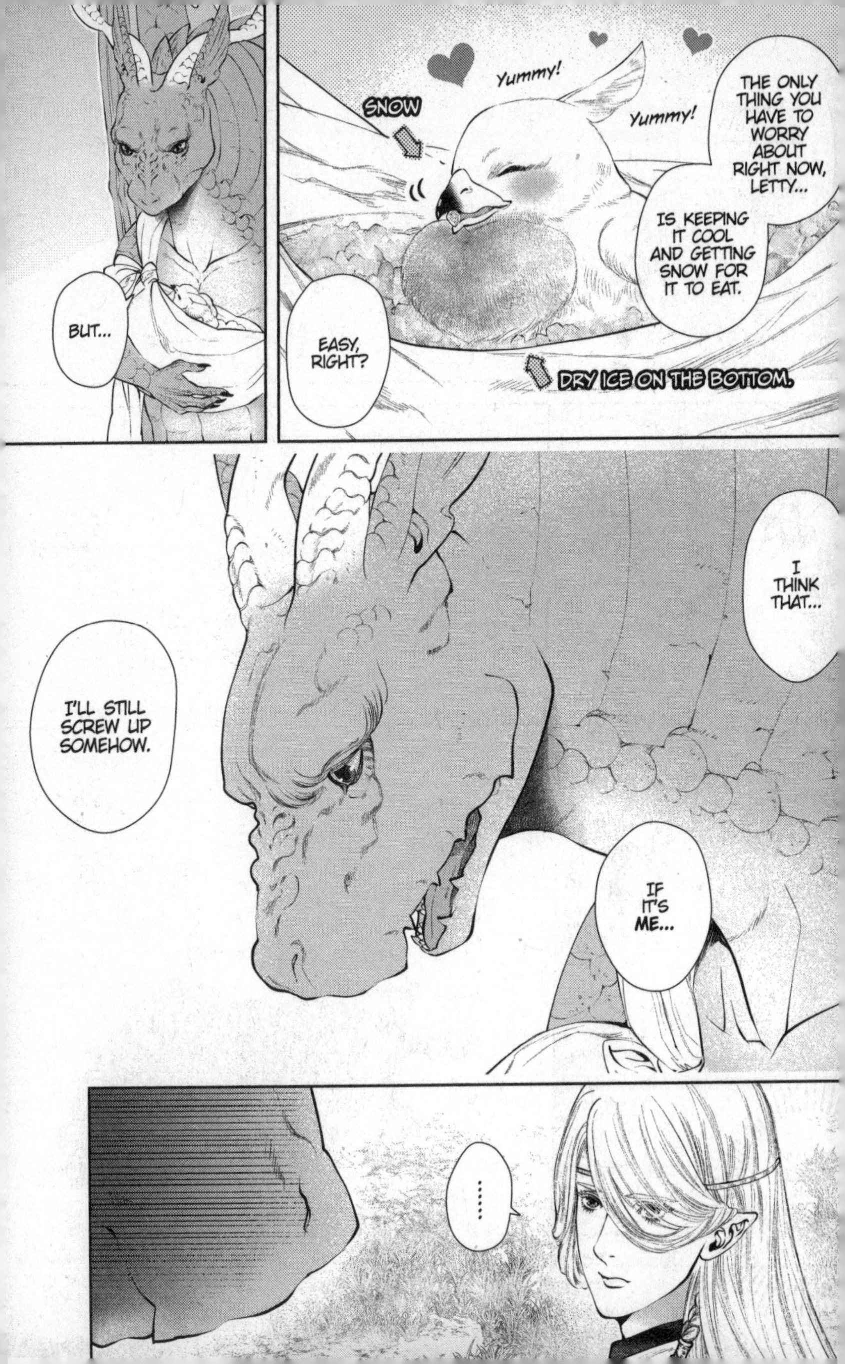
THE ONLY THING YOU HAVE TO WORRY ABOUT RIGHT NOW, LETTY...
IS KEEPING IT COOL AND GETTING SNOW FOR IT TO EAT.
Yummy!
Yummy!
SNOW
DRY ICE ON THE BOTTOM.
EASY, RIGHT?
BUT...
I THINK THAT...
IF IT'S ME...
I'LL STILL SCREW UP SOMEHOW.
......

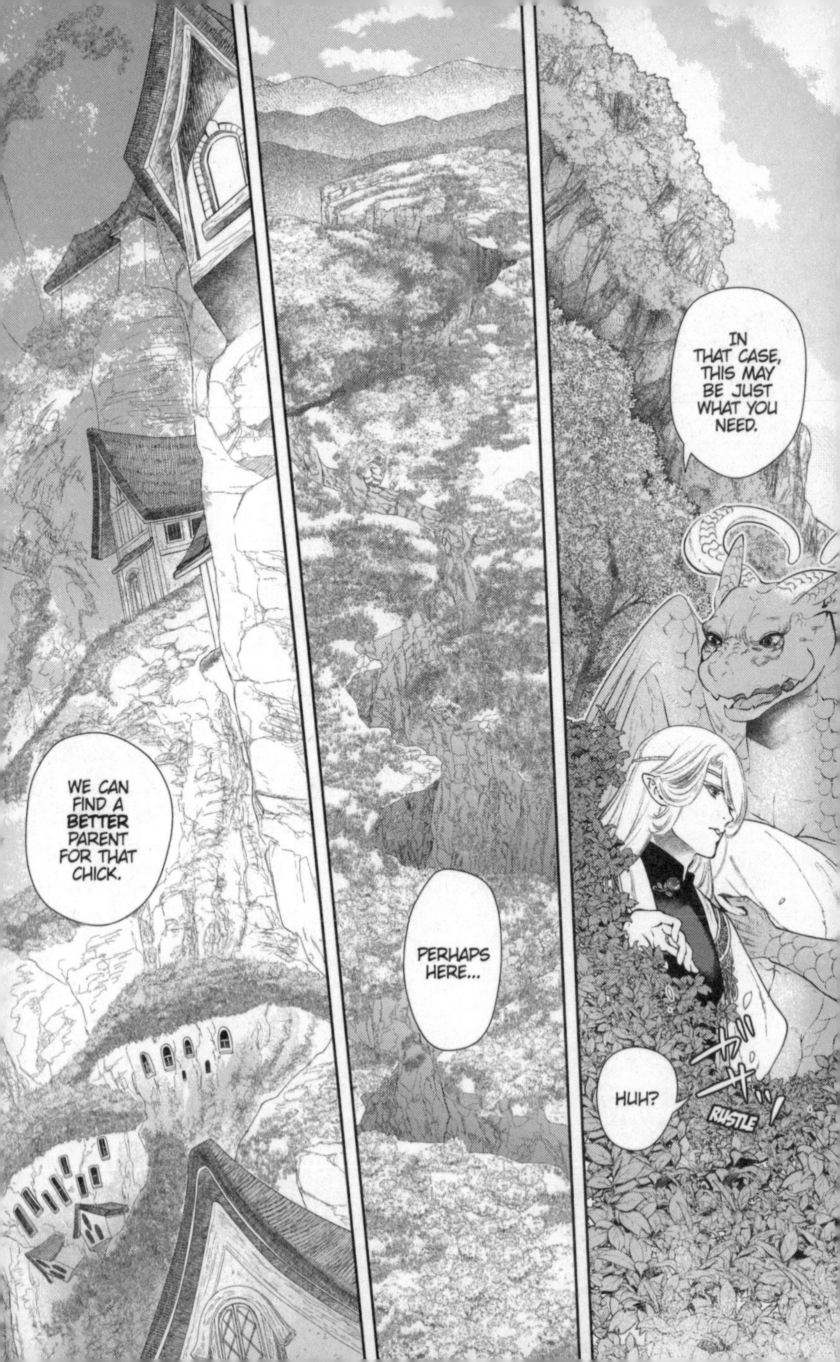
IN THAT CASE, THIS MAY BE JUST WHAT YOU NEED.
HUH?
RUSTLE
PERHAPS HERE...
WE CAN FIND A BETTER PARENT FOR THAT CHICK.

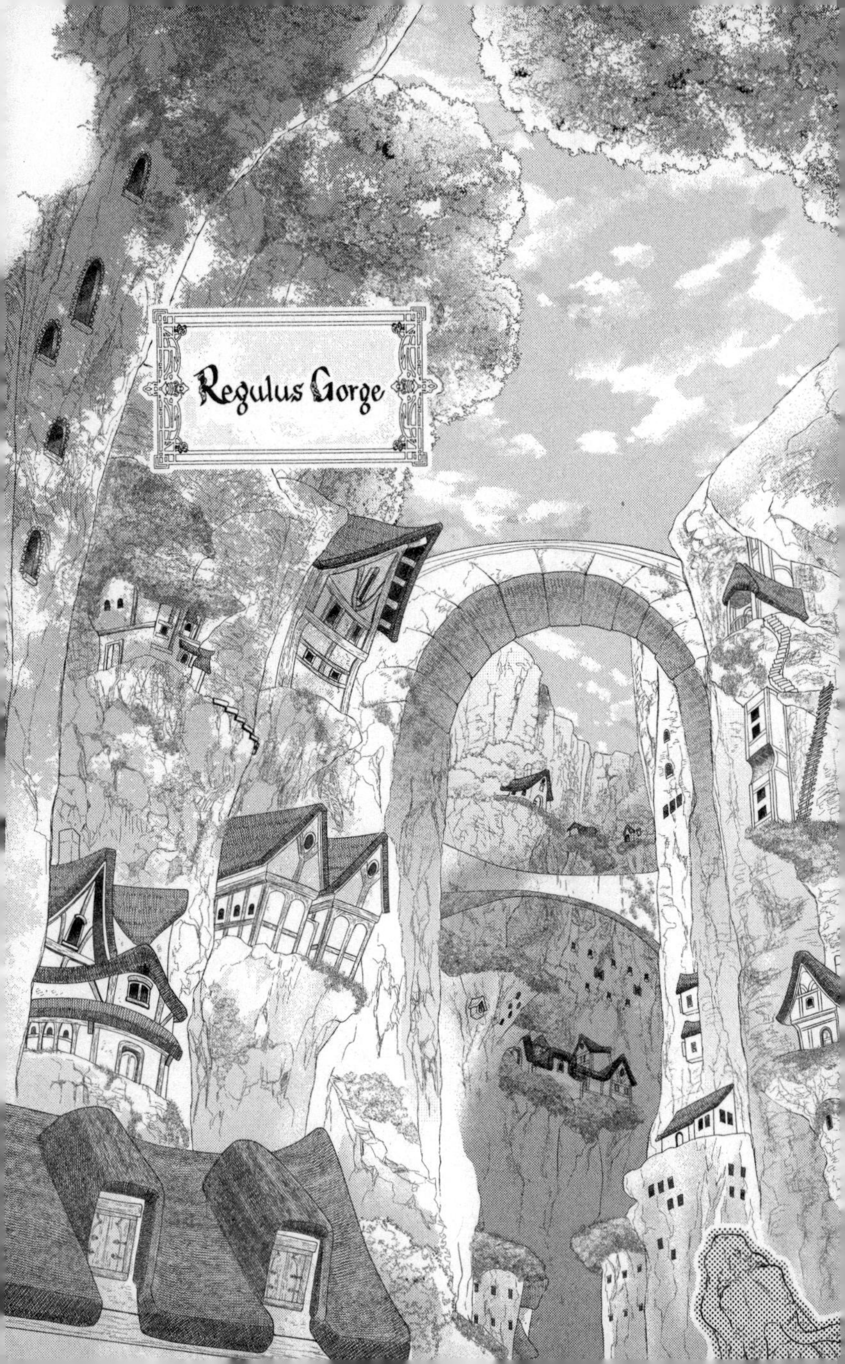
Regulus Gorge

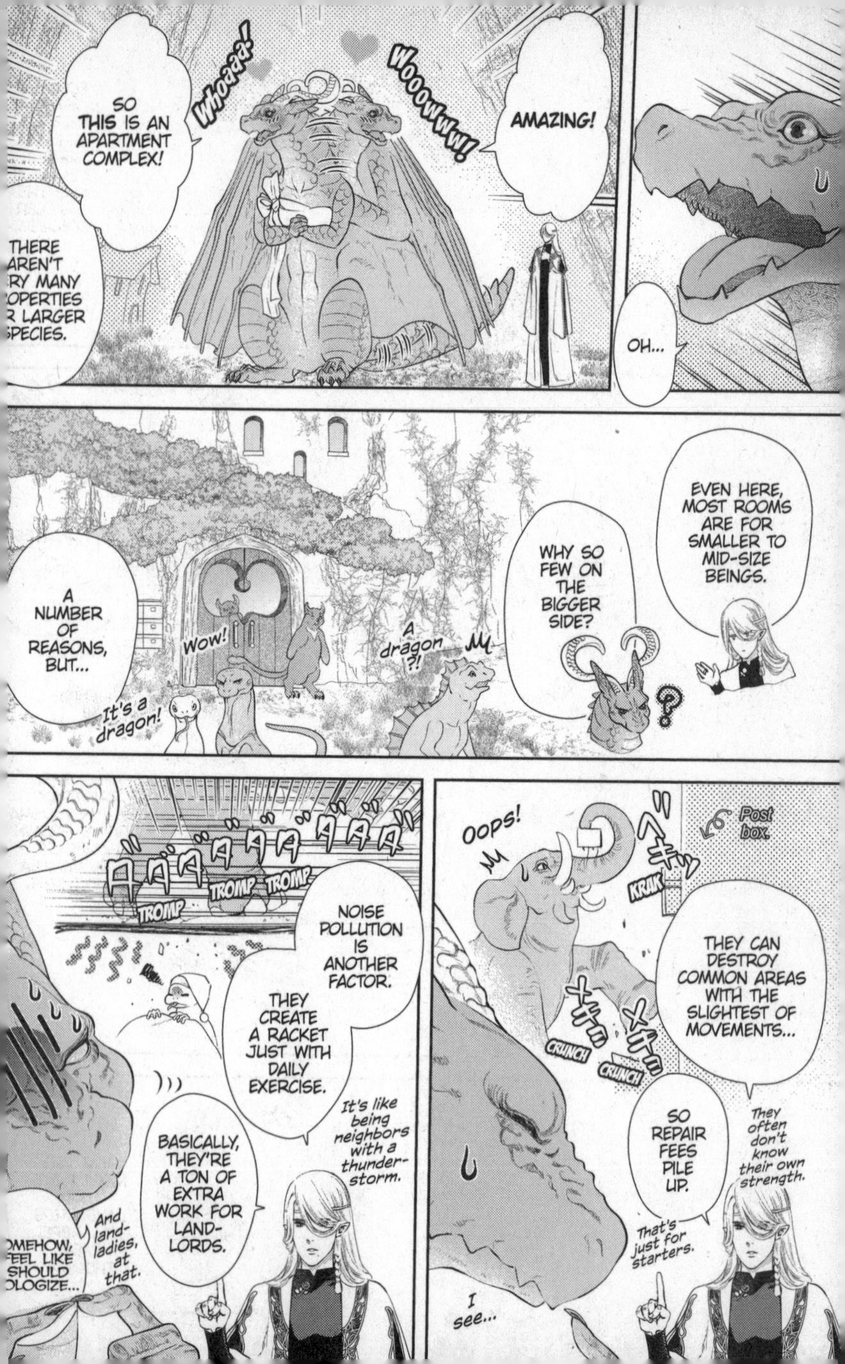
OH...
AMAZING!
Wooowww!
Whoaaa!
SO THIS IS AN APARTMENT COMPLEX!
THERE AREN'T RY MANY OPERTIES R LARGER PECIES.
EVEN HERE, MOST ROOMS ARE FOR SMALLER TO MID-SIZE BEINGS.
WHY SO FEW ON THE BIGGER SIDE?
A dragon?!
Wow!
It's a dragon!
A NUMBER OF REASONS, BUT...
Post box.
KRAK
OOPS!
THEY CAN DESTROY COMMON AREAS WITH THE SLIGHTEST OF MOVEMENTS...
CRUNCH
CRUNCH
They often don't know their own strength.
SO REPAIR FEES PILE UP.
That's just for starters.
I see...
TROMP
TROMP
TROMP
NOISE POLLUTION IS ANOTHER FACTOR.
THEY CREATE A RACKET JUST WITH DAILY EXERCISE.
It's like being neighbors with a thunder-storm.
BASICALLY, THEY'RE A TON OF EXTRA WORK FOR LAND-LORDS.
And land-ladies, at that.
OMEHOW, FEEL LIKE SHOULD OLOGIZE...

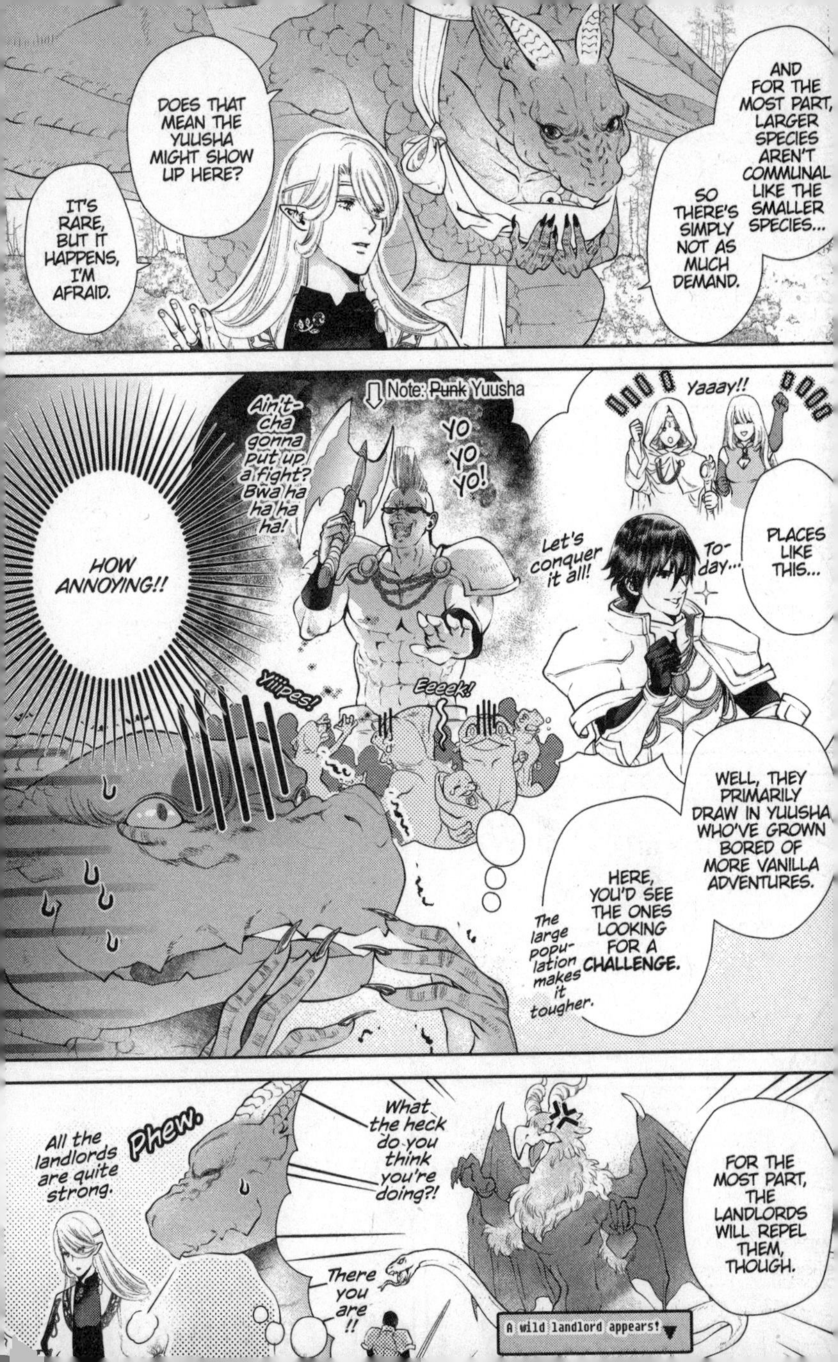
AND FOR THE MOST PART, LARGER SPECIES AREN'T COMMUNAL LIKE THE SMALLER SPECIES...
SO THERE'S SIMPLY NOT AS MUCH DEMAND.
DOES THAT MEAN THE YUUSHA MIGHT SHOW UP HERE?
IT'S RARE, BUT IT HAPPENS, I'M AFRAID.
PLACES LIKE THIS...
Yaaay!!
To-day...
Let's conquer it all!
WELL, THEY PRIMARILY DRAW IN YUUSHA WHO'VE GROWN BORED OF MORE VANILLA ADVENTURES.
HERE, YOU'D SEE THE ONES LOOKING FOR A CHALLENGE.
The large population makes it tougher.
Note: ~~Punk~~ Yuusha
YO YO YO!
Ain't-cha gonna put up a fight? Bwa ha ha ha ha!
Eeeek!
Yiiipes!
HOW ANNOYING!!
FOR THE MOST PART, THE LANDLORDS WILL REPEL THEM, THOUGH.
A wild landlord appears!
What the heck do you think you're doing?!
There you are!!
Phew.
All the landlords are quite strong.

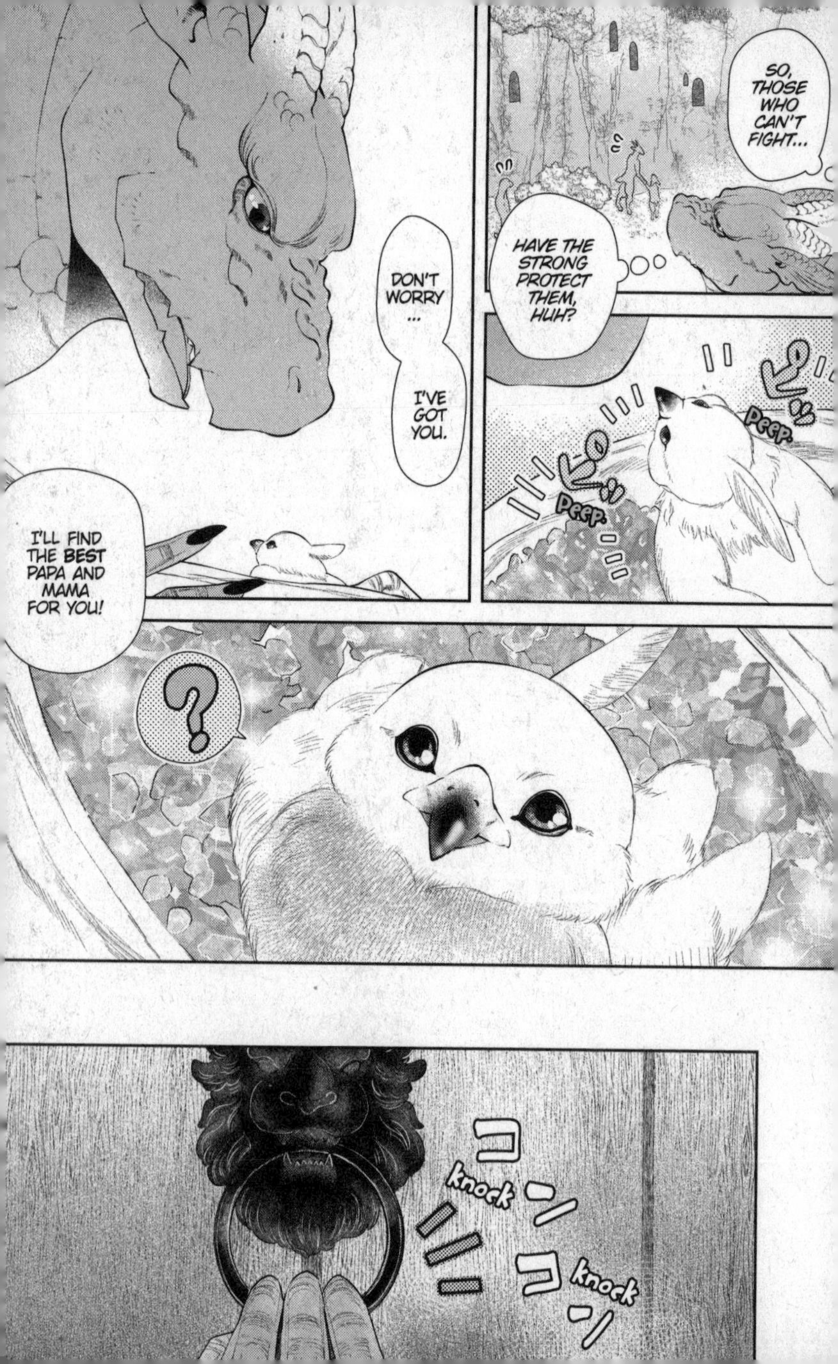
SO, THOSE WHO CAN'T FIGHT...
HAVE THE STRONG PROTECT THEM, HUH?
Peep.
Peep.
DON'T WORRY...
I'VE GOT YOU.
I'LL FIND THE BEST PAPA AND MAMA FOR YOU!
?
knock
knock

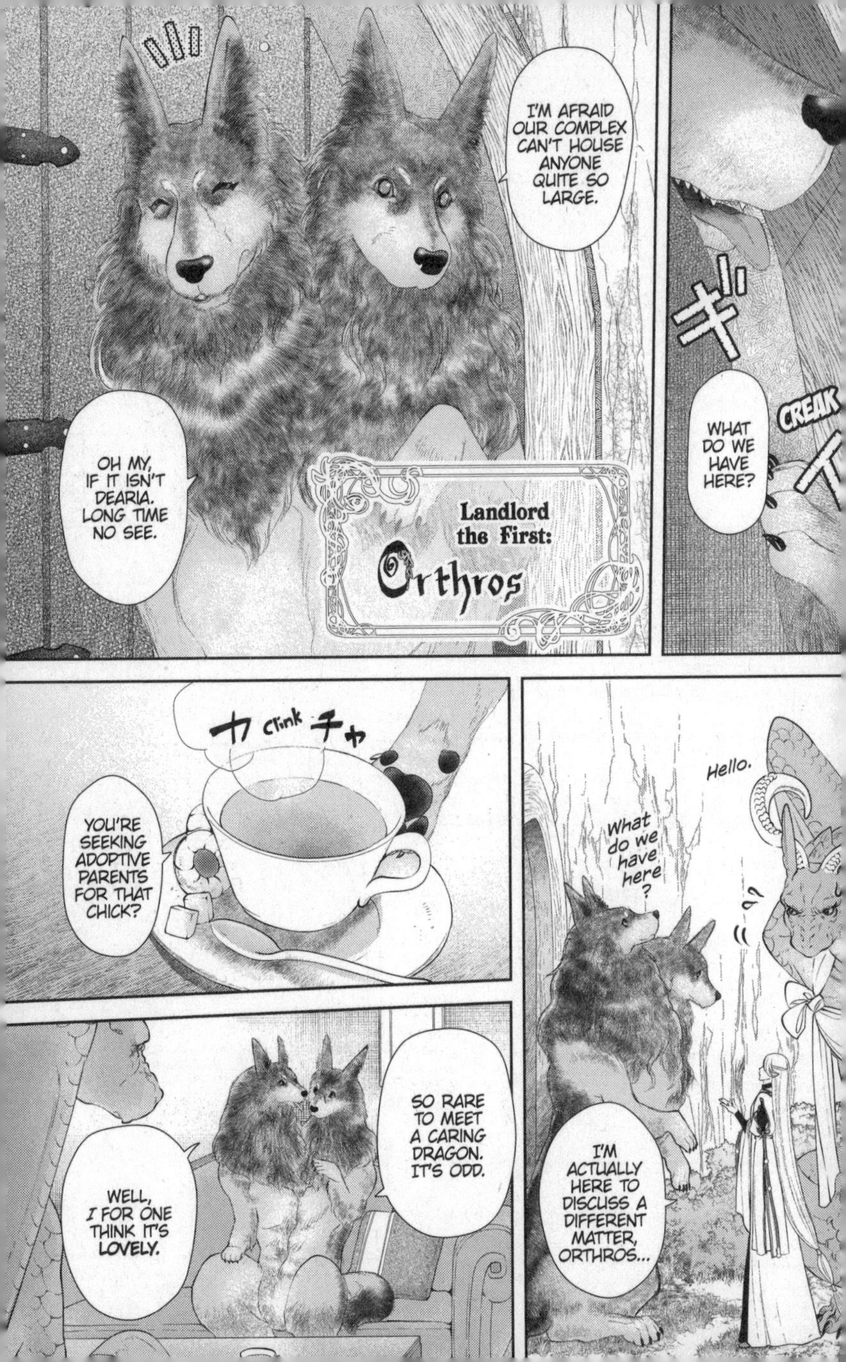
ギ
CREAK
イ
WHAT DO WE HAVE HERE?
I'M AFRAID OUR COMPLEX CAN'T HOUSE ANYONE QUITE SO LARGE.
Landlord the First:
Orthros
OH MY, IF IT ISN'T DEARIA. LONG TIME NO SEE.
Hello.
What do we have here?
I'M ACTUALLY HERE TO DISCUSS A DIFFERENT MATTER, ORTHROS...
カ clink チャ
YOU'RE SEEKING ADOPTIVE PARENTS FOR THAT CHICK?
SO RARE TO MEET A CARING DRAGON. IT'S ODD.
WELL, I FOR ONE THINK IT'S **LOVELY**.

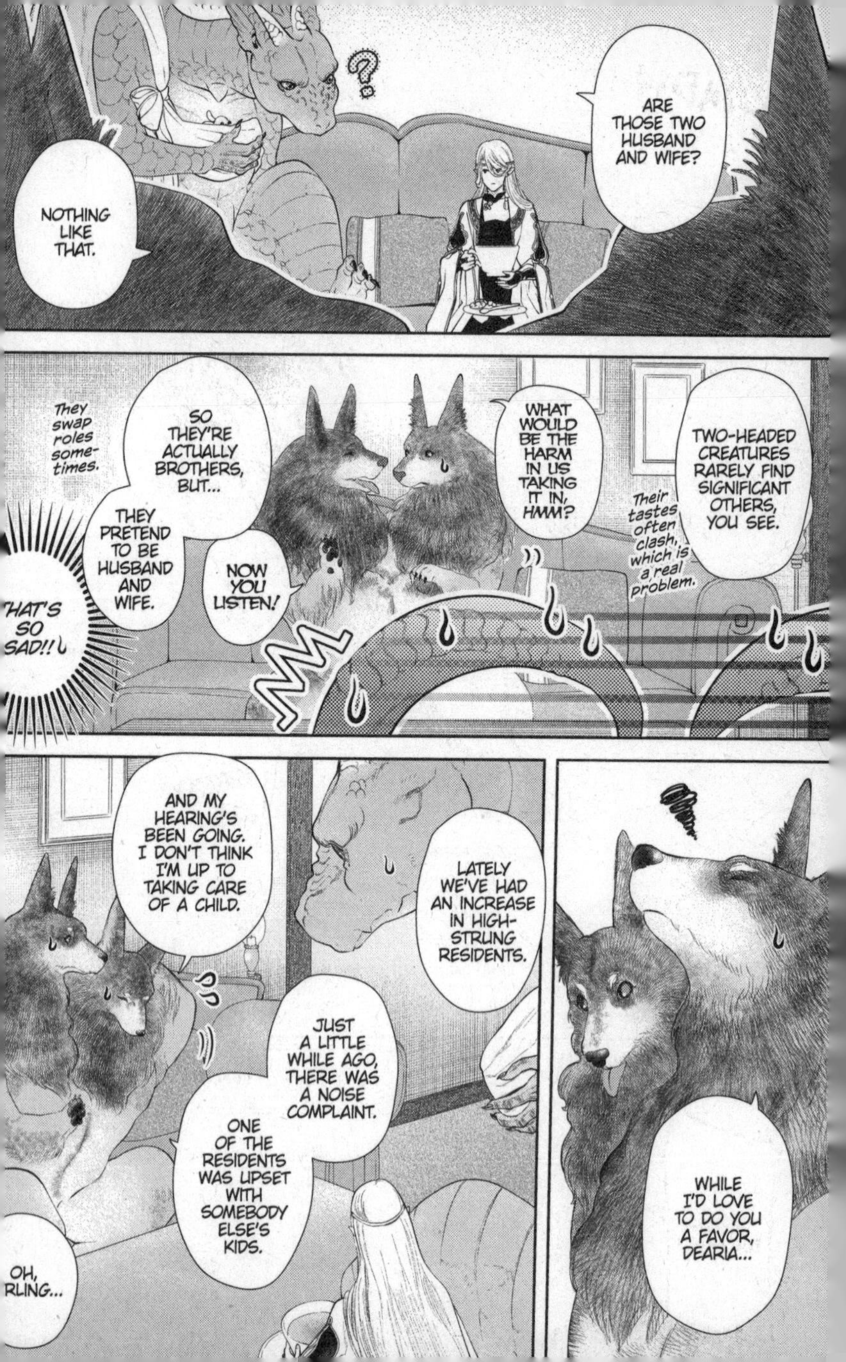
ARE THOSE TWO HUSBAND AND WIFE?
NOTHING LIKE THAT.
TWO-HEADED CREATURES RARELY FIND SIGNIFICANT OTHERS, YOU SEE.
Their tastes often clash, which is a real problem.
WHAT WOULD BE THE HARM IN US TAKING IT IN, HMM?
NOW YOU LISTEN!
SO THEY'RE ACTUALLY BROTHERS, BUT...
They swap roles sometimes.
THEY PRETEND TO BE HUSBAND AND WIFE.
HAT'S SO SAD!!
WHILE I'D LOVE TO DO YOU A FAVOR, DEARIA...
LATELY WE'VE HAD AN INCREASE IN HIGH-STRUNG RESIDENTS.
AND MY HEARING'S BEEN GOING. I DON'T THINK I'M UP TO TAKING CARE OF A CHILD.
JUST A LITTLE WHILE AGO, THERE WAS A NOISE COMPLAINT.
ONE OF THE RESIDENTS WAS UPSET WITH SOMEBODY ELSE'S KIDS.
OH, RLING...

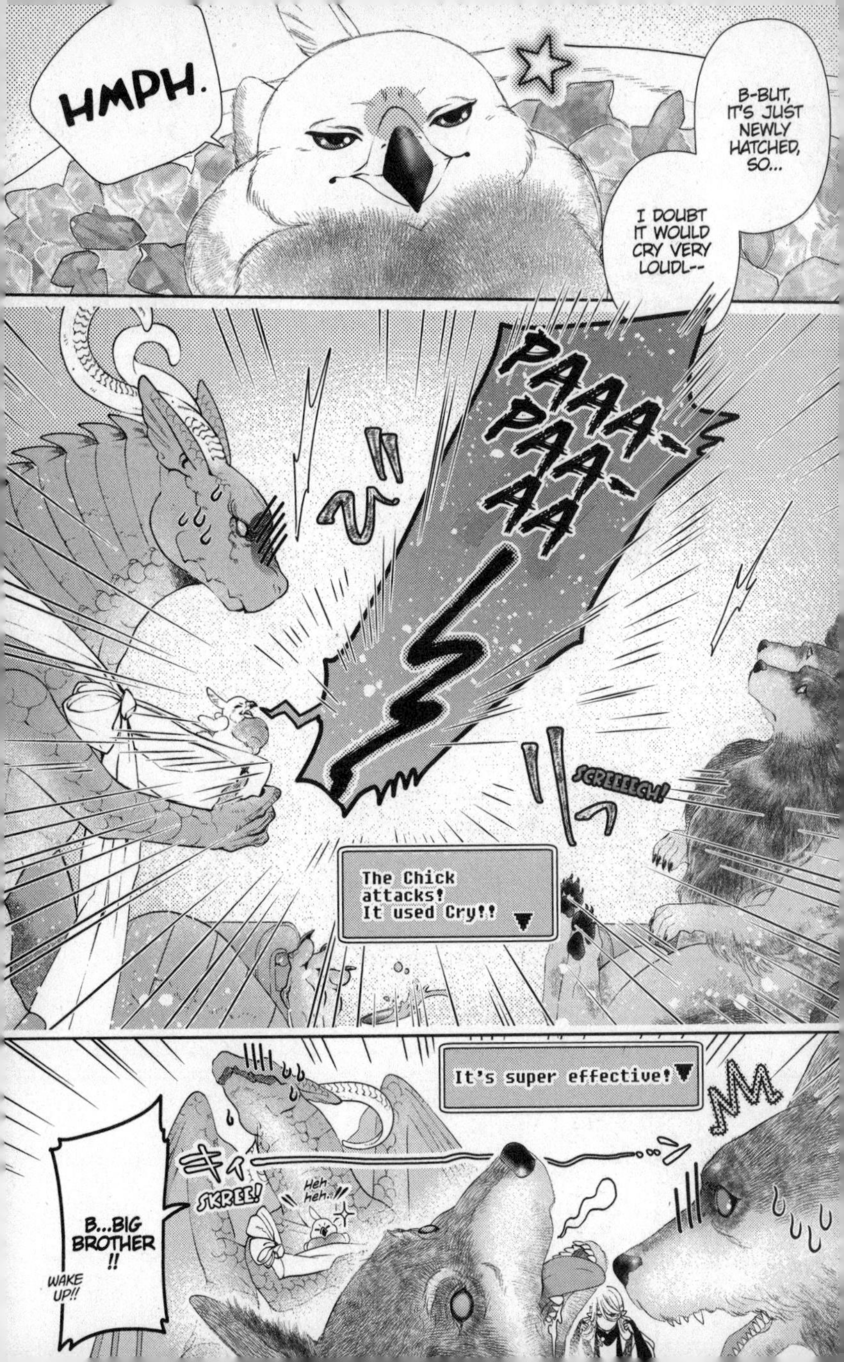
B-BUT, IT'S JUST NEWLY HATCHED, SO...
I DOUBT IT WOULD CRY VERY LOUDL--
HMPH.
PAAA-PAA-AA
SCREEEECH!
The Chick attacks! It used Cry!!
It's super effective!
キィ
SKREE!
Heh heh...
B...BIG BROTHER!!
WAKE UP!!

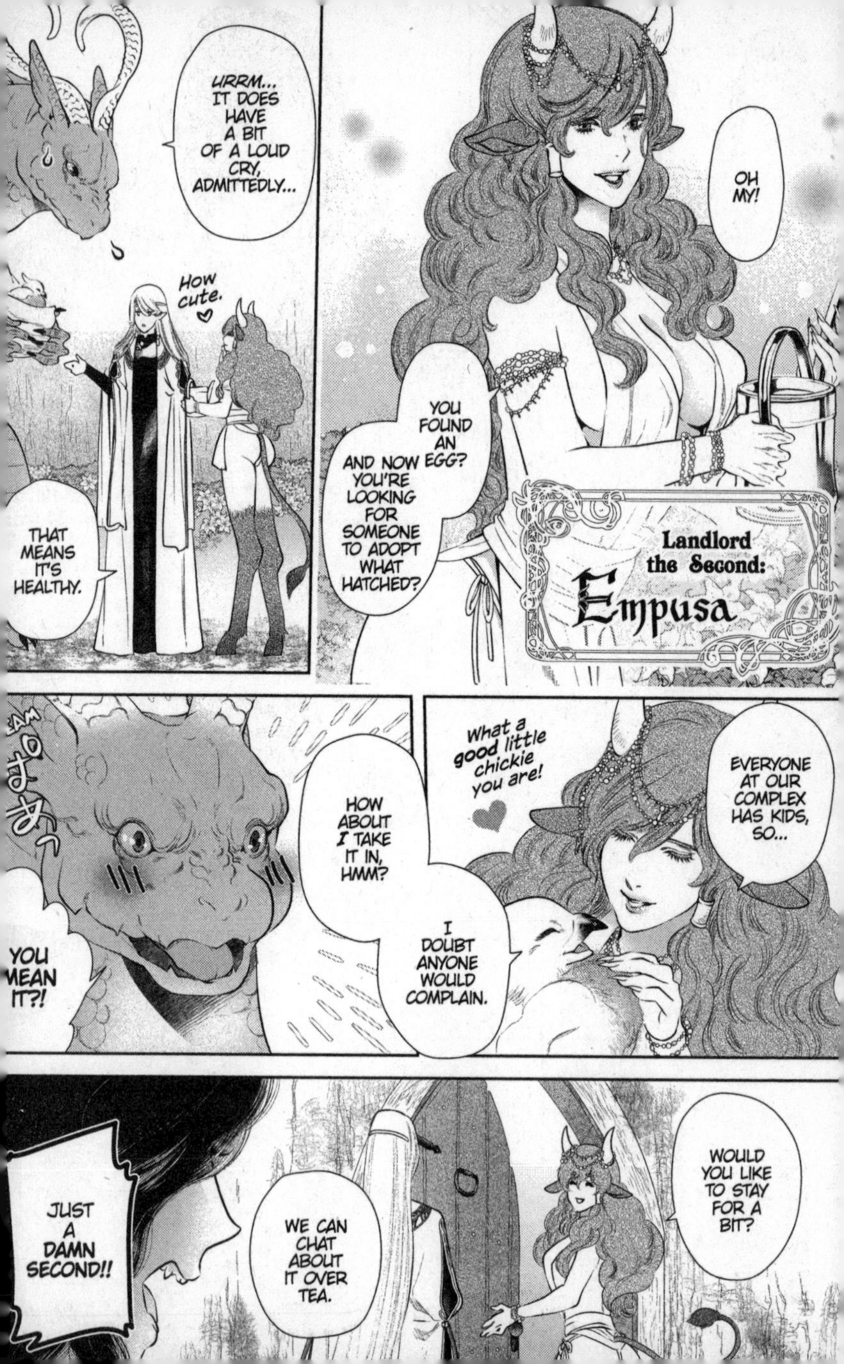
OH MY!
YOU FOUND AN EGG?
AND NOW YOU'RE LOOKING FOR SOMEONE TO ADOPT WHAT HATCHED?
Landlord the Second: Empusa
URRM... IT DOES HAVE A BIT OF A LOUD CRY, ADMITTEDLY...
How cute.
THAT MEANS IT'S HEALTHY.
EVERYONE AT OUR COMPLEX HAS KIDS, SO...
What a good little chickie you are!
HOW ABOUT I TAKE IT IN, HMM?
I DOUBT ANYONE WOULD COMPLAIN.
YOU MEAN IT?!
WOULD YOU LIKE TO STAY FOR A BIT?
WE CAN CHAT ABOUT IT OVER TEA.
JUST A DAMN SECOND!!

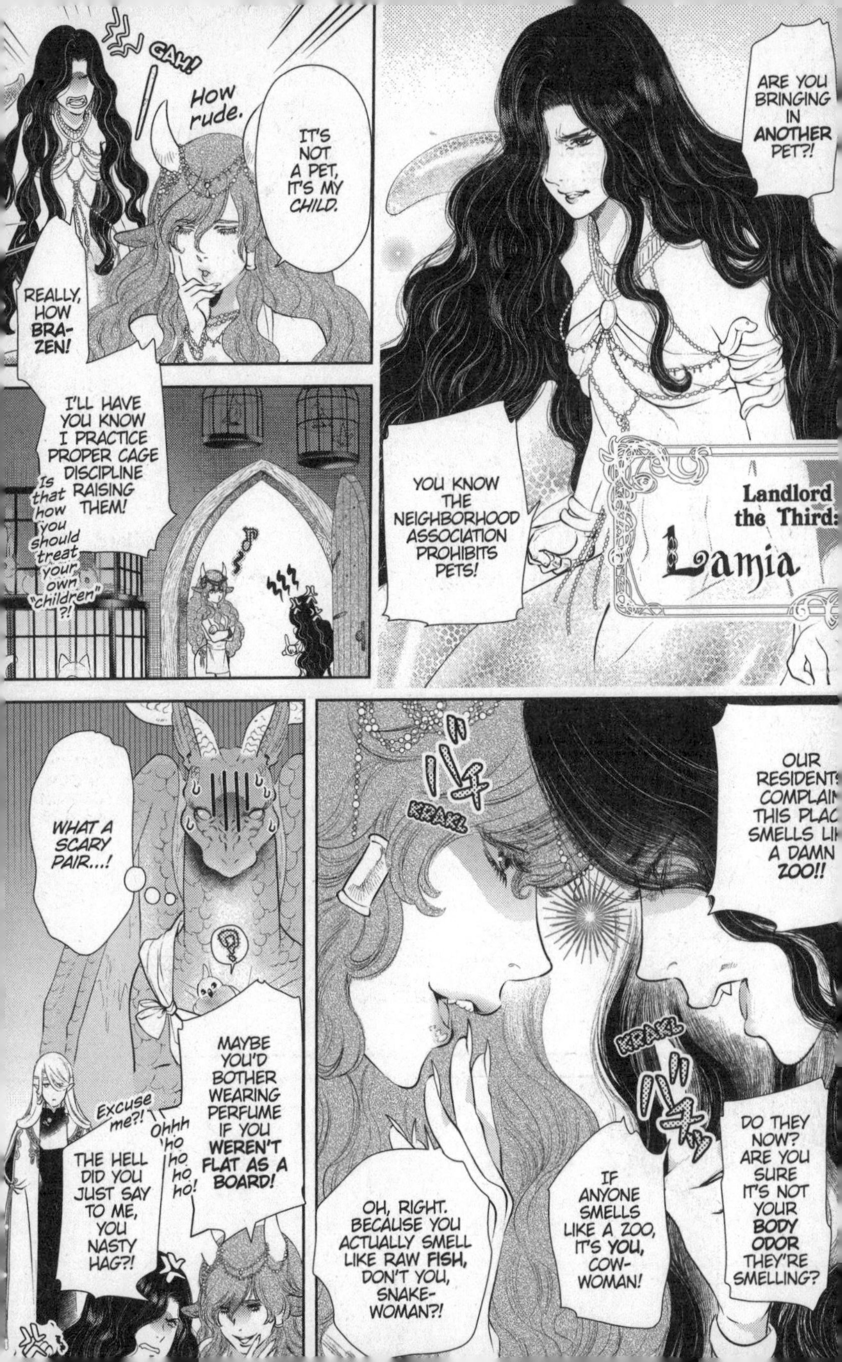
ARE YOU BRINGING IN ANOTHER PET?!
YOU KNOW THE NEIGHBORHOOD ASSOCIATION PROHIBITS PETS!
Landlord the Third:
Lamia
GAH!
How rude.
IT'S NOT A PET, IT'S MY CHILD.
REALLY, HOW BRA-ZEN!
I'LL HAVE YOU KNOW I PRACTICE PROPER CAGE DISCIPLINE RAISING THEM!
Is that how you should treat your own "children"?!
OUR RESIDENTS COMPLAIN THIS PLAC SMELLS LIK A DAMN ZOO!!
KRAKL
DO THEY NOW? ARE YOU SURE IT'S NOT YOUR BODY ODOR THEY'RE SMELLING?
KRAKL
IF ANYONE SMELLS LIKE A ZOO, IT'S YOU, COW-WOMAN!
OH, RIGHT. BECAUSE YOU ACTUALLY SMELL LIKE RAW FISH, DON'T YOU, SNAKE-WOMAN?!
WHAT A SCARY PAIR...!
MAYBE YOU'D BOTHER WEARING PERFUME IF YOU WEREN'T FLAT AS A BOARD!
Ohhh ho ho ho ho!
Excuse me?!
THE HELL DID YOU JUST SAY TO ME, YOU NASTY HAG?!

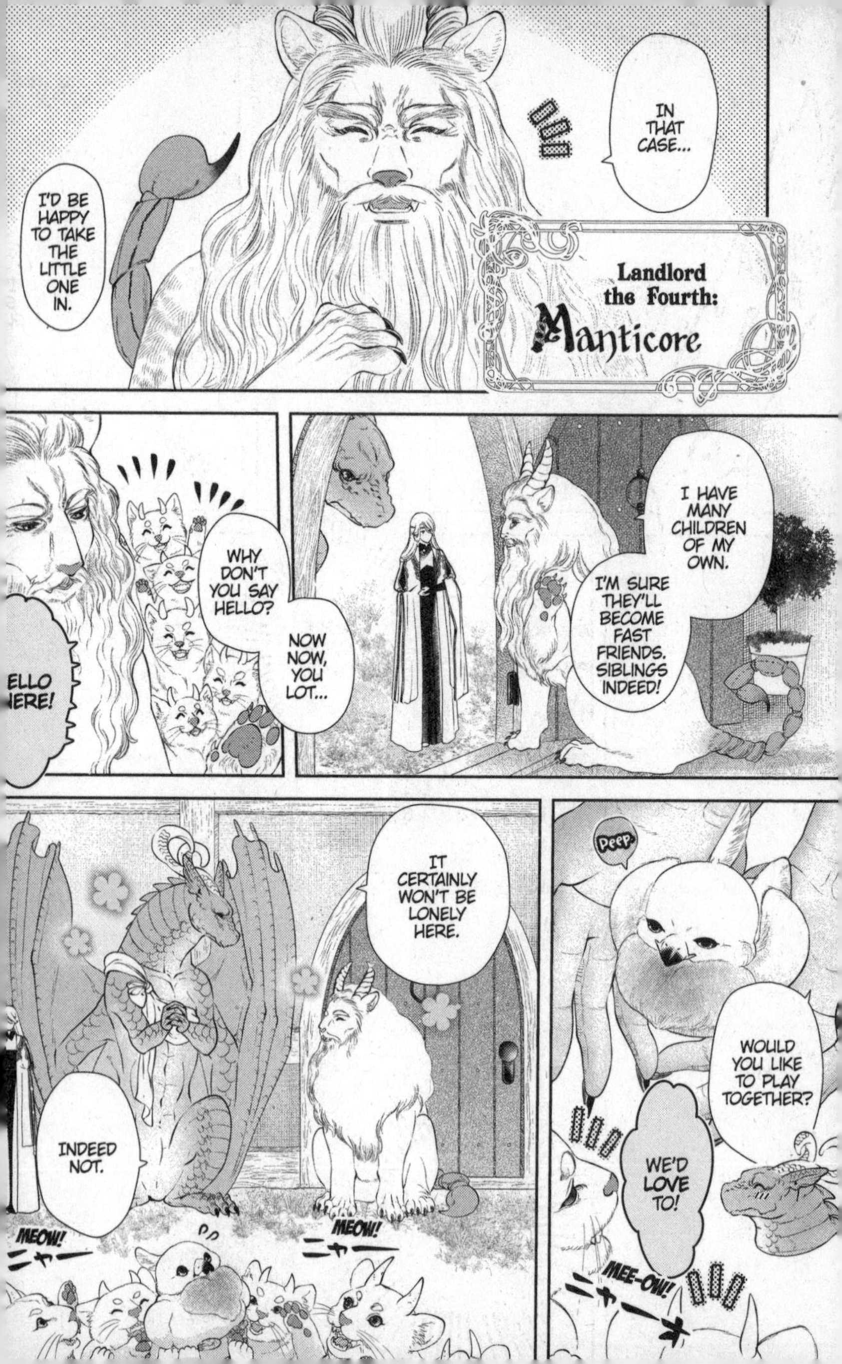
IN THAT CASE...
I'D BE HAPPY TO TAKE THE LITTLE ONE IN.
Landlord the Fourth: Manticore
I HAVE MANY CHILDREN OF MY OWN.
I'M SURE THEY'LL BECOME FAST FRIENDS. SIBLINGS INDEED!
WHY DON'T YOU SAY HELLO?
NOW NOW, YOU LOT...
ELLO HERE!
Peep.
WOULD YOU LIKE TO PLAY TOGETHER?
WE'D LOVE TO!
MEE-OW! ニャーオ
IT CERTAINLY WON'T BE LONELY HERE.
INDEED NOT.
MEOW! ニャー
MEOW! ニャー

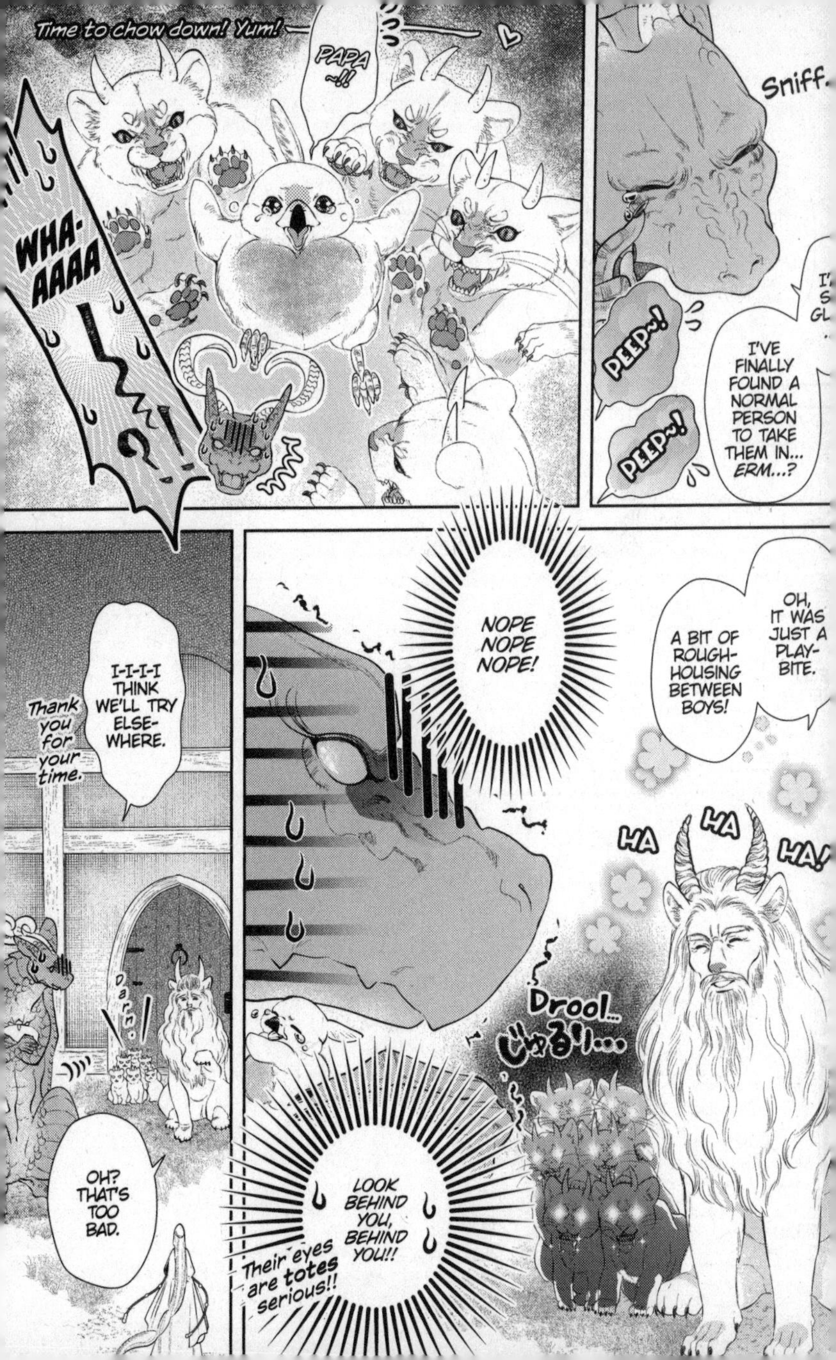
Sniff.
PEEP~!
I'VE FINALLY FOUND A NORMAL PERSON TO TAKE THEM IN... ERM...?
PEEP~!
Time to chow down! Yum!
PAPA ~!!
WHA-AAAA!?
OH, IT WAS JUST A PLAY-BITE.
A BIT OF ROUGH-HOUSING BETWEEN BOYS!
NOPE NOPE NOPE!
HA HA HA!
Drool... じゅるり...
LOOK BEHIND YOU, BEHIND YOU!!
Their eyes are totes serious!!
I-I-I-I THINK WE'LL TRY ELSE-WHERE.
Thank you for your time.
Darn.
OH? THAT'S TOO BAD.

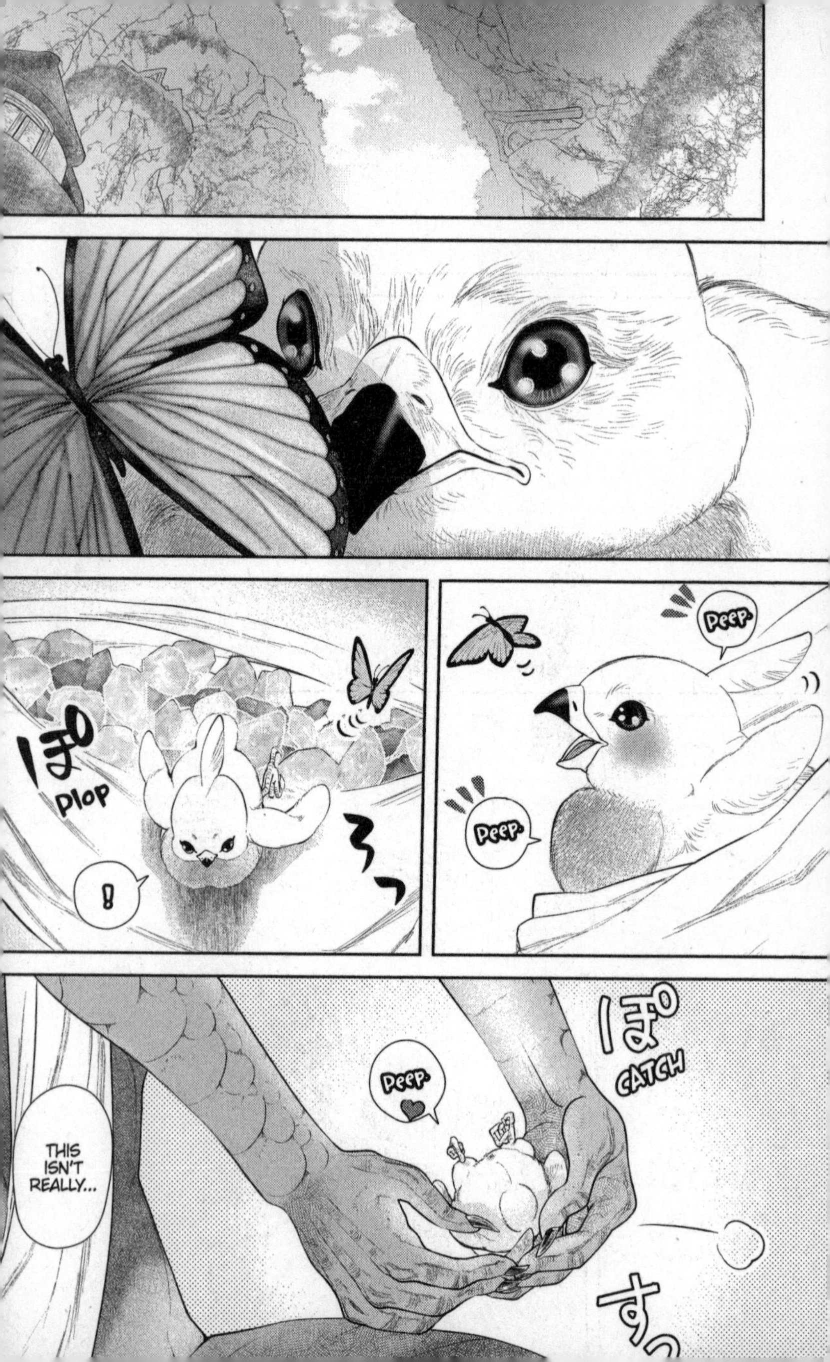

Peep.
Peep.
ぽ
plop
ろっ
!
ぽ
CATCH
Peep. ♥
THIS ISN'T REALLY...
すっ

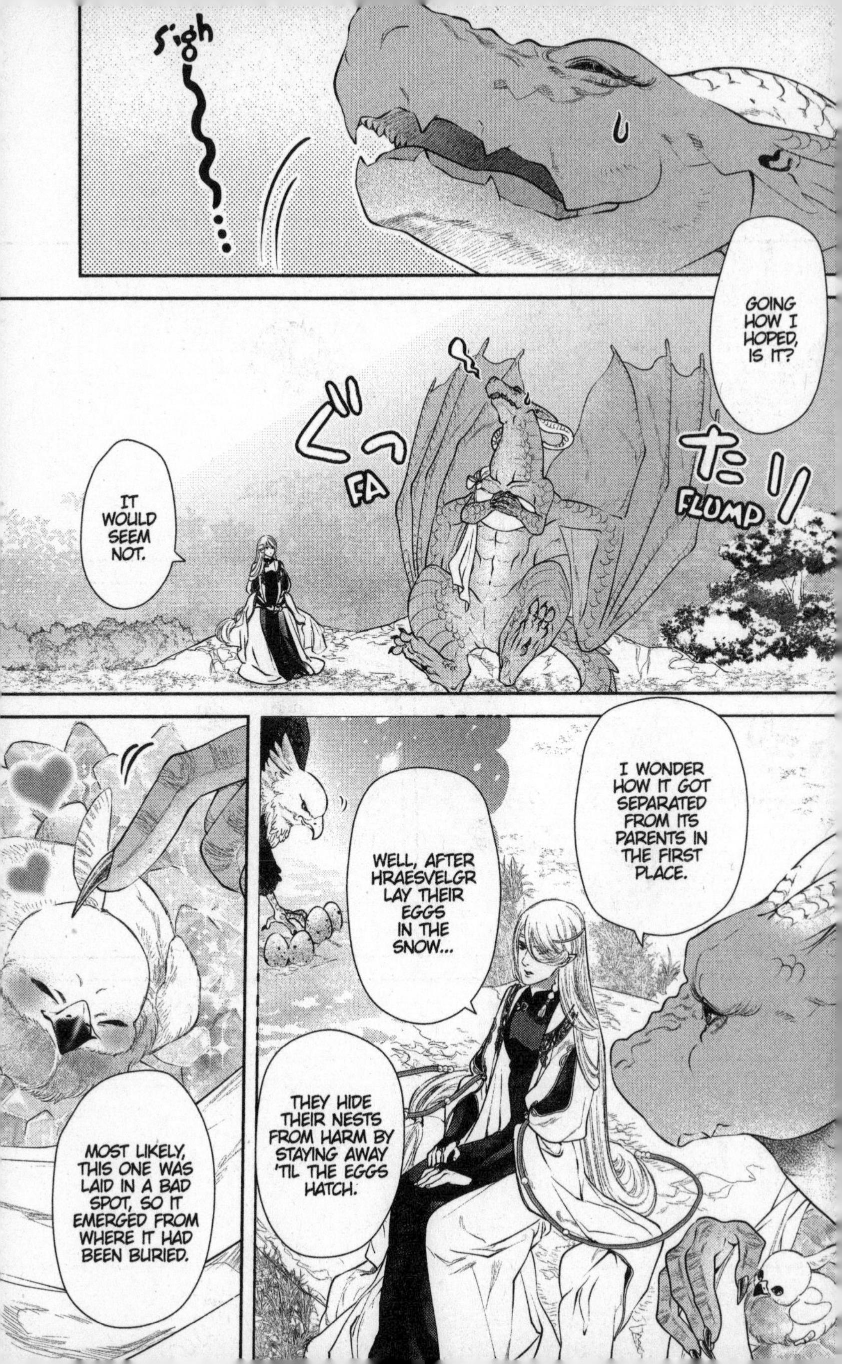
Sigh
GOING HOW I HOPED, IS IT?
FLUMP
FA
IT WOULD SEEM NOT.
I WONDER HOW IT GOT SEPARATED FROM ITS PARENTS IN THE FIRST PLACE.
WELL, AFTER HRAESVELGR LAY THEIR EGGS IN THE SNOW...
THEY HIDE THEIR NESTS FROM HARM BY STAYING AWAY 'TIL THE EGGS HATCH.
MOST LIKELY, THIS ONE WAS LAID IN A BAD SPOT, SO IT EMERGED FROM WHERE IT HAD BEEN BURIED.

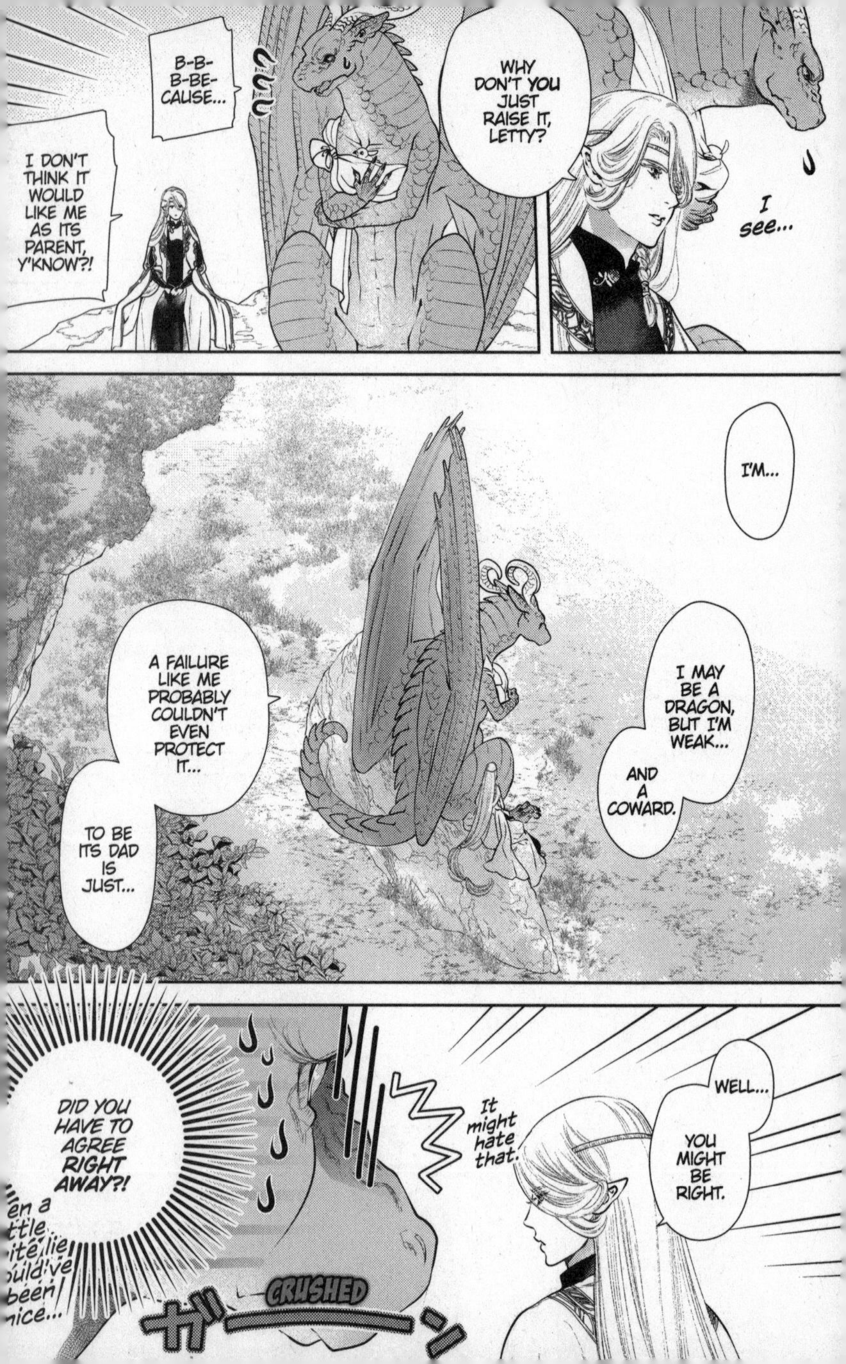
I see...
WHY DON'T YOU JUST RAISE IT, LETTY?
B-B-B-BE-CAUSE...
I DON'T THINK IT WOULD LIKE ME AS ITS PARENT, Y'KNOW?!
I'M...
I MAY BE A DRAGON, BUT I'M WEAK...
AND A COWARD.
A FAILURE LIKE ME PROBABLY COULDN'T EVEN PROTECT IT...
TO BE ITS DAD IS JUST...
WELL...
YOU MIGHT BE RIGHT.
It might hate that.
DID YOU HAVE TO AGREE RIGHT AWAY?!
en a ttle ite lie ould've been nice...
CRUSHED
ガーーン

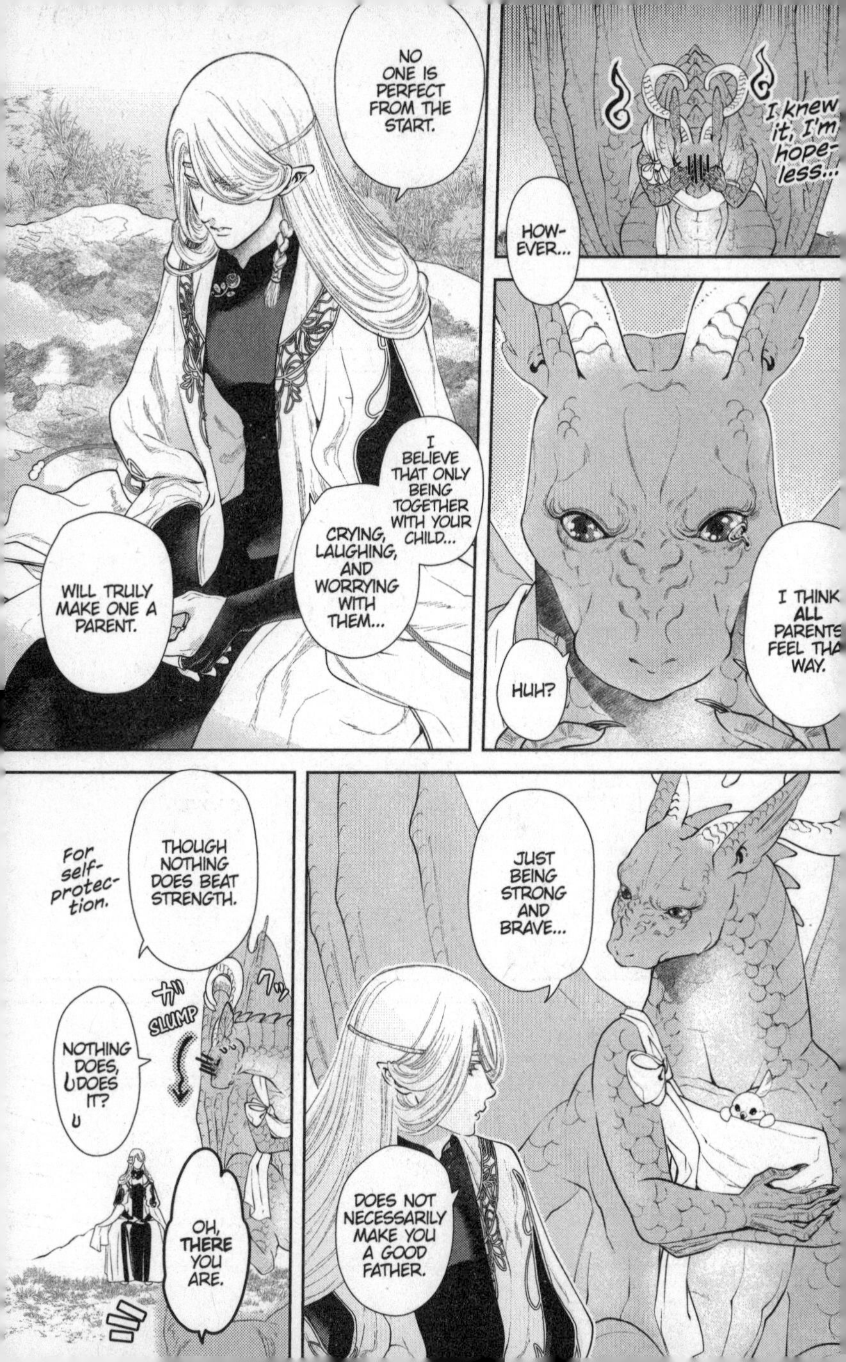
I knew it, I'm hope-less...
HOW-EVER...
I THINK ALL PARENTS FEEL THA WAY.
HUH?
NO ONE IS PERFECT FROM THE START.
I BELIEVE THAT ONLY BEING TOGETHER WITH YOUR CHILD...
CRYING, LAUGHING, AND WORRYING WITH THEM...
WILL TRULY MAKE ONE A PARENT.
JUST BEING STRONG AND BRAVE...
DOES NOT NECESSARILY MAKE YOU A GOOD FATHER.
THOUGH NOTHING DOES BEAT STRENGTH.
For self-protec-tion.
SLUMP
NOTHING DOES, DOES IT?
OH, THERE YOU ARE.

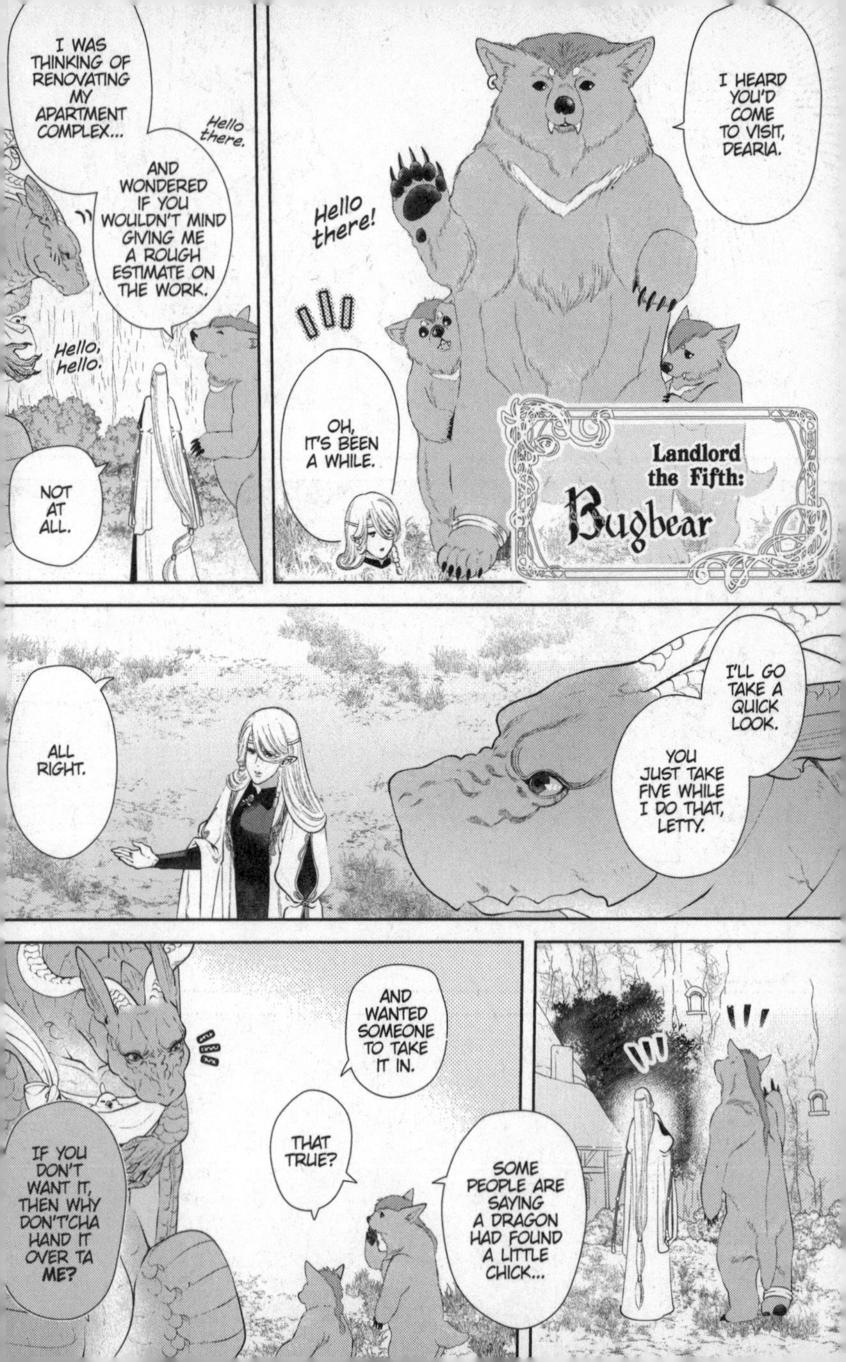
I HEARD YOU'D COME TO VISIT, DEARIA.
Hello there!
OH, IT'S BEEN A WHILE.
Landlord the Fifth: Bugbear
I WAS THINKING OF RENOVATING MY APARTMENT COMPLEX...
Hello there.
AND WONDERED IF YOU WOULDN'T MIND GIVING ME A ROUGH ESTIMATE ON THE WORK.
Hello, hello.
NOT AT ALL.
I'LL GO TAKE A QUICK LOOK.
YOU JUST TAKE FIVE WHILE I DO THAT, LETTY.
ALL RIGHT.
SOME PEOPLE ARE SAYING A DRAGON HAD FOUND A LITTLE CHICK...
AND WANTED SOMEONE TO TAKE IT IN.
THAT TRUE?
IF YOU DON'T WANT IT, THEN WHY DON'T'CHA HAND IT OVER TA ME?

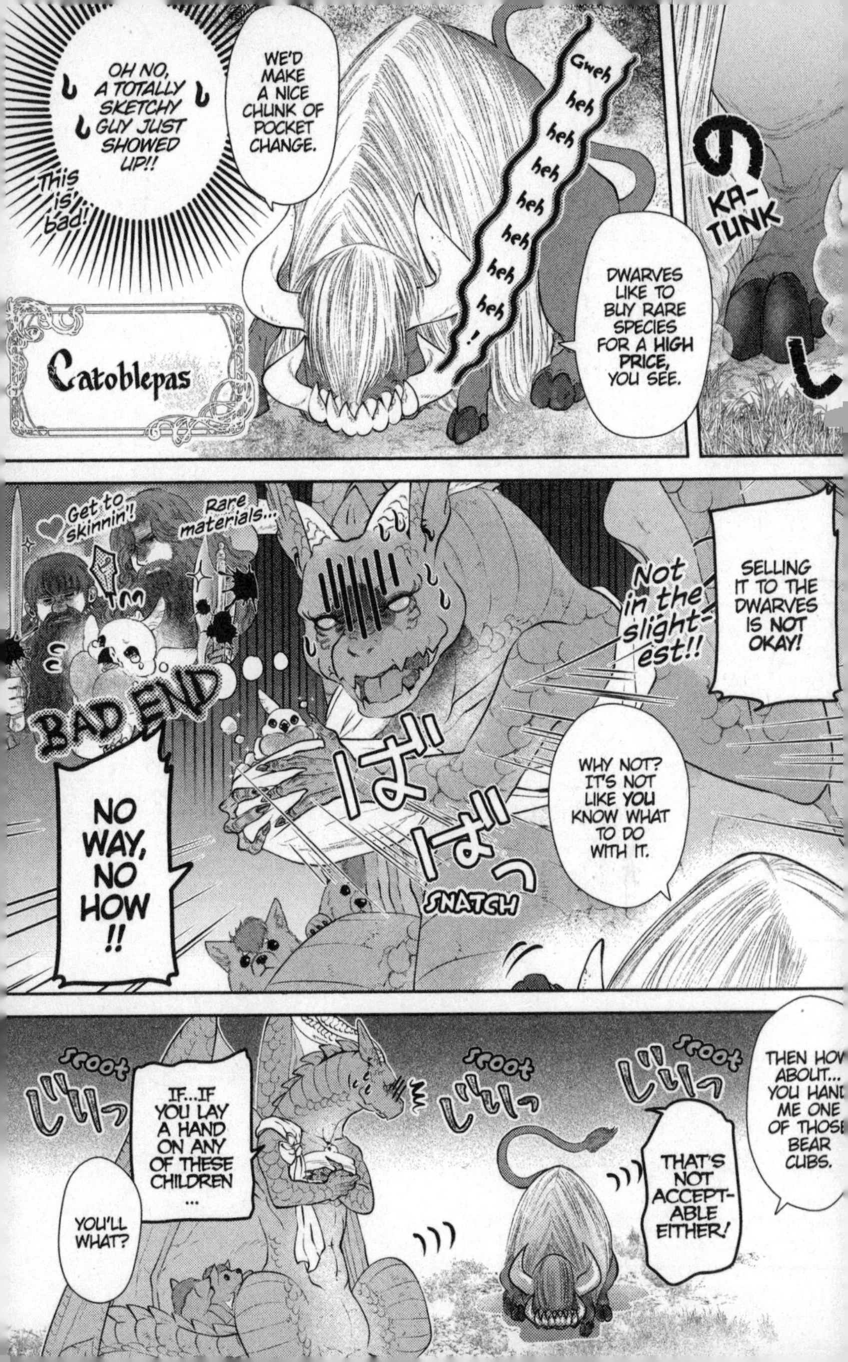
KA-TUNK
Gweh heh heh heh heh heh heh heh!
DWARVES LIKE TO BUY RARE SPECIES FOR A HIGH PRICE, YOU SEE.
WE'D MAKE A NICE CHUNK OF POCKET CHANGE.
OH NO, A TOTALLY SKETCHY GUY JUST SHOWED UP!!
This is bad!
Catoblepas
SELLING IT TO THE DWARVES IS NOT OKAY!
Not in the slight-est!!
WHY NOT? IT'S NOT LIKE YOU KNOW WHAT TO DO WITH IT.
Rare materials...
Get to skinnin'!
BAD END
NO WAY, NO HOW!!
SNATCH
THEN HOW ABOUT... YOU HAND ME ONE OF THOSE BEAR CUBS.
scoot
THAT'S NOT ACCEPT-ABLE EITHER!
scoot
IF...IF YOU LAY A HAND ON ANY OF THESE CHILDREN ...
scoot
YOU'LL WHAT?

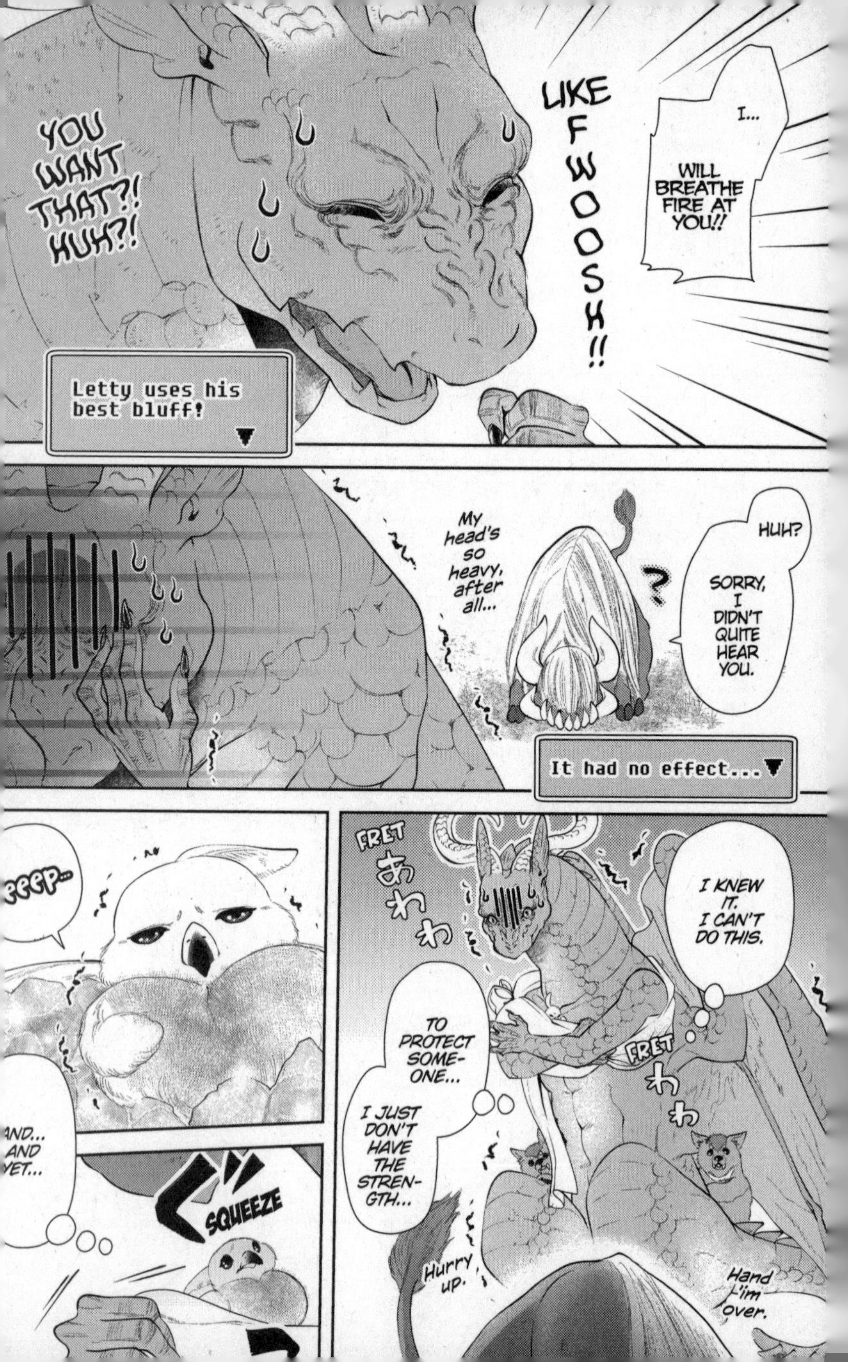
I...
WILL BREATHE FIRE AT YOU!!
LIKE FWOOSH!!
YOU WANT THAT?! HUH?!
Letty uses his best bluff!
HUH?
SORRY, I DIDN'T QUITE HEAR YOU.
My head's so heavy, after all...
It had no effect...
FRET
あわわ
I KNEW IT. I CAN'T DO THIS.
TO PROTECT SOME-ONE...
I JUST DON'T HAVE THE STREN-GTH...
FRET
わわ
Hand 'im over.
Hurry up.
eeep...
AND... AND YET...
SQUEEZE

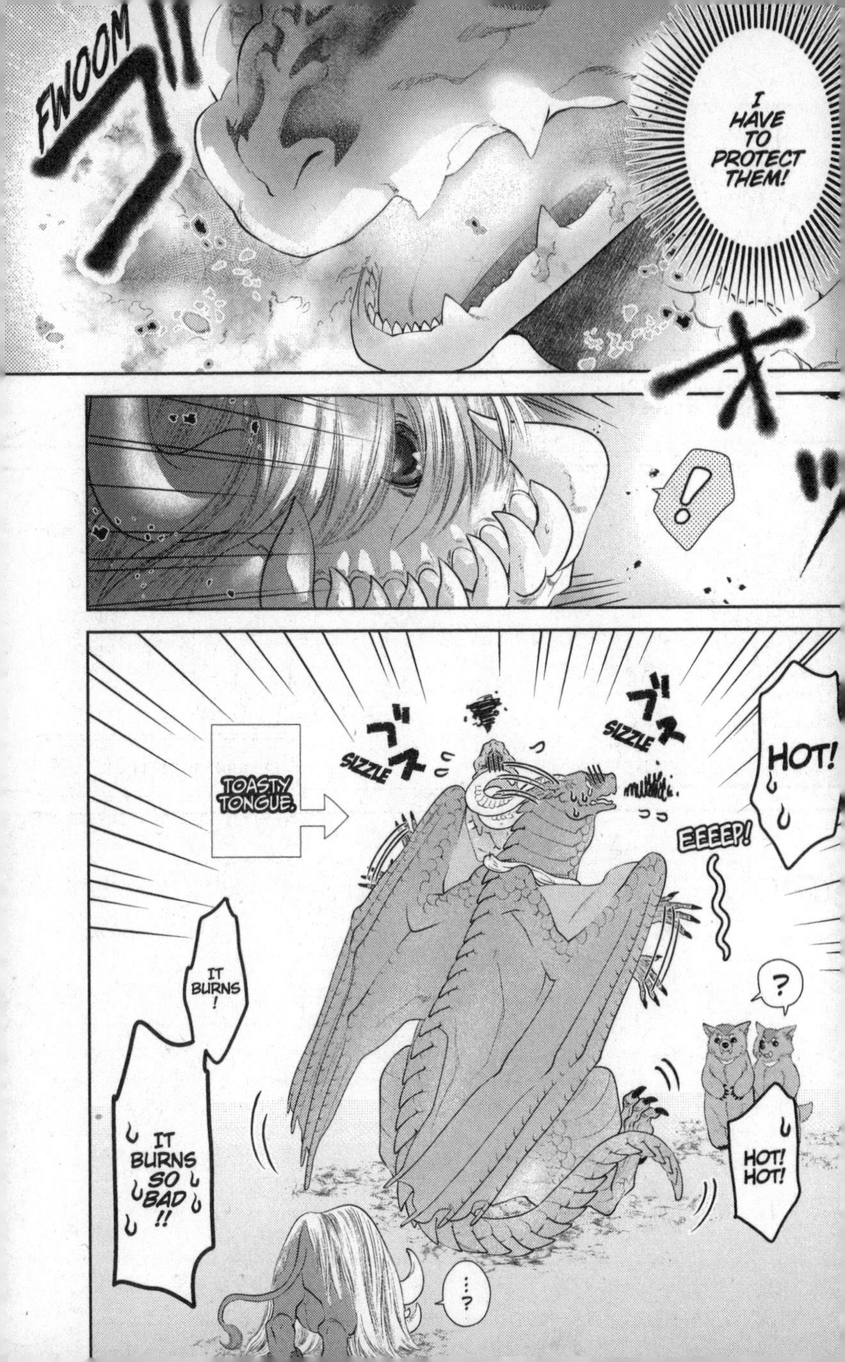

I HAVE TO PROTECT THEM!
FWOOM
!
HOT!
EEEEP!
SIZZLE
SIZZLE
?
HOT! HOT!
TOASTY TONGUE.
IT BURNS!
IT BURNS SO BAD!!
...?

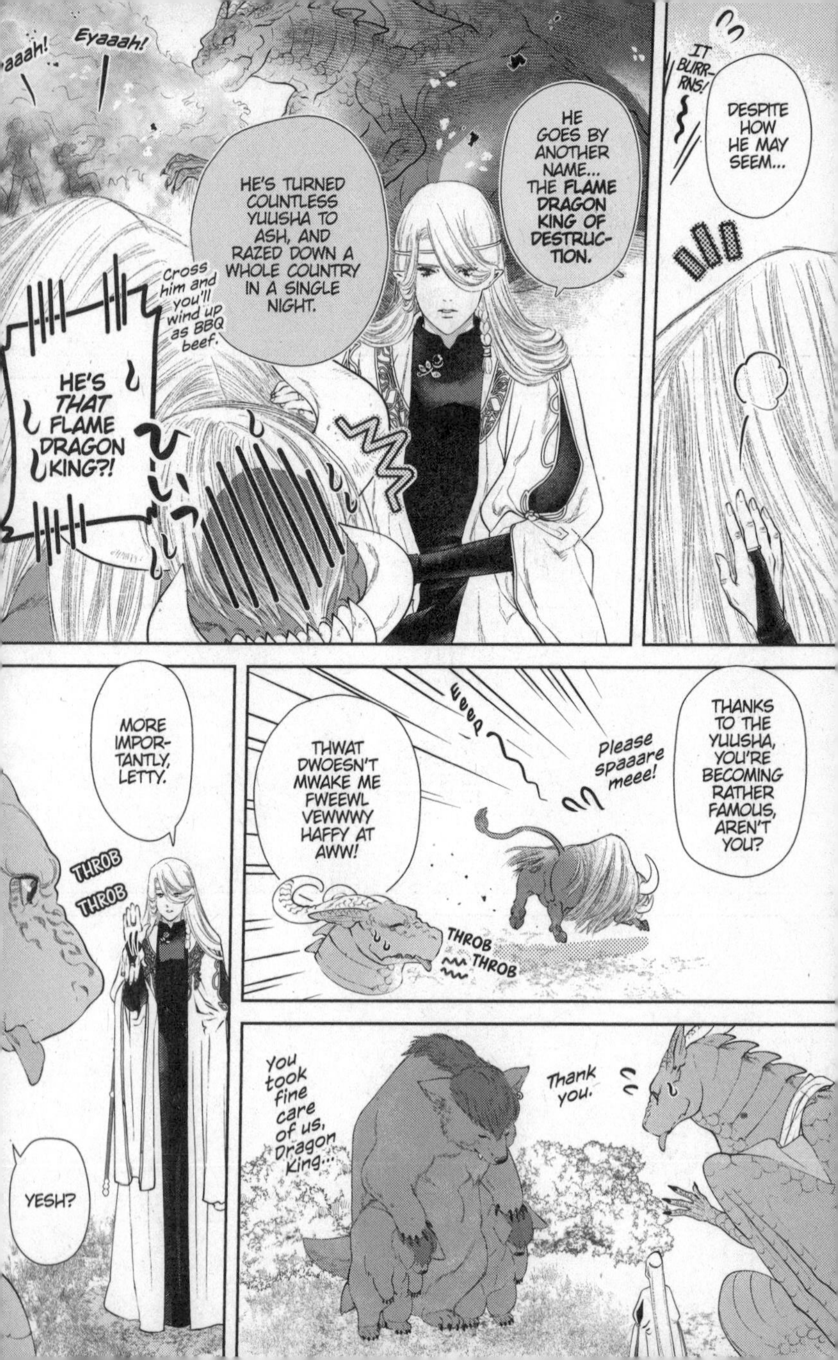
IT BURRRNS!
DESPITE HOW HE MAY SEEM...
HE GOES BY ANOTHER NAME... THE FLAME DRAGON KING OF DESTRUCTION.
Eyaaaah!
aaah!
HE'S TURNED COUNTLESS YUUSHA TO ASH, AND RAZED DOWN A WHOLE COUNTRY IN A SINGLE NIGHT.
Cross him and you'll wind up as BBQ beef.
HE'S THAT FLAME DRAGON KING?!
THANKS TO THE YUUSHA, YOU'RE BECOMING RATHER FAMOUS, AREN'T YOU?
Please spaaare meee!
THWAT DWOESN'T MWAKE ME FWEEWL VEWWWY HAFFY AT AWW!
THROB THROB
Thank you.
You took fine care of us, Dragon King...
MORE IMPORTANTLY, LETTY.
THROB THROB
YESH?

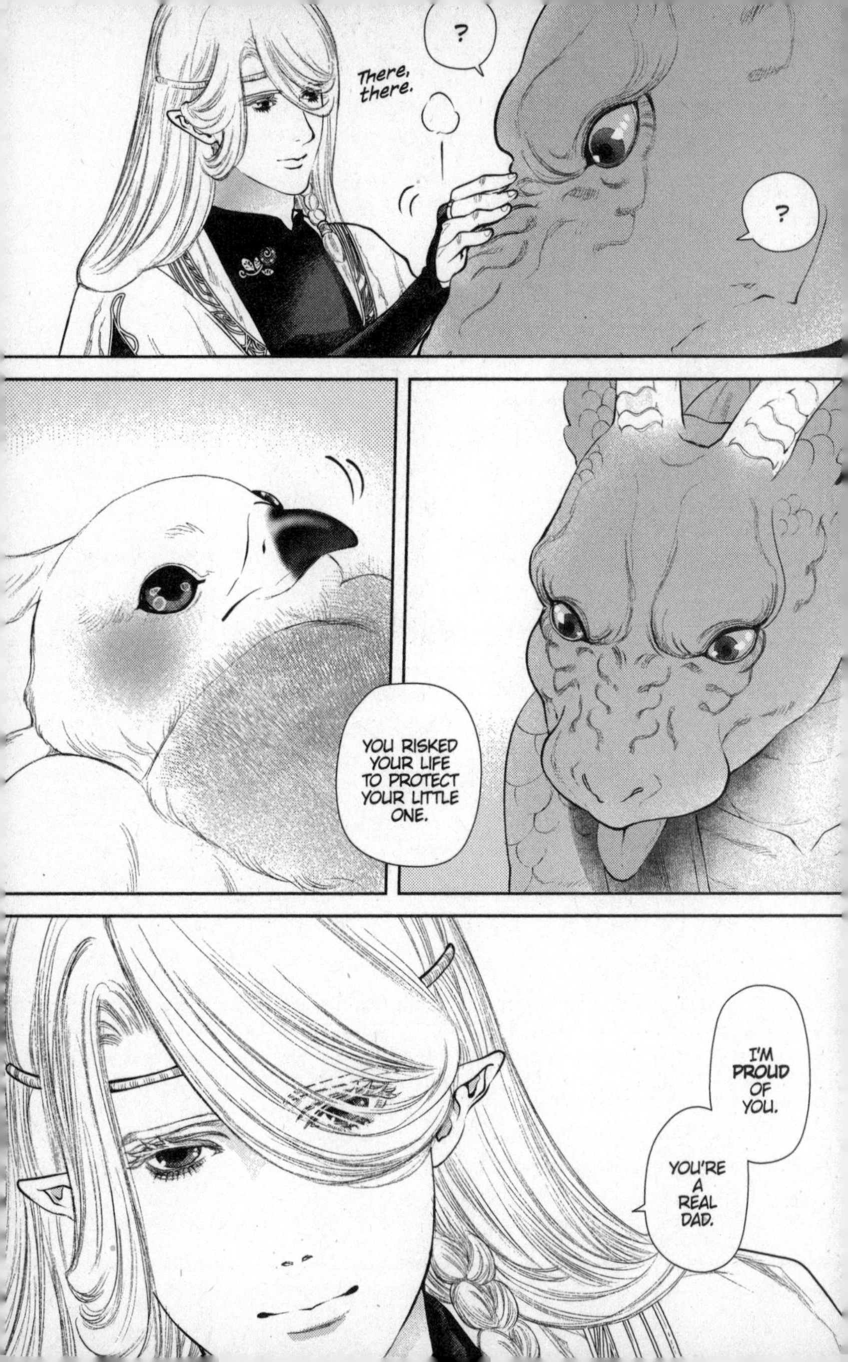
?
There, there.
?
YOU RISKED YOUR LIFE TO PROTECT YOUR LITTLE ONE.
I'M PROUD OF YOU.
YOU'RE A REAL DAD.

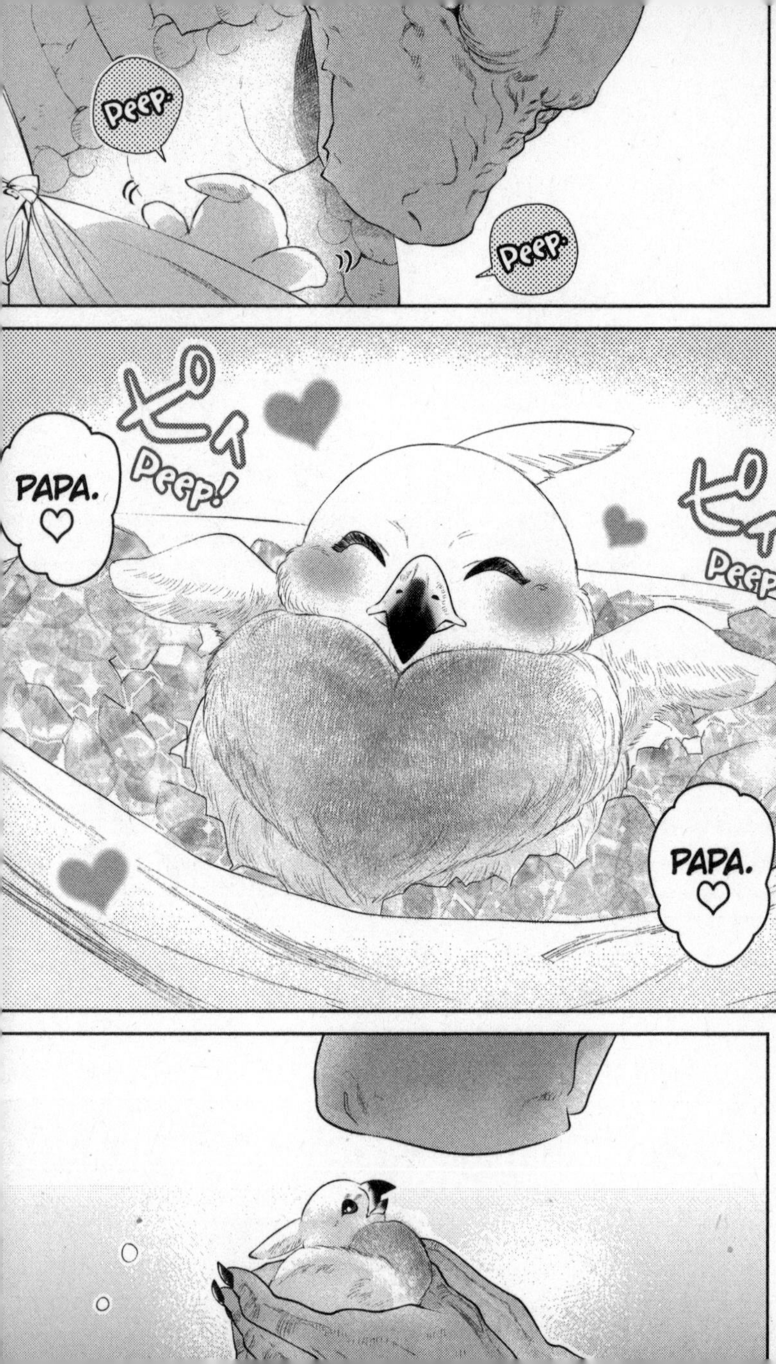

Peep.
Peep.
ピィ
Peep!
ピィ
Peep!
PAPA. ♡
PAPA. ♡

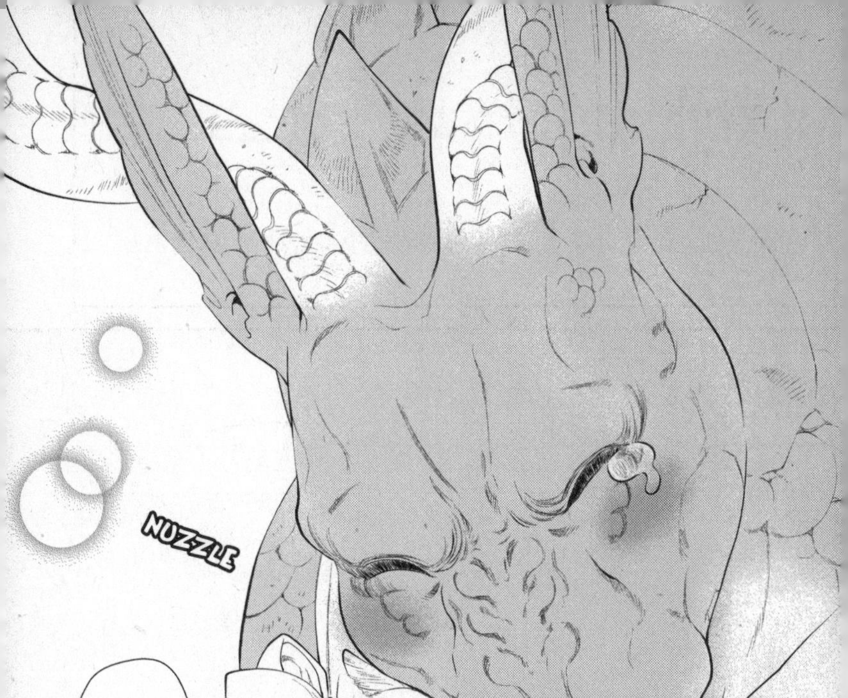
NUZZLE
YES, I AM!
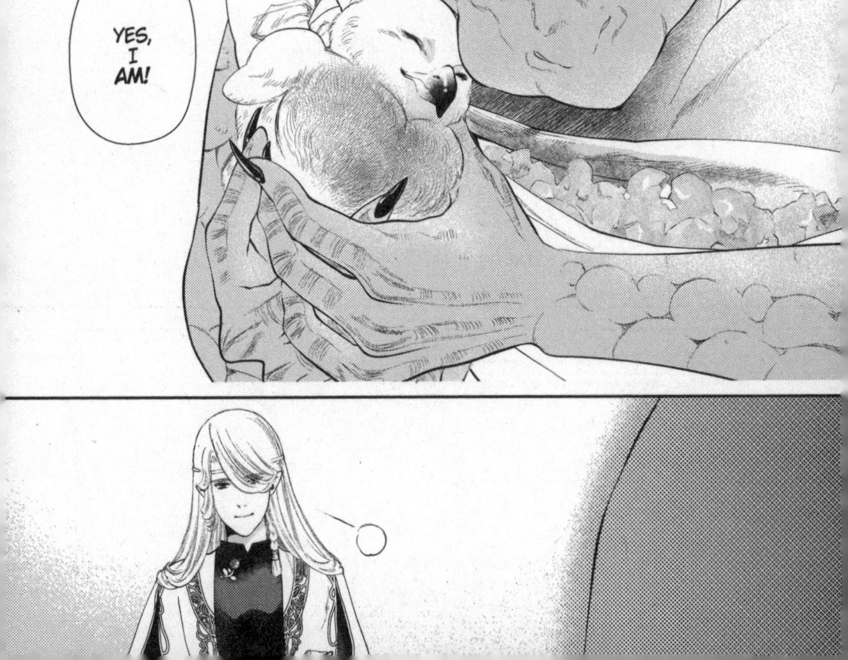

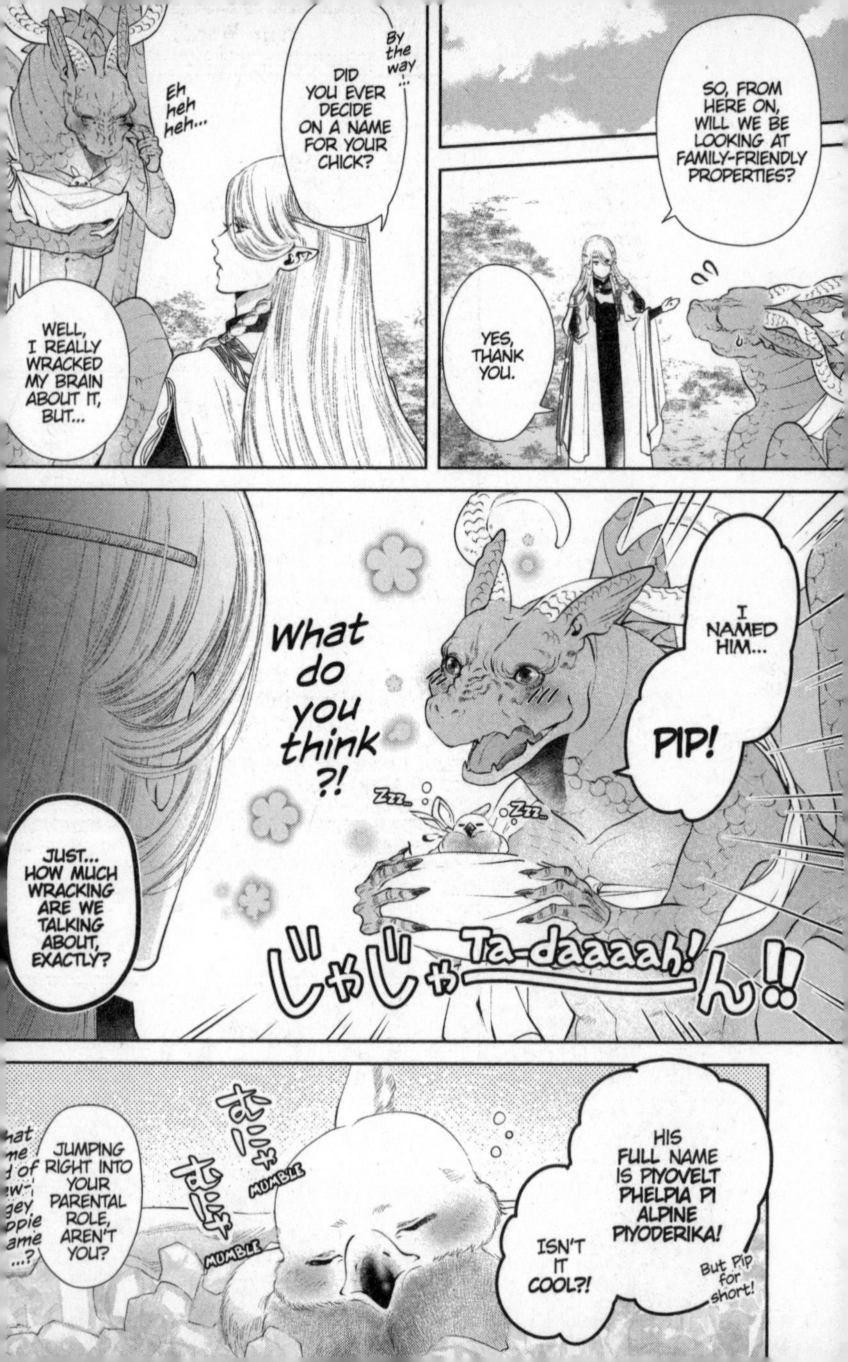
SO, FROM HERE ON, WILL WE BE LOOKING AT FAMILY-FRIENDLY PROPERTIES?
YES, THANK YOU.
By the way...
DID YOU EVER DECIDE ON A NAME FOR YOUR CHICK?
Eh heh heh...
WELL, I REALLY WRACKED MY BRAIN ABOUT IT, BUT...
I NAMED HIM...
PIP!
What do you think?!
Zzz...
Zzz...
じゃじゃーん!!
Ta-daaaah!
JUST... HOW MUCH WRACKING ARE WE TALKING ABOUT, EXACTLY?
HIS FULL NAME IS PIYOVELT PHELPIA PI ALPINE PIYODERIKA!
But Pip for short!
ISN'T IT COOL?!
むにゃむにゃ
MUMBLE
MUMBLE
JUMPING RIGHT INTO YOUR PARENTAL ROLE, AREN'T YOU?

Your Words

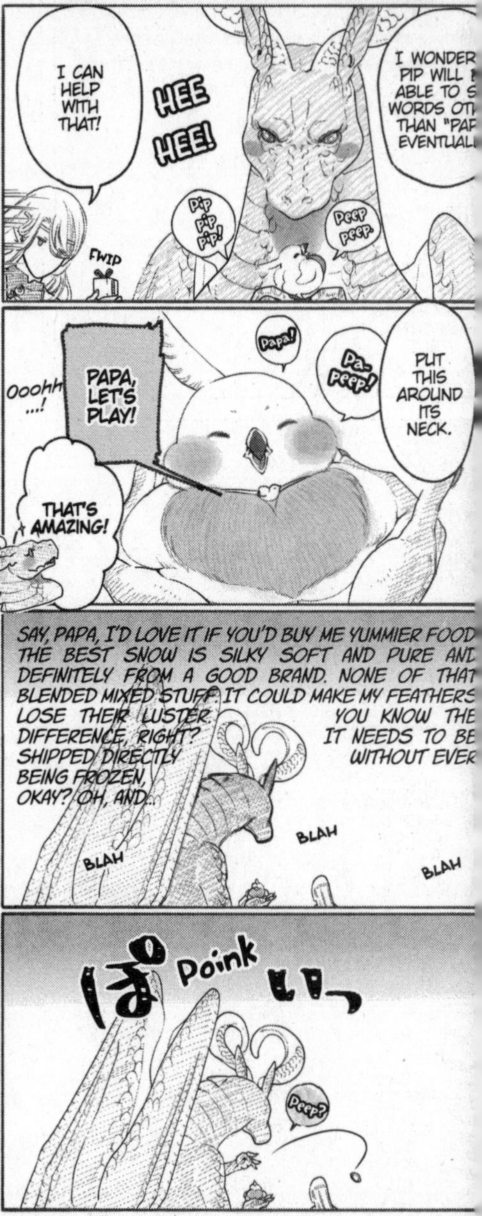
I WONDER
PIP WILL
ABLE TO
WORDS OTH
THAN "PAP
EVENTUALL
HEE HEE!
I CAN HELP WITH THAT!
Peep peep.
Pip pip pip!
FWIP
PUT THIS AROUND ITS NECK.
Papa!
Pa-peep!
PAPA, LET'S PLAY!
Ooohh...!
THAT'S AMAZING!
SAY, PAPA, I'D LOVE IT IF YOU'D BUY ME YUMMIER FOOD
THE BEST SNOW IS SILKY SOFT AND PURE AND
DEFINITELY FROM A GOOD BRAND. NONE OF THAT
BLENDED MIXED STUFF. IT COULD MAKE MY FEATHERS
LOSE THEIR LUSTER. YOU KNOW THE
DIFFERENCE, RIGHT? IT NEEDS TO BE
SHIPPED DIRECTLY WITHOUT EVER
BEING FROZEN,
OKAY? OH, AND...
BLAH
BLAH
BLAH
ぽいっ
Poink
Peep?

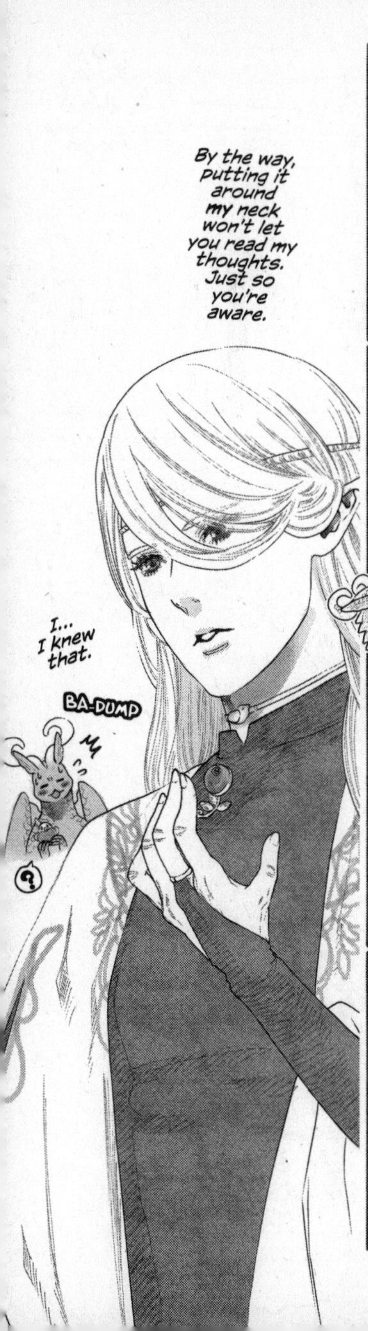
By the way, putting it around my neck won't let you read my thoughts. Just so you're aware.
I... I knew that.
BA-DUMP
?

Dragon
Goes
House-
Hunting

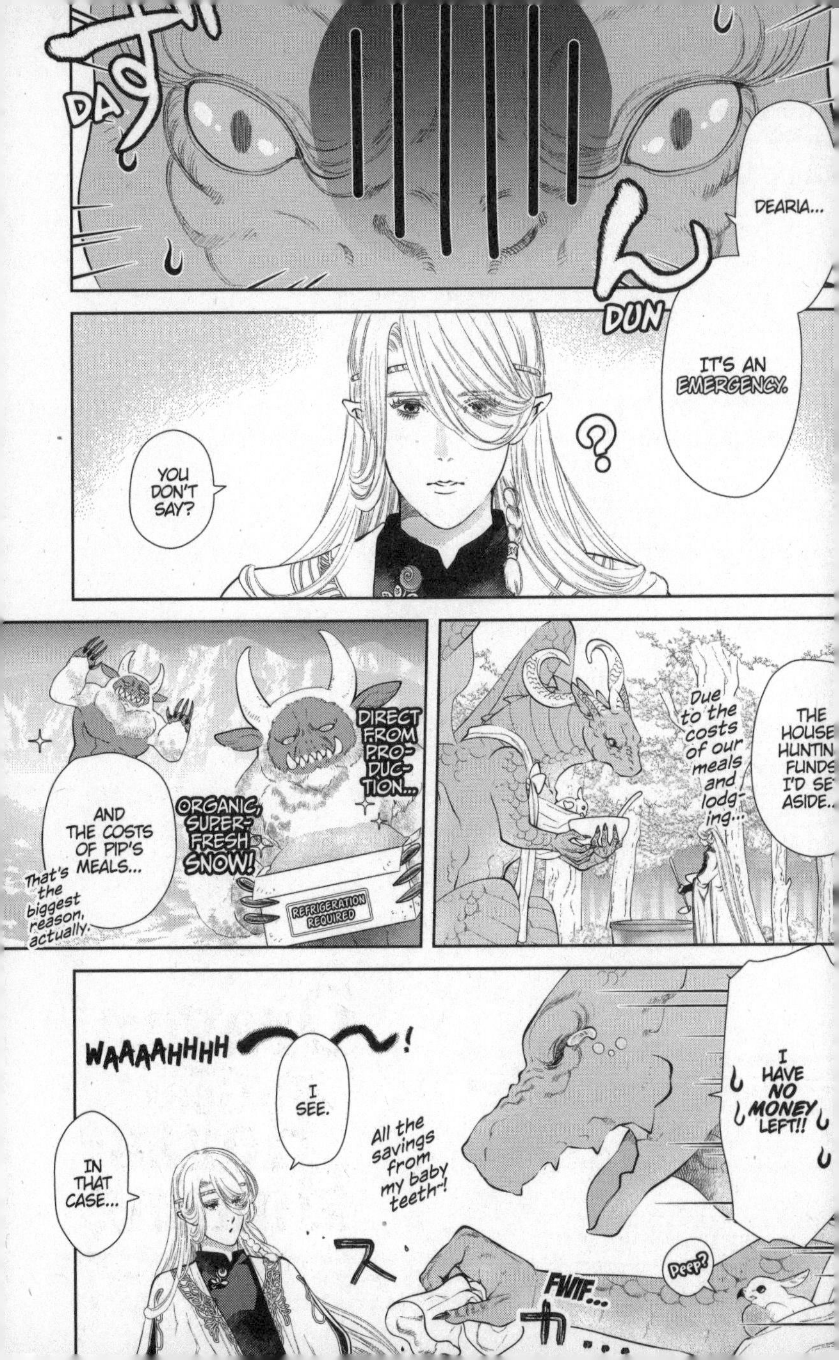
DA
DUN
DEARIA...
IT'S AN EMERGENCY.
?
YOU DON'T SAY?
THE HOUSE HUNTIN FUNDS I'D SE ASIDE...
Due to the costs of our meals and lodg-ing...
DIRECT FROM PRO-DUC-TION...
ORGANIC, SUPER-FRESH SNOW!
REFRIGERATION REQUIRED
AND THE COSTS OF PIP'S MEALS...
That's the biggest reason, actually.
I HAVE NO MONEY LEFT!!
WAAAAHHHH ~~!
All the savings from my baby teeth~!
I SEE.
IN THAT CASE...
Peep?
FWIF...

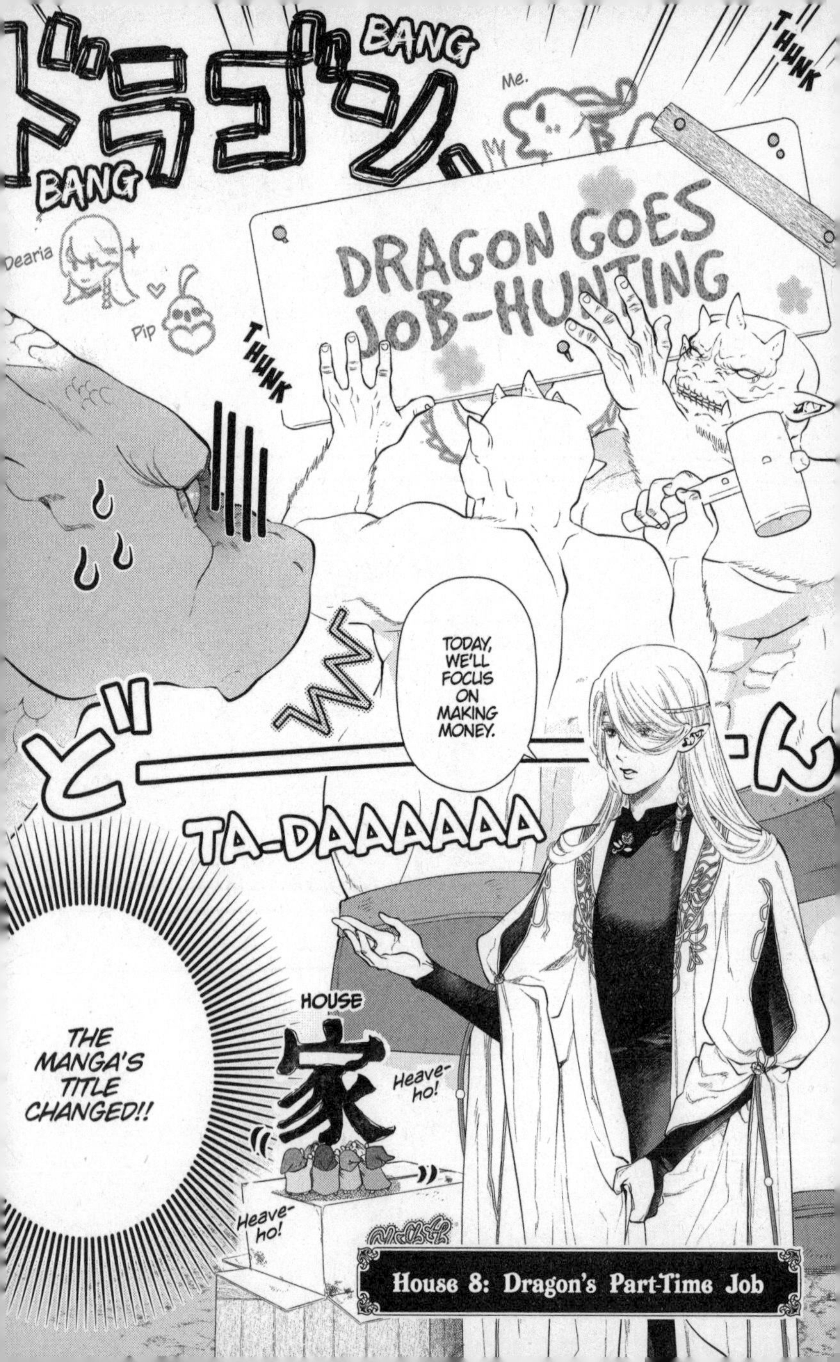
THUNK
Me.
BANG
ドラゴン
BANG
Dearia
Pip
DRAGON GOES JOB-HUNTING
THUNK
TODAY, WE'LL FOCUS ON MAKING MONEY.
どーーーん
TA-DAAAAAAA
HOUSE
家
Heave-ho!
Heave-ho!
THE MANGA'S TITLE CHANGED!!
House 8: Dragon's Part-Time Job

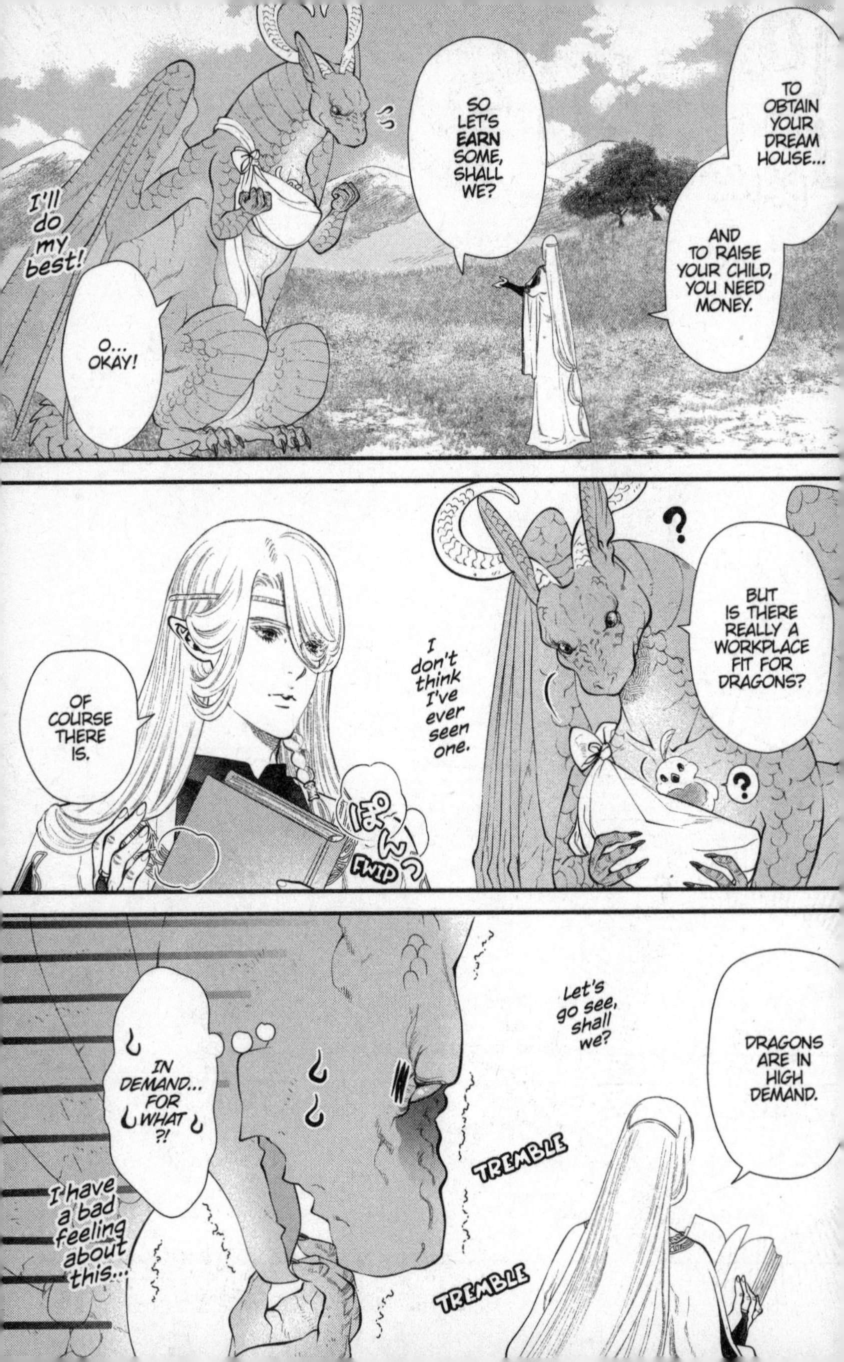
TO OBTAIN YOUR DREAM HOUSE...
AND TO RAISE YOUR CHILD, YOU NEED MONEY.
SO LET'S EARN SOME, SHALL WE?
I'll do my best!
O... OKAY!
BUT IS THERE REALLY A WORKPLACE FIT FOR DRAGONS?
I don't think I've ever seen one.
OF COURSE THERE IS.
ぽんっ
FWIP
DRAGONS ARE IN HIGH DEMAND.
Let's go see, shall we?
TREMBLE
TREMBLE
IN DEMAND... FOR WHAT?!
I have a bad feeling about this...

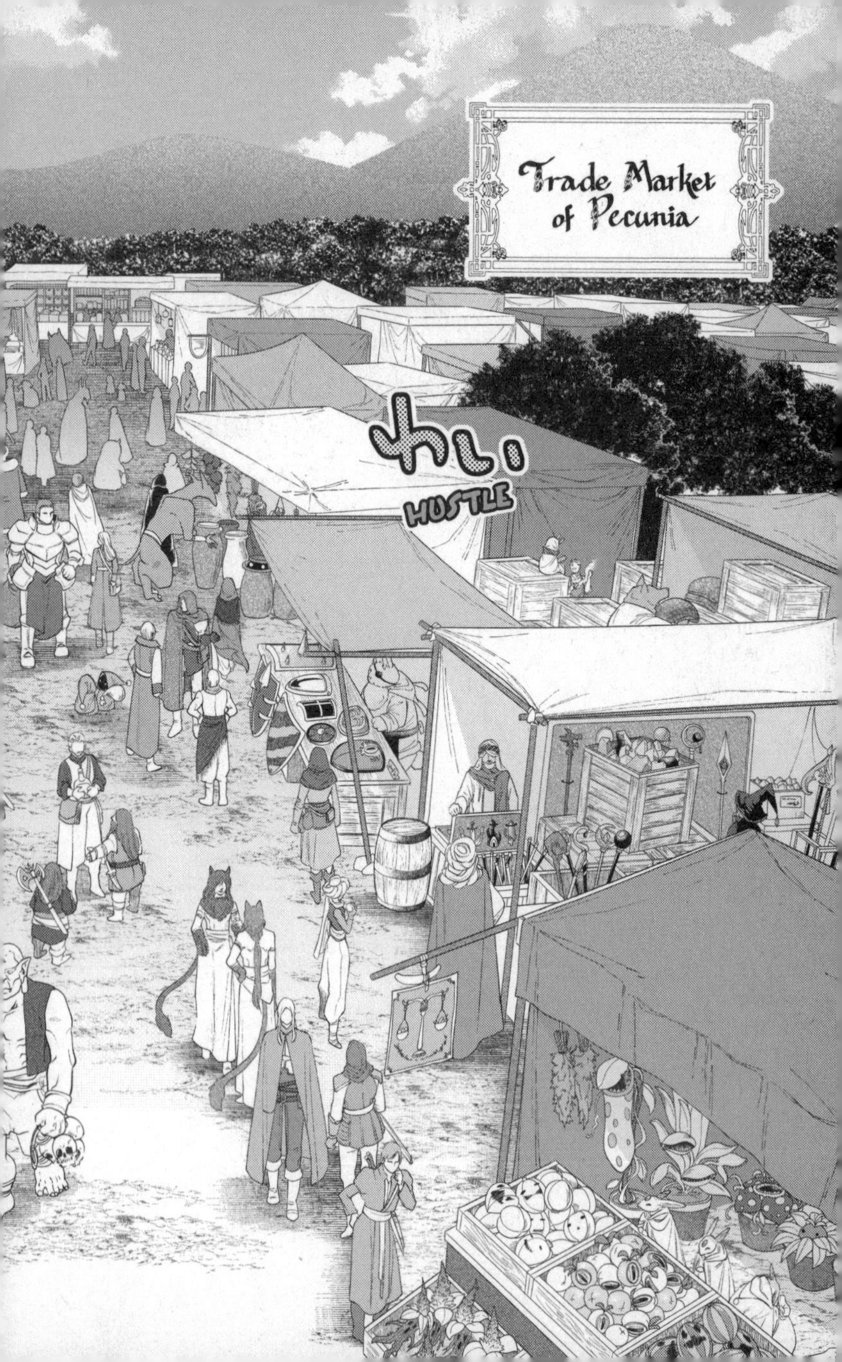

Trade Market of Pecunia
HUSTLE

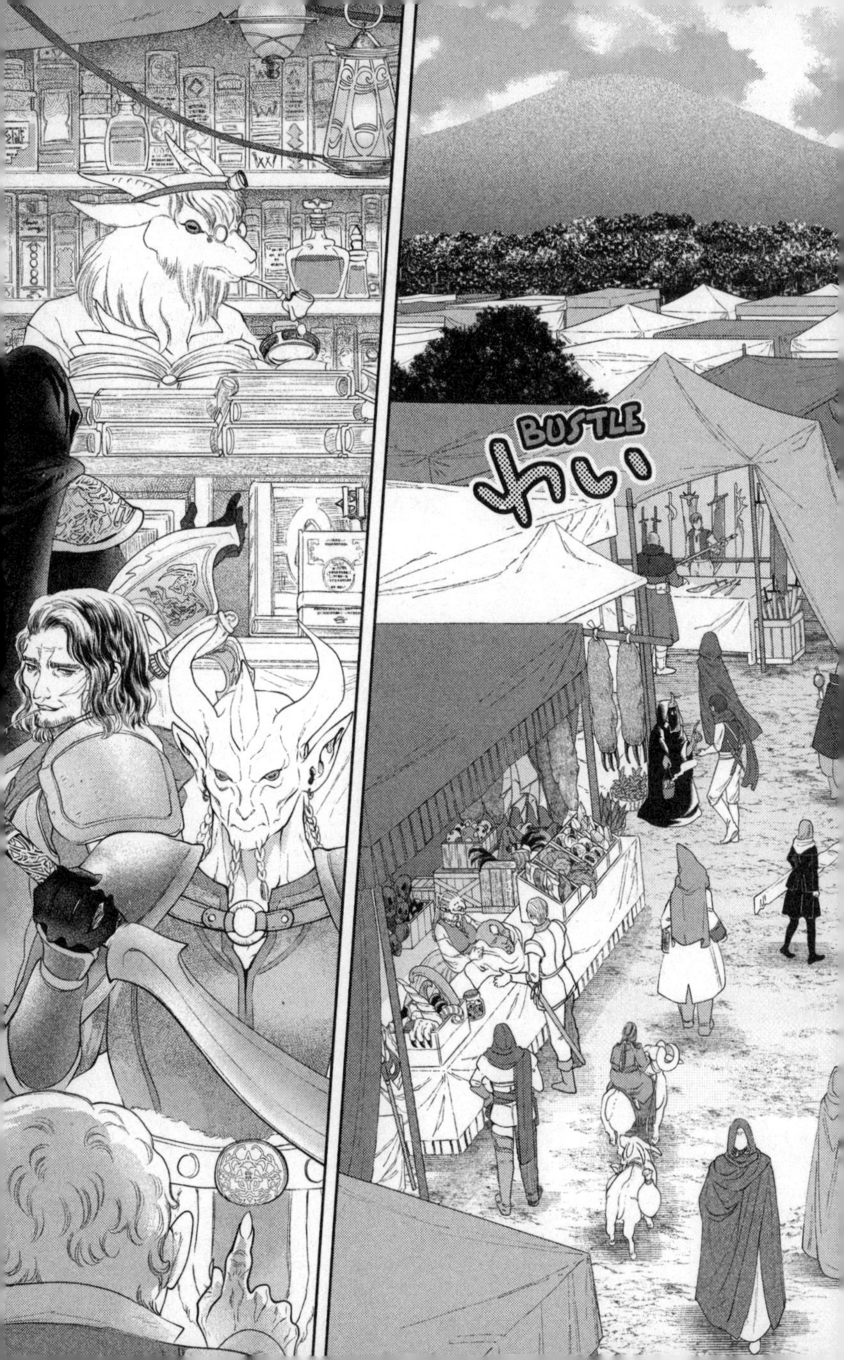
BUSTLE
わい

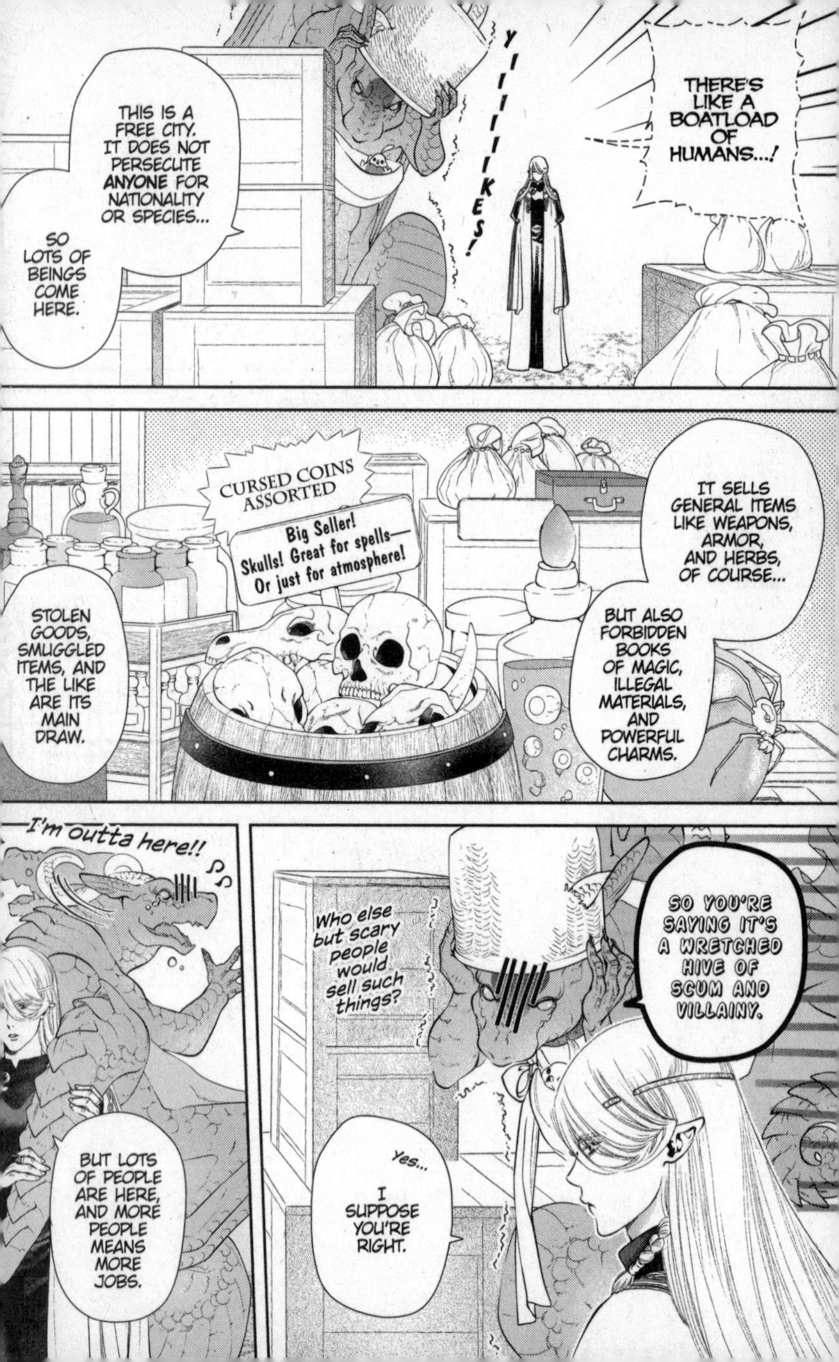
THERE'S LIKE A BOATLOAD OF HUMANS...!
YIIIIIKES!
THIS IS A FREE CITY. IT DOES NOT PERSECUTE ANYONE FOR NATIONALITY OR SPECIES...
SO LOTS OF BEINGS COME HERE.
IT SELLS GENERAL ITEMS LIKE WEAPONS, ARMOR, AND HERBS, OF COURSE...
BUT ALSO FORBIDDEN BOOKS OF MAGIC, ILLEGAL MATERIALS, AND POWERFUL CHARMS.
CURSED COINS ASSORTED
Big Seller! Skulls! Great for spells— Or just for atmosphere!
STOLEN GOODS, SMUGGLED ITEMS, AND THE LIKE ARE ITS MAIN DRAW.
SO YOU'RE SAYING IT'S A WRETCHED HIVE OF SCUM AND VILLAINY.
Who else but scary people would sell such things?
Yes...
I SUPPOSE YOU'RE RIGHT.
I'm outta here!!
BUT LOTS OF PEOPLE ARE HERE, AND MORE PEOPLE MEANS MORE JOBS.

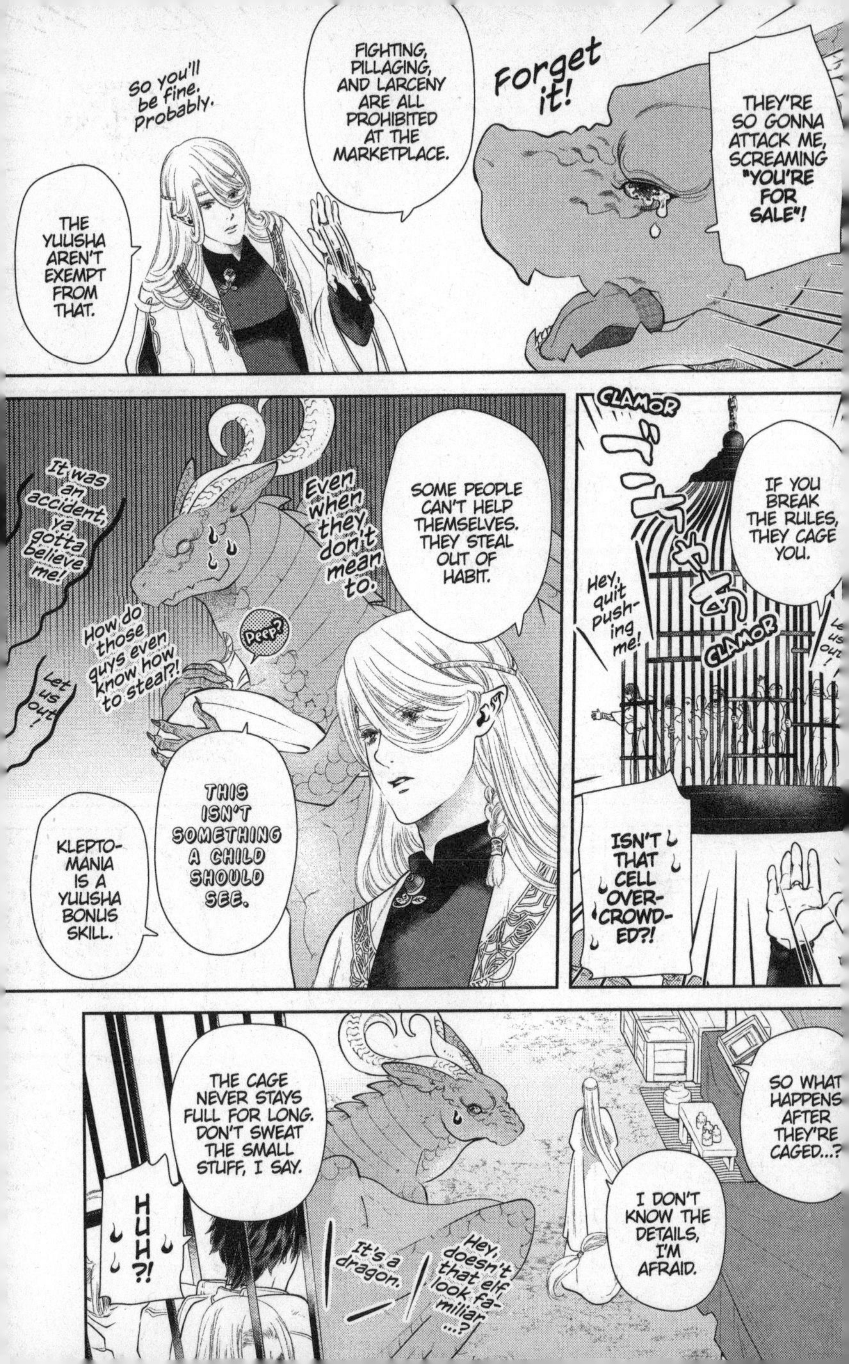
THEY'RE SO GONNA ATTACK ME, SCREAMING "YOU'RE FOR SALE"!
Forget it!
FIGHTING, PILLAGING, AND LARCENY ARE ALL PROHIBITED AT THE MARKETPLACE.
So you'll be fine. Probably.
THE YUUSHA AREN'T EXEMPT FROM THAT.
CLAMOR
IF YOU BREAK THE RULES, THEY CAGE YOU.
Hey, quit push-ing me!
CLAMOR
ISN'T THAT CELL OVER-CROWD-ED?!
SOME PEOPLE CAN'T HELP THEMSELVES. THEY STEAL OUT OF HABIT.
Even when they don't mean to.
It was an accident, ya gotta believe me!
How do those guys even know how to steal?!
Peep?
Let us out!
THIS ISN'T SOMETHING A CHILD SHOULD SEE.
KLEPTO-MANIA IS A YUUSHA BONUS SKILL.
SO WHAT HAPPENS AFTER THEY'RE CAGED...?
I DON'T KNOW THE DETAILS, I'M AFRAID.
Hey, doesn't that elf look fa-miliar...?
It's a dragon.
THE CAGE NEVER STAYS FULL FOR LONG. DON'T SWEAT THE SMALL STUFF, I SAY.
HUH?!

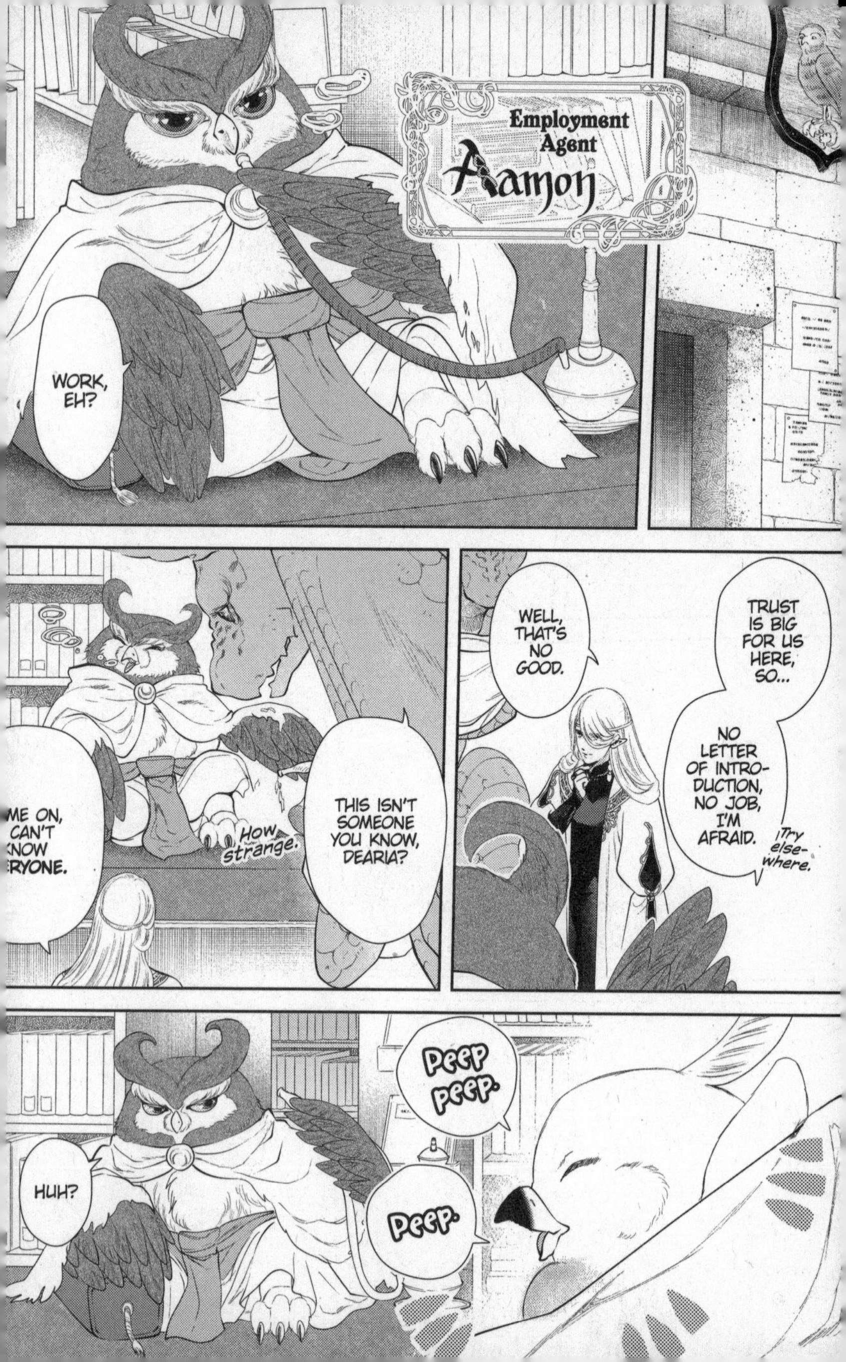
Employment Agent Aamon
WORK, EH?
TRUST IS BIG FOR US HERE, SO...
WELL, THAT'S NO GOOD.
NO LETTER OF INTRO-DUCTION, NO JOB, I'M AFRAID.
Try else-where.
THIS ISN'T SOMEONE YOU KNOW, DEARIA?
How strange.
ME ON, CAN'T KNOW ERYONE.
Peep peep.
Peep.
HUH?

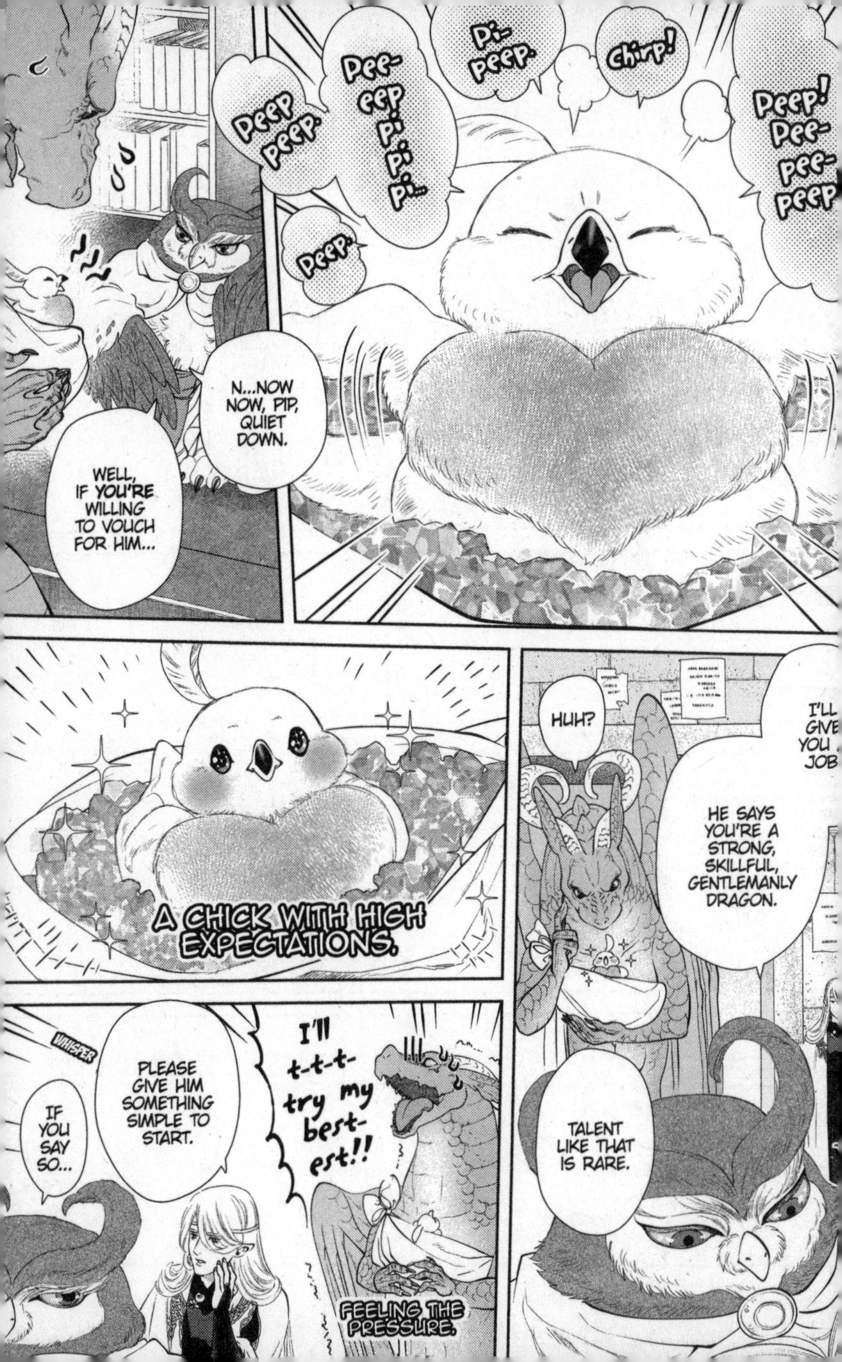

Peep! Pee-pee-peep
Chirp!
Pi-peep.
Pee-eep pi pi pi...
Peep peep.
Peep.
N...NOW NOW, PIP, QUIET DOWN.
WELL, IF YOU'RE WILLING TO VOUCH FOR HIM...
I'LL GIVE YOU JOB
HUH?
HE SAYS YOU'RE A STRONG, SKILLFUL, GENTLEMANLY DRAGON.
TALENT LIKE THAT IS RARE.
A CHICK WITH HIGH EXPECTATIONS.
I'll t-t-t-try my best-est!!
PLEASE GIVE HIM SOMETHING SIMPLE TO START.
WHISPER
IF YOU SAY SO...
FEELING THE PRESSURE.

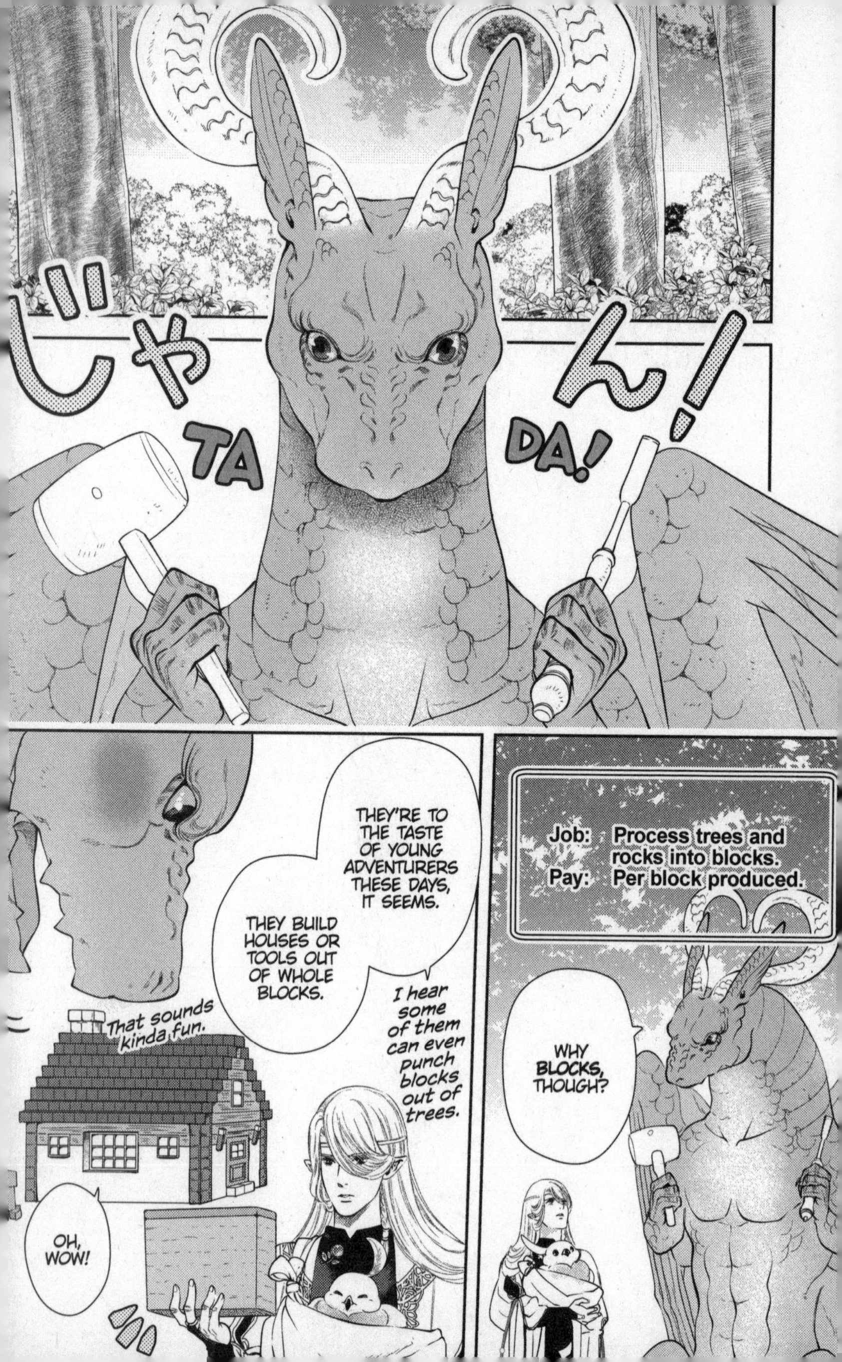
じゃん!
TA DA!
Job: Process trees and rocks into blocks.
Pay: Per block produced.
WHY BLOCKS, THOUGH?
THEY'RE TO THE TASTE OF YOUNG ADVENTURERS THESE DAYS, IT SEEMS.
THEY BUILD HOUSES OR TOOLS OUT OF WHOLE BLOCKS.
I hear some of them can even punch blocks out of trees.
That sounds kinda fun.
OH, WOW!

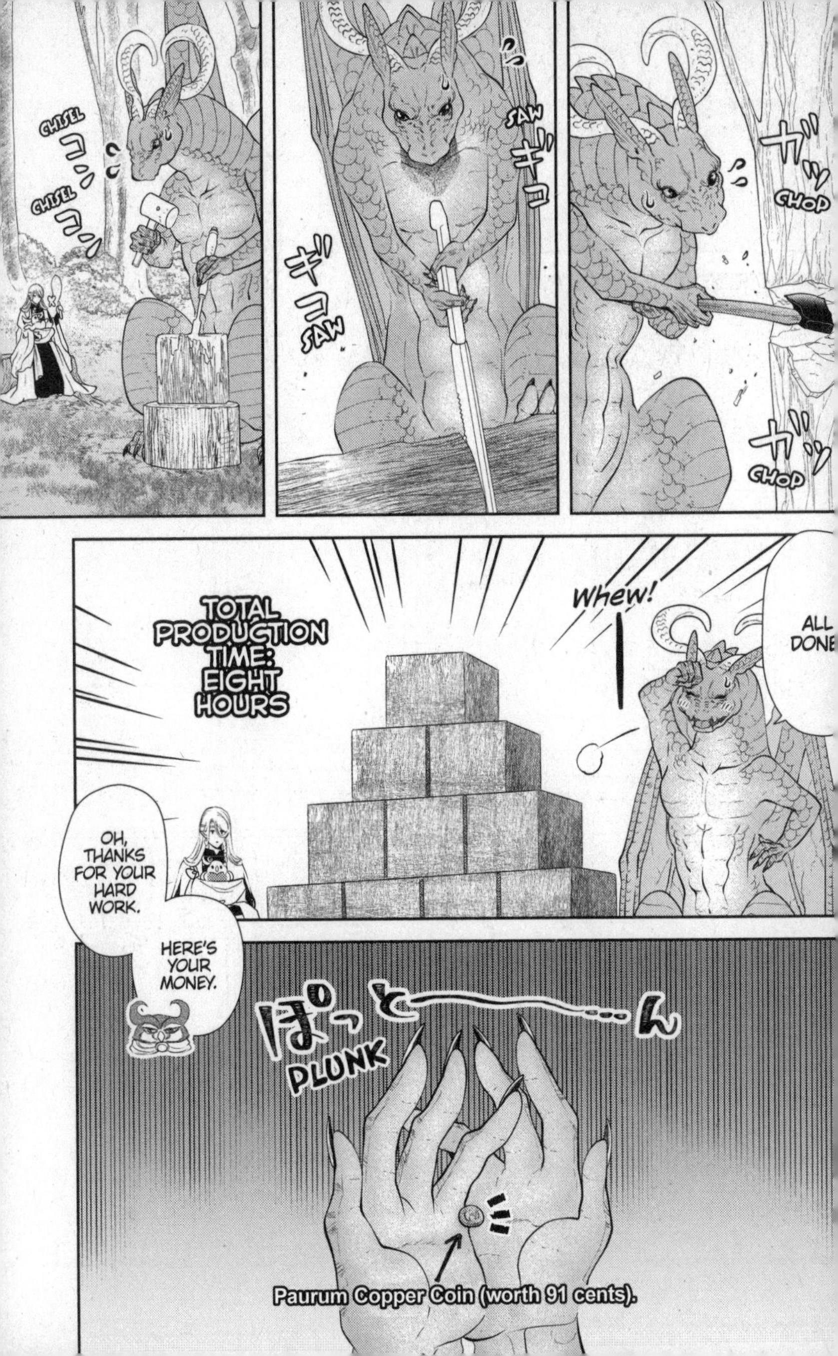
ガッ
CHOP
ガッ
CHOP
SAW
ギコ
ギコ
SAW
CHISEL
コッ
CHISEL
コッ
ALL DONE
Whew!
TOTAL PRODUCTION TIME: EIGHT HOURS
OH, THANKS FOR YOUR HARD WORK.
HERE'S YOUR MONEY.
ぽっと———ん
PLUNK
Paurum Copper Coin (worth 91 cents).

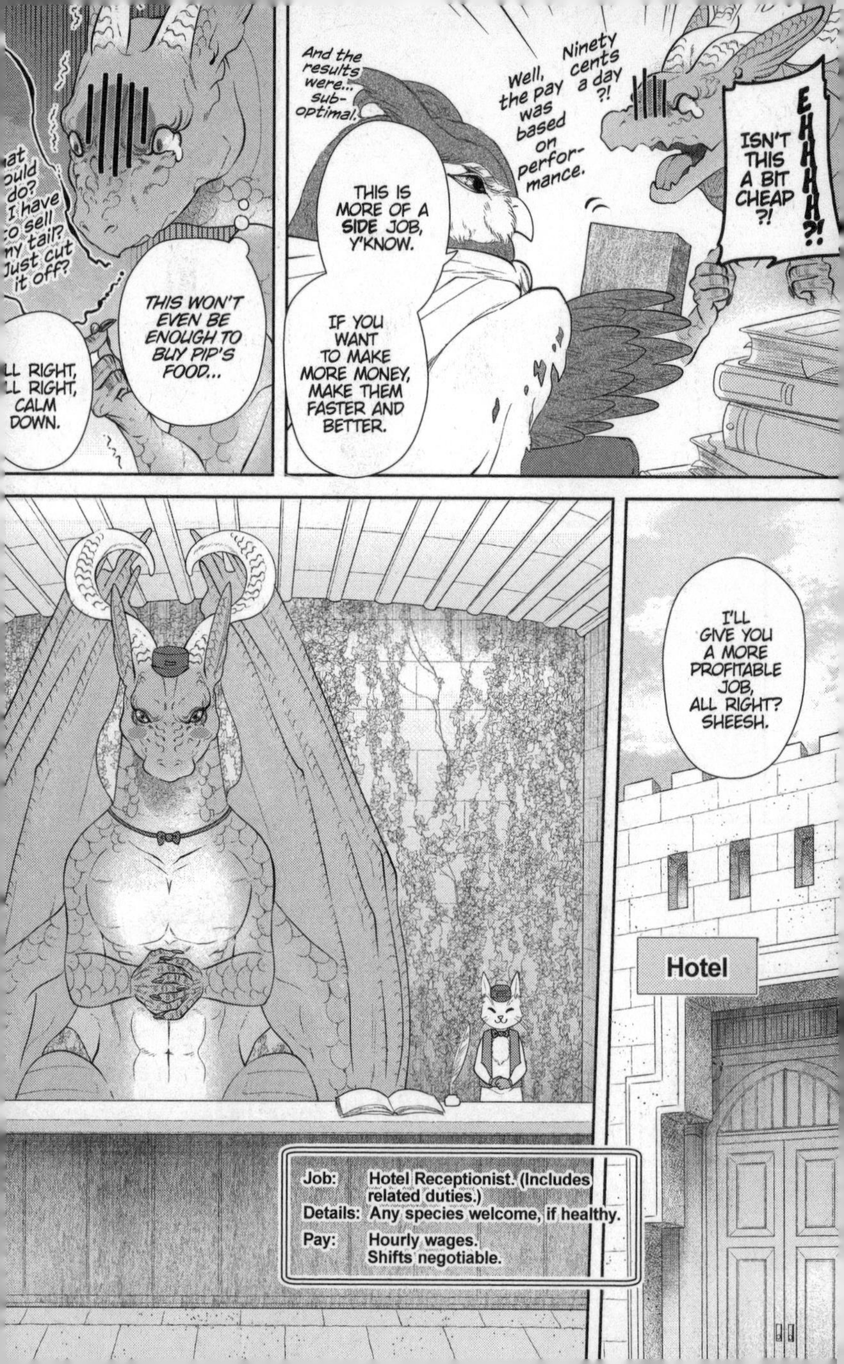
EHHHHH?!
ISN'T THIS A BIT CHEAP?!
Ninety cents a day?!
Well, the pay was based on performance.
And the results were... sub-optimal.
THIS IS MORE OF A SIDE JOB, Y'KNOW.
IF YOU WANT TO MAKE MORE MONEY, MAKE THEM FASTER AND BETTER.
do? I have to sell my tail? Just cut it off?
THIS WON'T EVEN BE ENOUGH TO BUY PIP'S FOOD...
LL RIGHT, LL RIGHT, CALM DOWN.
I'LL GIVE YOU A MORE PROFITABLE JOB, ALL RIGHT? SHEESH.
Hotel
Job: Hotel Receptionist. (Includes related duties.)
Details: Any species welcome, if healthy.
Pay: Hourly wages. Shifts negotiable.

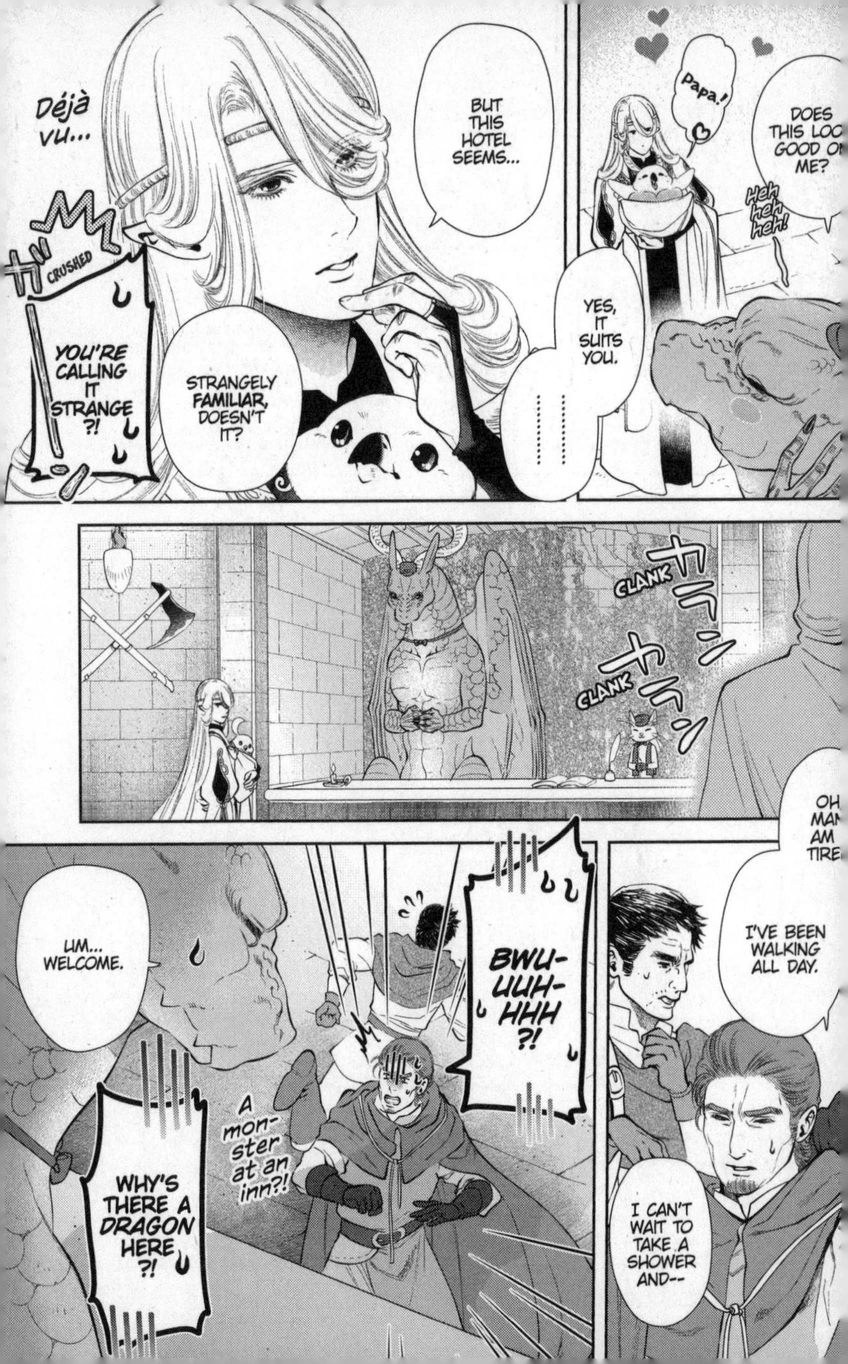
Papa!
DOES THIS LOO GOOD O ME?
Heh heh heh!
YES, IT SUITS YOU.
......
BUT THIS HOTEL SEEMS...
STRANGELY FAMILIAR, DOESN'T IT?
Déjà vu...
CRUSHED
YOU'RE CALLING IT STRANGE?!
CLANK
CLANK
OH MAN AM TIRE
I'VE BEEN WALKING ALL DAY.
I CAN'T WAIT TO TAKE A SHOWER AND--
BWU-UUH-HHH?!
A mon-ster at an inn?!
UM... WELCOME.
WHY'S THERE A DRAGON HERE?!

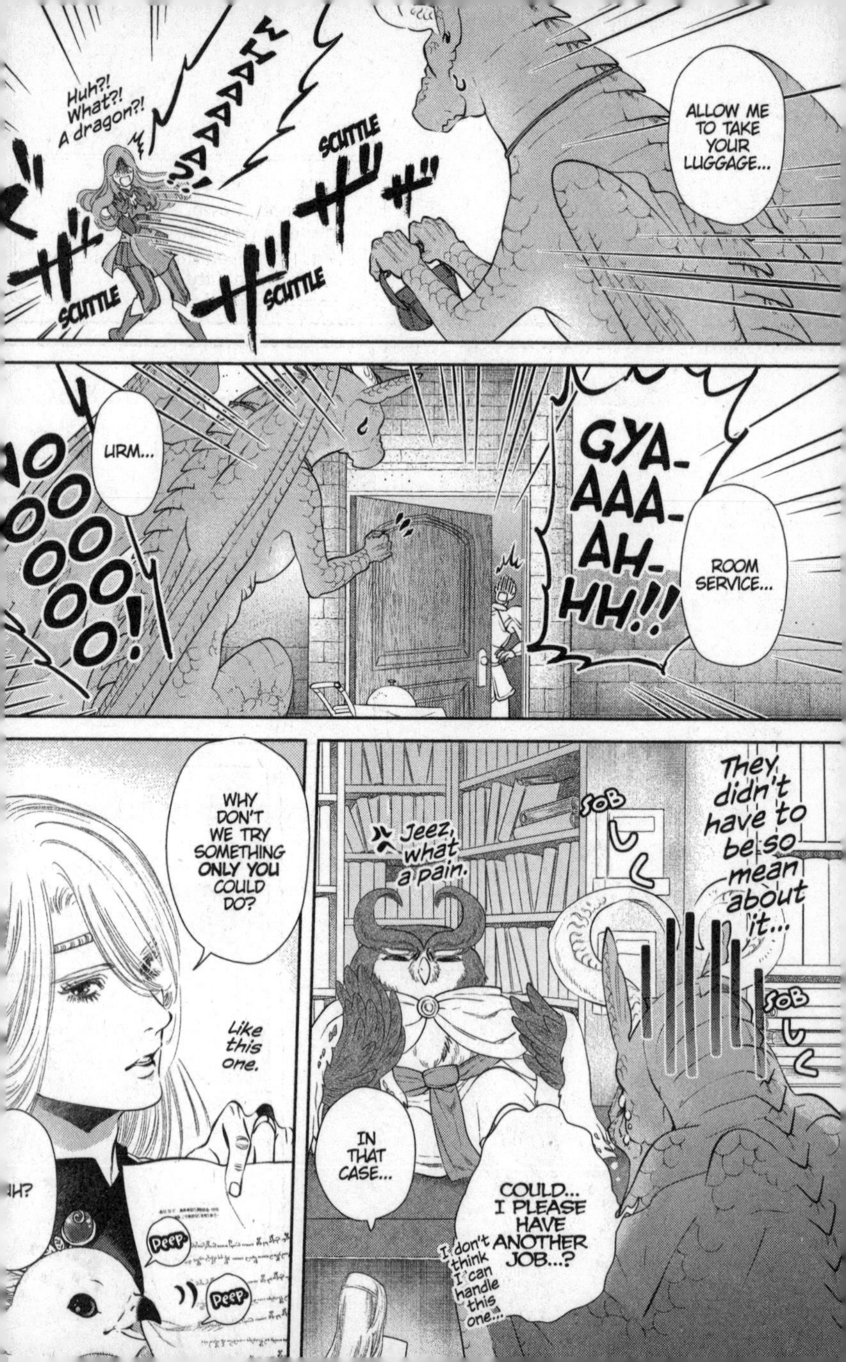
ALLOW ME TO TAKE YOUR LUGGAGE...
SCUTTLE
SCUTTLE
WHAAAAA?!
Huh?! What?! A dragon?!
SCUTTLE
ROOM SERVICE...
GYA-AAA-AH-HH!!
URM...
OOOOOOOOOOO!
They didn't have to be so mean about it...
SOB
SOB
Jeez, what a pain.
COULD... I PLEASE HAVE ANOTHER JOB...?
I don't think I can handle this one...
IN THAT CASE...
WHY DON'T WE TRY SOMETHING ONLY YOU COULD DO?
Like this one.
NH?
PEEP
PEEP

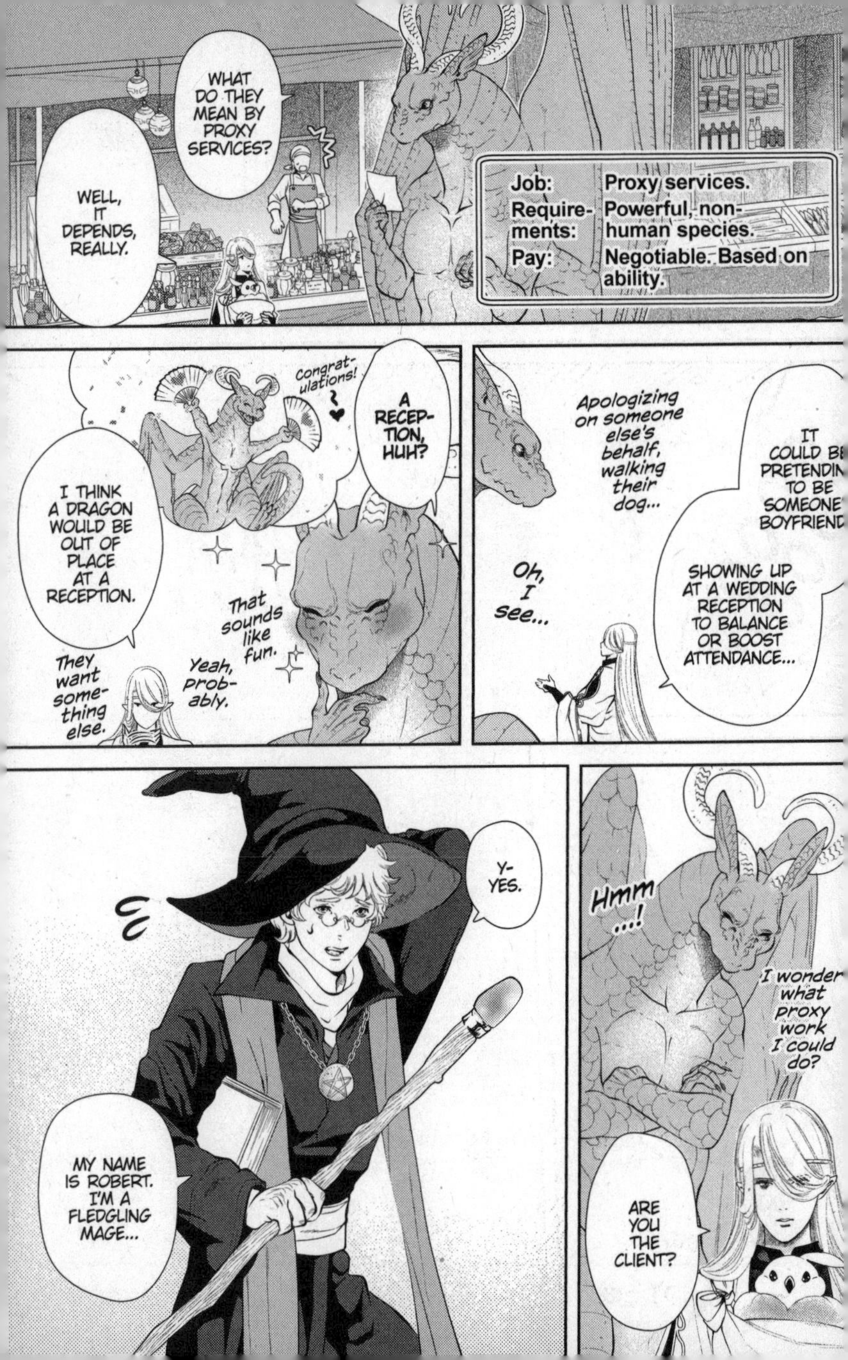
Job: Proxy services.
Requirements: Powerful, non-human species.
Pay: Negotiable. Based on ability.
WHAT DO THEY MEAN BY PROXY SERVICES?
WELL, IT DEPENDS, REALLY.
IT COULD BE PRETENDIN TO BE SOMEONE BOYFRIEND
Apologizing on someone else's behalf, walking their dog...
SHOWING UP AT A WEDDING RECEPTION TO BALANCE OR BOOST ATTENDANCE...
Oh, I see...
A RECEPTION, HUH?
Congratulations!
I THINK A DRAGON WOULD BE OUT OF PLACE AT A RECEPTION.
That sounds like fun.
Yeah, probably.
They want something else.
Hmm...!
I wonder what proxy work I could do?
ARE YOU THE CLIENT?
Y-YES.
MY NAME IS ROBERT. I'M A FLEDGLING MAGE...

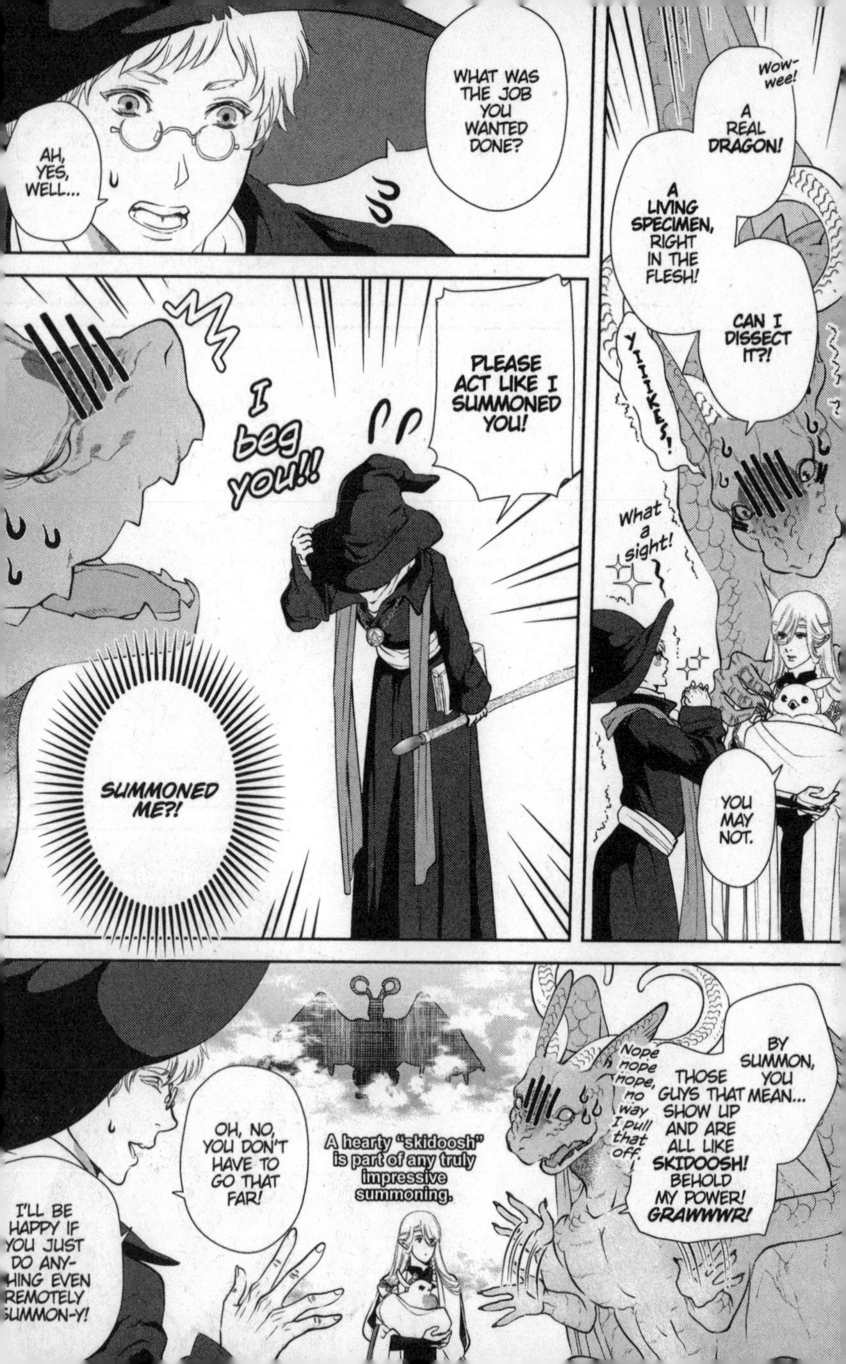
Wow-wee!
A REAL DRAGON!
A LIVING SPECIMEN, RIGHT IN THE FLESH!
CAN I DISSECT IT?!
YIIIIKES!
What a sight!
YOU MAY NOT.
WHAT WAS THE JOB YOU WANTED DONE?
AH, YES, WELL...
PLEASE ACT LIKE I SUMMONED YOU!
I beg you!!
SUMMONED ME?!
BY SUMMON, YOU MEAN... THOSE GUYS THAT SHOW UP AND ARE ALL LIKE SKIDOOSH! BEHOLD MY POWER! GRAWWWR!
Nope nope nope, no way I pull that off.
A hearty "skidoosh" is part of any truly impressive summoning.
OH, NO, YOU DON'T HAVE TO GO THAT FAR!
I'LL BE HAPPY IF YOU JUST DO ANY-HING EVEN REMOTELY SUMMON-Y!

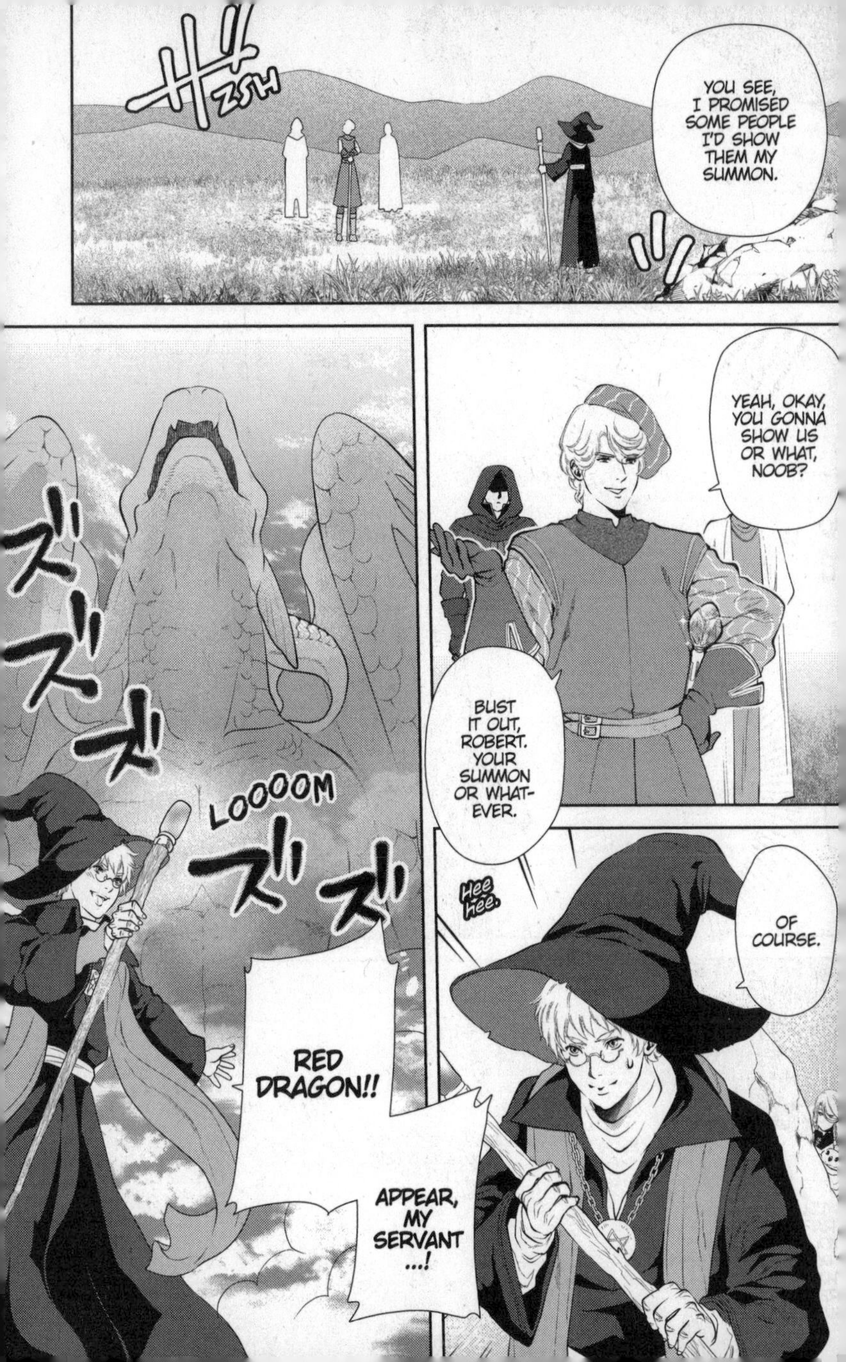

YOU SEE, I PROMISED SOME PEOPLE I'D SHOW THEM MY SUMMON.
ZSH
YEAH, OKAY, YOU GONNA SHOW US OR WHAT, NOOB?
BUST IT OUT, ROBERT. YOUR SUMMON OR WHAT-EVER.
OF COURSE.
Hee hee.
LOOOOM
RED DRAGON!!
APPEAR, MY SERVANT ...!

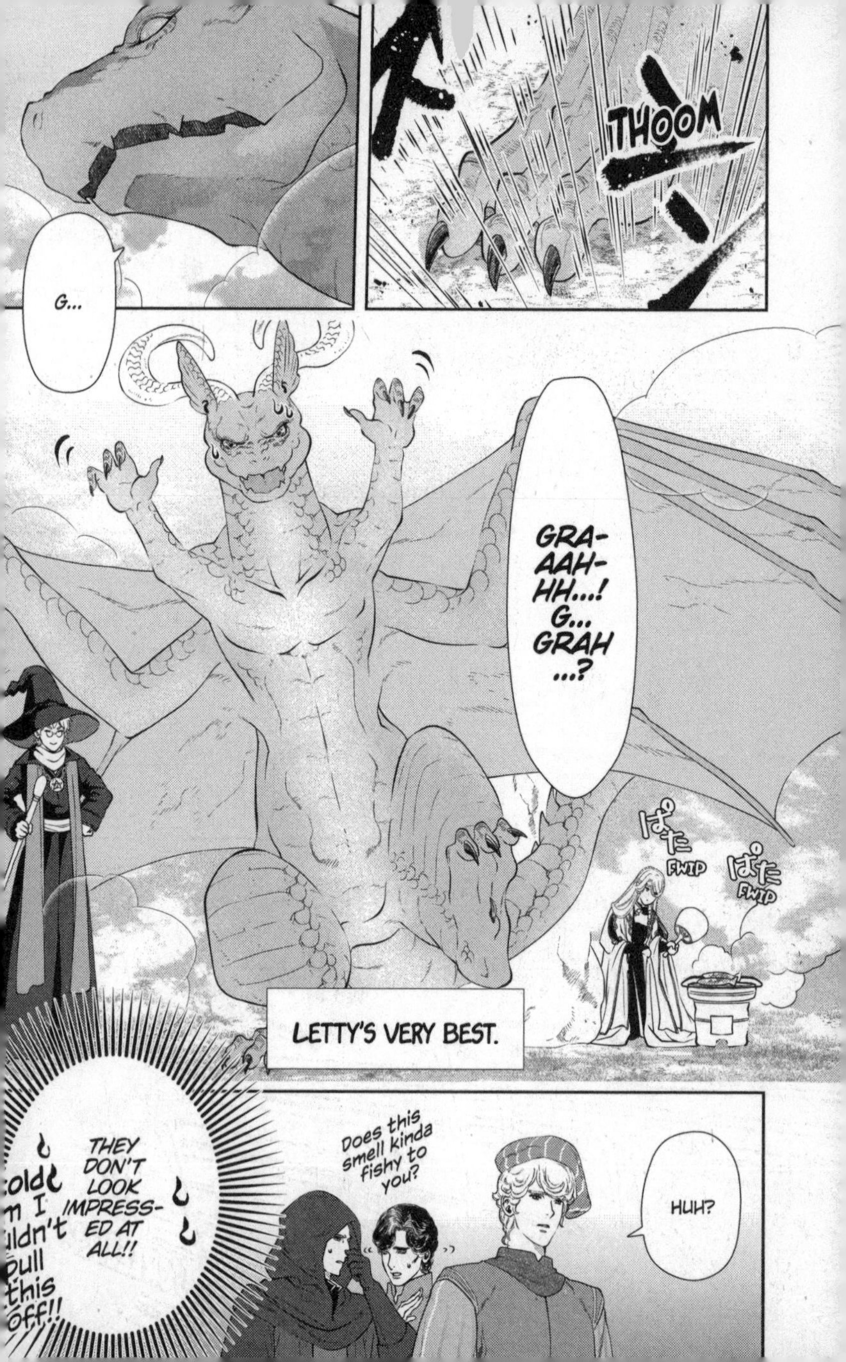
THOOM
G...
GRA-AAH-HH...! G... GRAH ...?
ぱた FWIP
ぱた FWIP
LETTY'S VERY BEST.
HUH?
Does this smell kinda fishy to you?
THEY DON'T LOOK IMPRESSED AT ALL!!
old n I ldn't pull this off!!

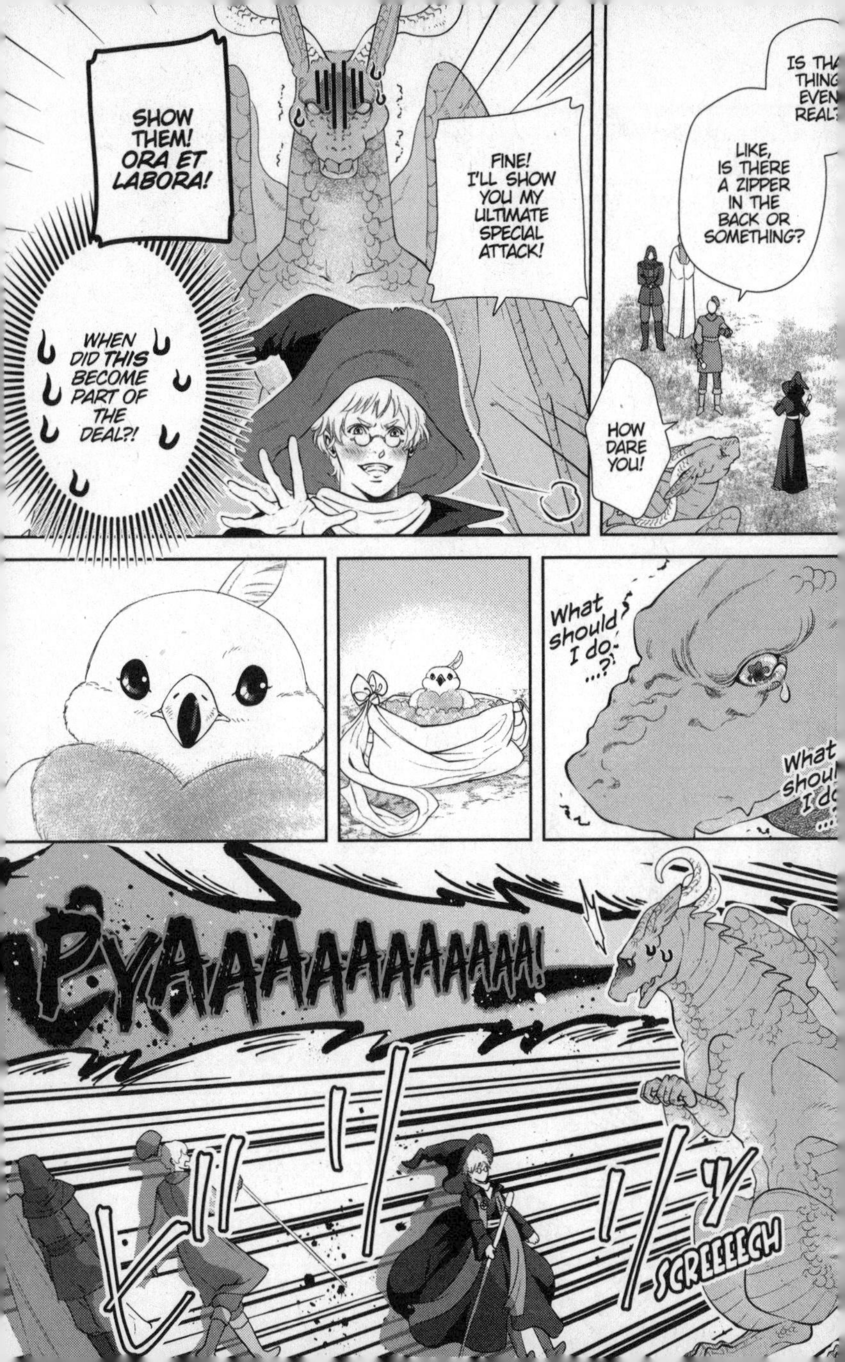
IS THA THING EVEN REAL?
LIKE, IS THERE A ZIPPER IN THE BACK OR SOMETHING?
HOW DARE YOU!
FINE! I'LL SHOW YOU MY ULTIMATE SPECIAL ATTACK!
SHOW THEM! ORA ET LABORA!
WHEN DID THIS BECOME PART OF THE DEAL?!
What should I do-...?!
What shoul I do ...?
PYAAAAAAAAAA!
SCREEEECH

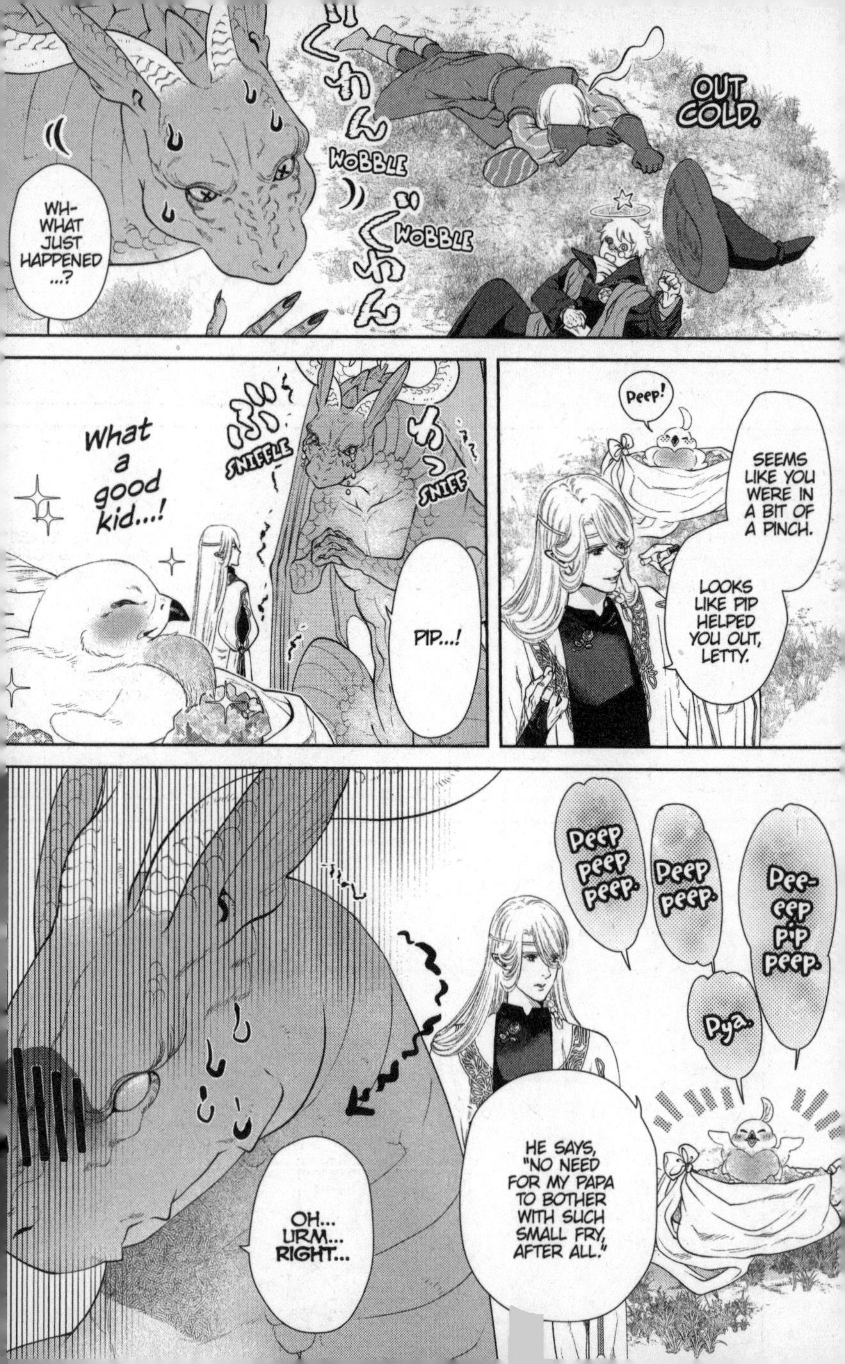
OUT COLD.
くわん
WOBBLE
ぐわん
WOBBLE
WH-WHAT JUST HAPPENED ...?
Peep!
SEEMS LIKE YOU WERE IN A BIT OF A PINCH.
LOOKS LIKE PIP HELPED YOU OUT, LETTY.
SNIFF
SNIFFLE
PIP...!
What a good kid...!
Pee-eep pip peep.
Peep peep.
Peep peep peep.
Pya.
HE SAYS, "NO NEED FOR MY PAPA TO BOTHER WITH SUCH SMALL FRY, AFTER ALL."
OH... URM... RIGHT...

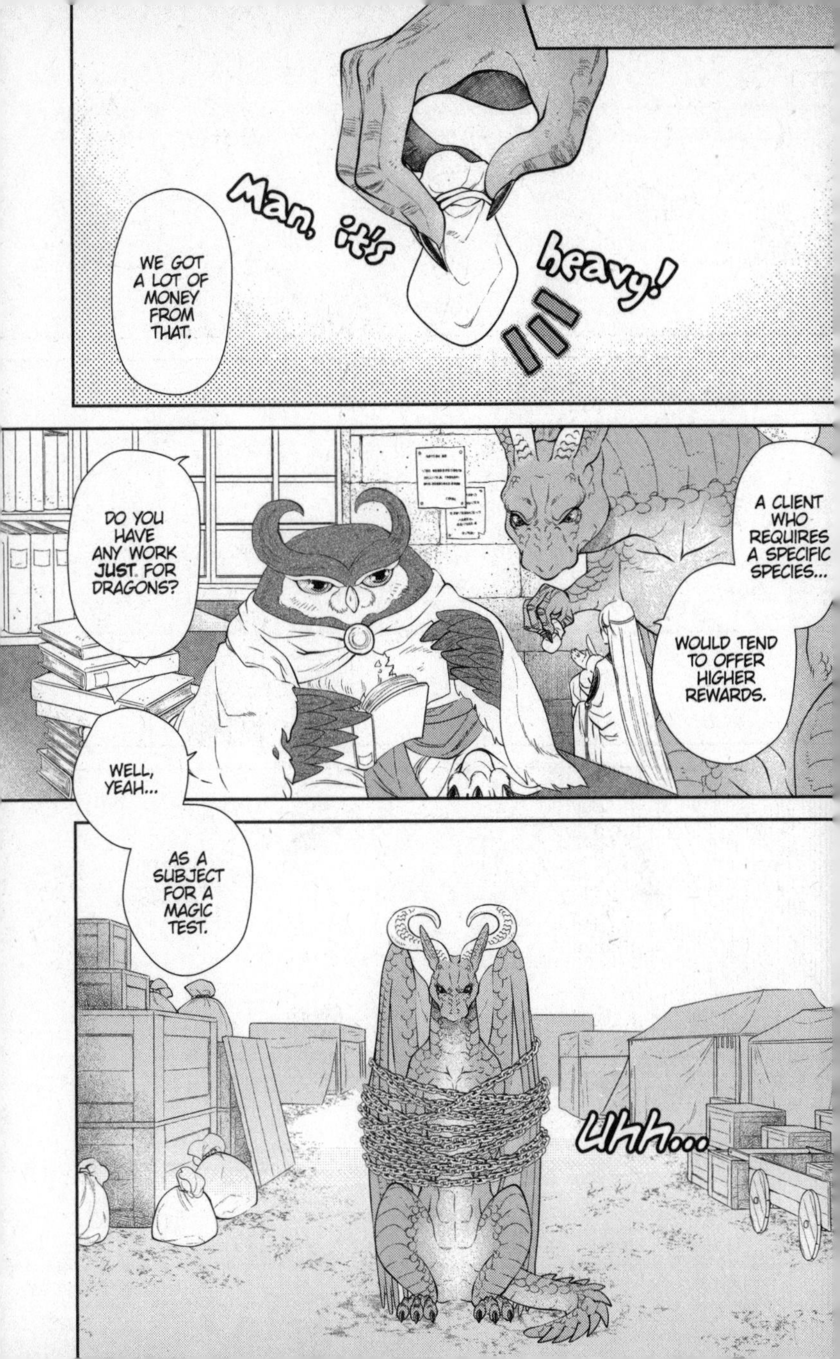
Man, it's heavy!
WE GOT A LOT OF MONEY FROM THAT.
A CLIENT WHO REQUIRES A SPECIFIC SPECIES...
WOULD TEND TO OFFER HIGHER REWARDS.
DO YOU HAVE ANY WORK JUST FOR DRAGONS?
WELL, YEAH...
AS A SUBJECT FOR A MAGIC TEST.
Uhh...

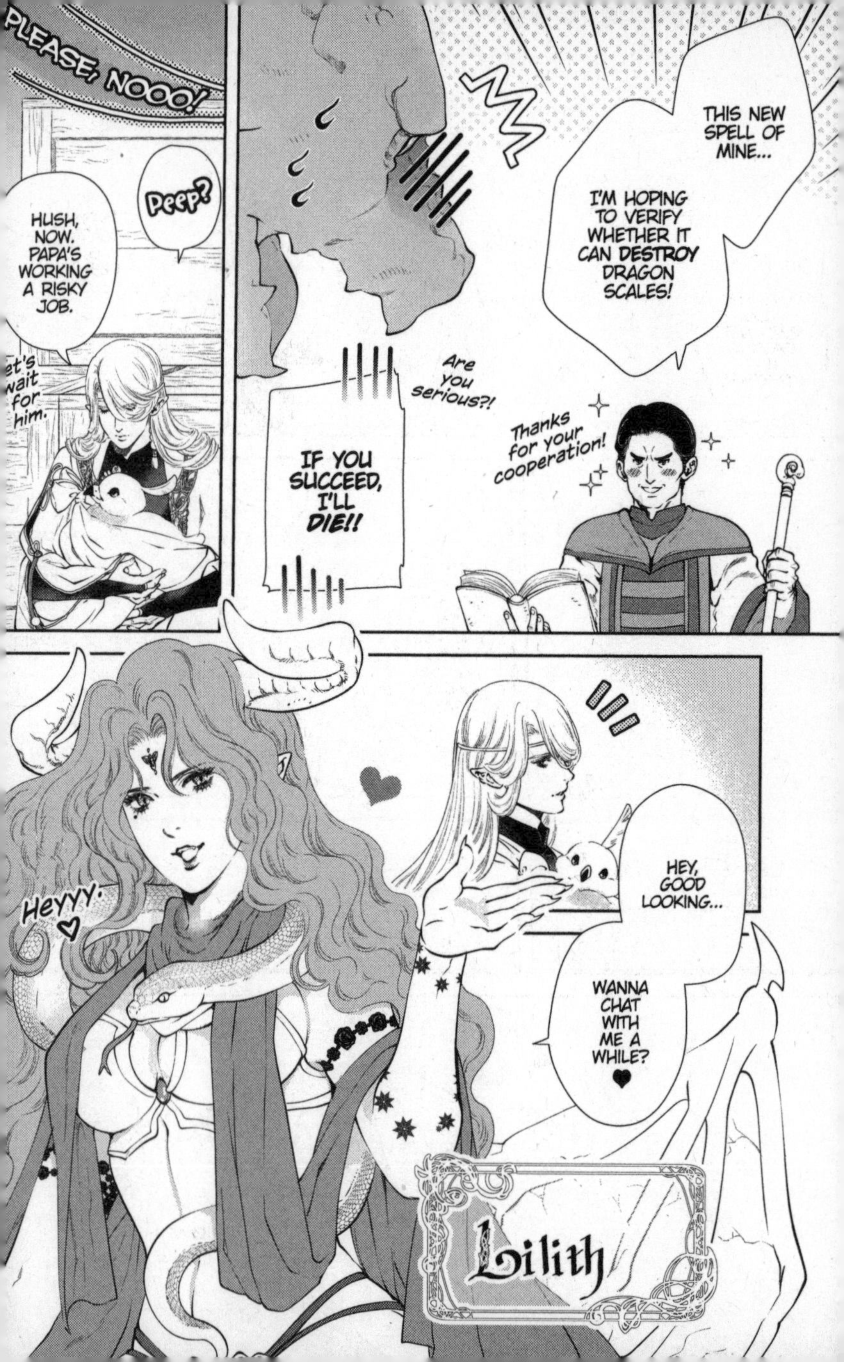
THIS NEW SPELL OF MINE...
I'M HOPING TO VERIFY WHETHER IT CAN DESTROY DRAGON SCALES!
Thanks for your cooperation!
Are you serious?!
IF YOU SUCCEED, I'LL DIE!!
PLEASE, NOOO!
Peep?
HUSH, NOW. PAPA'S WORKING A RISKY JOB.
et's wait for him.
HEY, GOOD LOOKING...
WANNA CHAT WITH ME A WHILE?
Heyyy.
Lilith

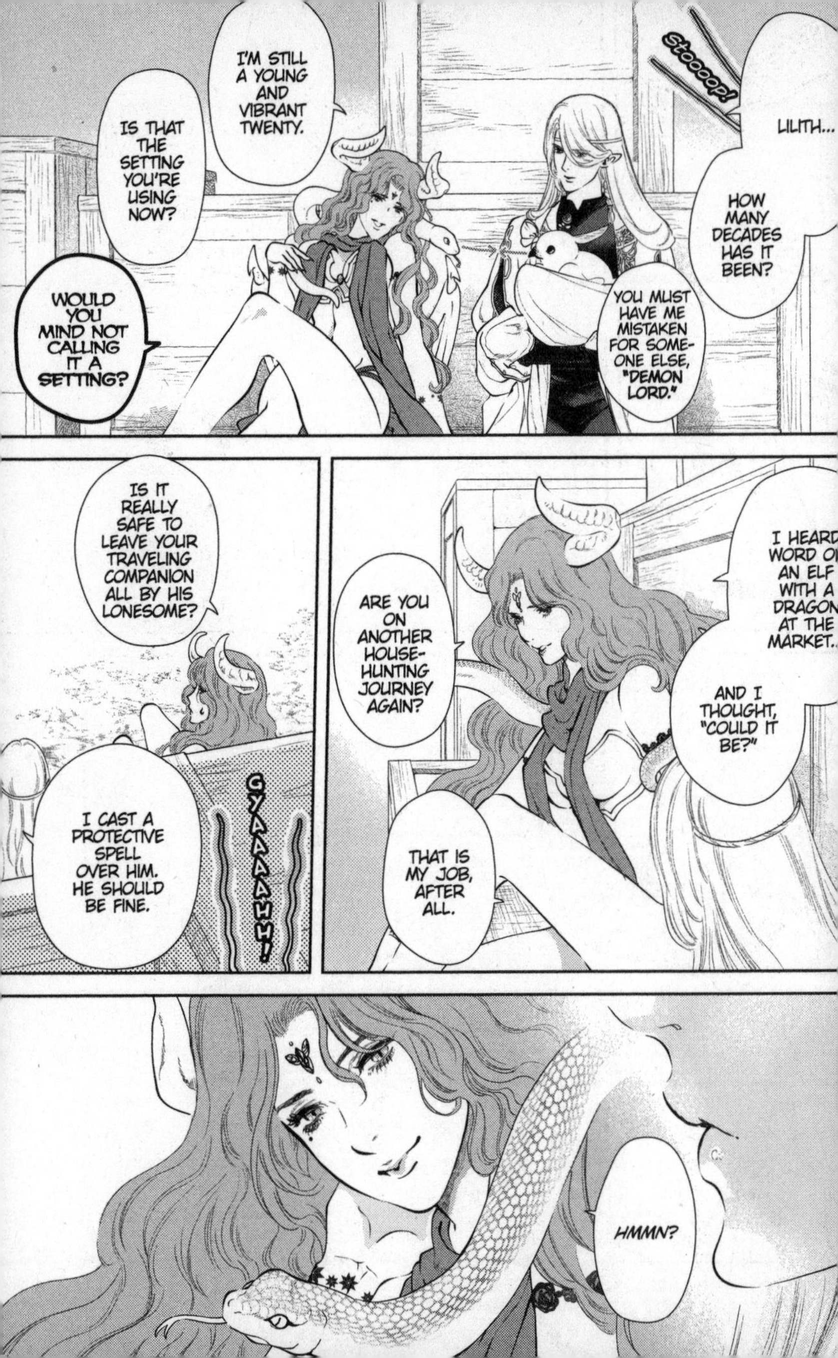
Stoooop!
LILITH...
HOW MANY DECADES HAS IT BEEN?
YOU MUST HAVE ME MISTAKEN FOR SOMEONE ELSE, "DEMON LORD."
I'M STILL A YOUNG AND VIBRANT TWENTY.
IS THAT THE SETTING YOU'RE USING NOW?
WOULD YOU MIND NOT CALLING IT A SETTING?
I HEARD WORD OF AN ELF WITH A DRAGON AT THE MARKET..
AND I THOUGHT, "COULD IT BE?"
ARE YOU ON ANOTHER HOUSE-HUNTING JOURNEY AGAIN?
THAT IS MY JOB, AFTER ALL.
IS IT REALLY SAFE TO LEAVE YOUR TRAVELING COMPANION ALL BY HIS LONESOME?
GYAAAAAHH!
I CAST A PROTECTIVE SPELL OVER HIM. HE SHOULD BE FINE.
HMMN?

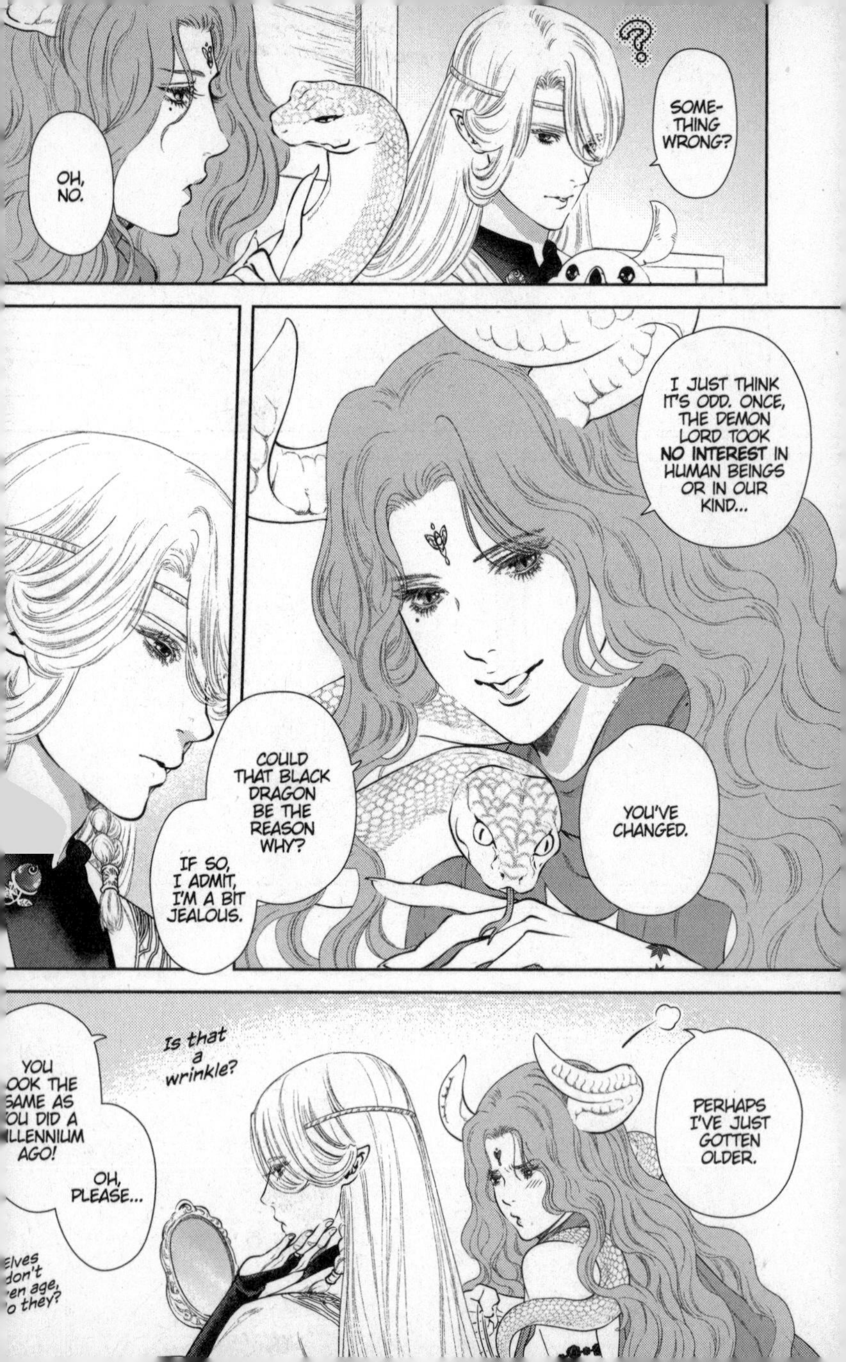
?
SOME-THING WRONG?
OH, NO.
I JUST THINK IT'S ODD. ONCE, THE DEMON LORD TOOK **NO INTEREST** IN HUMAN BEINGS OR IN OUR KIND...
YOU'VE CHANGED.
COULD THAT BLACK DRAGON BE THE REASON WHY?
IF SO, I ADMIT, I'M A BIT JEALOUS.
PERHAPS I'VE JUST GOTTEN OLDER.
Is that a wrinkle?
YOU OOK THE SAME AS OU DID A ILLENNIUM AGO!
OH, PLEASE...
Elves don't en age, o they?

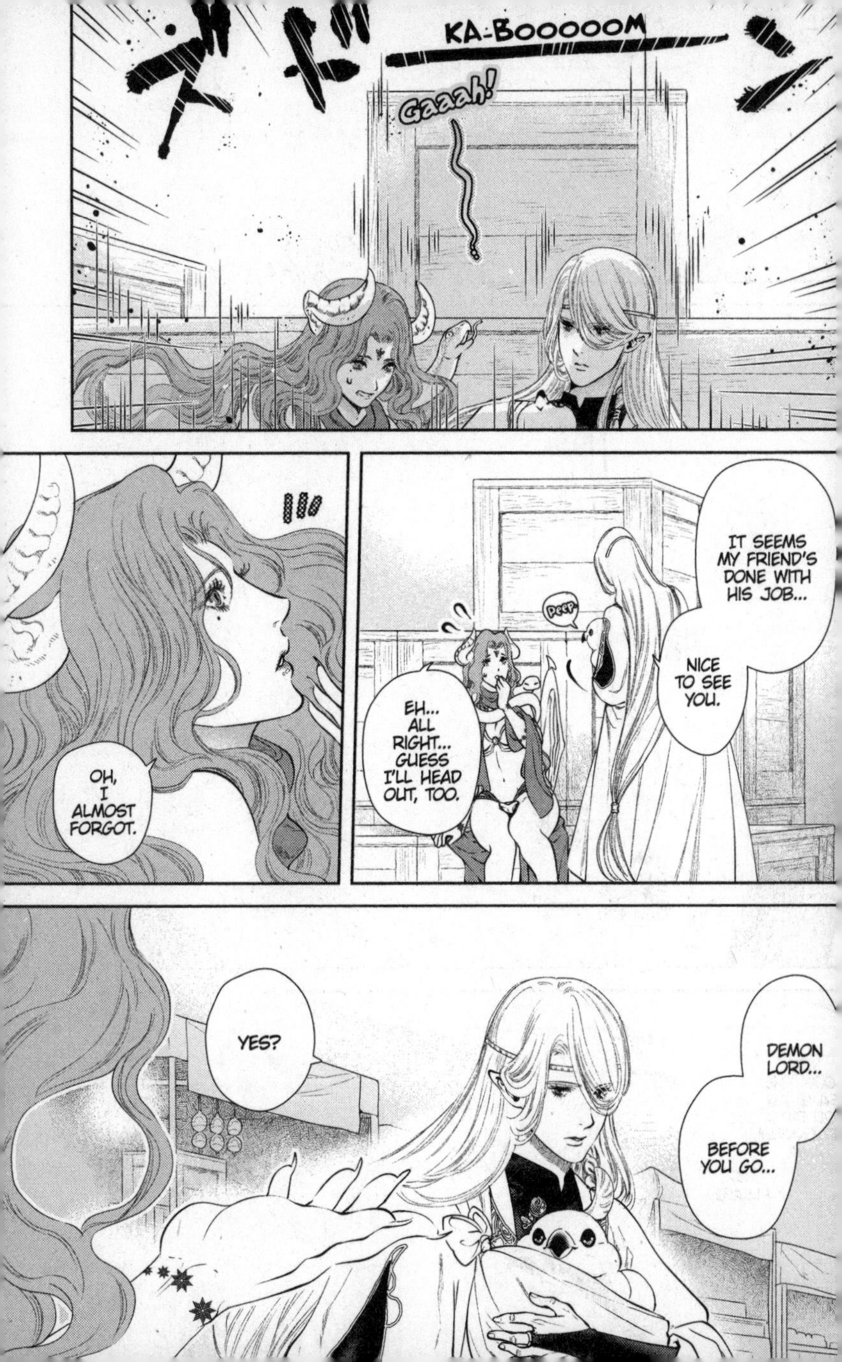
KA-BOOOOOM
Gaaah!
IT SEEMS MY FRIEND'S DONE WITH HIS JOB...
NICE TO SEE YOU.
Peep
EH... ALL RIGHT... GUESS I'LL HEAD OUT, TOO.
OH, I ALMOST FORGOT.
DEMON LORD...
BEFORE YOU GO...
YES?

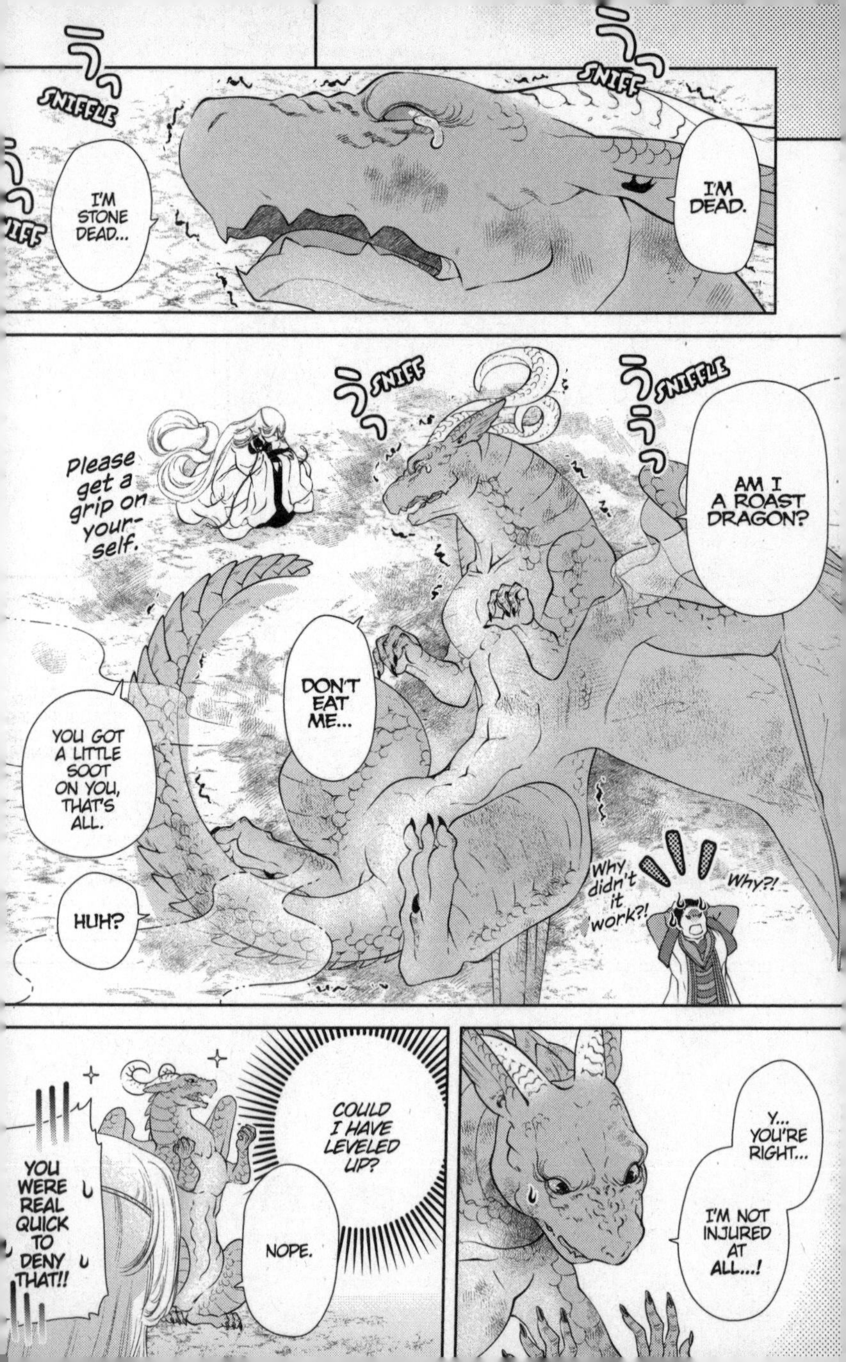
SNIFF
I'M DEAD.
SNIFFLE
I'M STONE DEAD...
SNIFF
SNIFFLE
AM I A ROAST DRAGON?
SNIFF
Please get a grip on your-self.
Why?!
Why didn't it work?!
DON'T EAT ME...
YOU GOT A LITTLE SOOT ON YOU, THAT'S ALL.
HUH?
Y... YOU'RE RIGHT...
I'M NOT INJURED AT ALL...!
COULD I HAVE LEVELED UP?
NOPE.
YOU WERE REAL QUICK TO DENY THAT!!

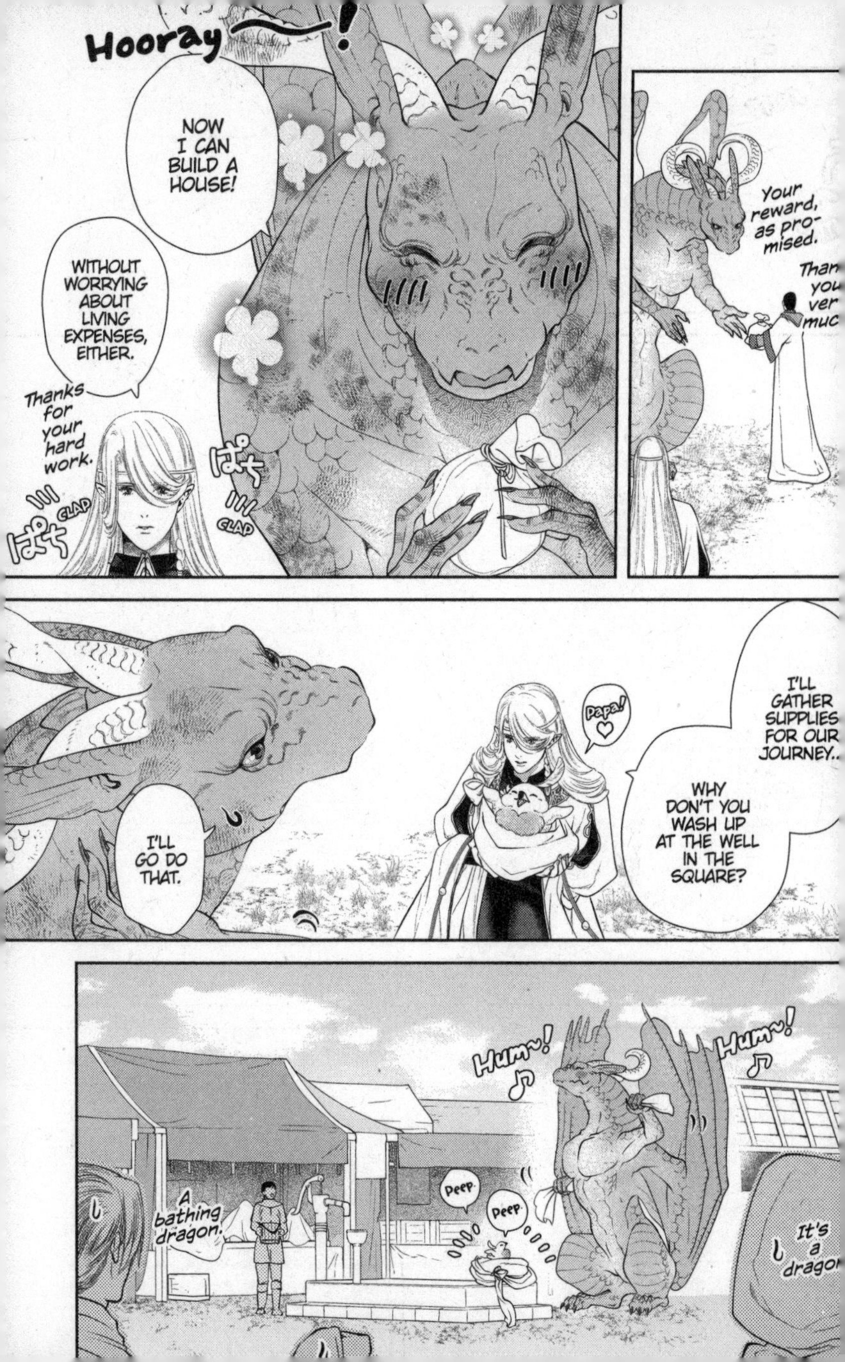
Your reward, as promised.
Than you ver muc
Hooray—!
NOW I CAN BUILD A HOUSE!
WITHOUT WORRYING ABOUT LIVING EXPENSES, EITHER.
Thanks for your hard work.
ぱち CLAP
ぱち CLAP
I'LL GATHER SUPPLIES FOR OUR JOURNEY..
WHY DON'T YOU WASH UP AT THE WELL IN THE SQUARE?
Papa! ♡
I'LL GO DO THAT.
It's a dragon
Hum~! ♪
Hum~! ♪
Peep.
Peep.
A bathing dragon.

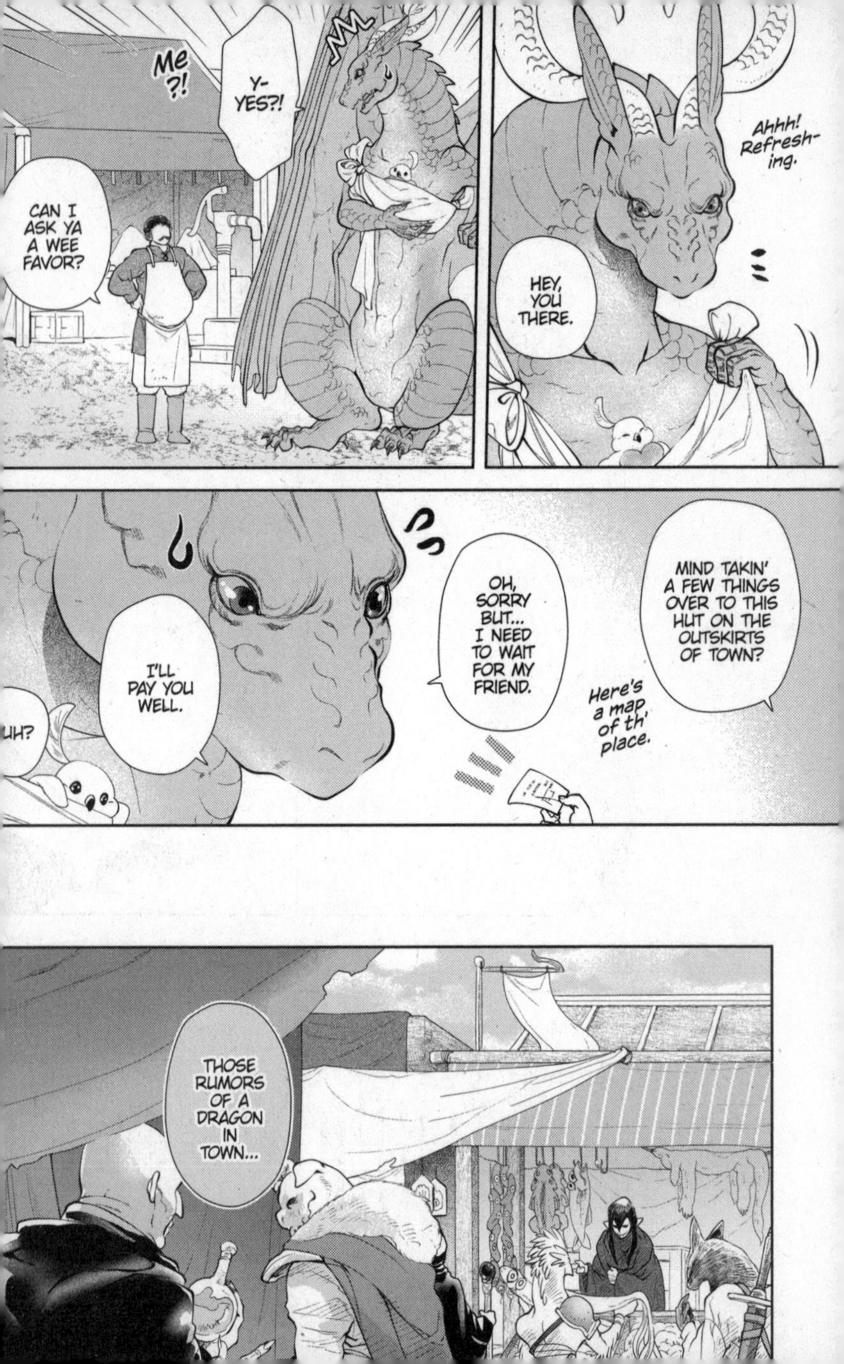
Ahhh! Refresh-ing.
HEY, YOU THERE.
Y-YES?!
Me ?!
CAN I ASK YA A WEE FAVOR?
MIND TAKIN' A FEW THINGS OVER TO THIS HUT ON THE OUTSKIRTS OF TOWN?
Here's a map of th' place.
OH, SORRY BUT... I NEED TO WAIT FOR MY FRIEND.
I'LL PAY YOU WELL.
UH?
THOSE RUMORS OF A DRAGON IN TOWN...

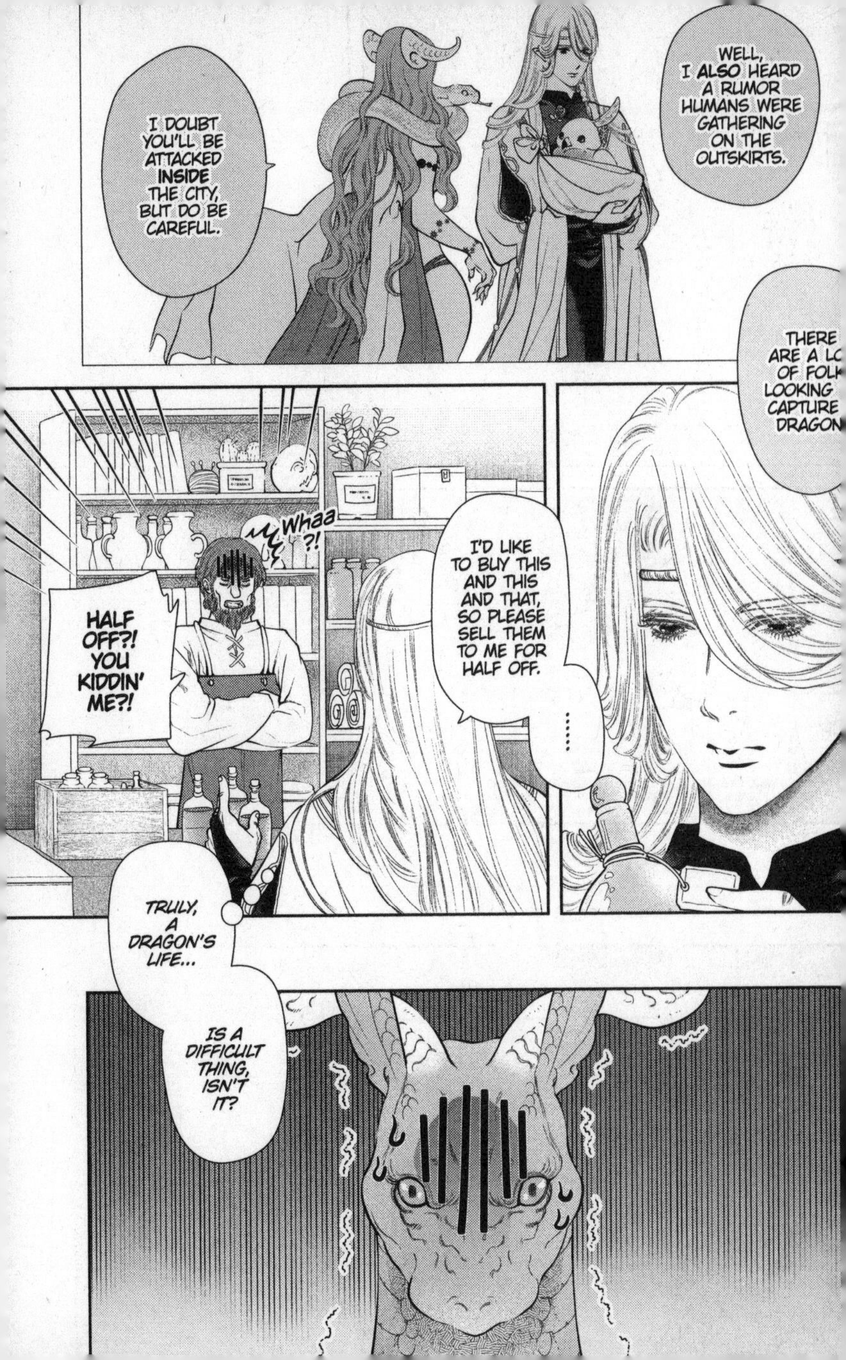
WELL, I ALSO HEARD A RUMOR HUMANS WERE GATHERING ON THE OUTSKIRTS.
I DOUBT YOU'LL BE ATTACKED **INSIDE** THE CITY, BUT DO BE CAREFUL.
THERE ARE A LO OF FOLK LOOKING CAPTURE DRAGON
I'D LIKE TO BUY THIS AND THIS AND THAT, SO PLEASE SELL THEM TO ME FOR HALF OFF.
......
Whaa ?!
HALF OFF?! YOU KIDDIN' ME?!
TRULY, A DRAGON'S LIFE...
IS A DIFFICULT THING, ISN'T IT?

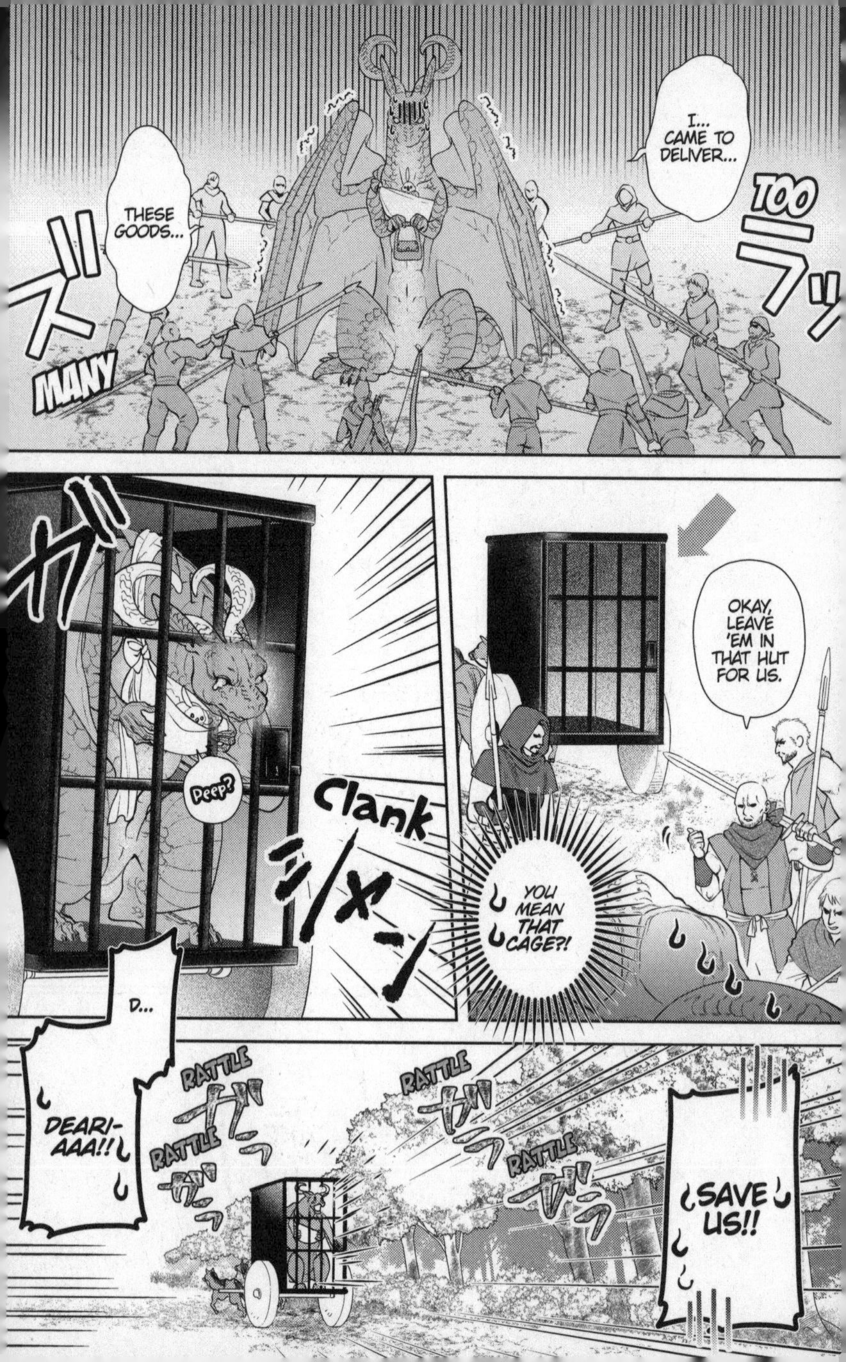
I... CAME TO DELIVER...
TOO
MANY
THESE GOODS...
OKAY, LEAVE 'EM IN THAT HUT FOR US.
YOU MEAN THAT CAGE?!
Clank
Deep?
SAVE US!!
RATTLE
RATTLE
RATTLE
RATTLE
D...
DEARI-AAA!!

I Really Want It

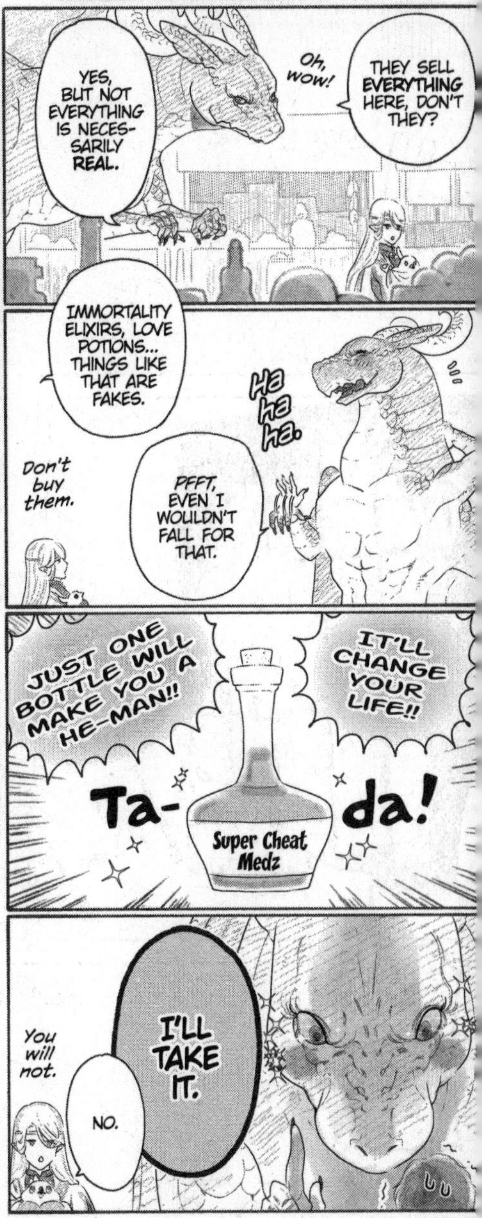
THEY SELL EVERYTHING HERE, DON'T THEY?
Oh, wow!
YES, BUT NOT EVERYTHING IS NECES-SARILY REAL.
IMMORTALITY ELIXIRS, LOVE POTIONS... THINGS LIKE THAT ARE FAKES.
Ha ha ha.
PFFT, EVEN I WOULDN'T FALL FOR THAT.
Don't buy them.
IT'LL CHANGE YOUR LIFE!!
JUST ONE BOTTLE WILL MAKE YOU A HE-MAN!!
Ta- da!
Super Cheat Medz
I'LL TAKE IT.
You will not.
NO.

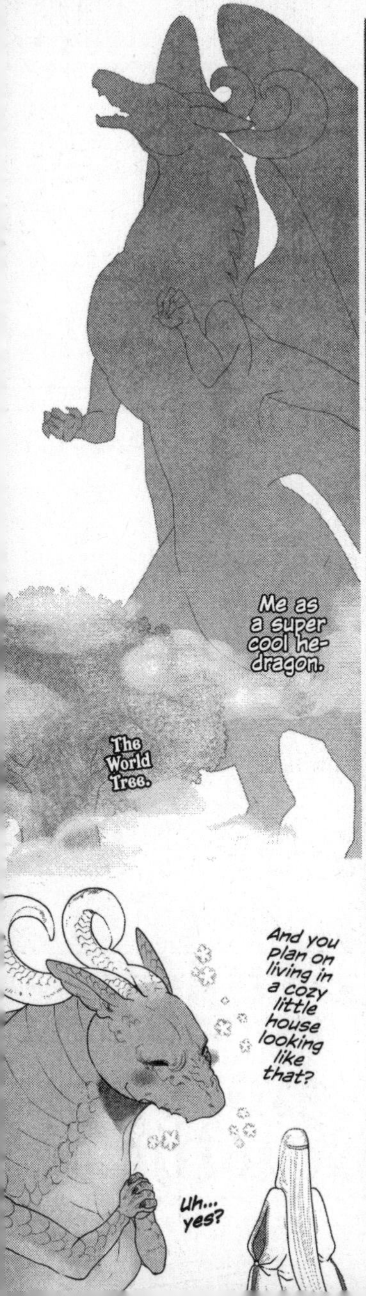
Me as a super cool he-dragon.
The World Tree.
And you plan on living in a cozy little house looking like that?
Uh... yes?

Dragon Goes House-Hunting

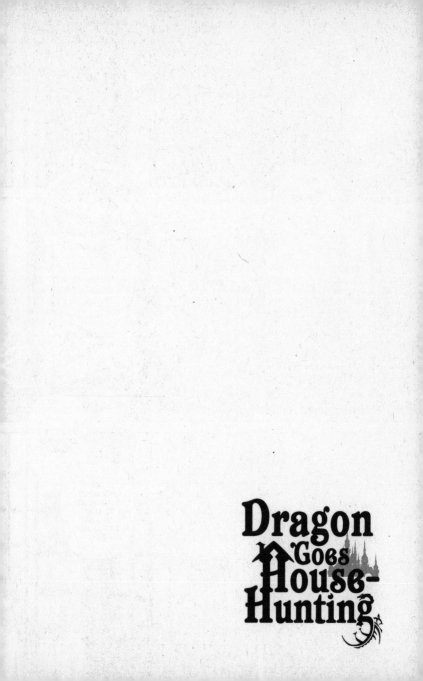

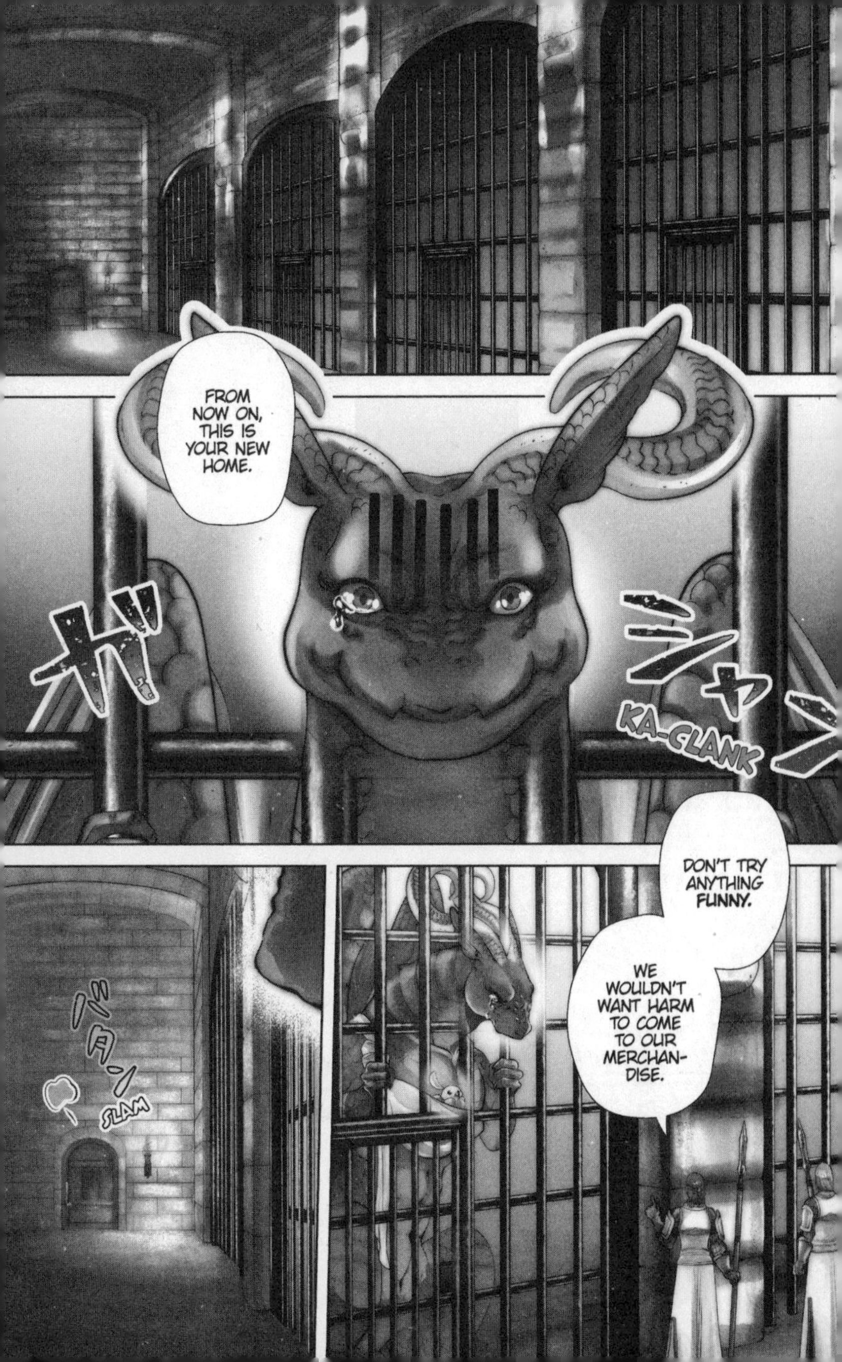

FROM NOW ON, THIS IS YOUR NEW HOME.
ガシャン
KA-CLANK
ガッ
DON'T TRY ANYTHING FUNNY.
WE WOULDN'T WANT HARM TO COME TO OUR MERCHAN-DISE.
バタン
SLAM

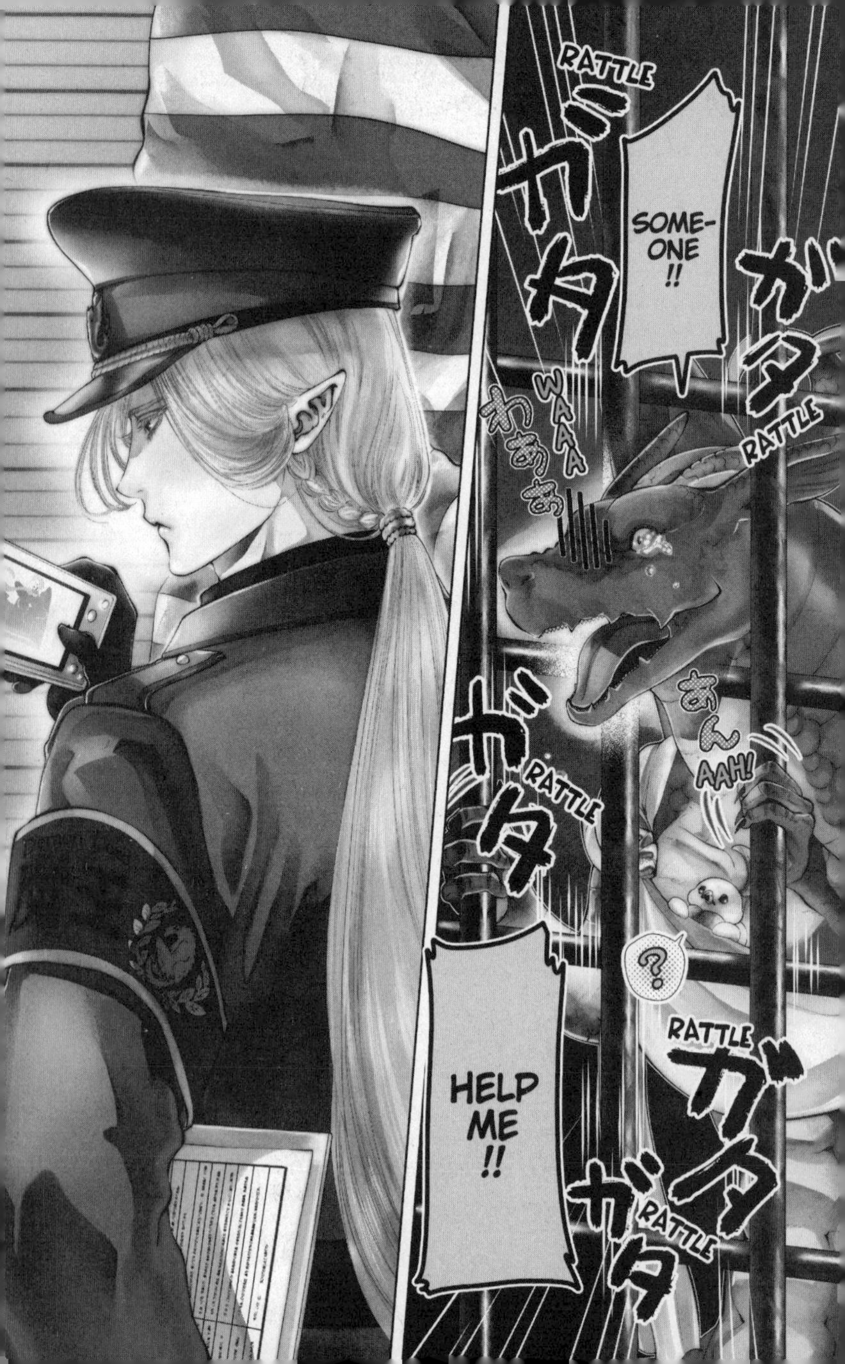
RATTLE
SOME-ONE!!
RATTLE
WAAAA
AAH!
RATTLE
?
RATTLE
HELP ME!!
RATTLE

House 9: The Big House (Part 1)

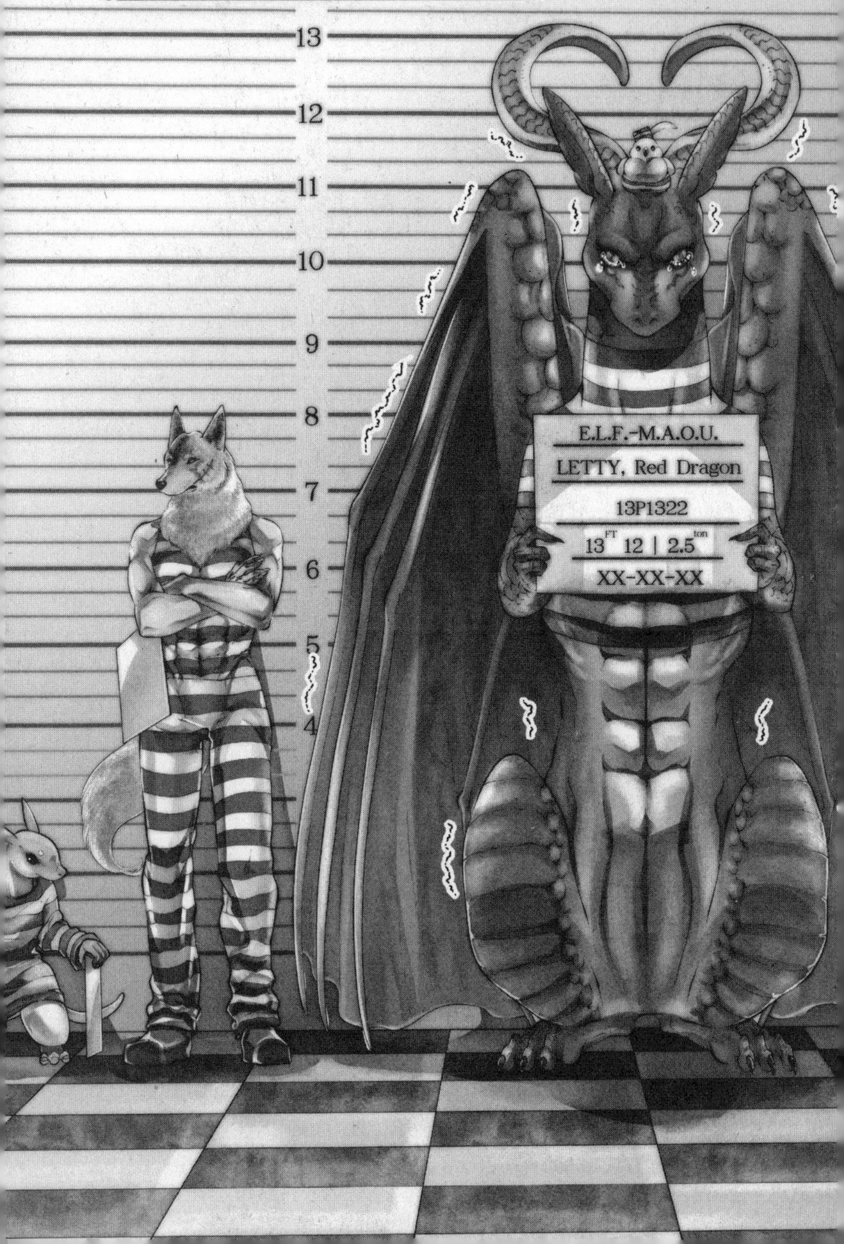
E.L.F.-M.A.O.U.
LETTY, Red Dragon
13P1322
13 FT 12 | 2.5 ton
XX-XX-XX

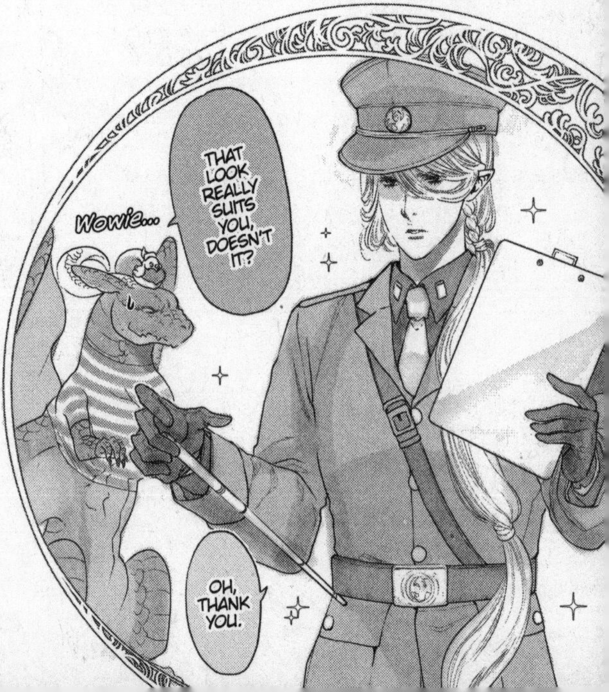
THAT LOOK REALLY SUITS YOU, DOESN'T IT?
Wowie...
OH, THANK YOU.

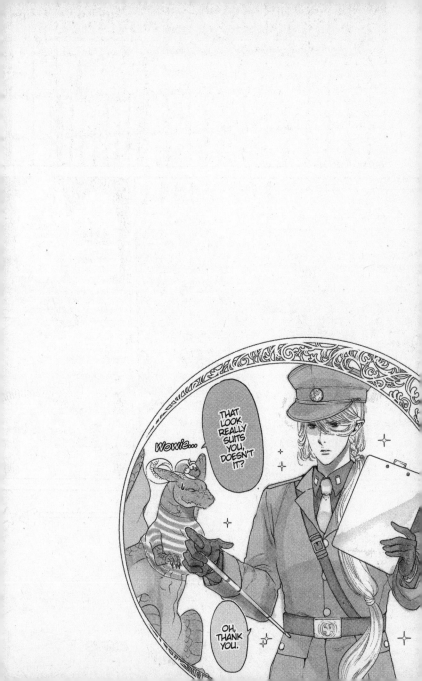

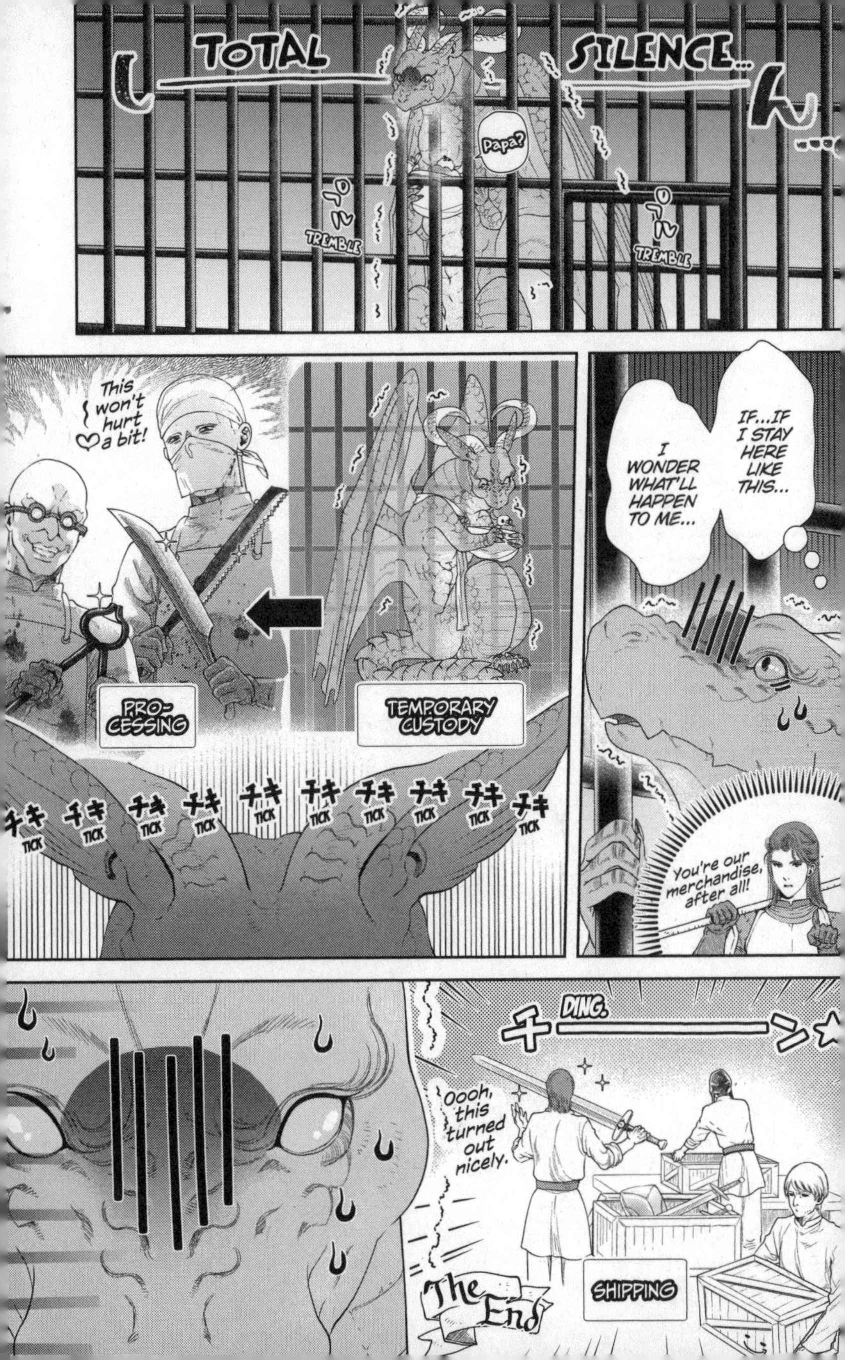

TOTAL SILENCE...
Papa?
プル
TREMBLE
プル
TREMBLE
IF...IF I STAY HERE LIKE THIS...
I WONDER WHAT'LL HAPPEN TO ME...
You're our merchandise, after all!
TEMPORARY CUSTODY
PRO-CESSING
This won't hurt a bit!
チキ TICK チキ TICK チキ TICK チキ TICK チキ TICK チキ TICK チキ TICK チキ TICK チキ TICK チキ TICK
DING.
Oooh, this turned out nicely.
SHIPPING
The End

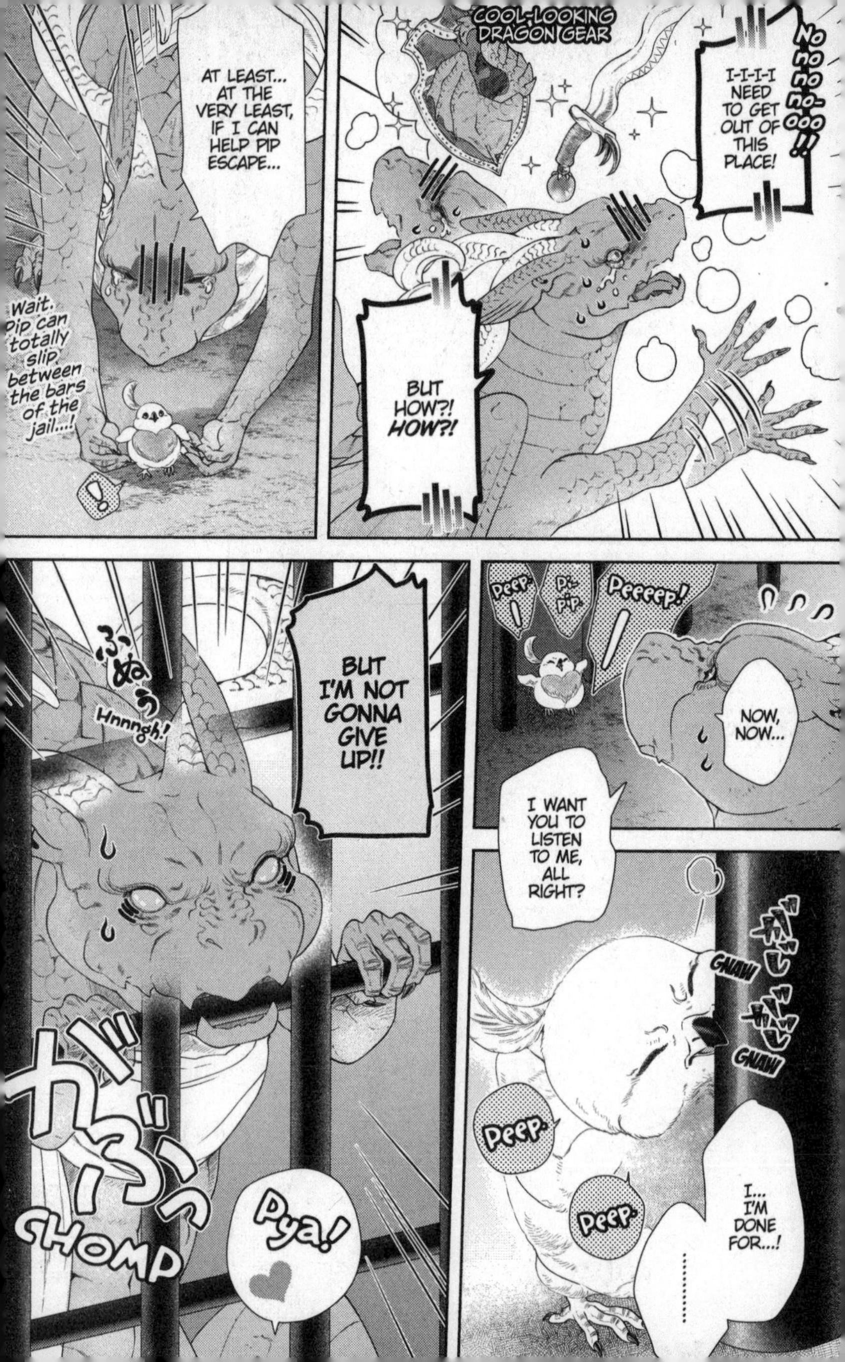
No no no no-ooo!!
I-I-I-I NEED TO GET OUT OF THIS PLACE!
COOL-LOOKING DRAGON GEAR
BUT HOW?! HOW?!
AT LEAST... AT THE VERY LEAST, IF I CAN HELP PIP ESCAPE...
Wait. Pip can totally slip between the bars of the jail...!
Peeeep!
Pi-pip.
Peep.
NOW, NOW...
I WANT YOU TO LISTEN TO ME, ALL RIGHT?
GNAW
GNAW
Peep.
Peep.
I... I'M DONE FOR...!
......
BUT I'M NOT GONNA GIVE UP!!
Hnnngh!
CHOMP
Pya!

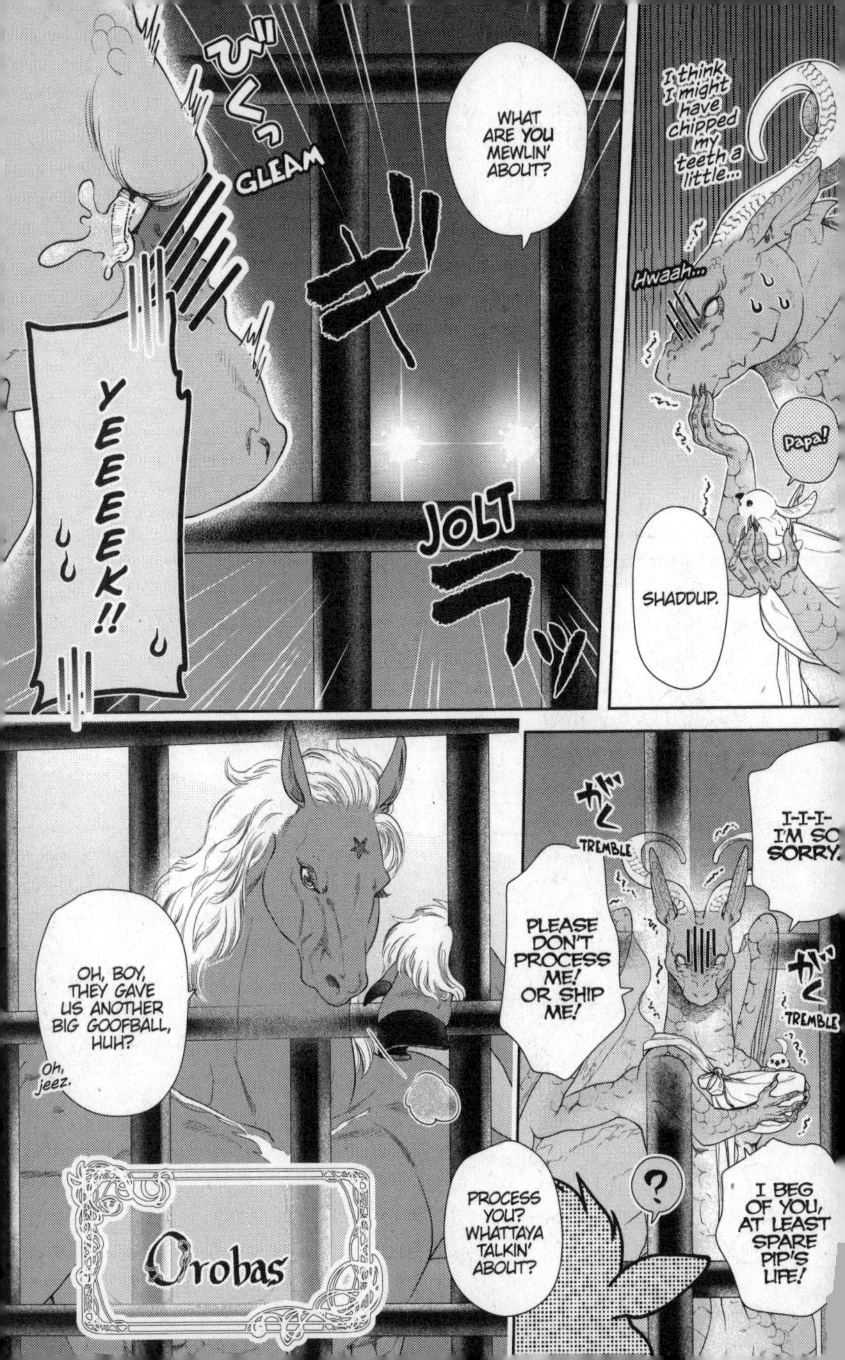
I think I might have chipped my teeth a little...
Hwaah...
Papa!
SHADDUP.
WHAT ARE YOU MEWLIN' ABOUT?
ギ
びくっ
GLEAM
JOLT
ラッ
YEEEEEK!!
I-I-I-I'M SO SORRY.
がく
TREMBLE
がく
TREMBLE
PLEASE DON'T PROCESS ME! OR SHIP ME!
I BEG OF YOU, AT LEAST SPARE PIP'S LIFE!
?
PROCESS YOU? WHATTAYA TALKIN' ABOUT?
OH, BOY, THEY GAVE US ANOTHER BIG GOOFBALL, HUH?
Oh, jeez.
Orobas

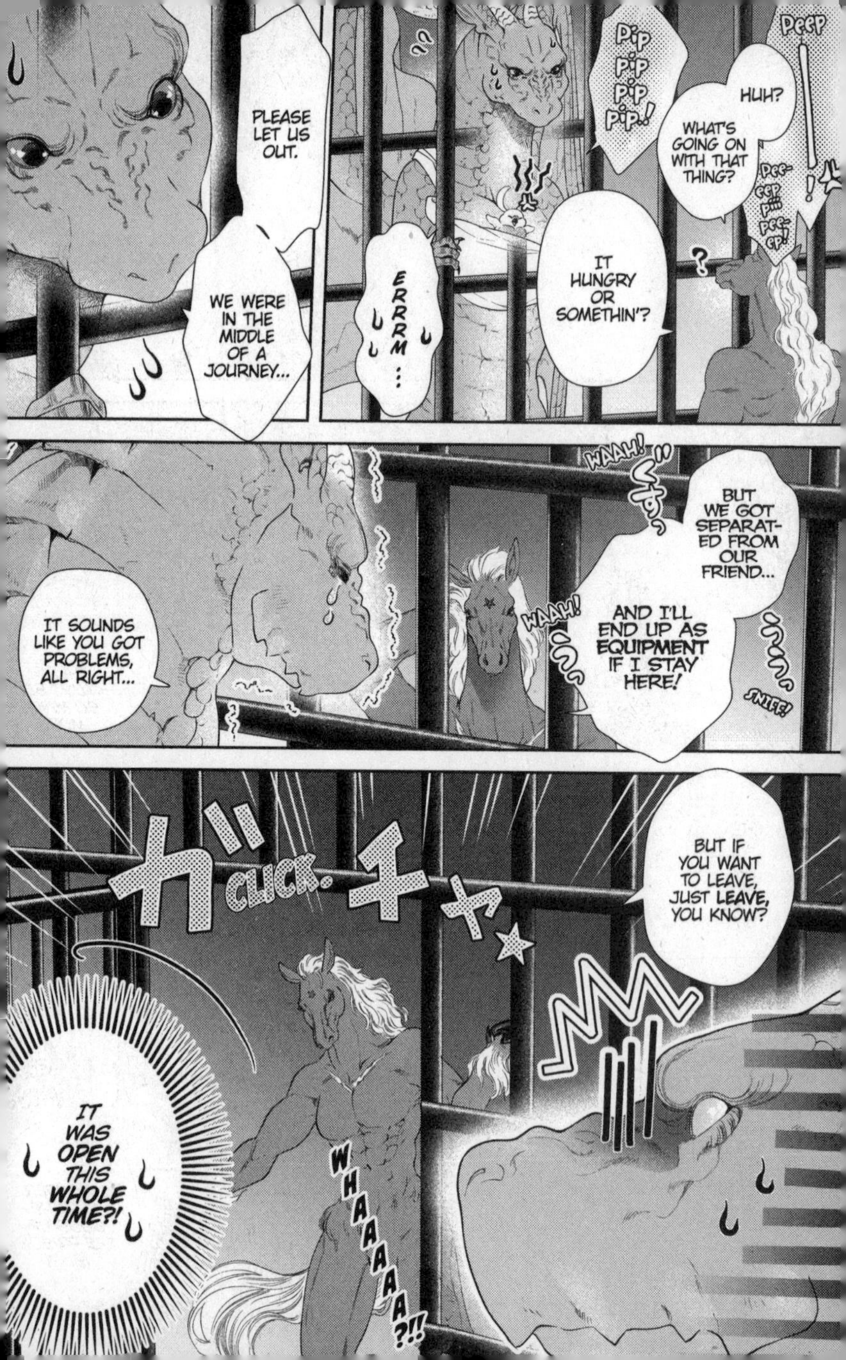
Peep!
Pip pip pip pip!
HUH?
WHAT'S GOING ON WITH THAT THING?
Pee-eep p!!! pee-ep!
IT HUNGRY OR SOMETHIN'?
ERRRM...
PLEASE LET US OUT.
WE WERE IN THE MIDDLE OF A JOURNEY...
WAAH!
BUT WE GOT SEPARATED FROM OUR FRIEND...
AND I'LL END UP AS EQUIPMENT IF I STAY HERE!
WAAH!
SNIFF!
IT SOUNDS LIKE YOU GOT PROBLEMS, ALL RIGHT...
BUT IF YOU WANT TO LEAVE, JUST LEAVE, YOU KNOW?
CLICK.
IT WAS OPEN THIS WHOLE TIME?!
WHAAAAAA?!!

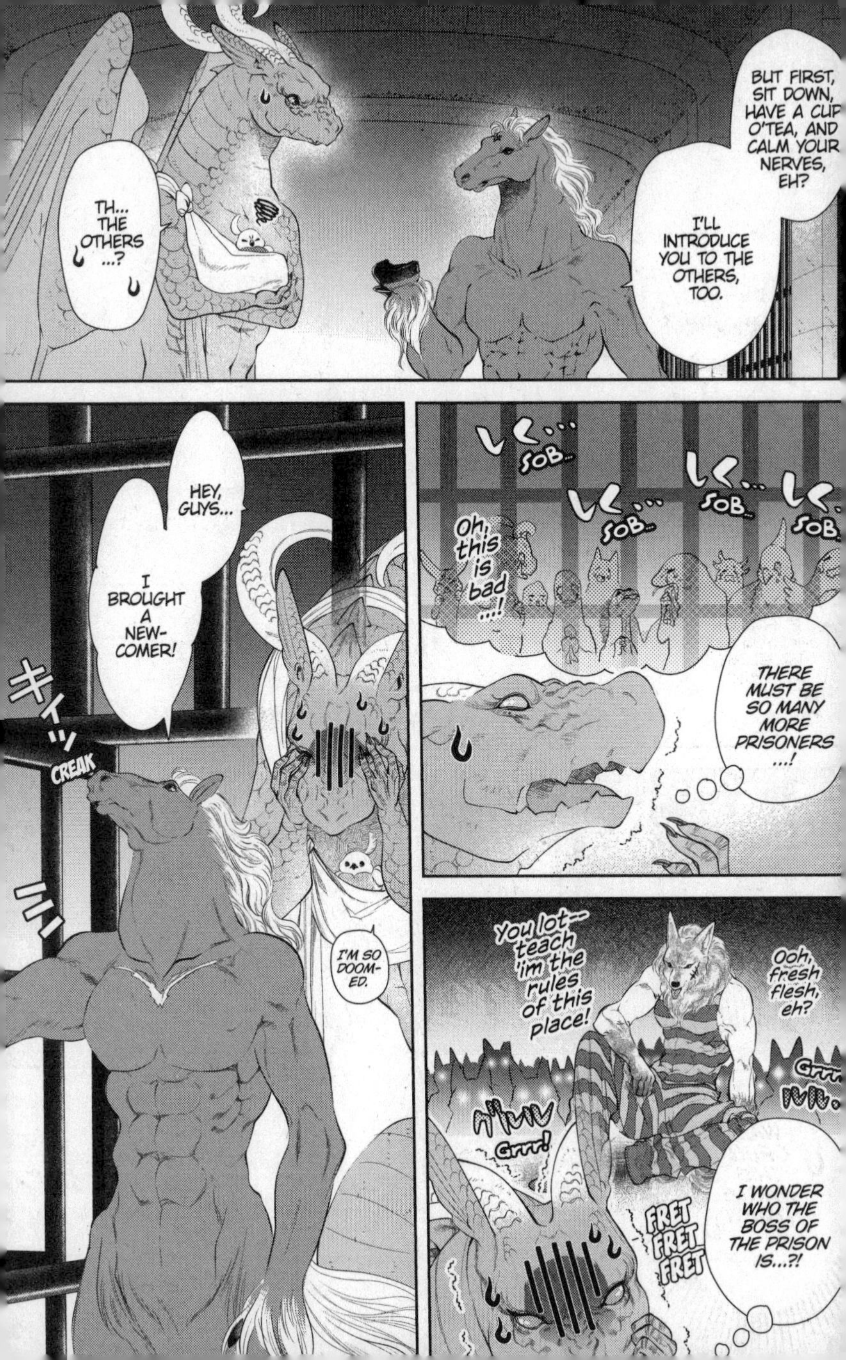
BUT FIRST, SIT DOWN, HAVE A CUP O'TEA, AND CALM YOUR NERVES, EH?
I'LL INTRODUCE YOU TO THE OTHERS, TOO.
TH... THE OTHERS ...?
SOB...
SOB...
SOB...
SOB...
Oh, this is bad ...!
THERE MUST BE SO MANY MORE PRISONERS ...!
Ooh, fresh flesh, eh?
You lot-- teach 'im the rules of this place!
Grrr...
Grrr!
FRET FRET FRET
I WONDER WHO THE BOSS OF THE PRISON IS...?!
HEY, GUYS...
I BROUGHT A NEW-COMER!
CREAK
I'M SO DOOM-ED.

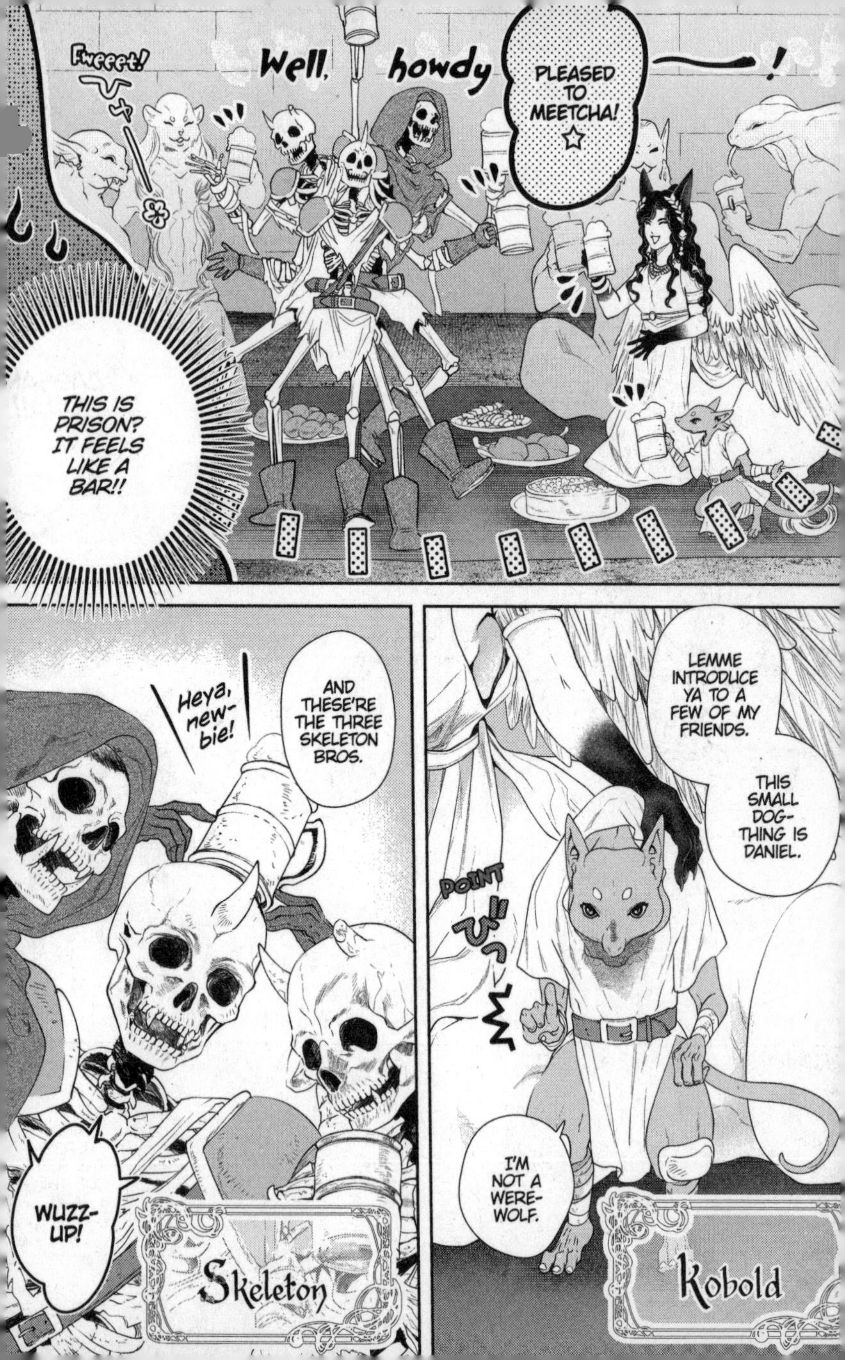
Well, howdy ——!
PLEASED TO MEETCHA! ☆
Fweeet!
THIS IS PRISON? IT FEELS LIKE A BAR!!
LEMME INTRODUCE YA TO A FEW OF MY FRIENDS.
THIS SMALL DOG-THING IS DANIEL.
POINT
I'M NOT A WERE-WOLF.
Kobold
AND THESE'RE THE THREE SKELETON BROS.
Heya, newbie!
WUZZ-UP!
Skeleton

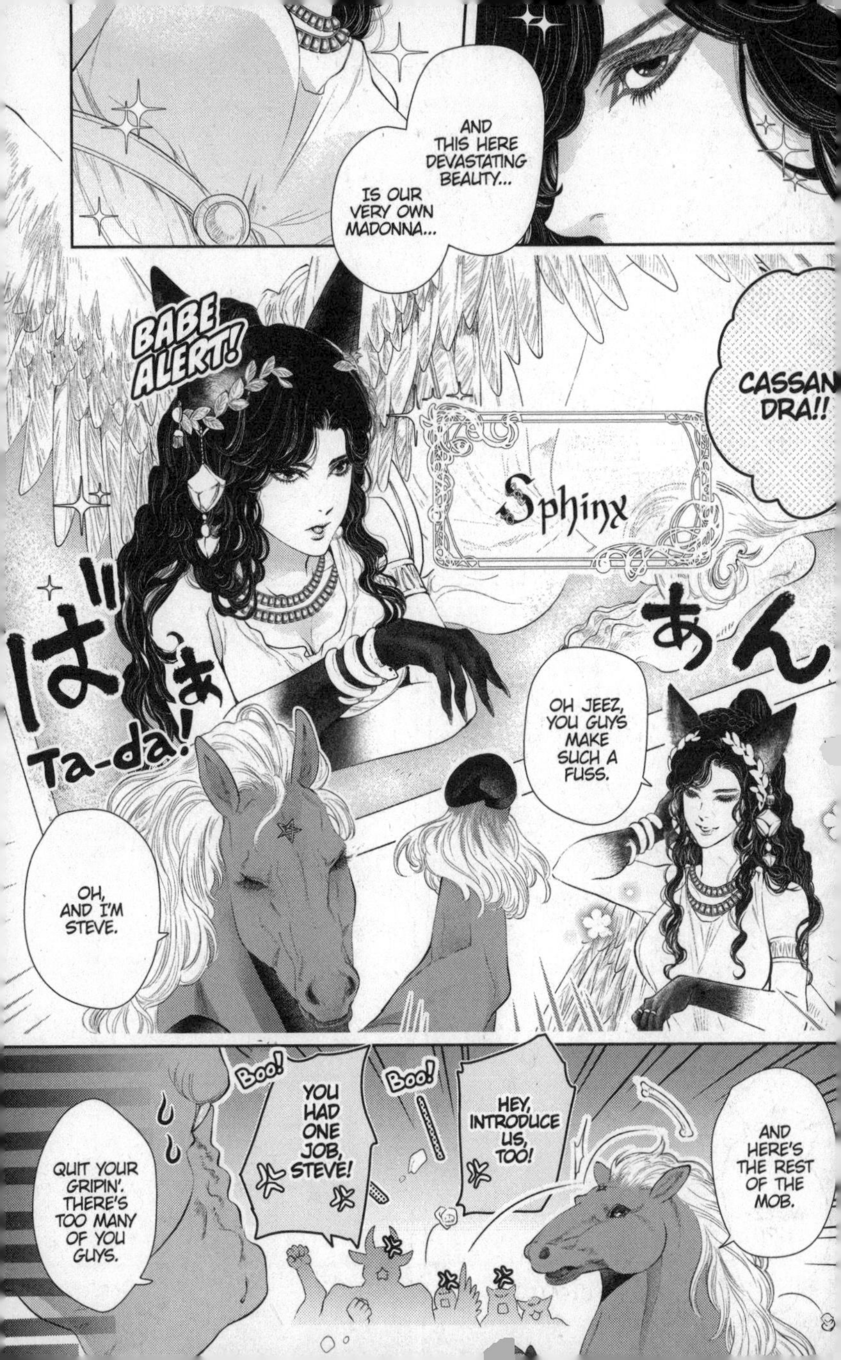
AND THIS HERE DEVASTATING BEAUTY...
IS OUR VERY OWN MADONNA...
CASSANDRA!!
BABE ALERT!
Sphinx
あん
ばぁ
Ta-da!
OH JEEZ, YOU GUYS MAKE SUCH A FUSS.
OH, AND I'M STEVE.
AND HERE'S THE REST OF THE MOB.
HEY, INTRODUCE US, TOO!
Boo!
YOU HAD ONE JOB, STEVE!
Boo!
QUIT YOUR GRIPIN'. THERE'S TOO MANY OF YOU GUYS.

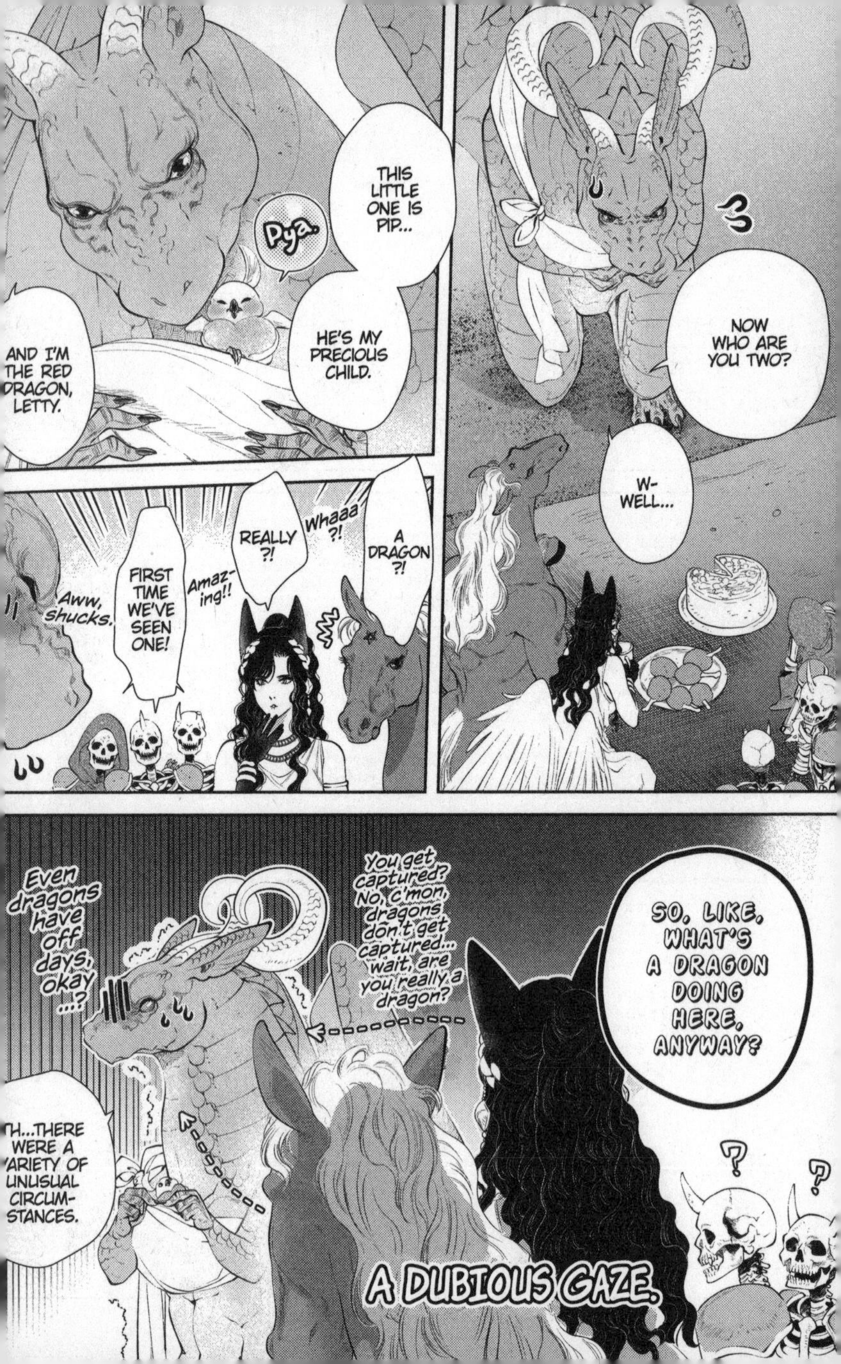
NOW WHO ARE YOU TWO?
W-WELL...
THIS LITTLE ONE IS PIP...
Pya.
HE'S MY PRECIOUS CHILD.
AND I'M THE RED DRAGON, LETTY.
A DRAGON?!
Whaaa?!
REALLY?!
Amazing!!
FIRST TIME WE'VE SEEN ONE!
Aww, shucks.
SO, LIKE, WHAT'S A DRAGON DOING HERE, ANYWAY?
TH...THERE WERE A ARIETY OF UNUSUAL CIRCUM-STANCES.
You get captured? No, c'mon, dragons don't get captured... wait, are you really a dragon?
Even dragons have off days, okay...?
A DUBIOUS GAZE.

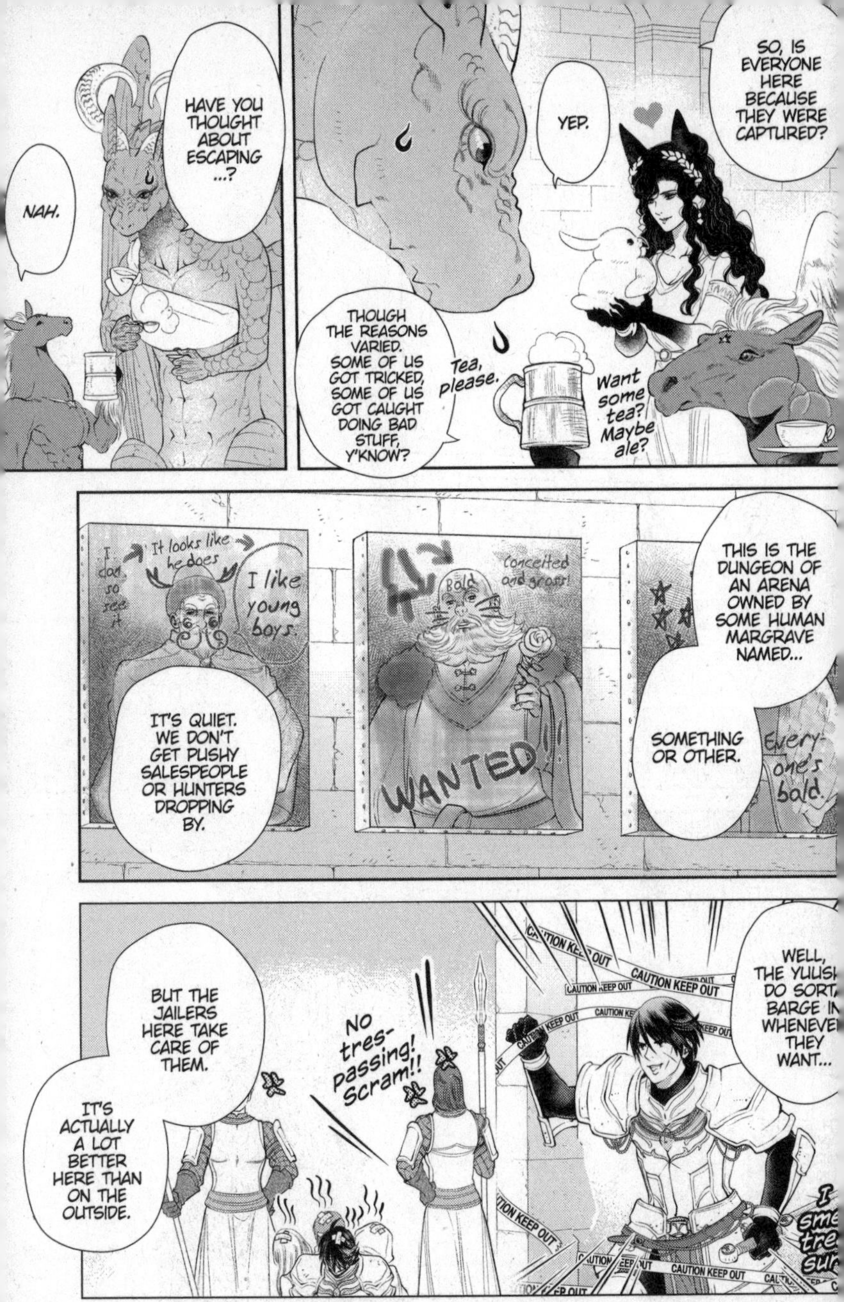
SO, IS EVERYONE HERE BECAUSE THEY WERE CAPTURED?
YEP.
Want some tea? Maybe ale?
Tea, please.
THOUGH THE REASONS VARIED. SOME OF US GOT TRICKED, SOME OF US GOT CAUGHT DOING BAD STUFF, Y'KNOW?
HAVE YOU THOUGHT ABOUT ESCAPING ...?
NAH.
THIS IS THE DUNGEON OF AN ARENA OWNED BY SOME HUMAN MARGRAVE NAMED...
SOMETHING OR OTHER.
Every-one's bald.
Conceited and gross!
Bald
WANTED
I like young boys.
It looks like he does
I don so see it
IT'S QUIET. WE DON'T GET PUSHY SALESPEOPLE OR HUNTERS DROPPING BY.
WELL, THE YUUSH DO SORT BARGE IN WHENEVE THEY WANT...
CAUTION KEEP OUT
No tres-passing! Scram!!
BUT THE JAILERS HERE TAKE CARE OF THEM.
IT'S ACTUALLY A LOT BETTER HERE THAN ON THE OUTSIDE.

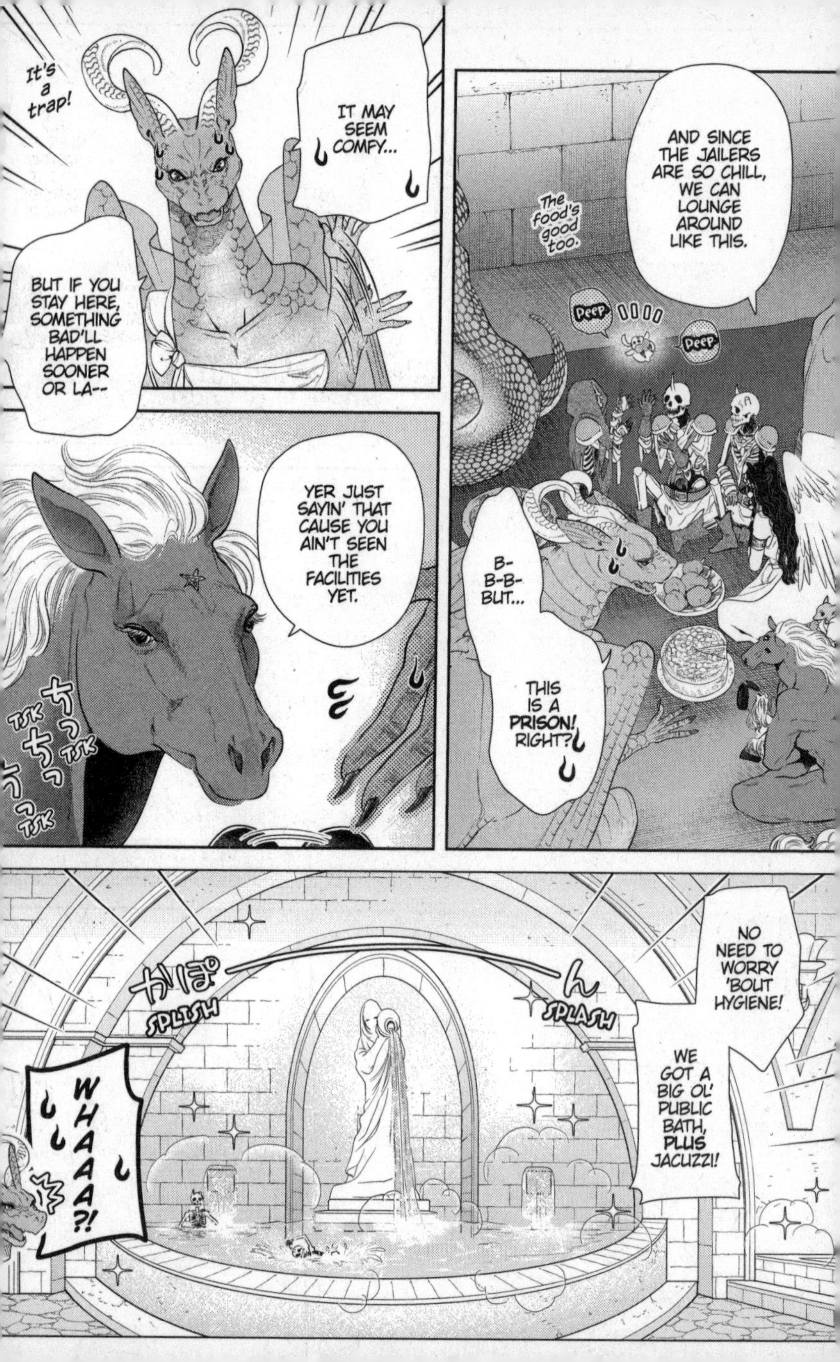
It's a trap!
IT MAY SEEM COMFY...
BUT IF YOU STAY HERE, SOMETHING BAD'LL HAPPEN SOONER OR LA--
YER JUST SAYIN' THAT CAUSE YOU AIN'T SEEN THE FACILITIES YET.
ちっ TSK
ちっ TSK
ちっ TSK
AND SINCE THE JAILERS ARE SO CHILL, WE CAN LOUNGE AROUND LIKE THIS.
The food's good too.
PEEP
PEEP
B-B-B-BUT...
THIS IS A PRISON! RIGHT?
NO NEED TO WORRY 'BOUT HYGIENE!
WE GOT A BIG OL' PUBLIC BATH, PLUS JACUZZI!
かぽ SPLISH
ん SPLASH
WHAAAA?!

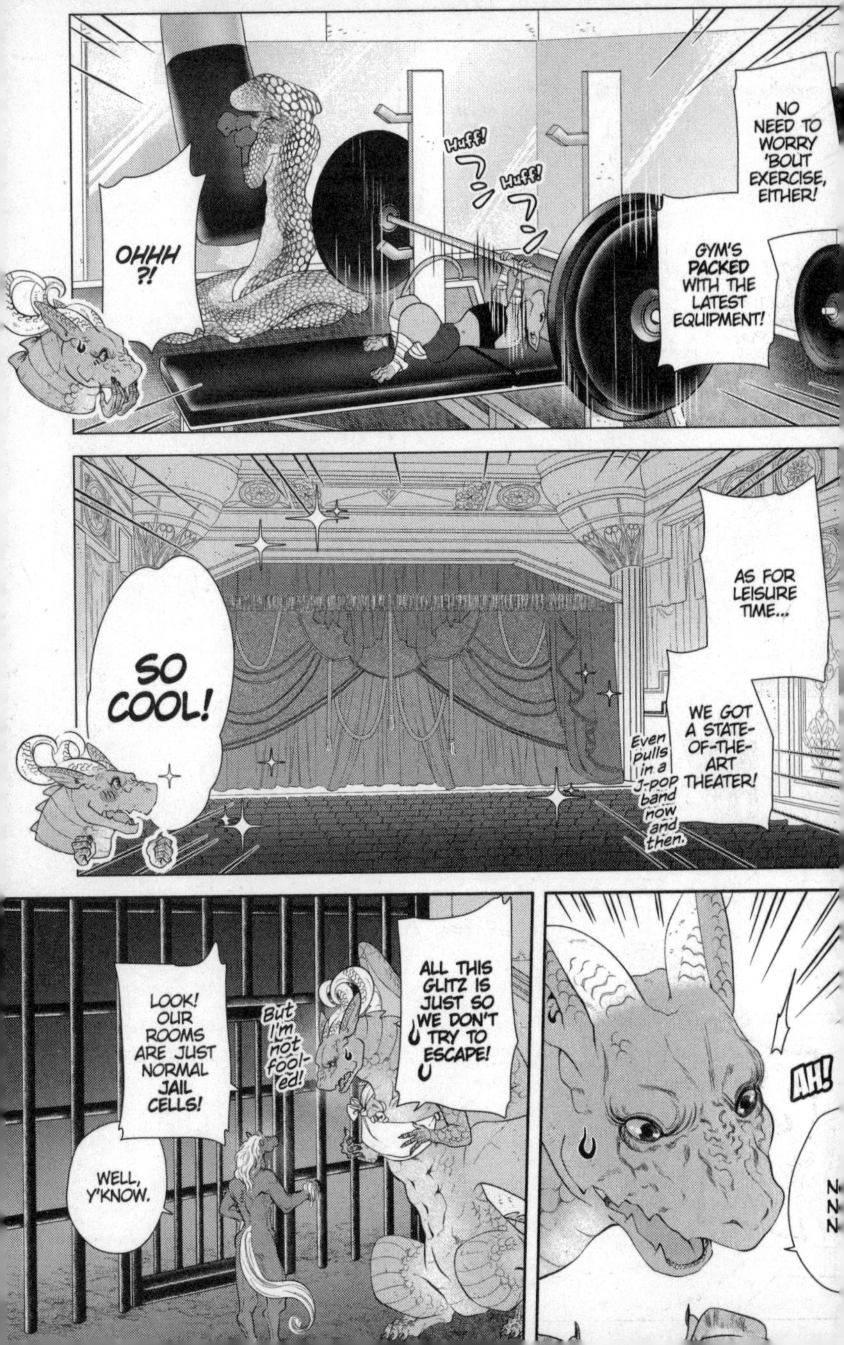
NO NEED TO WORRY 'BOUT EXERCISE, EITHER!
GYM'S PACKED WITH THE LATEST EQUIPMENT!
Huff!
Huff!
OHHH ?!
AS FOR LEISURE TIME...
WE GOT A STATE-OF-THE-ART THEATER!
Even pulls in a J-pop band now and then.
SO COOL!
AH!
NNN
ALL THIS GLITZ IS JUST SO WE DON'T TRY TO ESCAPE!
But I'm not fooled!
LOOK! OUR ROOMS ARE JUST NORMAL JAIL CELLS!
WELL, Y'KNOW.

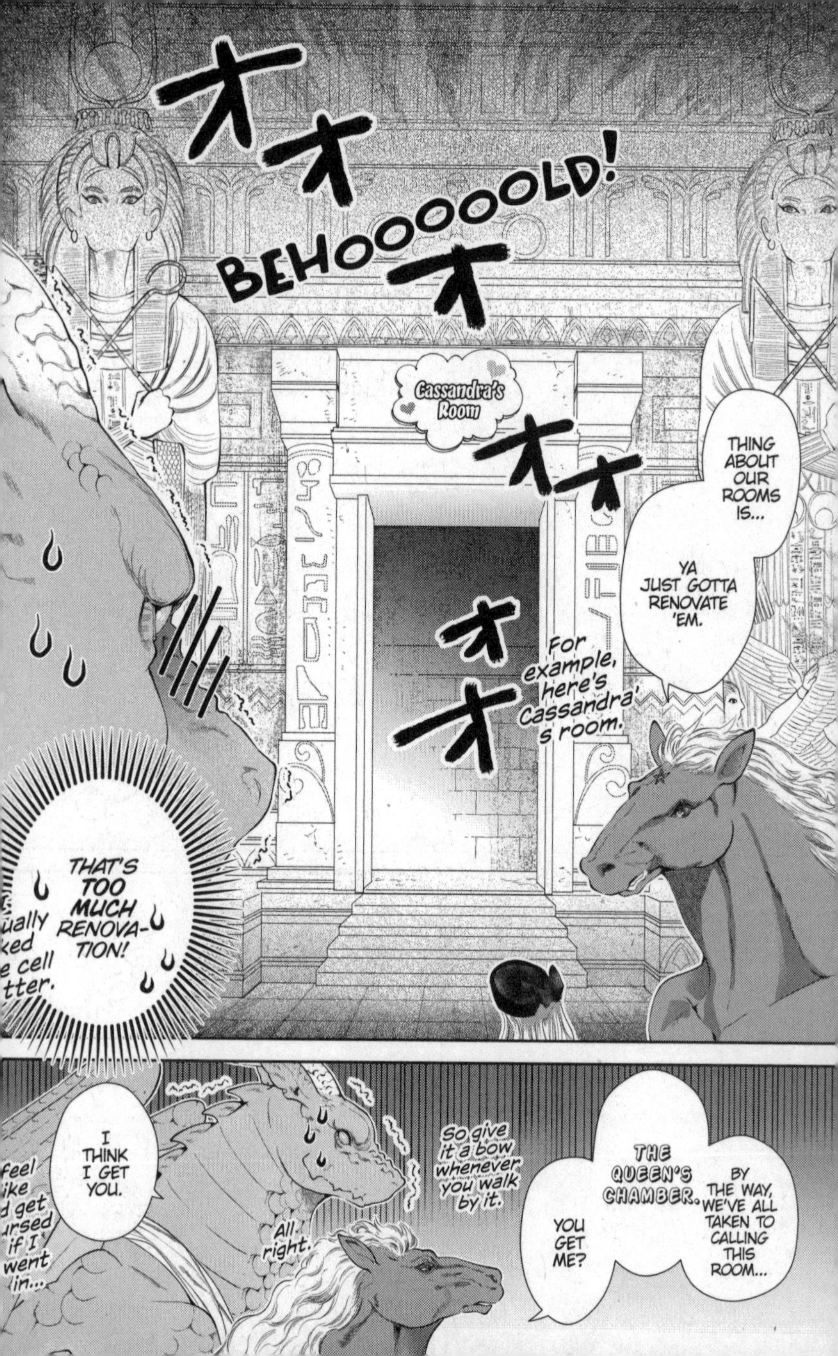

THING ABOUT OUR ROOMS IS...
YA JUST GOTTA RENOVATE 'EM.
For example, here's Cassandra's room.
Cassandra's Room
オオ
BEHOOOOOOLD!
オオ
オオ
THAT'S TOO MUCH RENOVATION!
ually ked e cell tter.
BY THE WAY, WE'VE ALL TAKEN TO CALLING THIS ROOM...
THE QUEEN'S CHAMBER.
YOU GET ME?
So give it a bow whenever you walk by it.
All right.
I THINK I GET YOU.
feel ike d get ursed if I went in...

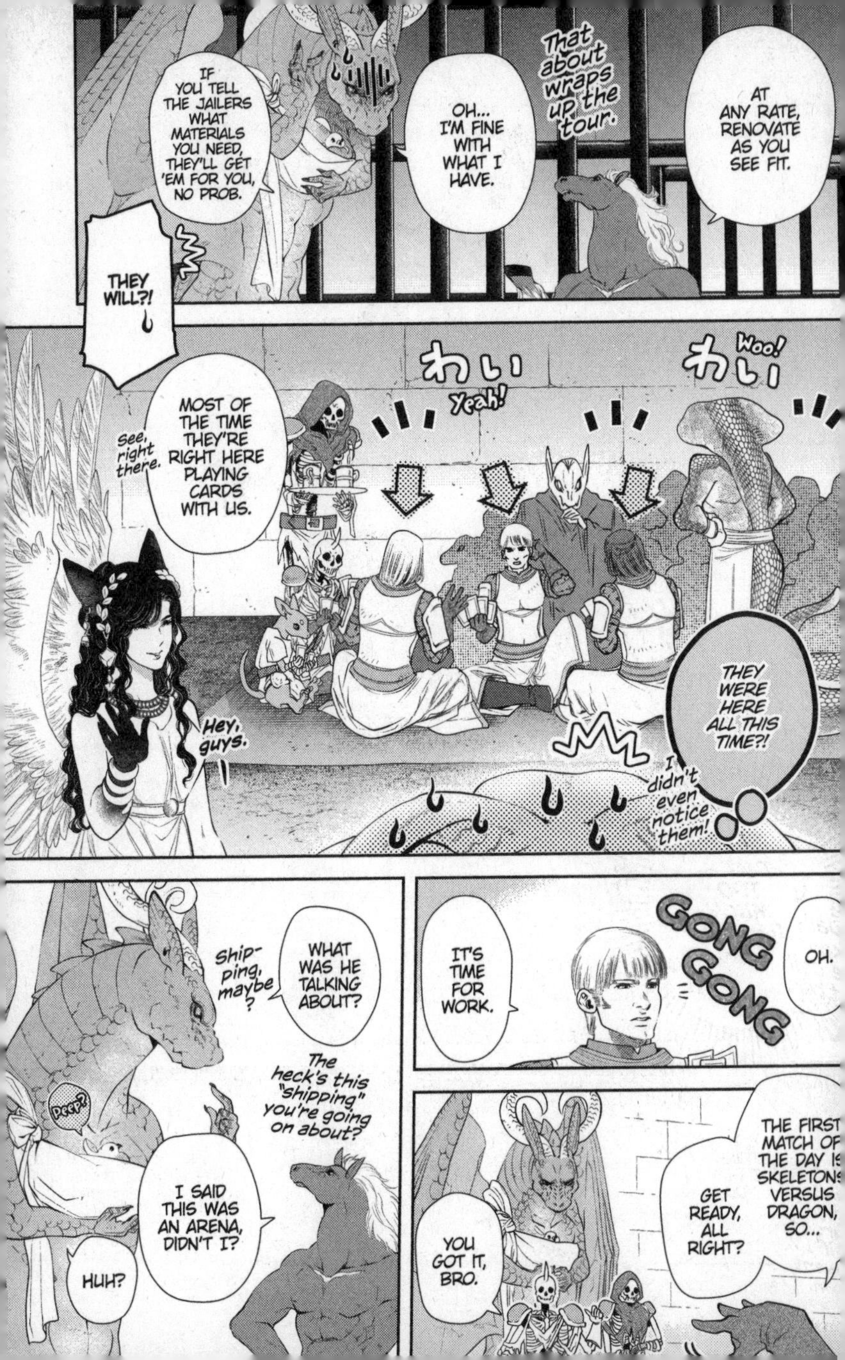
AT ANY RATE, RENOVATE AS YOU SEE FIT.
That about wraps up the tour.
OH... I'M FINE WITH WHAT I HAVE.
IF YOU TELL THE JAILERS WHAT MATERIALS YOU NEED, THEY'LL GET 'EM FOR YOU, NO PROB.
THEY WILL?!
わい
Woo!
わい
Yeah!
THEY WERE HERE ALL THIS TIME?!
I didn't even notice them!
MOST OF THE TIME THEY'RE RIGHT HERE PLAYING CARDS WITH US.
See, right there.
Hey, guys.
OH.
GONG GONG
IT'S TIME FOR WORK.
THE FIRST MATCH OF THE DAY IS SKELETONS VERSUS DRAGON, SO...
GET READY, ALL RIGHT?
YOU GOT IT, BRO.
WHAT WAS HE TALKING ABOUT?
Ship-ping, maybe?
The heck's this "shipping" you're going on about?
Peep?
I SAID THIS WAS AN ARENA, DIDN'T I?
HUH?

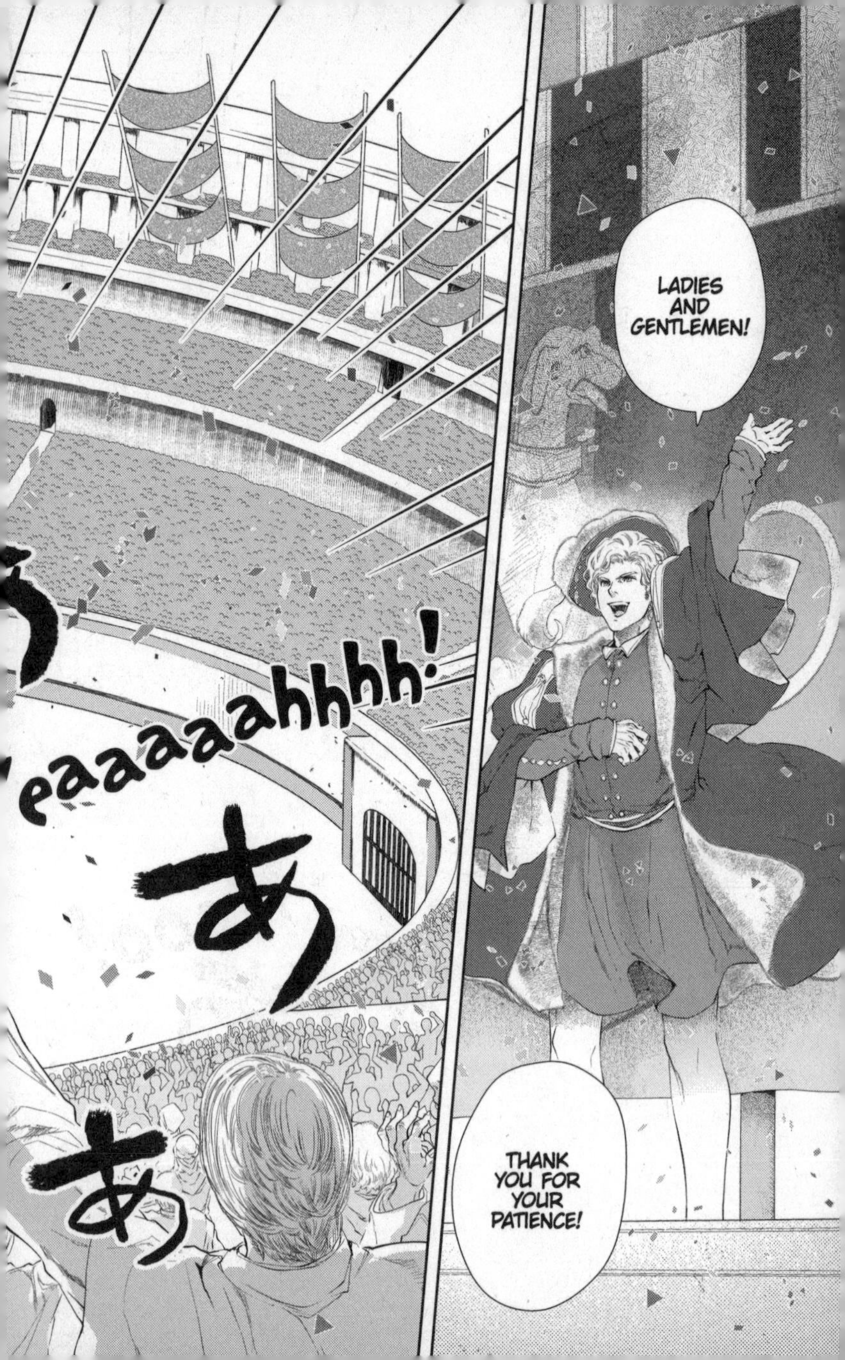
LADIES AND GENTLEMEN!
THANK YOU FOR YOUR PATIENCE!
eaaaaahhhhh!
あ
あ

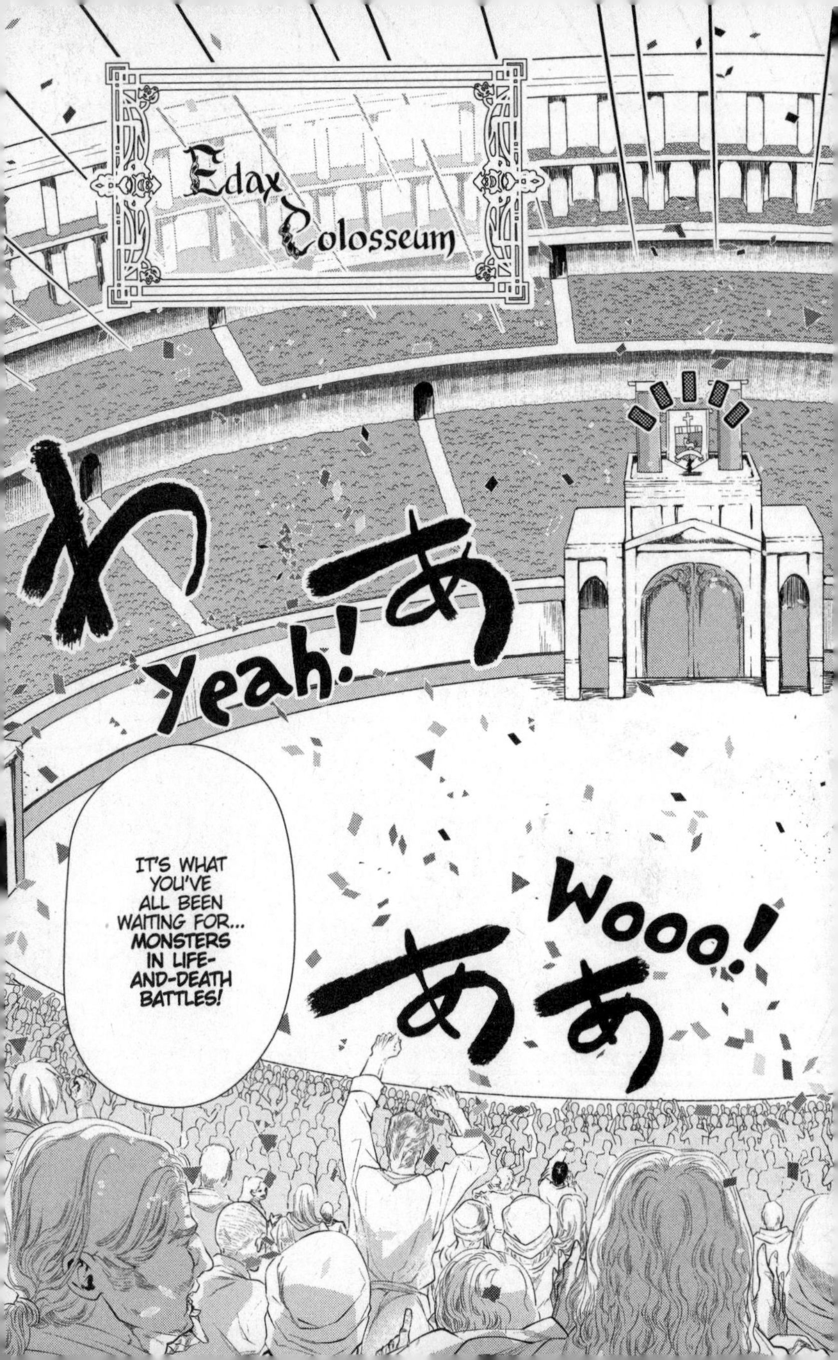
Edax Colosseum
わあ
Yeah!
ああ
Wooo!
IT'S WHAT YOU'VE ALL BEEN WAITING FOR... MONSTERS IN LIFE-AND-DEATH BATTLES!

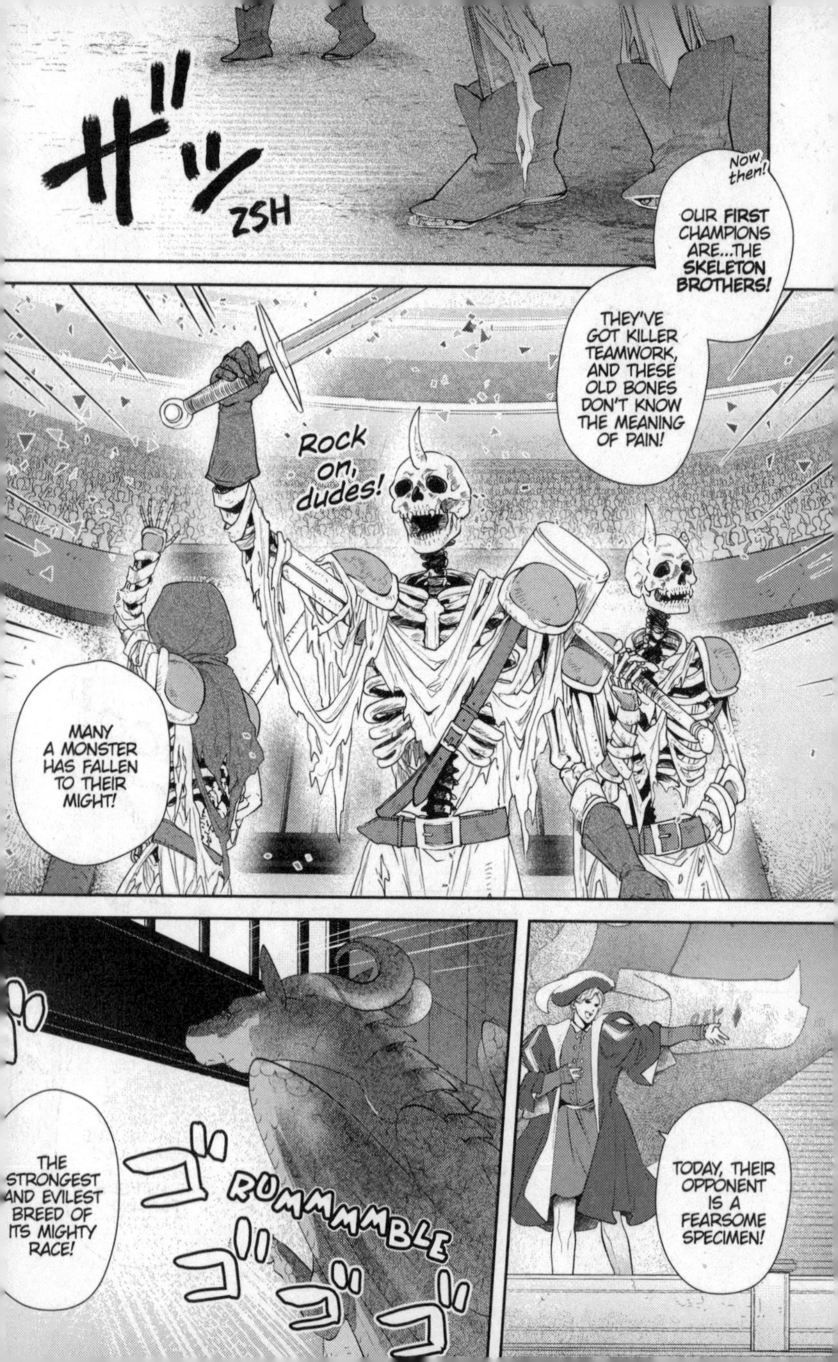
ザッ
ZSH
Now, then!
OUR FIRST CHAMPIONS ARE...THE SKELETON BROTHERS!
THEY'VE GOT KILLER TEAMWORK, AND THESE OLD BONES DON'T KNOW THE MEANING OF PAIN!
Rock on, dudes!
MANY A MONSTER HAS FALLEN TO THEIR MIGHT!
TODAY, THEIR OPPONENT IS A FEARSOME SPECIMEN!
ゴゴゴゴ
RUMMMMBLE
THE STRONGEST AND EVILEST BREED OF ITS MIGHTY RACE!

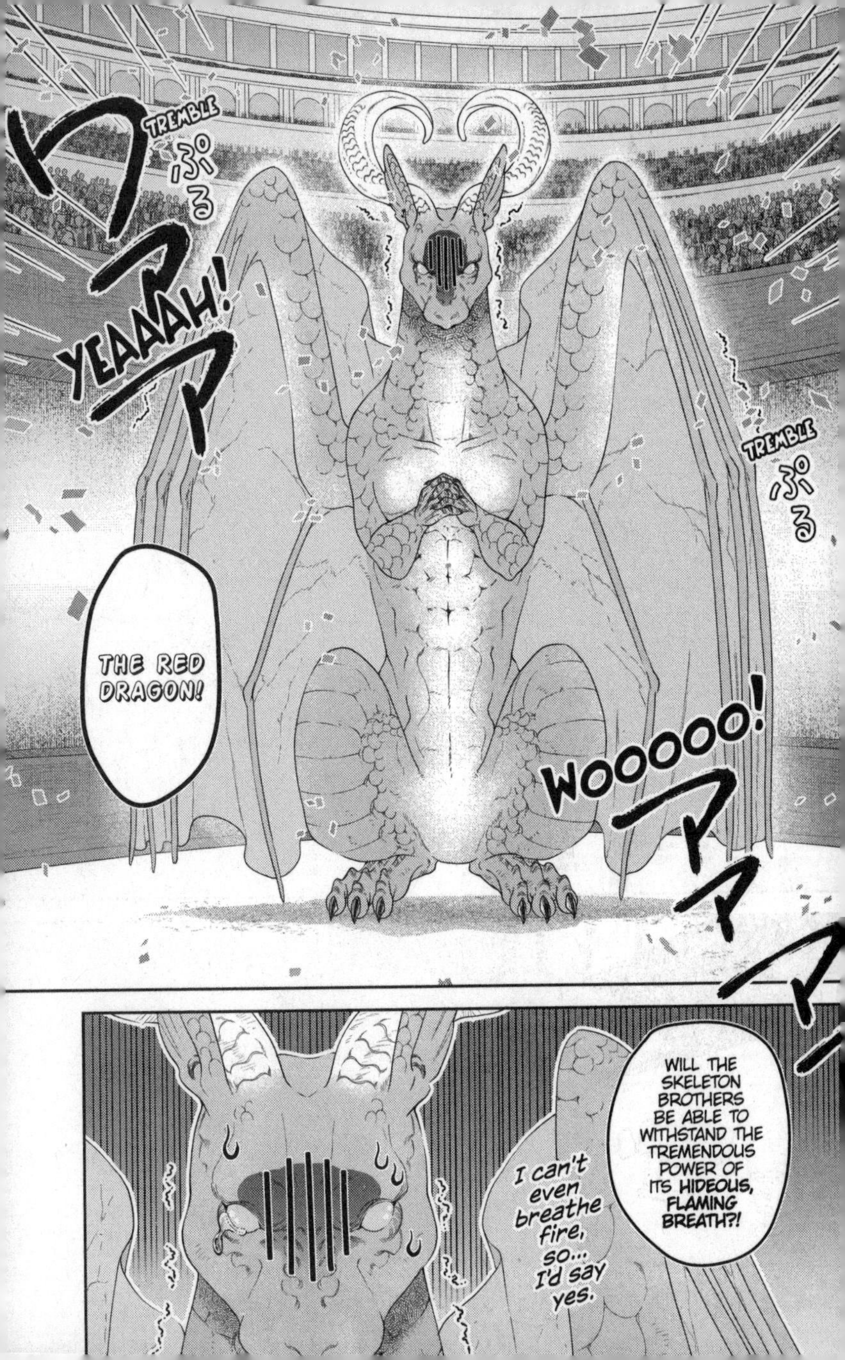
TREMBLE
ぷる
YEAAAH!
TREMBLE
ぷる
THE RED DRAGON!
WOOOOO!
WILL THE SKELETON BROTHERS BE ABLE TO WITHSTAND THE TREMENDOUS POWER OF ITS HIDEOUS, FLAMING BREATH?!
I can't even breathe fire, so... I'd say yes.

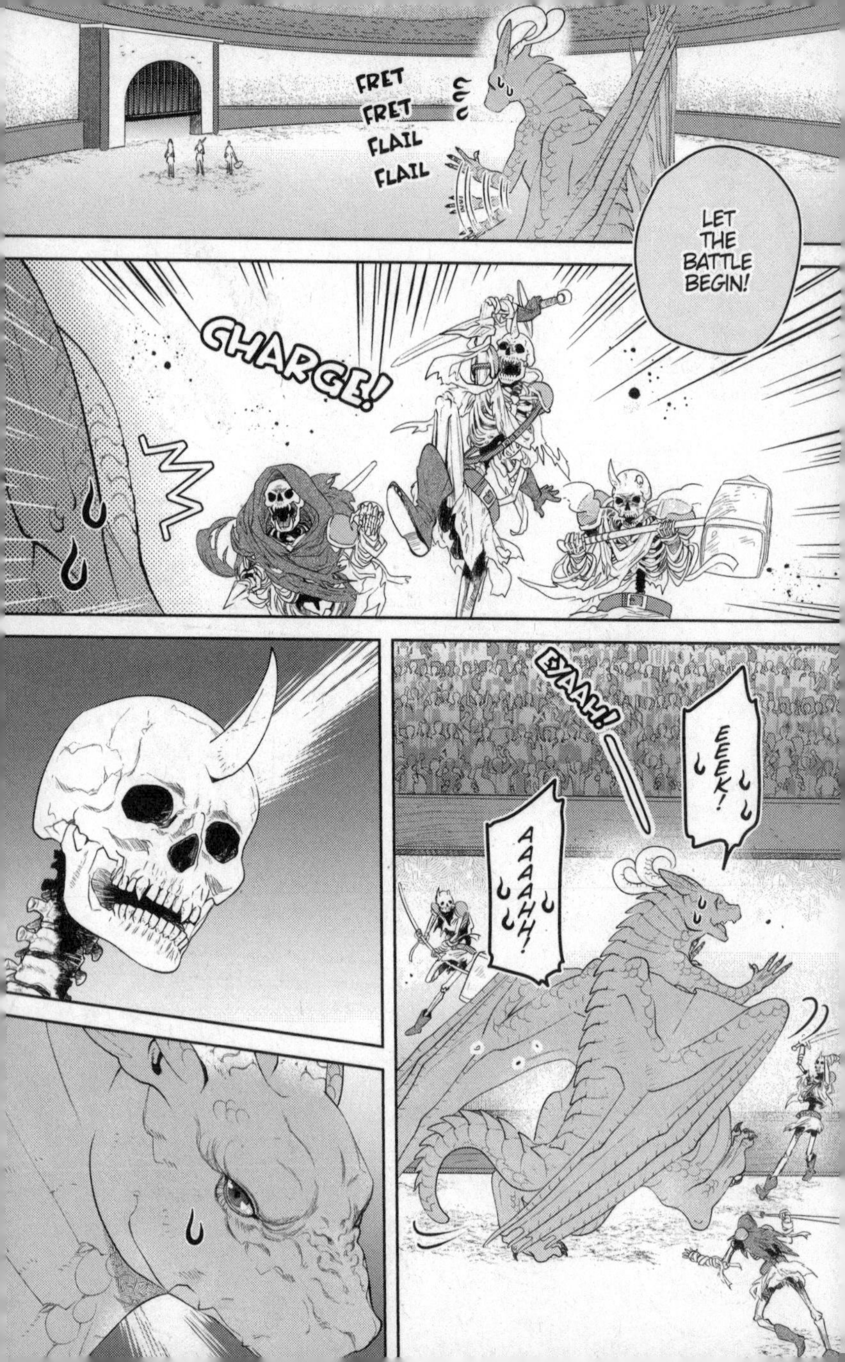
FRET
FRET
FLAIL
FLAIL
LET THE BATTLE BEGIN!
CHARGE!
EYAAH!
EEEK!
AAAAHH!

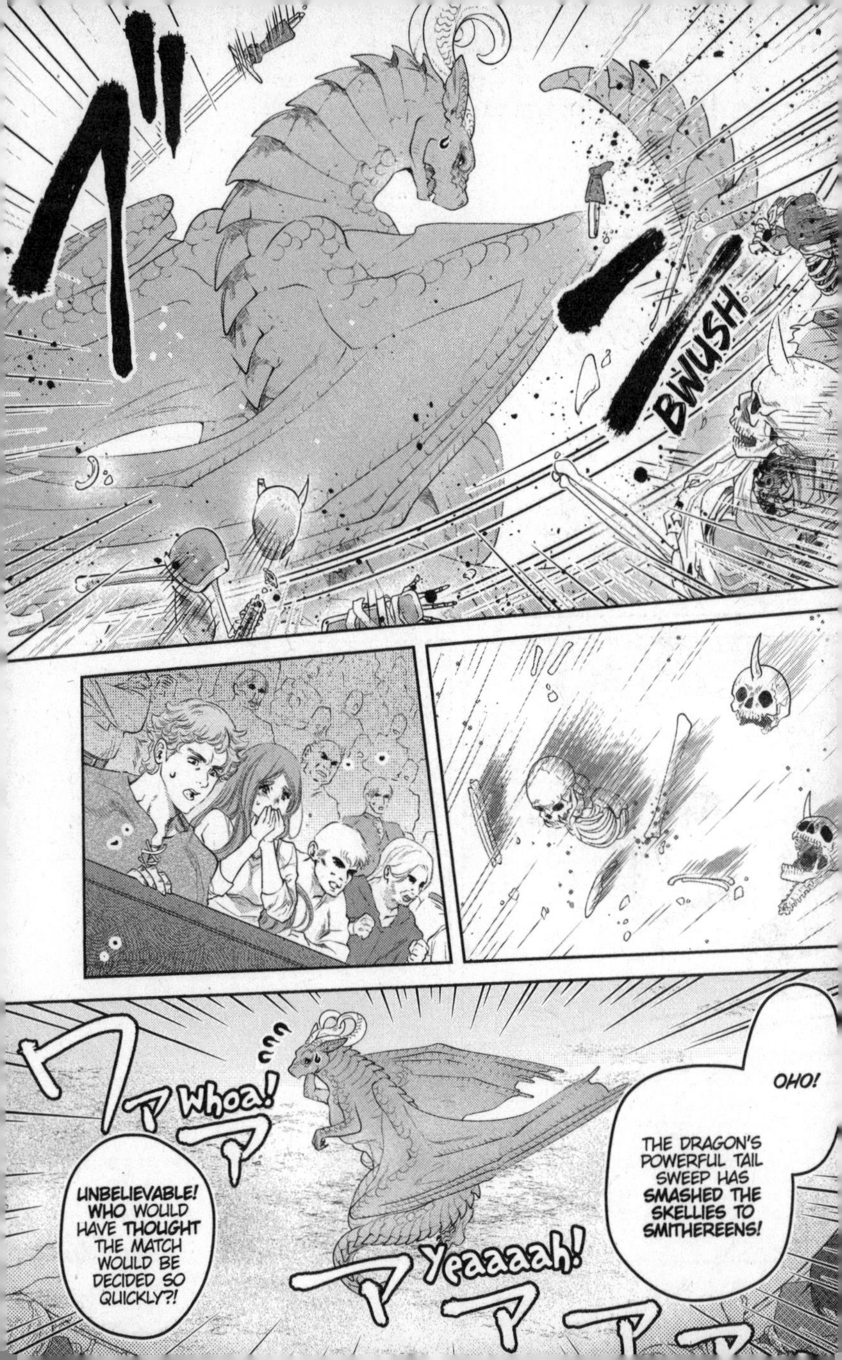
BWUSH
OHO!
THE DRAGON'S POWERFUL TAIL SWEEP HAS SMASHED THE SKELLIES TO SMITHEREENS!
Whoa!
UNBELIEVABLE! WHO WOULD HAVE THOUGHT THE MATCH WOULD BE DECIDED SO QUICKLY?!
Yeaaaah!

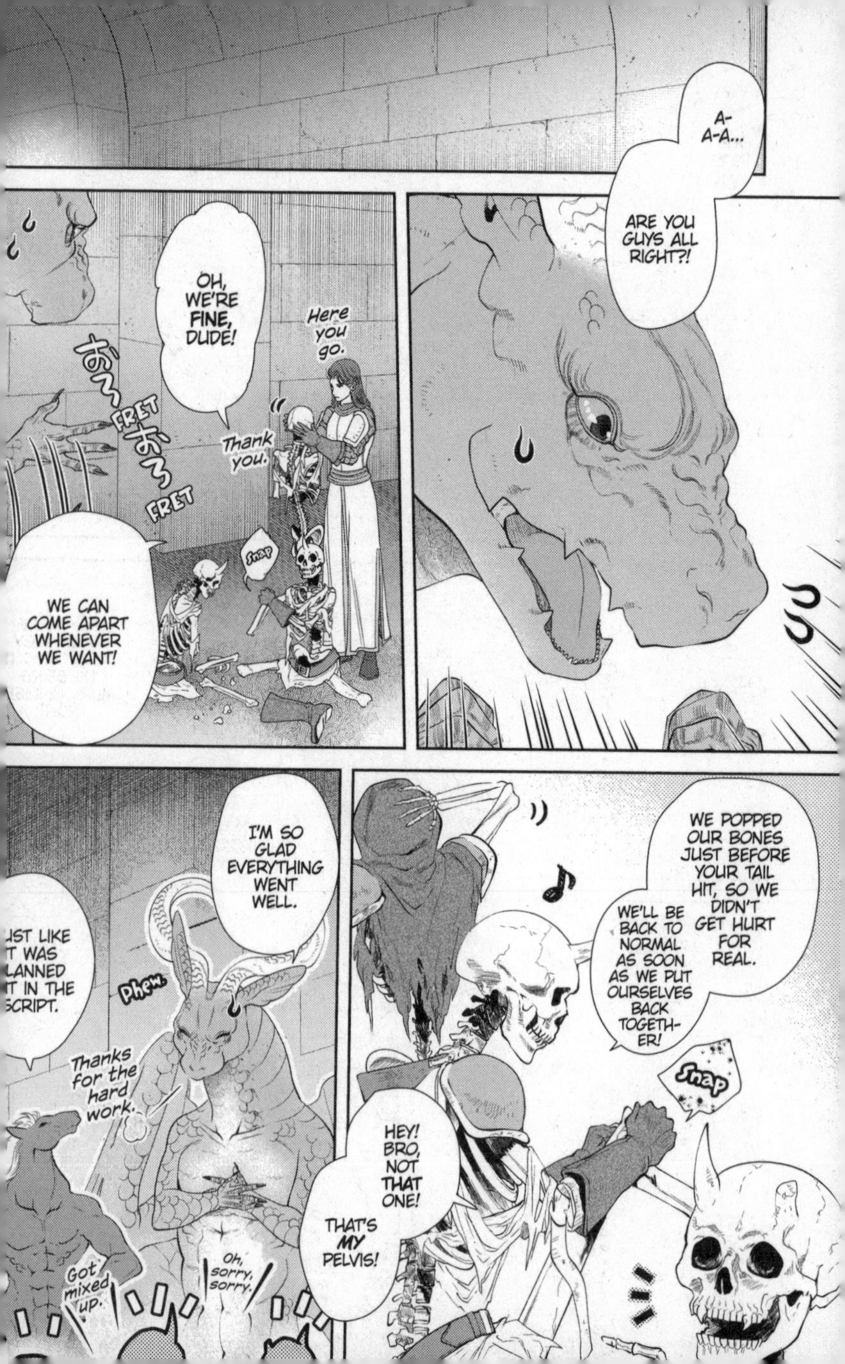
A-
A-A...
ARE YOU GUYS ALL RIGHT?!
OH, WE'RE FINE, DUDE!
Here you go.
Thank you.
おろ FRET おろ FRET
Snap
WE CAN COME APART WHENEVER WE WANT!
WE POPPED OUR BONES JUST BEFORE YOUR TAIL HIT, SO WE DIDN'T GET HURT FOR REAL.
WE'LL BE BACK TO NORMAL AS SOON AS WE PUT OURSELVES BACK TOGETH-ER!
Snap
HEY! BRO, NOT THAT ONE!
THAT'S MY PELVIS!
I'M SO GLAD EVERYTHING WENT WELL.
Phew.
Thanks for the hard work.
Oh, sorry, sorry.
Got mixed up.

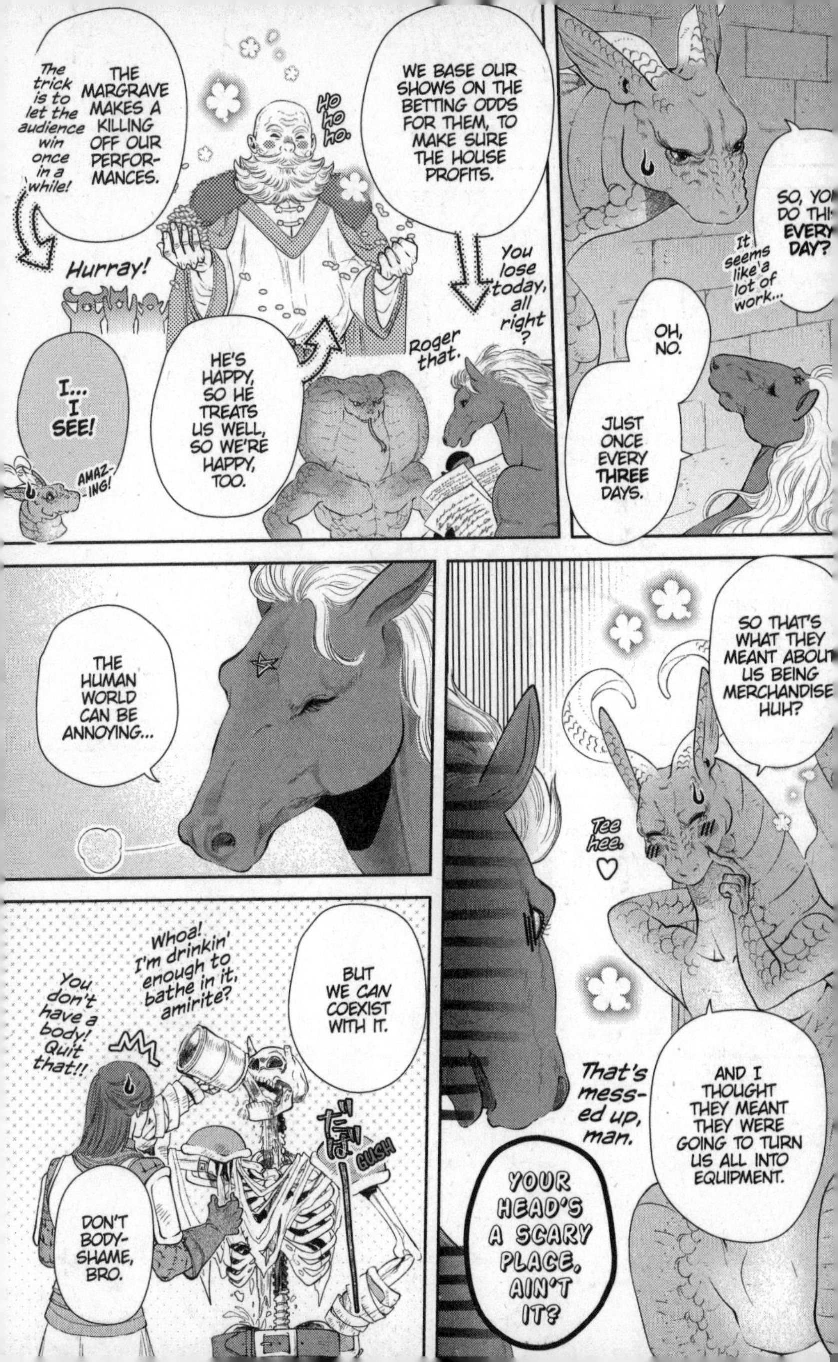
SO, YO DO THI EVERY DAY?
It seems like a lot of work...
OH, NO.
JUST ONCE EVERY THREE DAYS.
WE BASE OUR SHOWS ON THE BETTING ODDS FOR THEM, TO MAKE SURE THE HOUSE PROFITS.
Ho ho ho.
THE MARGRAVE MAKES A KILLING OFF OUR PERFORMANCES.
The trick is to let the audience win once in a while!
You lose today, all right?
Roger that.
Hurray!
HE'S HAPPY, SO HE TREATS US WELL, SO WE'RE HAPPY, TOO.
I... I SEE!
AMAZ-ING!
SO THAT'S WHAT THEY MEANT ABOUT US BEING MERCHANDISE HUH?
Tee hee. ♡
AND I THOUGHT THEY MEANT THEY WERE GOING TO TURN US ALL INTO EQUIPMENT.
That's mess-ed up, man.
YOUR HEAD'S A SCARY PLACE, AIN'T IT?
THE HUMAN WORLD CAN BE ANNOYING...
BUT WE CAN COEXIST WITH IT.
Whoa! I'm drinkin' enough to bathe in it, amirite?
GUSH
You don't have a body! Quit that!!
DON'T BODY-SHAME, BRO.

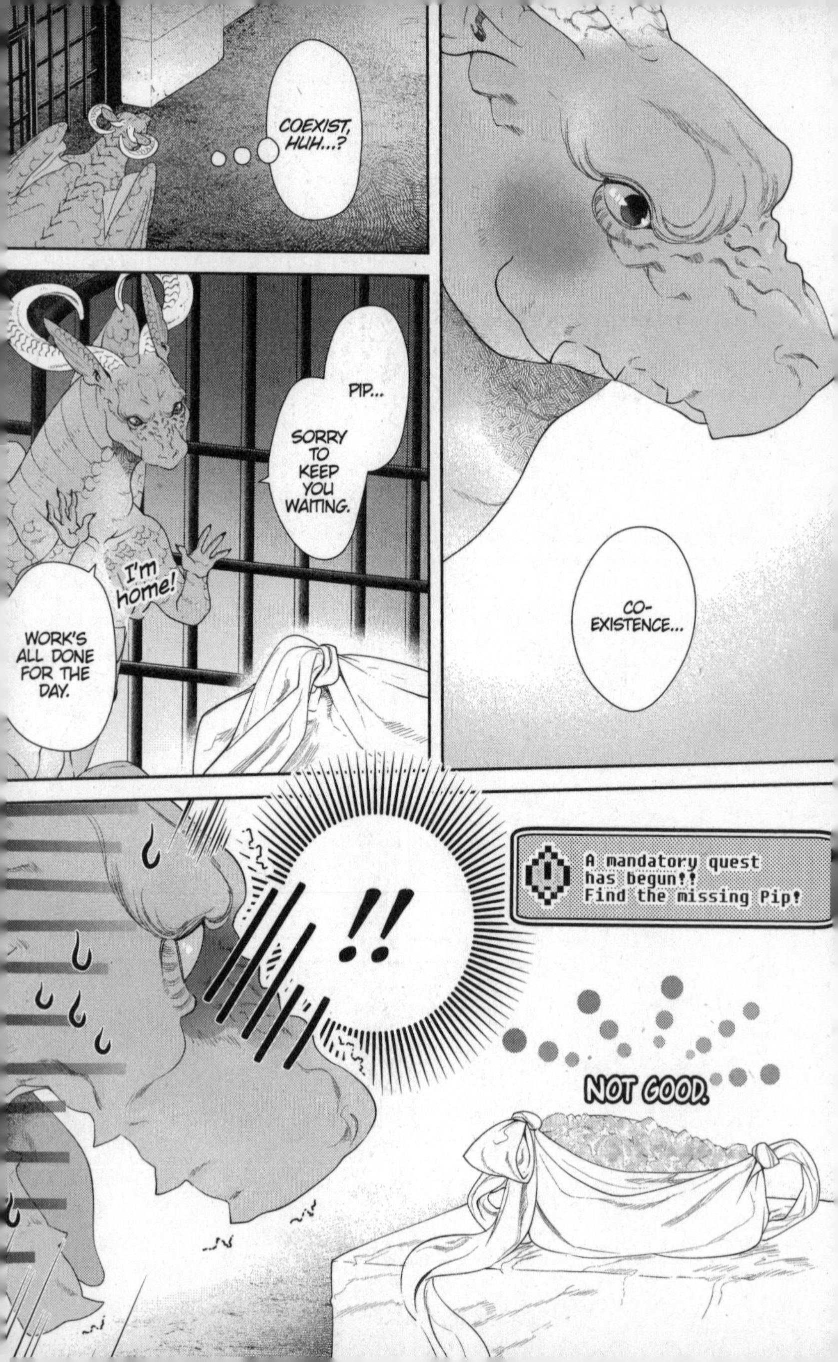
CO-EXISTENCE...
COEXIST, HUH...?
PIP... SORRY TO KEEP YOU WAITING.
I'm home!
WORK'S ALL DONE FOR THE DAY.
A mandatory quest has begun!! Find the missing Pip!
!!
NOT GOOD.

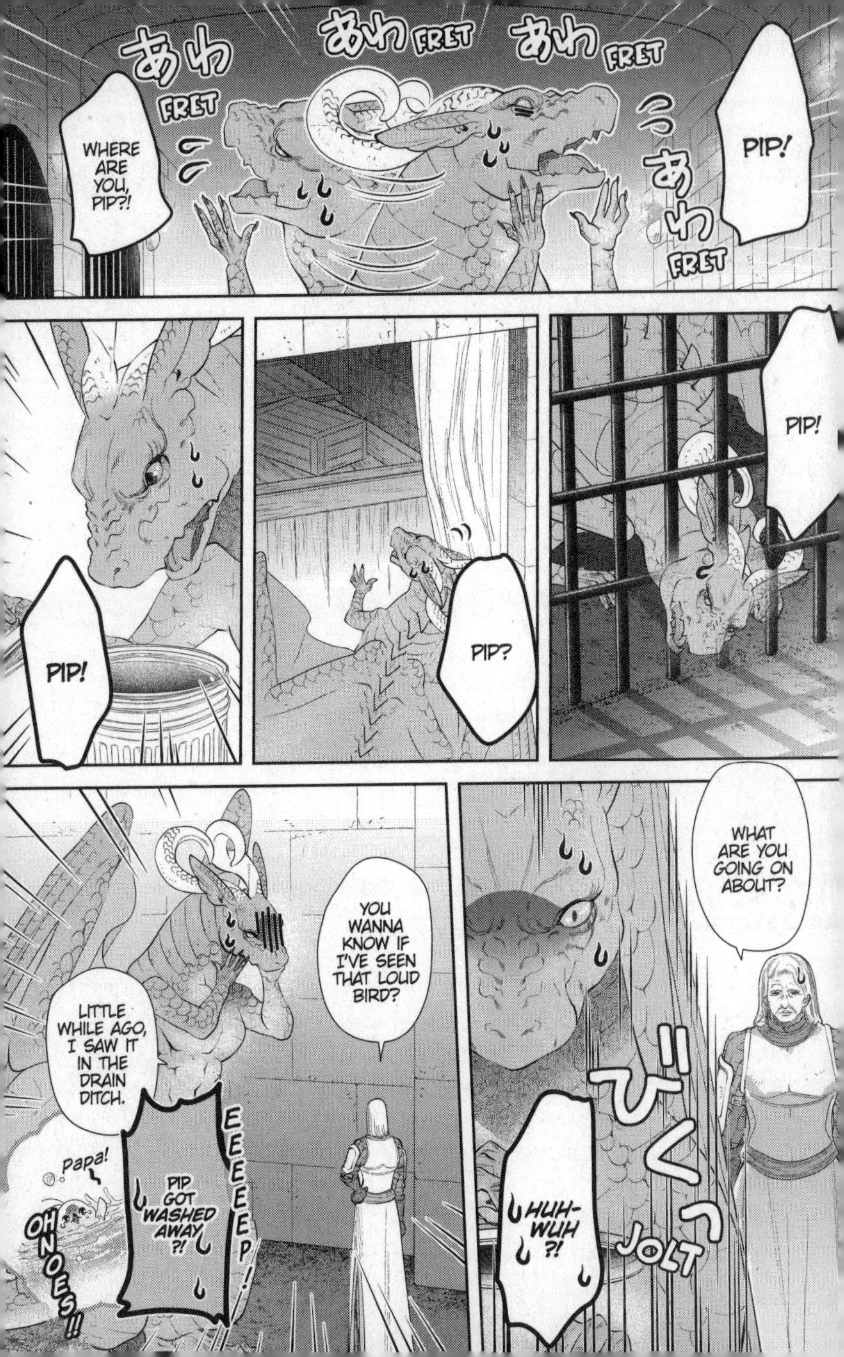
あわ FRET
あわ FRET
あわ FRET
PIP!
あわ FRET
WHERE ARE YOU, PIP?!
PIP!
PIP?
PIP!
WHAT ARE YOU GOING ON ABOUT?
びくっ JOLT
HUH-WUH?!
YOU WANNA KNOW IF I'VE SEEN THAT LOUD BIRD?
LITTLE WHILE AGO, I SAW IT IN THE DRAIN DITCH.
EEEEEEP!
PIP GOT WASHED AWAY?!
Papa!
OH NOES!!

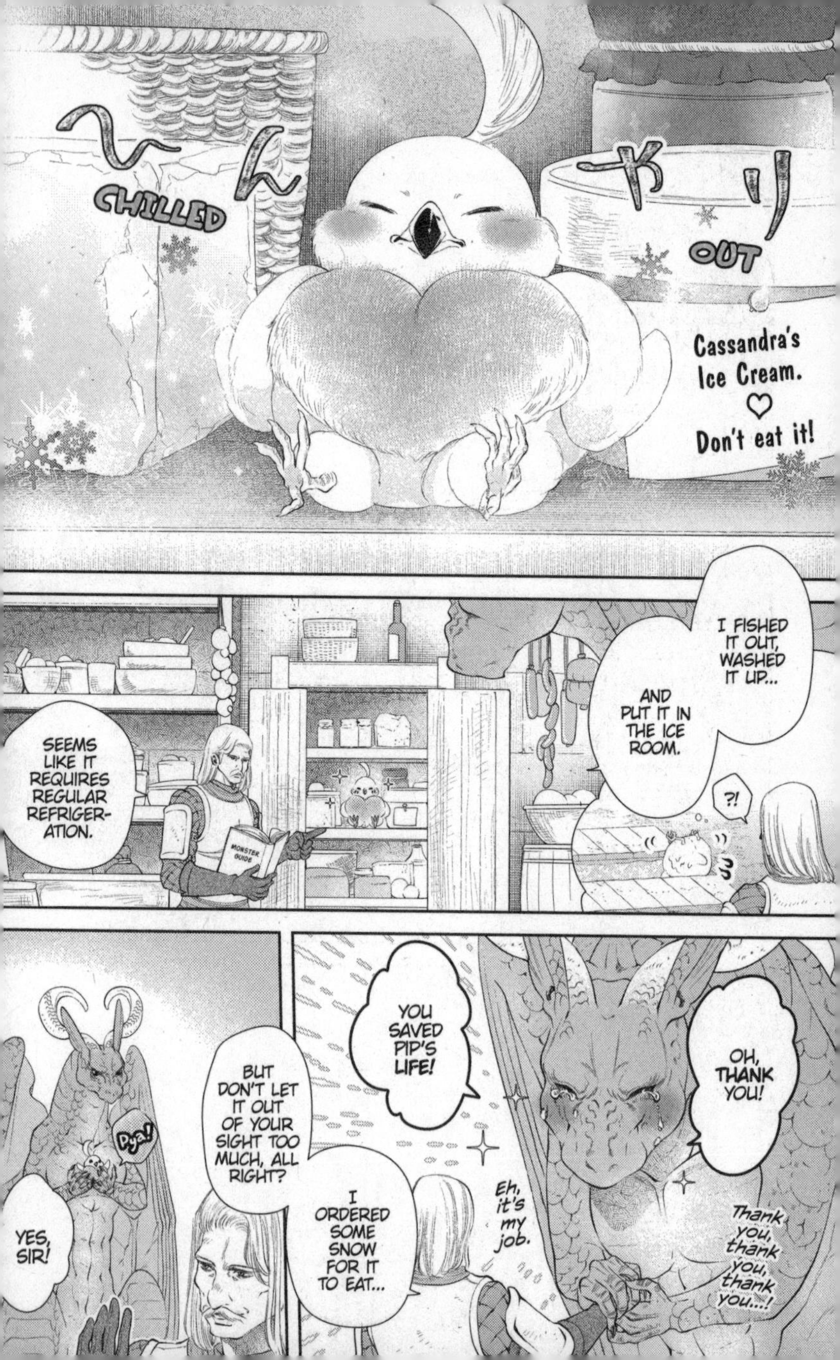
OUT
Cassandra's Ice Cream. ♡ Don't eat it!
CHILLED
I FISHED IT OUT, WASHED IT UP...
AND PUT IT IN THE ICE ROOM.
?!
SEEMS LIKE IT REQUIRES REGULAR REFRIGER-ATION.
MONSTER GUIDE
OH, THANK YOU!
YOU SAVED PIP'S LIFE!
Thank you, thank you, thank you...!
Eh, it's my job.
BUT DON'T LET IT OUT OF YOUR SIGHT TOO MUCH, ALL RIGHT?
I ORDERED SOME SNOW FOR IT TO EAT...
Pya!
YES, SIR!

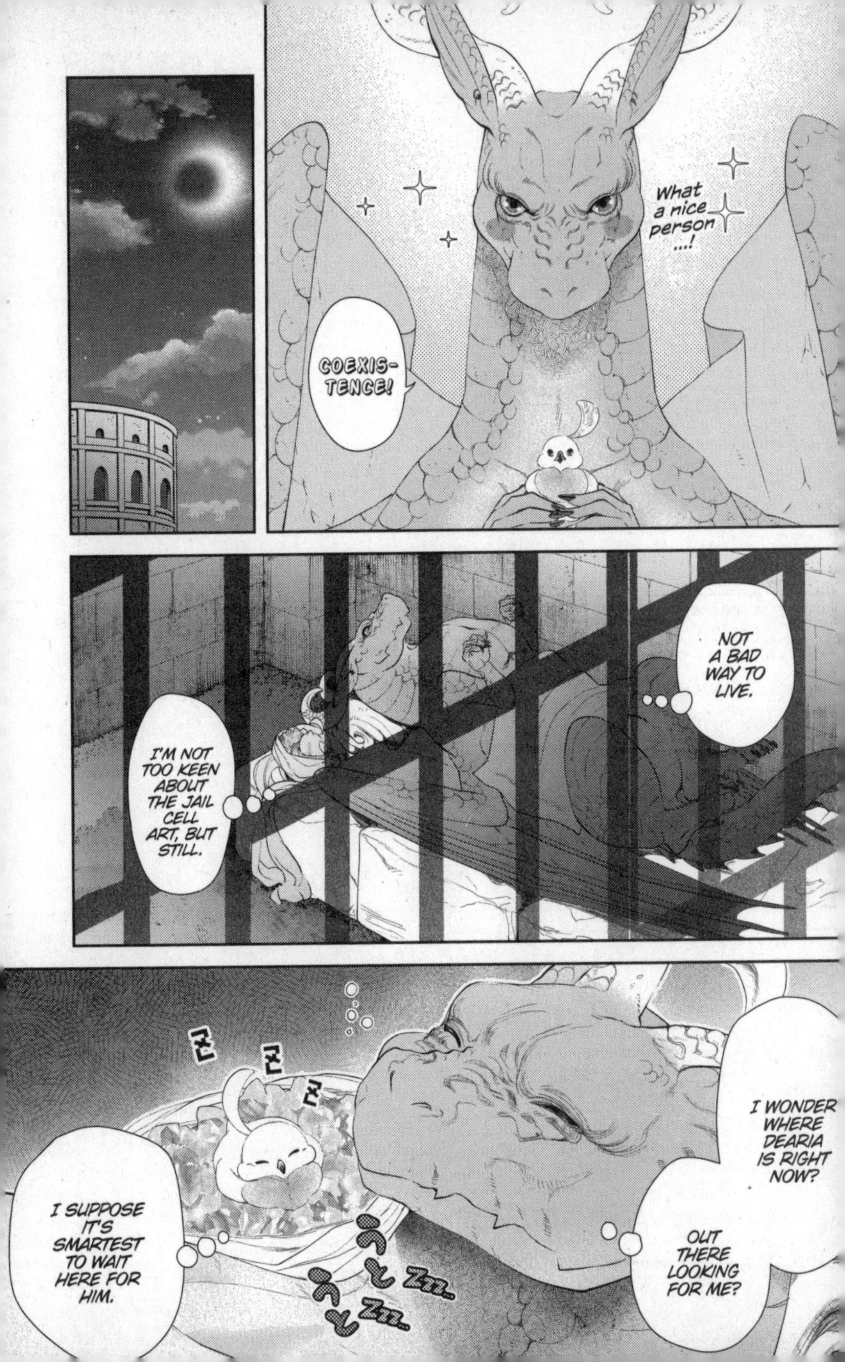
What a nice person ...!
COEXIS-TENCE!
NOT A BAD WAY TO LIVE.
I'M NOT TOO KEEN ABOUT THE JAIL CELL ART, BUT STILL.
I WONDER WHERE DEARIA IS RIGHT NOW?
OUT THERE LOOKING FOR ME?
I SUPPOSE IT'S SMARTEST TO WAIT HERE FOR HIM.
Zzz...
Zzz...

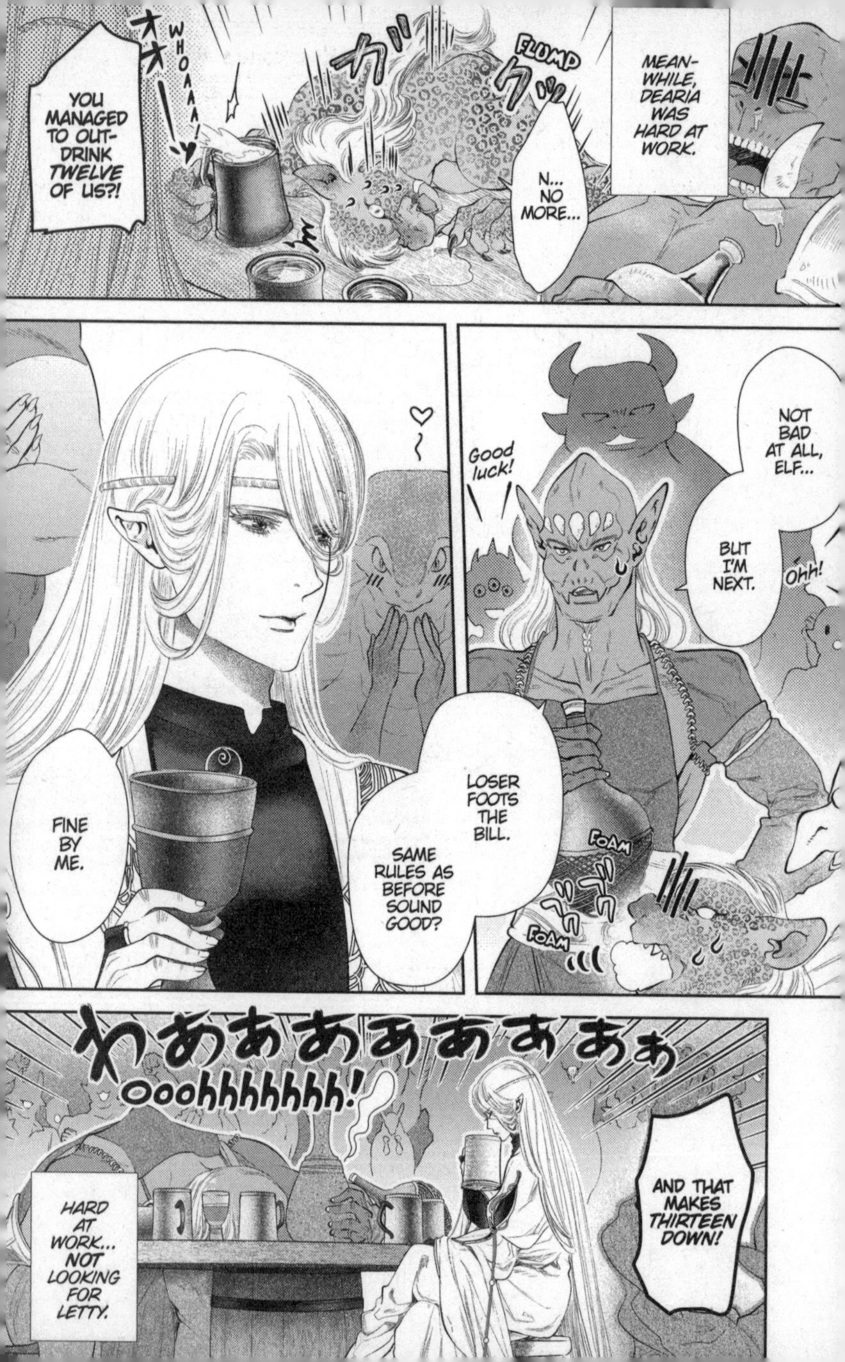
MEAN-WHILE, DEARIA WAS HARD AT WORK.
N... NO MORE...
FLUMP
WHOAAAA!
YOU MANAGED TO OUT-DRINK TWELVE OF US?!
NOT BAD AT ALL, ELF...
BUT I'M NEXT.
Ohh!
Good luck!
FOAM
FOAM
LOSER FOOTS THE BILL.
SAME RULES AS BEFORE SOUND GOOD?
FINE BY ME.
わあああああああぁ
Oooohhhhhhhh!
AND THAT MAKES THIRTEEN DOWN!
HARD AT WORK... NOT LOOKING FOR LETTY.

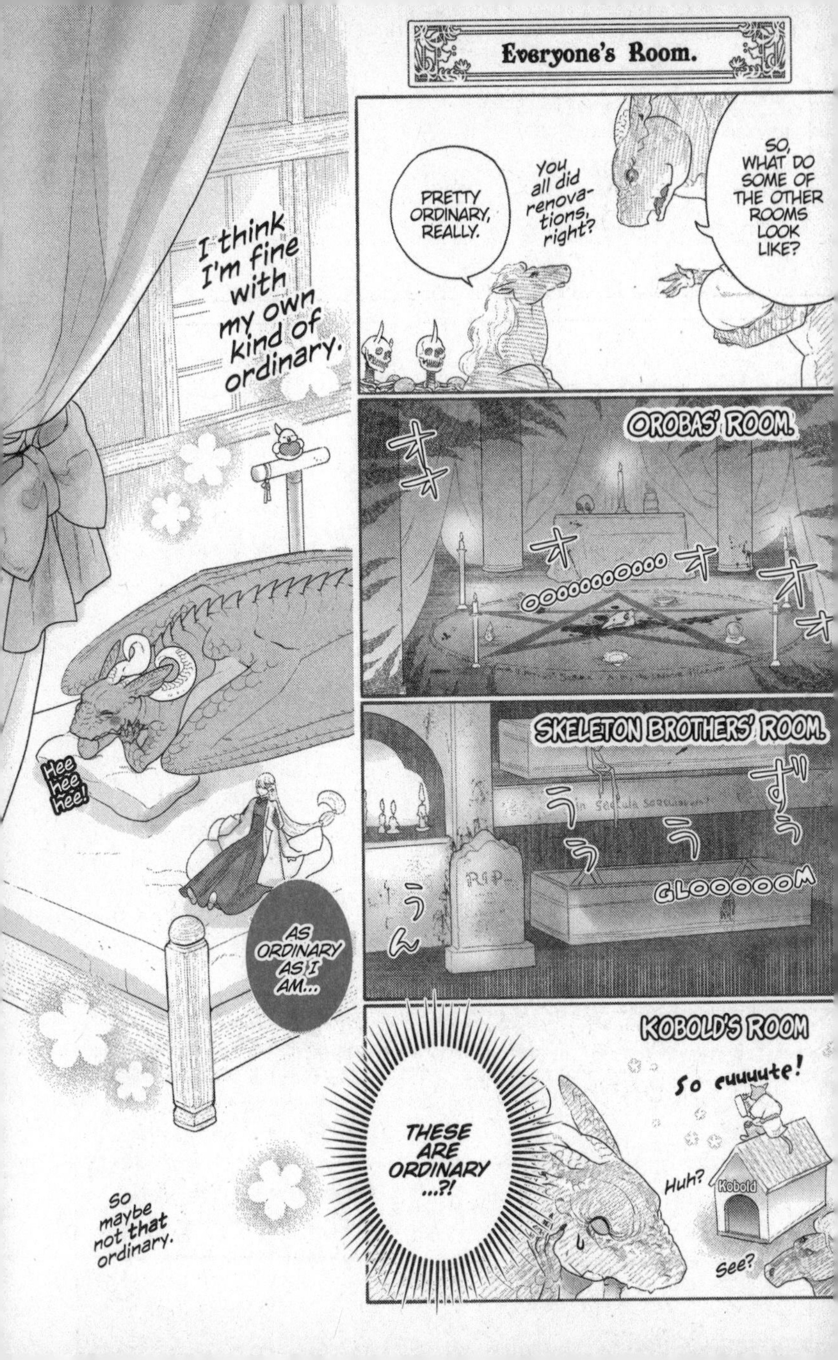
Everyone's Room.
SO, WHAT DO SOME OF THE OTHER ROOMS LOOK LIKE?
You all did renova-tions, right?
PRETTY ORDINARY, REALLY.
OROBAS' ROOM.
OOOOOOOOOOO
SKELETON BROTHERS' ROOM.
GLOOOOOM
KOBOLD'S ROOM
So cuuuute!
THESE ARE ORDINARY ...?!
Huh?
Kobold
See?
I think I'm fine with my own kind of ordinary.
Hee hee hee!
AS ORDINARY AS I AM...
So maybe not that ordinary.

Dragon Goes House-Hunting

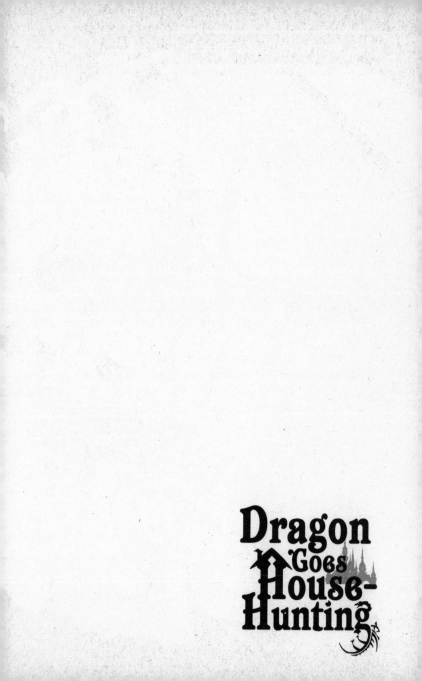

House 10: The Big House (Part 2)

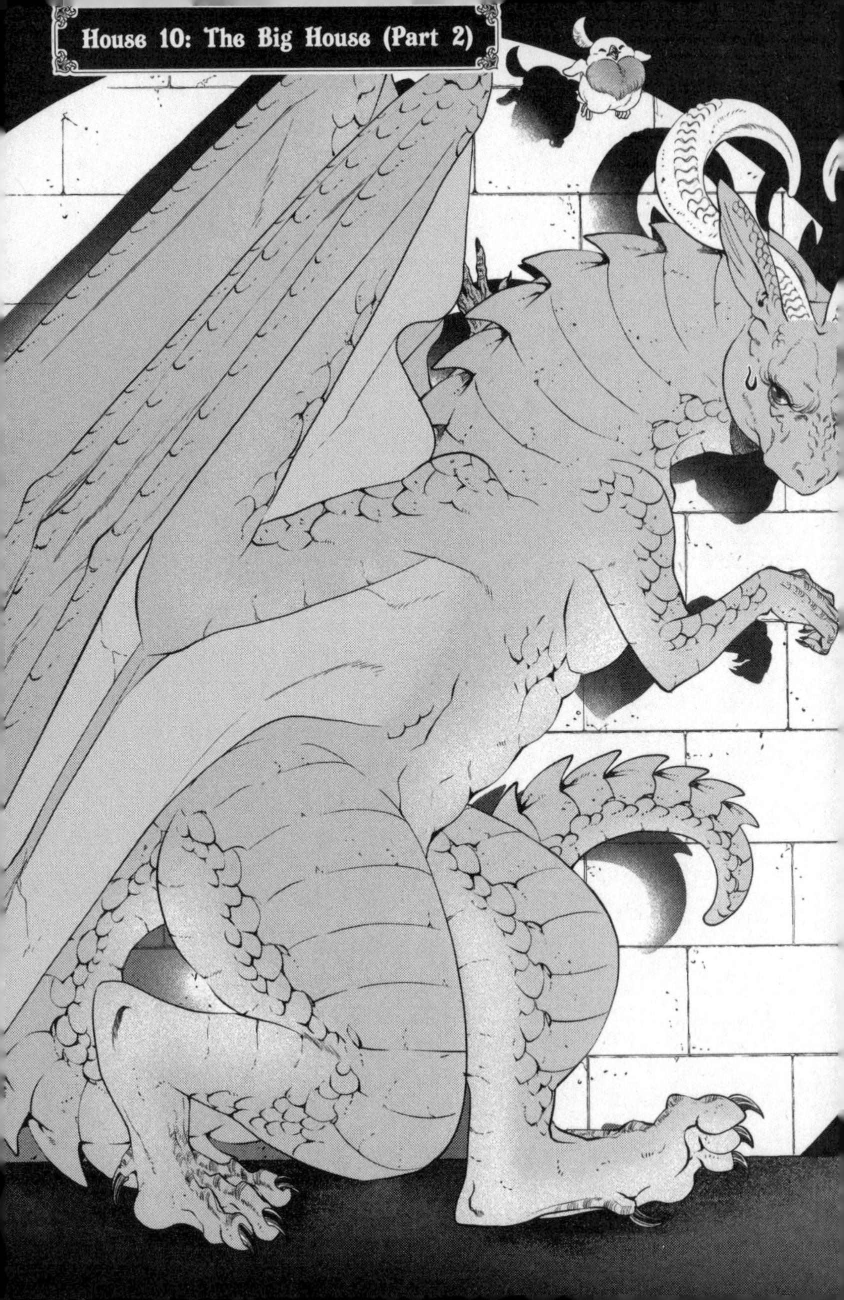

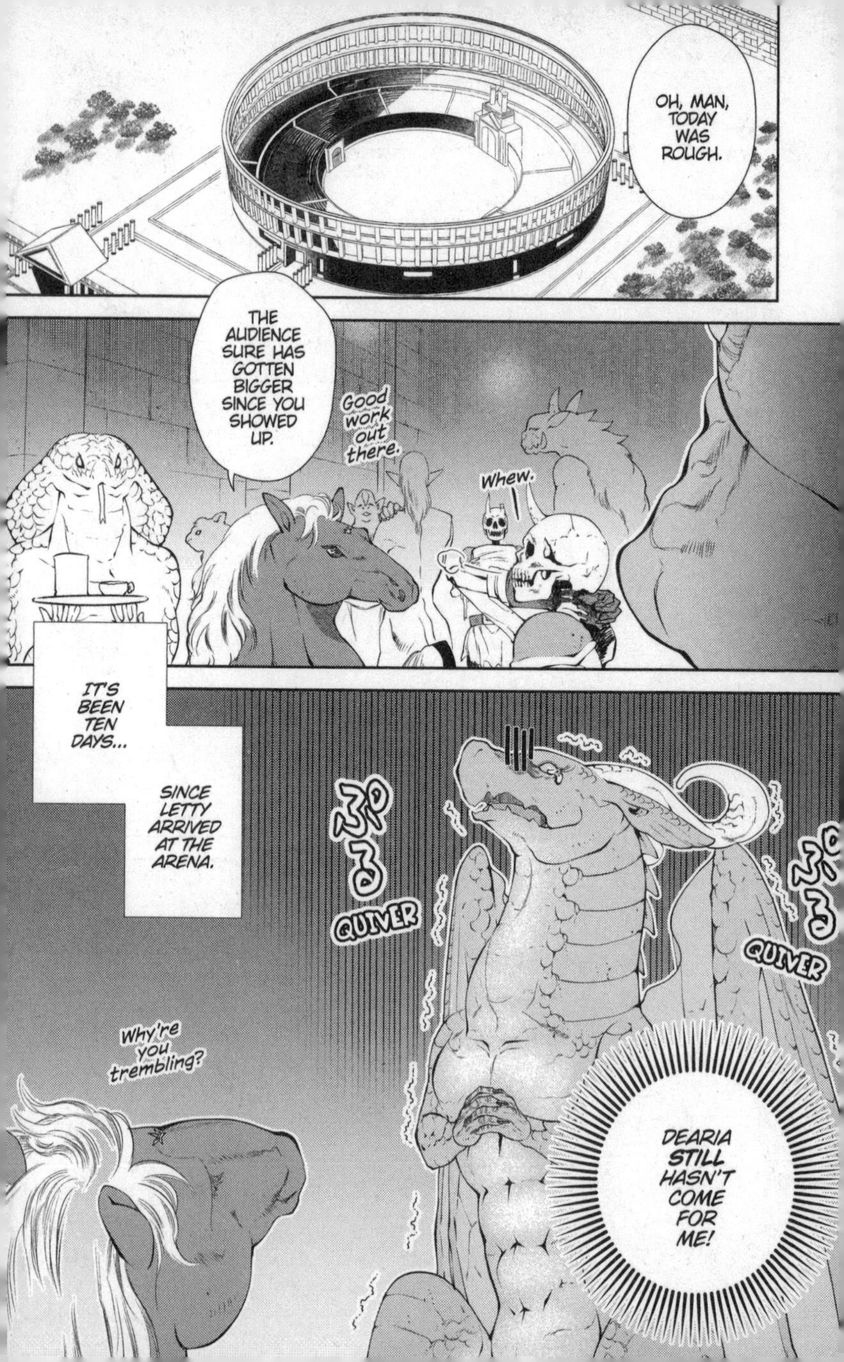
OH, MAN, TODAY WAS ROUGH.
THE AUDIENCE SURE HAS GOTTEN BIGGER SINCE YOU SHOWED UP.
Good work out there.
Whew.
IT'S BEEN TEN DAYS...
SINCE LETTY ARRIVED AT THE ARENA.
QUIVER
QUIVER
DEARIA STILL HASN'T COME FOR ME!
Why're you trembling?

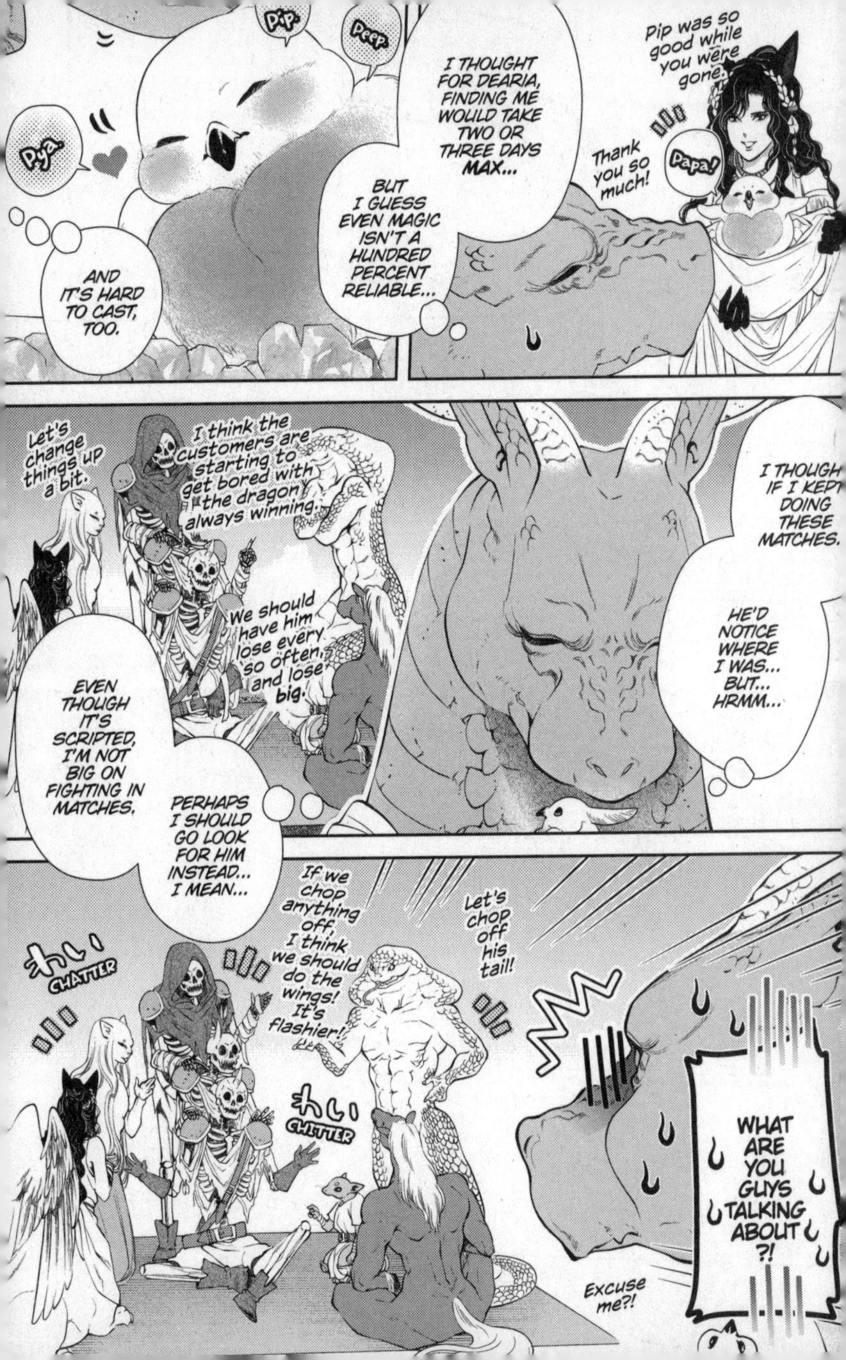
Pip was so good while you were gone.
Papa!
Thank you so much!
I THOUGHT FOR DEARIA, FINDING ME WOULD TAKE TWO OR THREE DAYS MAX...
BUT I GUESS EVEN MAGIC ISN'T A HUNDRED PERCENT RELIABLE...
Pip.
Peep.
Pya.
AND IT'S HARD TO CAST, TOO.
I THOUGH IF I KEPT DOING THESE MATCHES.
HE'D NOTICE WHERE I WAS... BUT... HRMM...
I think the customers are starting to get bored with the dragon always winning.
Let's change things up a bit.
We should have him lose every so often, and lose big.
EVEN THOUGH IT'S SCRIPTED, I'M NOT BIG ON FIGHTING IN MATCHES.
PERHAPS I SHOULD GO LOOK FOR HIM INSTEAD... I MEAN...
WHAT ARE YOU GUYS TALKING ABOUT?!
Excuse me?!
Let's chop off his tail!
If we chop anything off, I think we should do the wings! It's flashier!
CHITTER
CHATTER

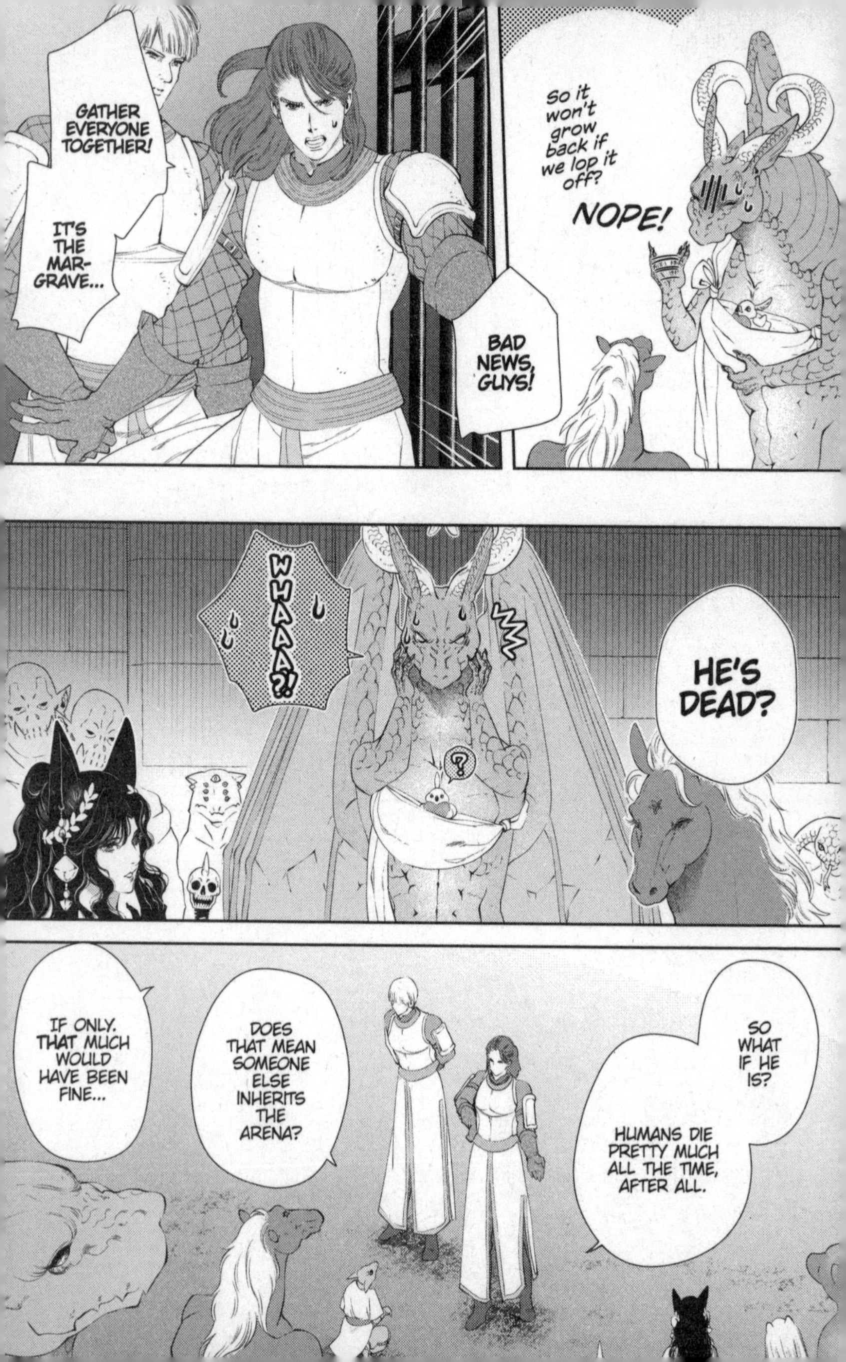
So it won't grow back if we lop it off?
NOPE!
BAD NEWS, GUYS!
GATHER EVERYONE TOGETHER!
IT'S THE MAR-GRAVE...
HE'S DEAD?
WHAAAA?!
?
SO WHAT IF HE IS?
HUMANS DIE PRETTY MUCH ALL THE TIME, AFTER ALL.
DOES THAT MEAN SOMEONE ELSE INHERITS THE ARENA?
IF ONLY. THAT MUCH WOULD HAVE BEEN FINE...

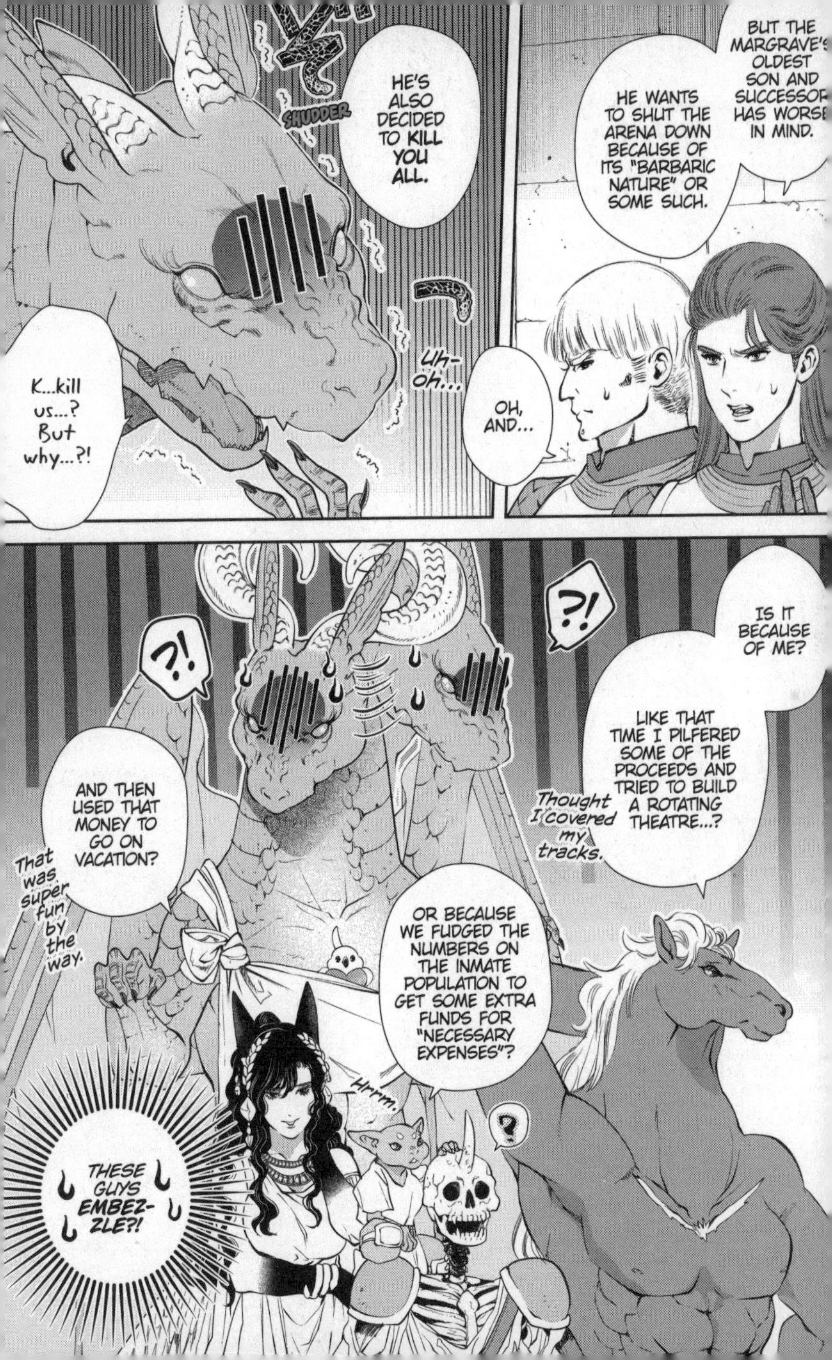
BUT THE MARGRAVE'S OLDEST SON AND SUCCESSOR HAS WORSE IN MIND.
HE WANTS TO SHUT THE ARENA DOWN BECAUSE OF ITS "BARBARIC NATURE" OR SOME SUCH.
OH, AND...
HE'S ALSO DECIDED TO KILL YOU ALL.
SHUDDER
Uh-oh...
K...kill us...? But why...?!
?!
IS IT BECAUSE OF ME?
LIKE THAT TIME I PILFERED SOME OF THE PROCEEDS AND TRIED TO BUILD A ROTATING THEATRE...?
Thought I covered my tracks.
?!
AND THEN USED THAT MONEY TO GO ON VACATION?
That was super fun by the way.
OR BECAUSE WE FUDGED THE NUMBERS ON THE INMATE POPULATION TO GET SOME EXTRA FUNDS FOR "NECESSARY EXPENSES"?
Hrrrm.
?
THESE GUYS EMBEZZLE?!

IT'S CALLED A PRE-EMPTIVE STRIKE.

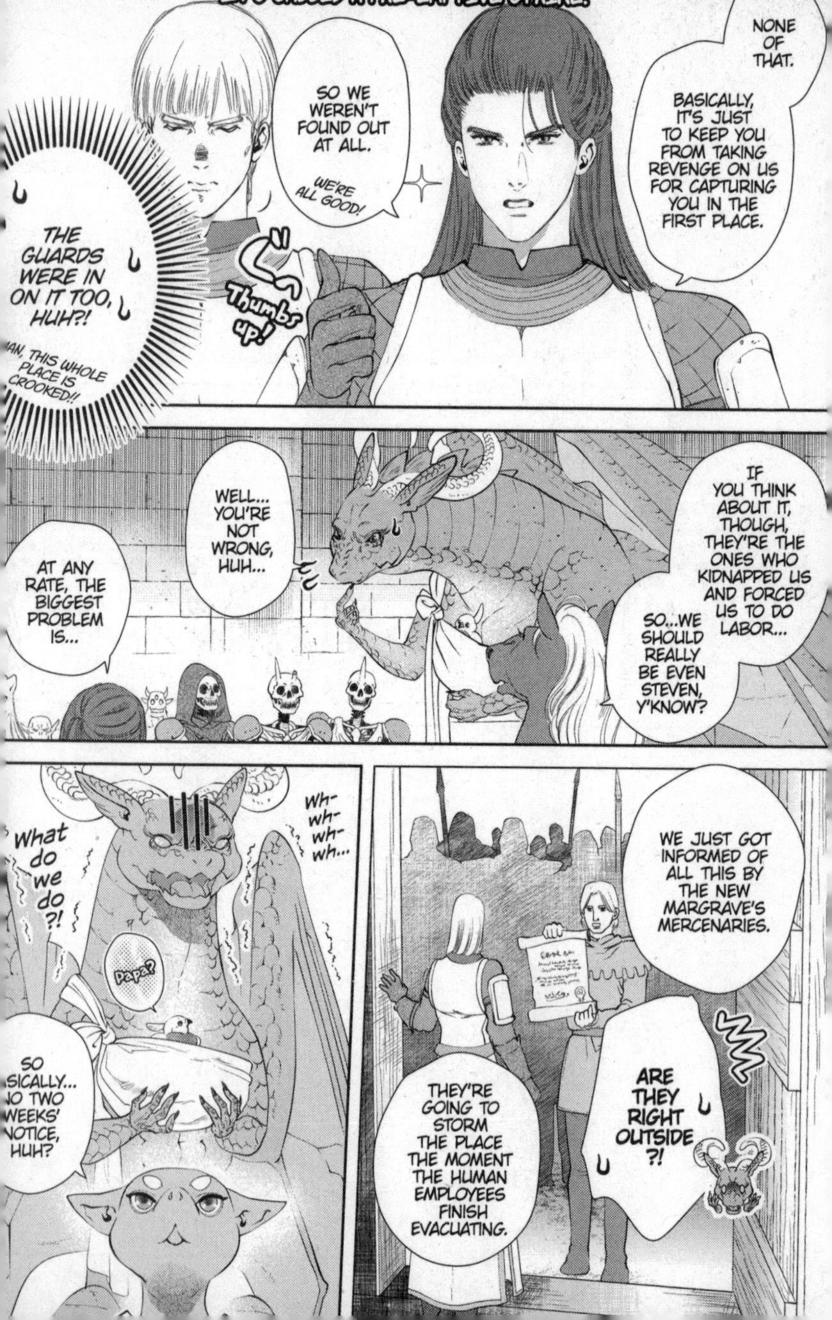

NONE OF THAT.
BASICALLY, IT'S JUST TO KEEP YOU FROM TAKING REVENGE ON US FOR CAPTURING YOU IN THE FIRST PLACE.
SO WE WEREN'T FOUND OUT AT ALL.
WE'RE ALL GOOD!
Thumbs up!
THE GUARDS WERE IN ON IT TOO, HUH?!
AN, THIS WHOLE PLACE IS CROOKED!!
IF YOU THINK ABOUT IT, THOUGH, THEY'RE THE ONES WHO KIDNAPPED US AND FORCED US TO DO LABOR...
SO...WE SHOULD REALLY BE EVEN STEVEN, Y'KNOW?
WELL... YOU'RE NOT WRONG, HUH...
AT ANY RATE, THE BIGGEST PROBLEM IS...
WE JUST GOT INFORMED OF ALL THIS BY THE NEW MARGRAVE'S MERCENARIES.
ARE THEY RIGHT OUTSIDE?!
THEY'RE GOING TO STORM THE PLACE THE MOMENT THE HUMAN EMPLOYEES FINISH EVACUATING.
Wh-wh-wh-wh...
What do we do?!
Papa?
SO SICALLY... O TWO WEEKS' OTICE, HUH?

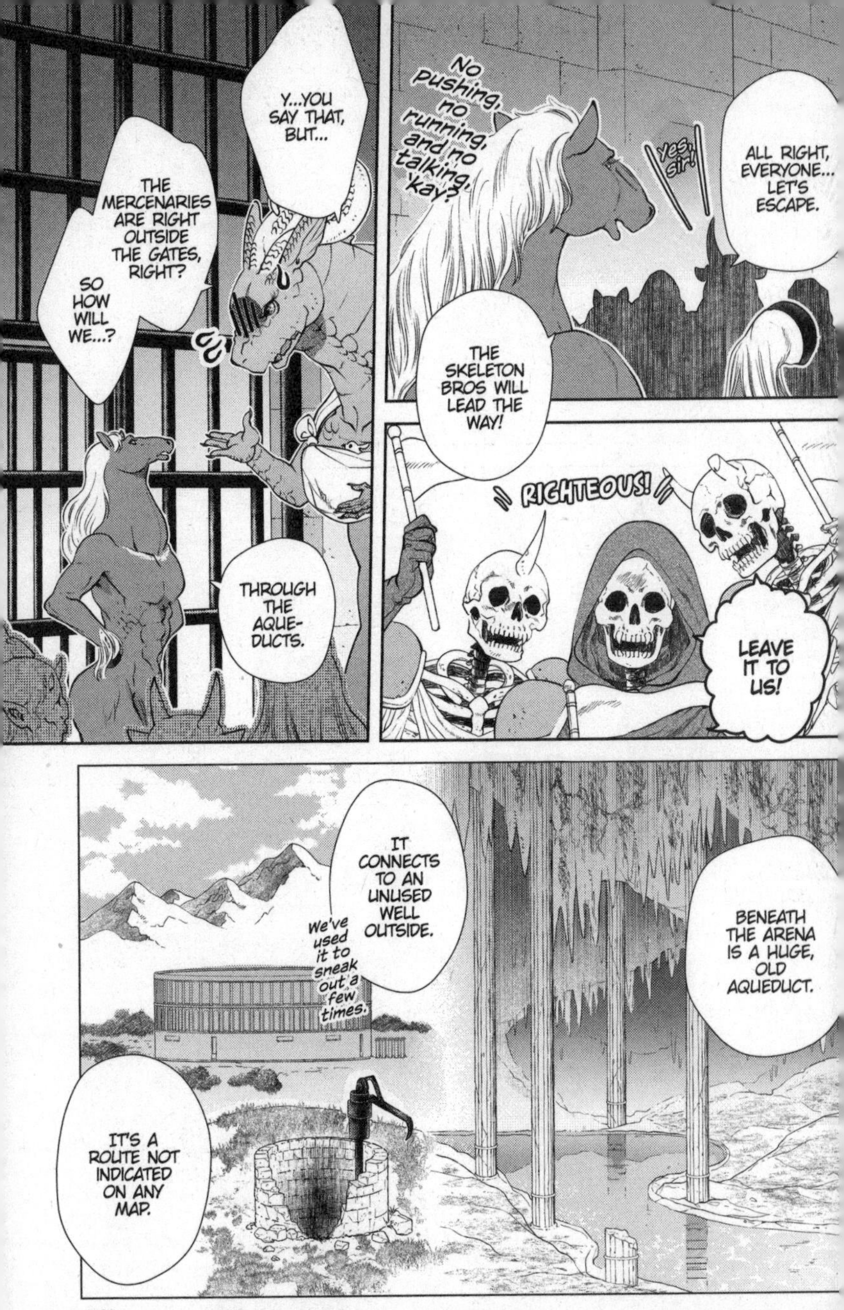
ALL RIGHT, EVERYONE... LET'S ESCAPE.
Yes, sir!
No pushing, no running, and no talking, 'kay?
THE SKELETON BROS WILL LEAD THE WAY!
RIGHTEOUS!
LEAVE IT TO US!
Y...YOU SAY THAT, BUT...
THE MERCENARIES ARE RIGHT OUTSIDE THE GATES, RIGHT?
SO HOW WILL WE...?
THROUGH THE AQUE-DUCTS.
BENEATH THE ARENA IS A HUGE, OLD AQUEDUCT.
IT CONNECTS TO AN UNUSED WELL OUTSIDE.
We've used it to sneak out a few times.
IT'S A ROUTE NOT INDICATED ON ANY MAP.

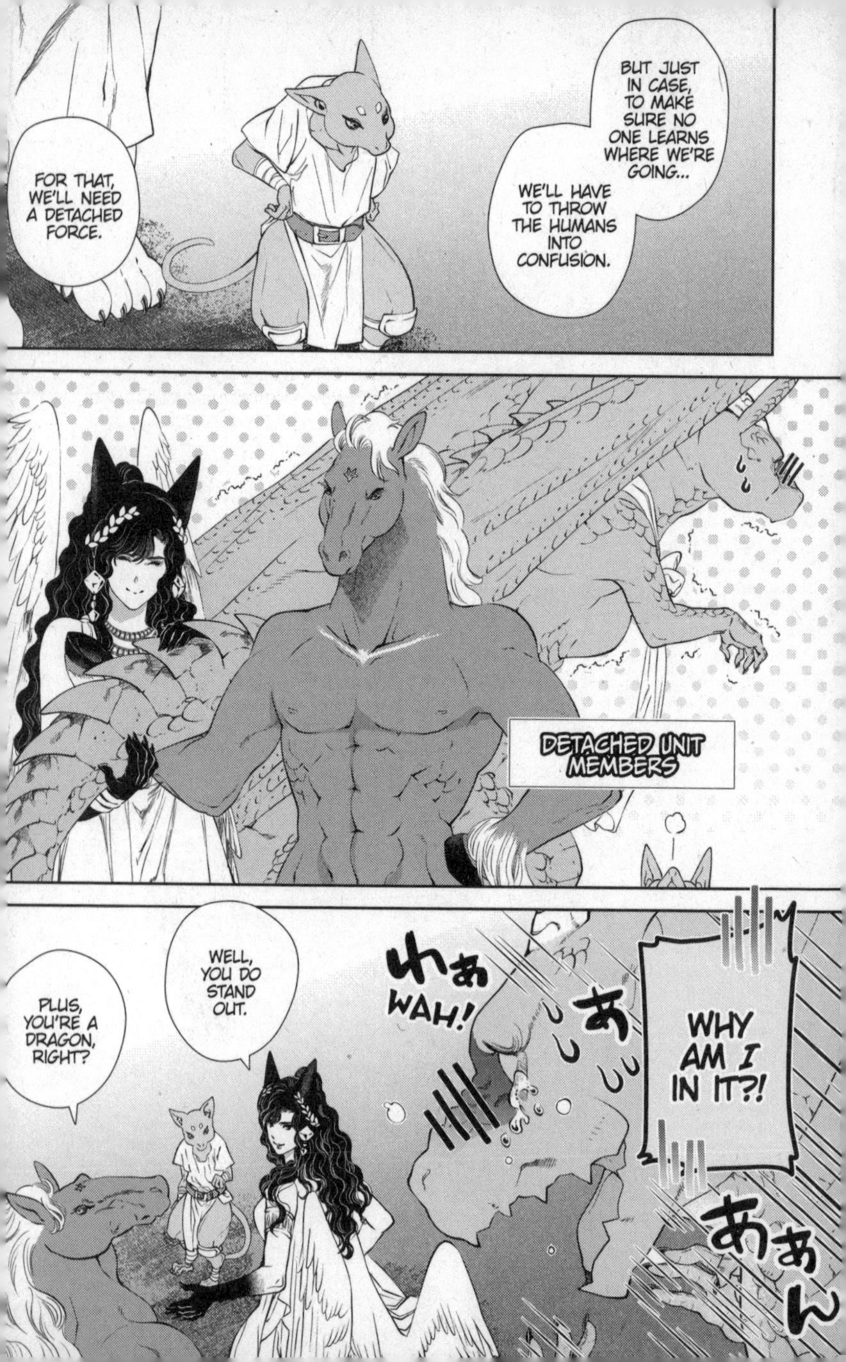
BUT JUST IN CASE, TO MAKE SURE NO ONE LEARNS WHERE WE'RE GOING...
WE'LL HAVE TO THROW THE HUMANS INTO CONFUSION.
FOR THAT, WE'LL NEED A DETACHED FORCE.
DETACHED UNIT MEMBERS
WHY AM I IN IT?!
ああん
あ
わぁ WAH!
WELL, YOU DO STAND OUT.
PLUS, YOU'RE A DRAGON, RIGHT?

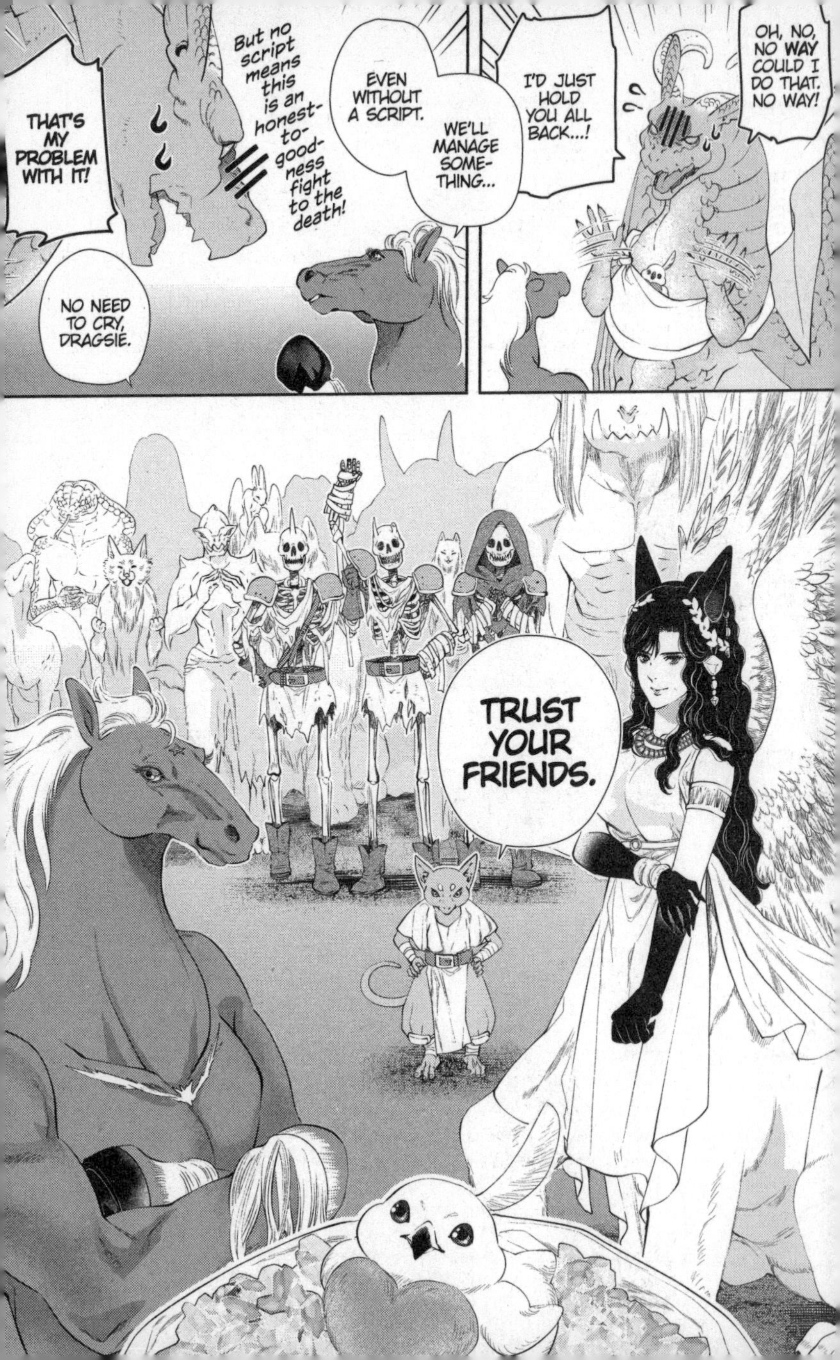
OH, NO, NO WAY COULD I DO THAT. NO WAY!
I'D JUST HOLD YOU ALL BACK...!
WE'LL MANAGE SOME-THING...
EVEN WITHOUT A SCRIPT.
But no script means this is an honest-to-good-ness fight to the death!
THAT'S MY PROBLEM WITH IT!
NO NEED TO CRY, DRAGSIE.
TRUST YOUR FRIENDS.

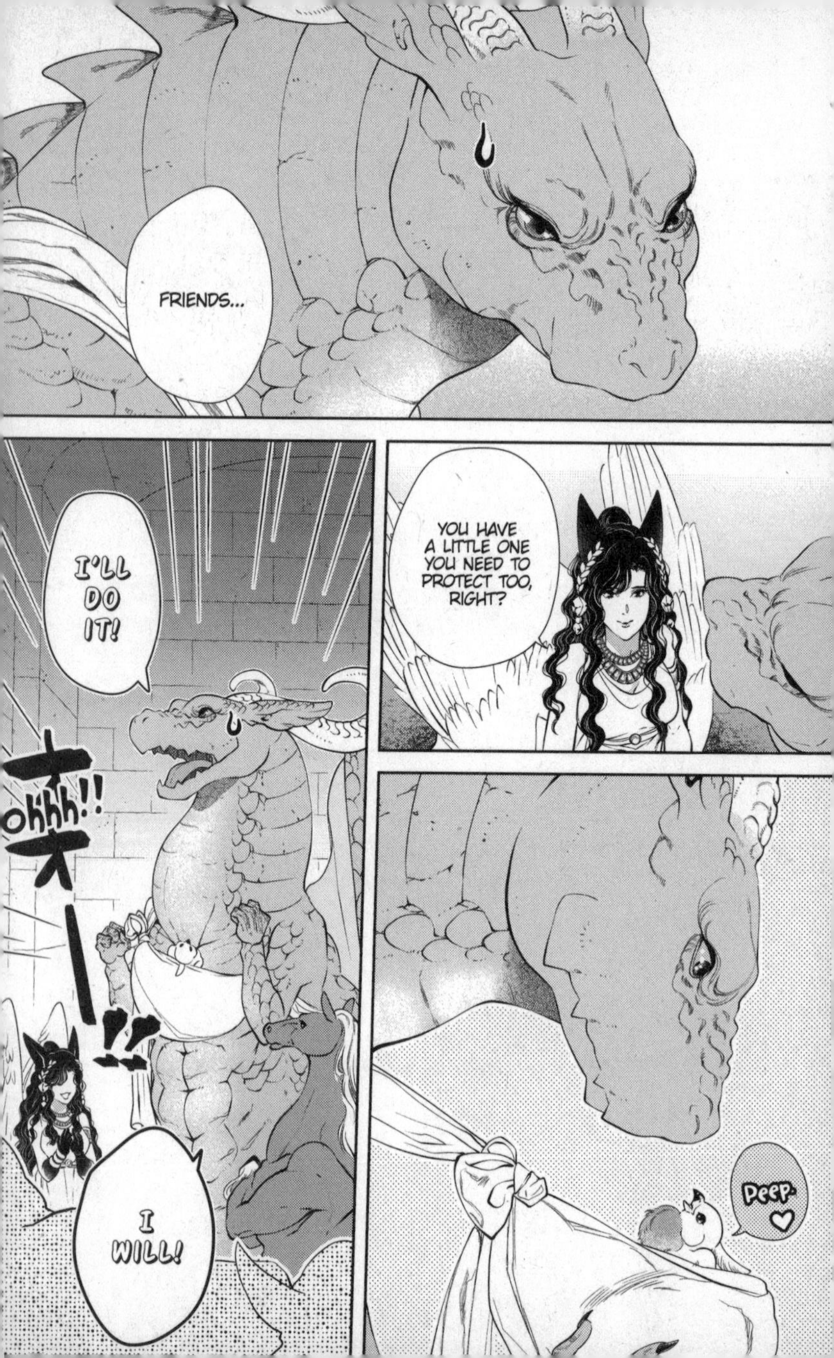
FRIENDS...
YOU HAVE A LITTLE ONE YOU NEED TO PROTECT TOO, RIGHT?
Peep. ♥
I'LL DO IT!
Ohhh!!
I WILL!

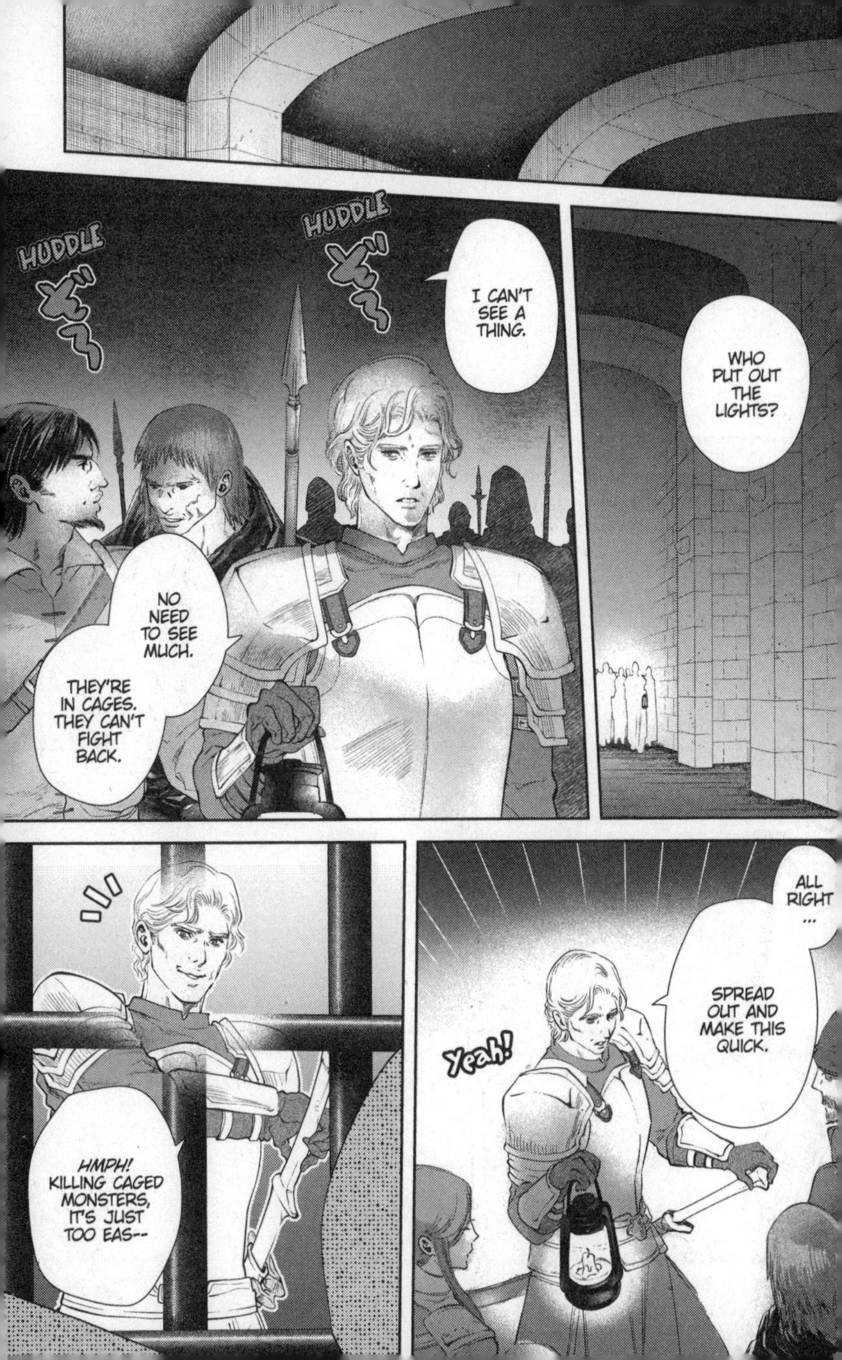
WHO PUT OUT THE LIGHTS?
I CAN'T SEE A THING.
HUDDLE
HUDDLE
NO NEED TO SEE MUCH.
THEY'RE IN CAGES. THEY CAN'T FIGHT BACK.
ALL RIGHT ...
SPREAD OUT AND MAKE THIS QUICK.
Yeah!
HMPH! KILLING CAGED MONSTERS, IT'S JUST TOO EAS--

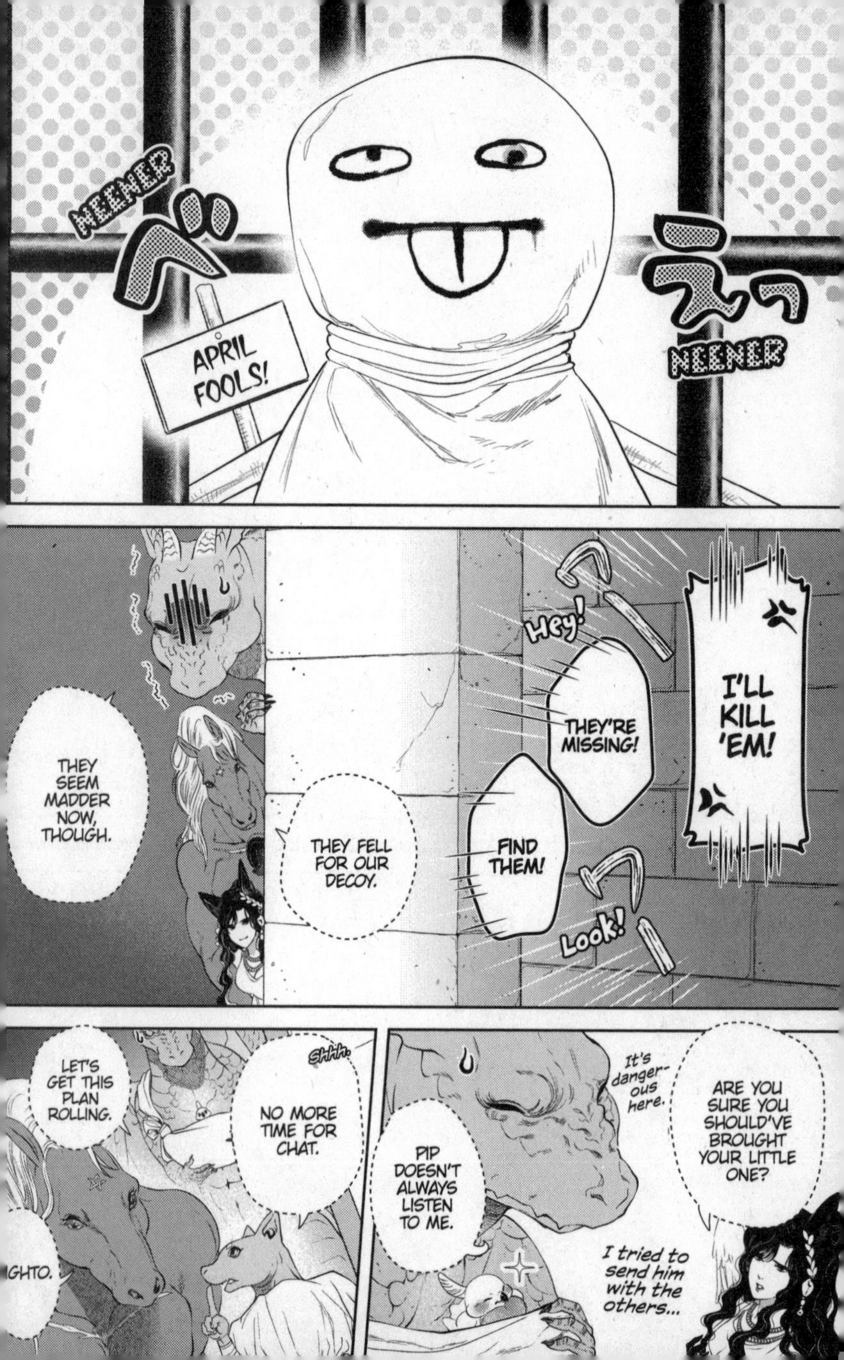
NEENER
NEENER
APRIL FOOLS!
I'LL KILL 'EM!
Hey!
THEY'RE MISSING!
FIND THEM!
Look!
THEY FELL FOR OUR DECOY.
THEY SEEM MADDER NOW, THOUGH.
ARE YOU SURE YOU SHOULD'VE BROUGHT YOUR LITTLE ONE?
It's danger-ous here.
I tried to send him with the others...
PIP DOESN'T ALWAYS LISTEN TO ME.
Shhh.
NO MORE TIME FOR CHAT.
LET'S GET THIS PLAN ROLLING.

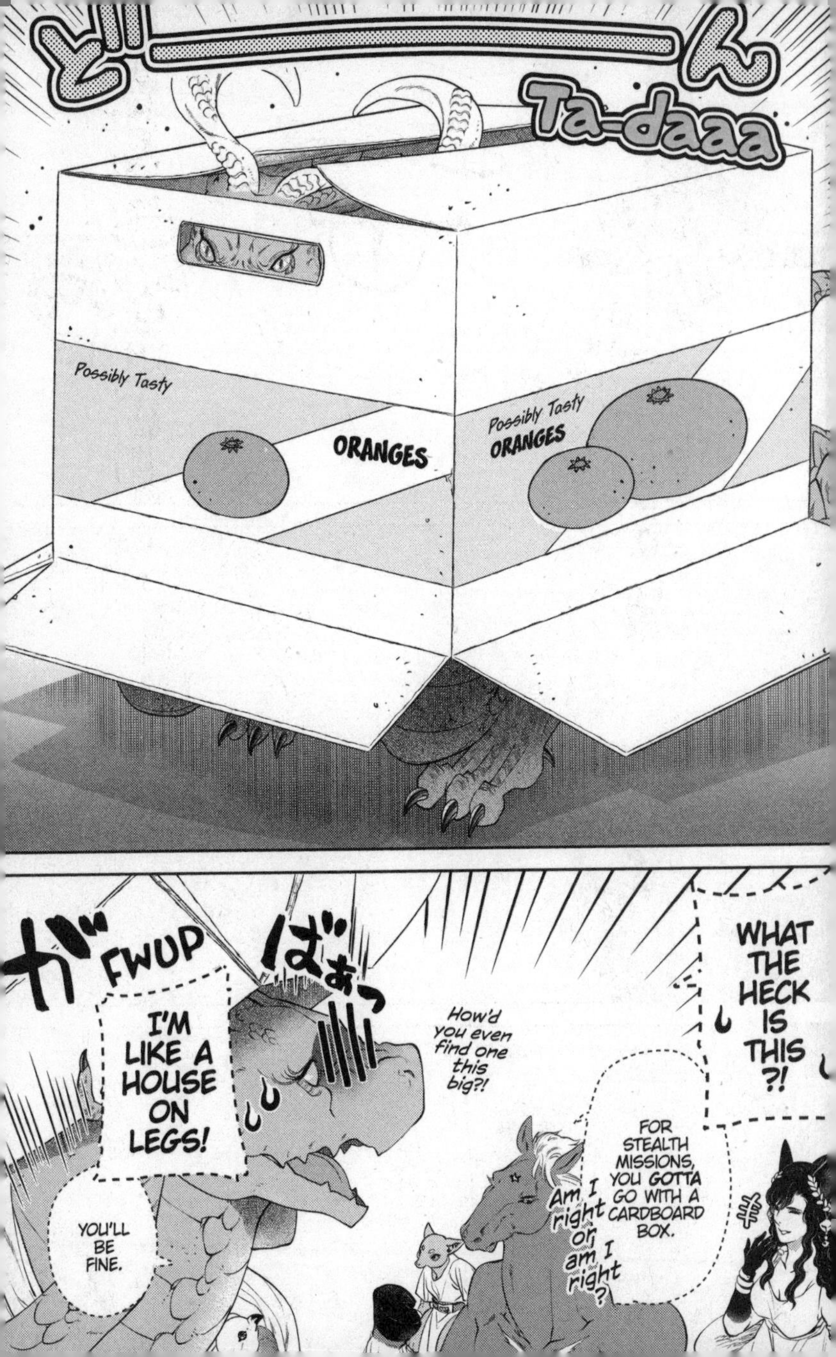
どーーーん
Ta-daaa
Possibly Tasty
ORANGES
Possibly Tasty
ORANGES
WHAT THE HECK IS THIS?!
FOR STEALTH MISSIONS, YOU GOTTA GO WITH A CARDBOARD BOX.
Am I right or am I right?
How'd you even find one this big?!
ばあっ
FWUP
が
I'M LIKE A HOUSE ON LEGS!
YOU'LL BE FINE.

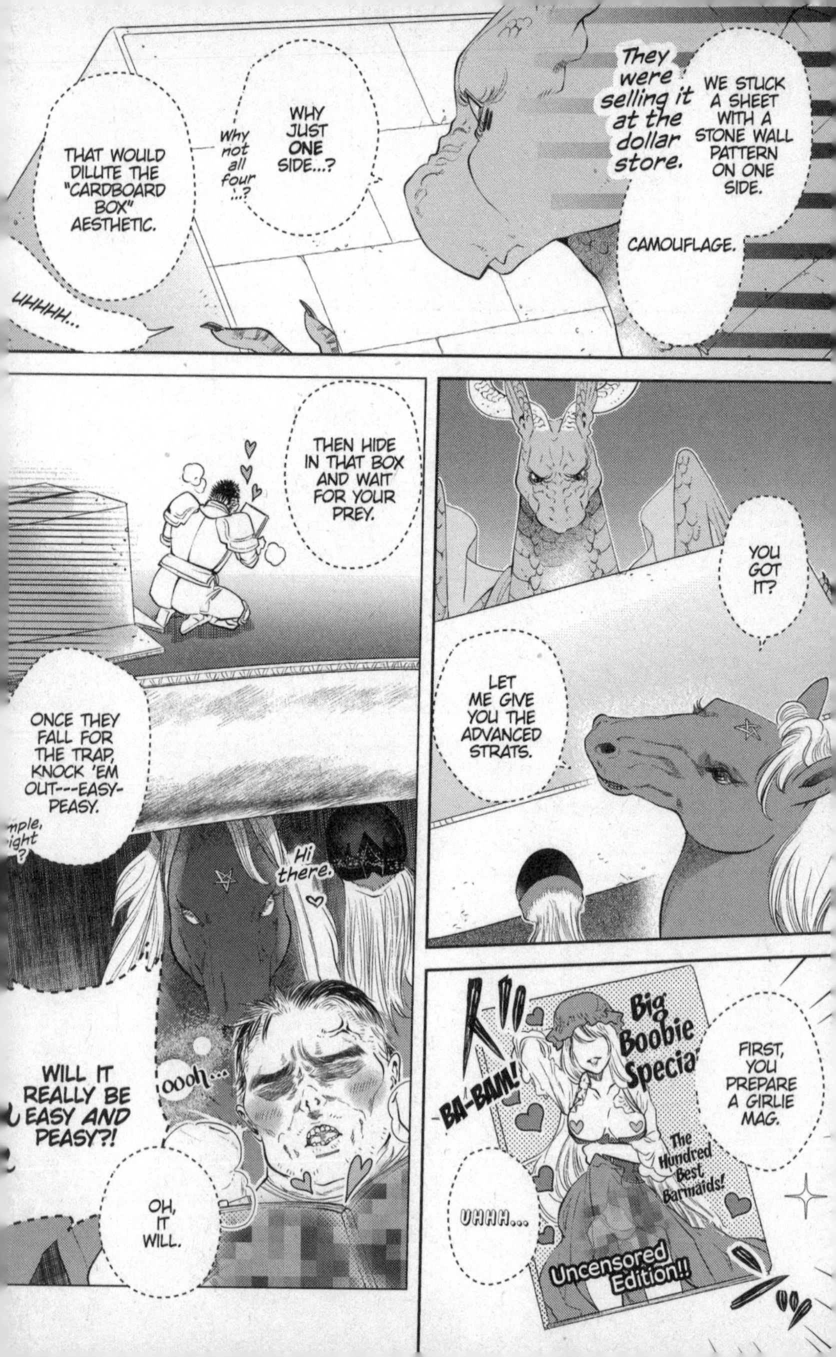

WE STUCK A SHEET WITH A STONE WALL PATTERN ON ONE SIDE.
CAMOUFLAGE.
They were selling it at the dollar store.
WHY JUST ONE SIDE...?
Why not all four...?
THAT WOULD DILUTE THE "CARDBOARD BOX" AESTHETIC.
UHHHH...
YOU GOT IT?
LET ME GIVE YOU THE ADVANCED STRATS.
THEN HIDE IN THAT BOX AND WAIT FOR YOUR PREY.
ONCE THEY FALL FOR THE TRAP, KNOCK 'EM OUT---EASY-PEASY.
Hi there.
FIRST, YOU PREPARE A GIRLIE MAG.
BA-BAM!
Big Boobie Specia
The Hundred Best Barmaids!
Uncensored Edition!!
UHHH...
WILL IT REALLY BE EASY AND PEASY?!
oooh...
OH, IT WILL.

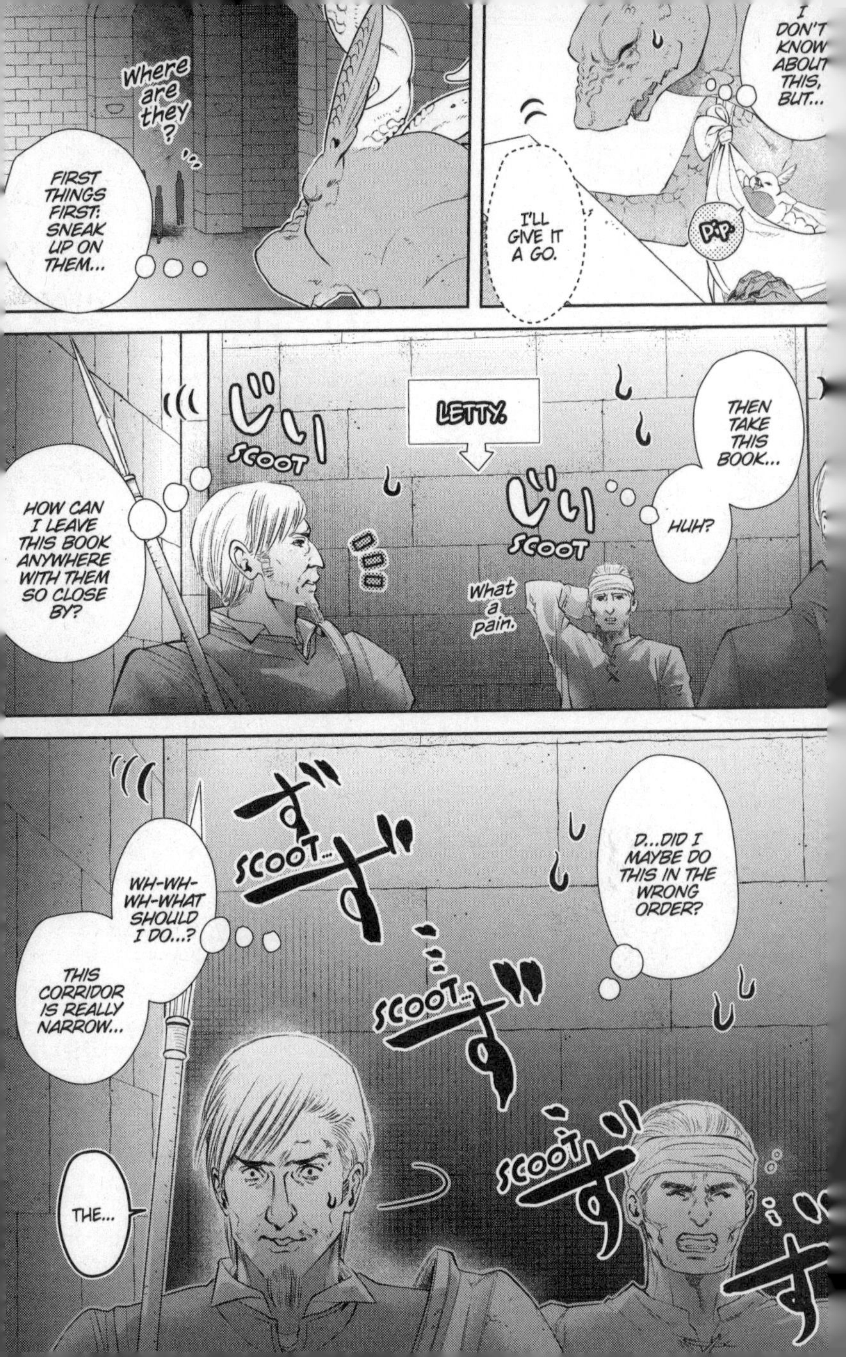
I DON'T KNOW ABOUT THIS, BUT...
I'LL GIVE IT A GO.
PIP
Where are they?
FIRST THINGS FIRST: SNEAK UP ON THEM...
THEN TAKE THIS BOOK...
HUH?
LETTY.
SCOOT
What a pain.
SCOOT
HOW CAN I LEAVE THIS BOOK ANYWHERE WITH THEM SO CLOSE BY?
D...DID I MAYBE DO THIS IN THE WRONG ORDER?
SCOOT
SCOOT...
WH-WH-WH-WHAT SHOULD I DO...?
THIS CORRIDOR IS REALLY NARROW...
SCOOT...
THE...

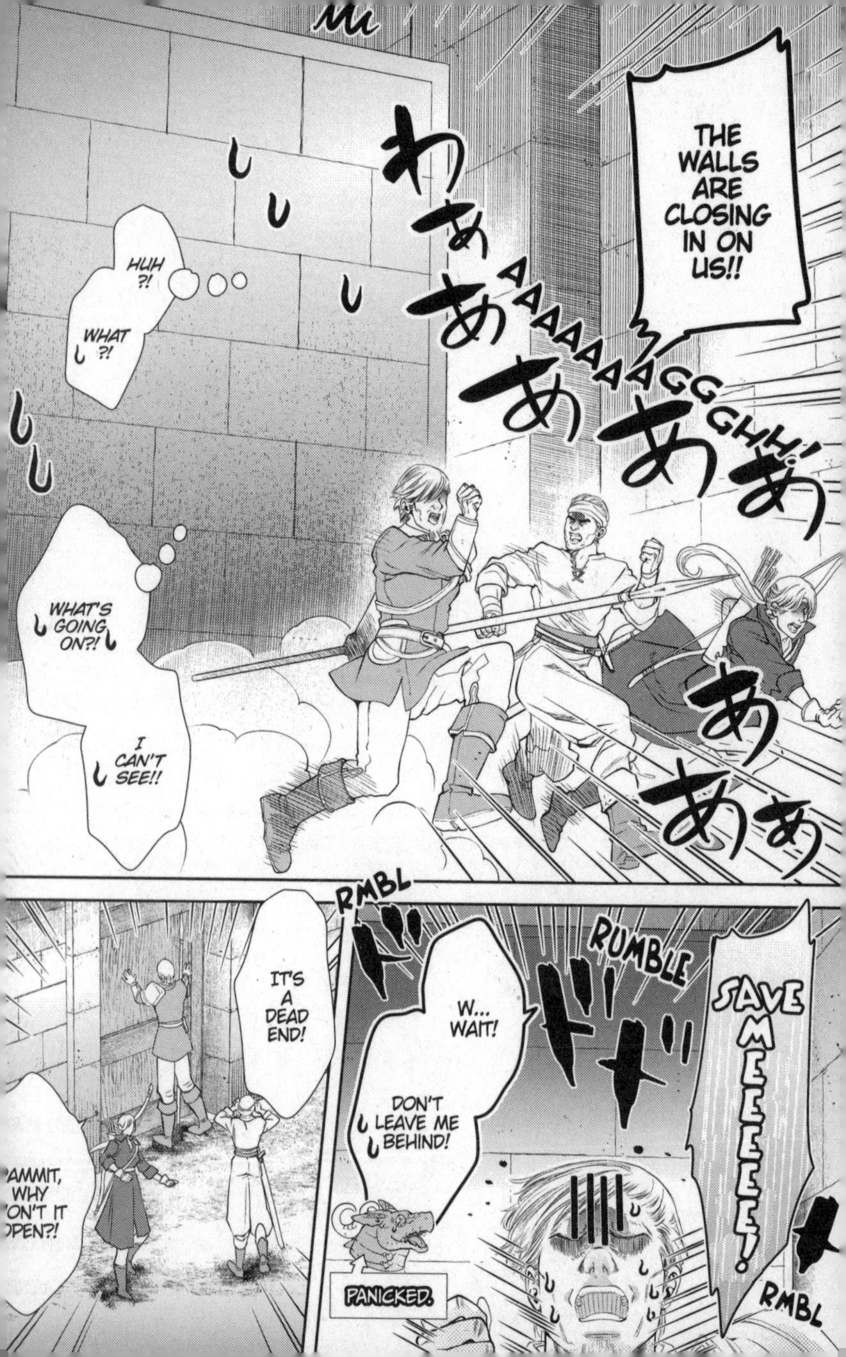
THE WALLS ARE CLOSING IN ON US!!
AAAAAAAGGGHH!
HUH ?!
WHAT ?!
WHAT'S GOING ON?!
I CAN'T SEE!!
SAVE MEEEEEE!
RMBL
RUMBLE
RMBL
W... WAIT!
DON'T LEAVE ME BEHIND!
PANICKED.
IT'S A DEAD END!
AMMIT, WHY ON'T IT OPEN?!

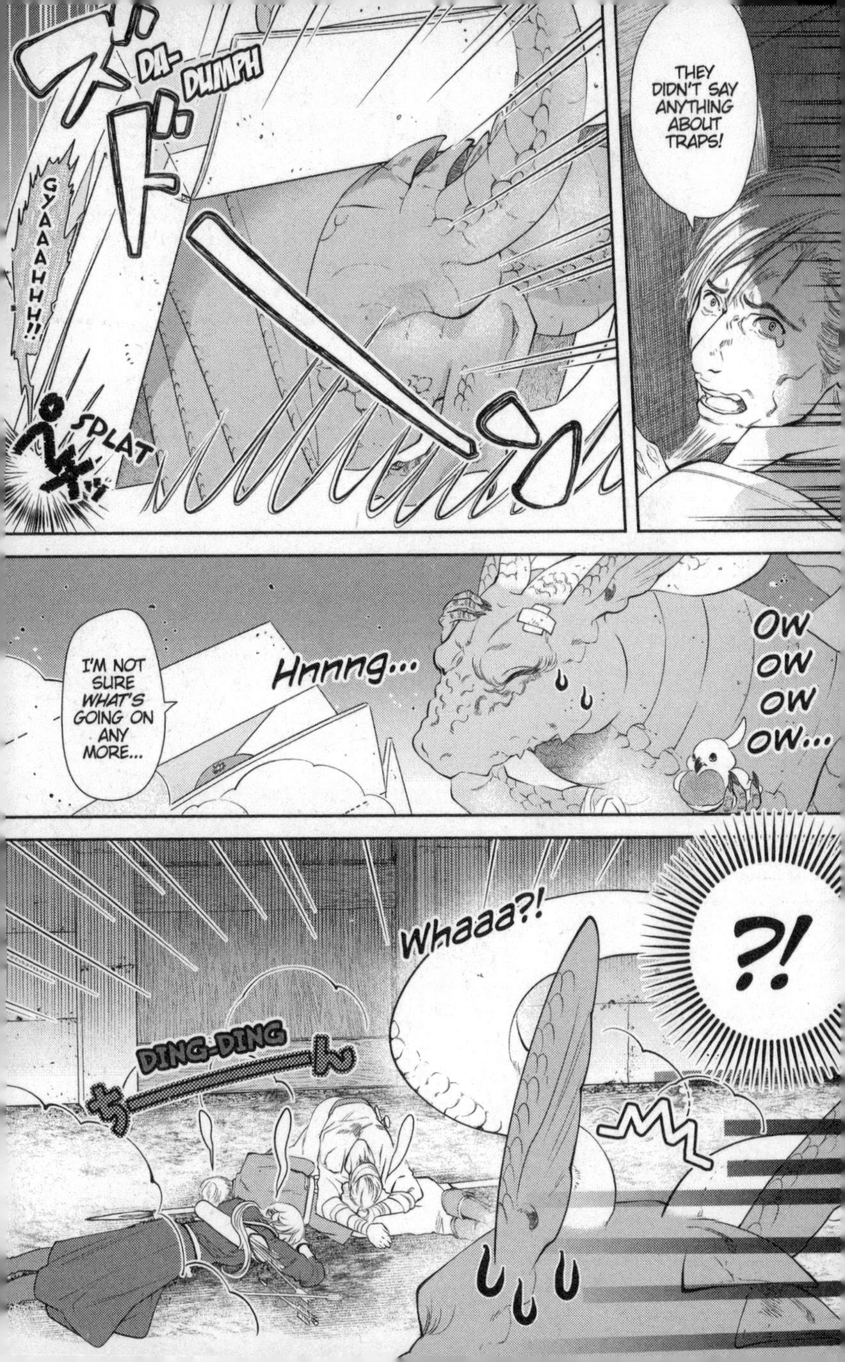
THEY DIDN'T SAY ANYTHING ABOUT TRAPS!
DA-DUMPH
GYAAAAHHH!!
SPLAT
OW OW OW OW...
Hnnng...
I'M NOT SURE WHAT'S GOING ON ANY MORE...
?!
Whaaa?!
DING-DING

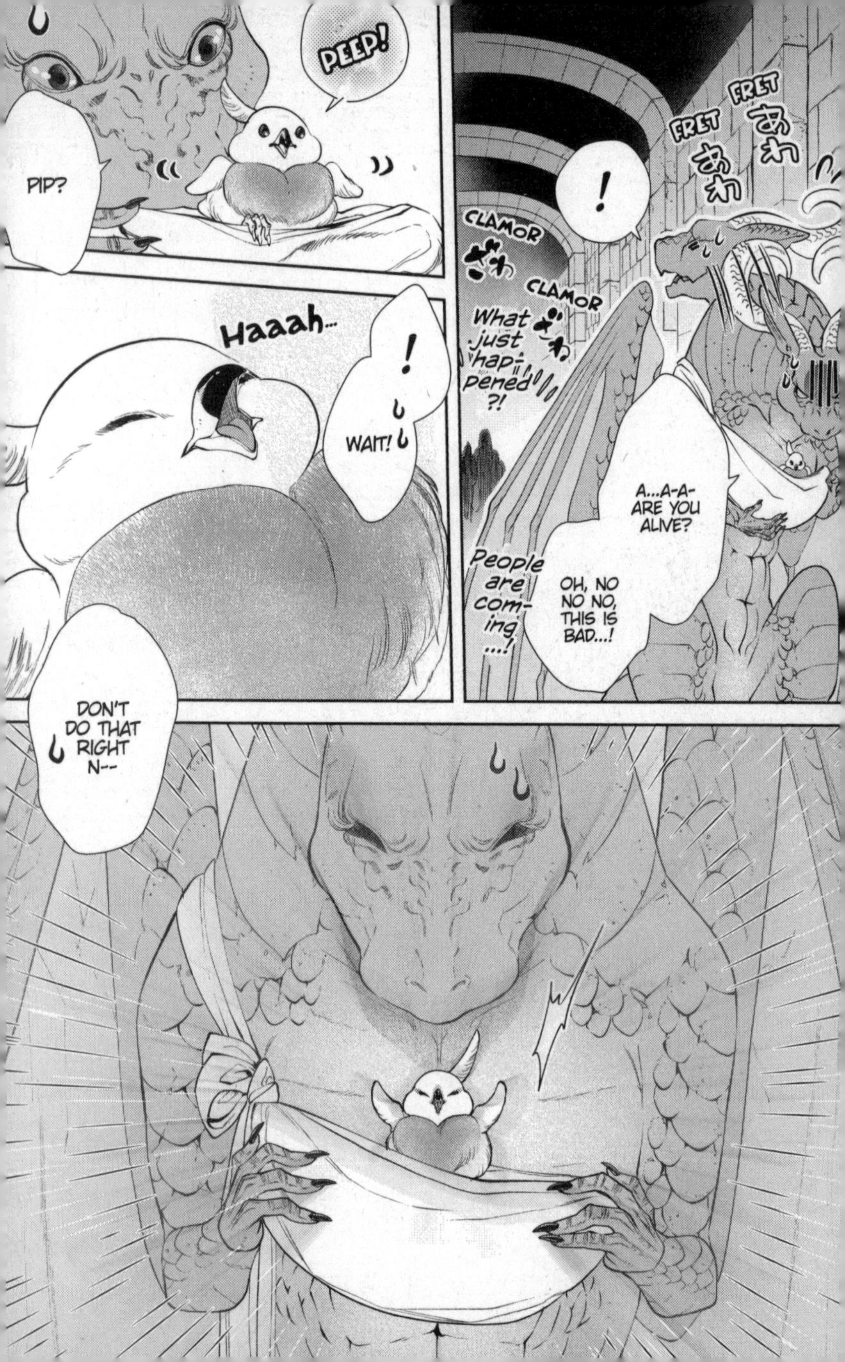
FRET FRET
あわ あわ
!
CLAMOR
ざわ
CLAMOR
ざわ
What just hap-pened?!
A...A-A-ARE YOU ALIVE?
OH, NO NO NO, THIS IS BAD...!
People are com-ing...!
PEEP!
PIP?
!
WAIT!
Haaah...
DON'T DO THAT RIGHT N--

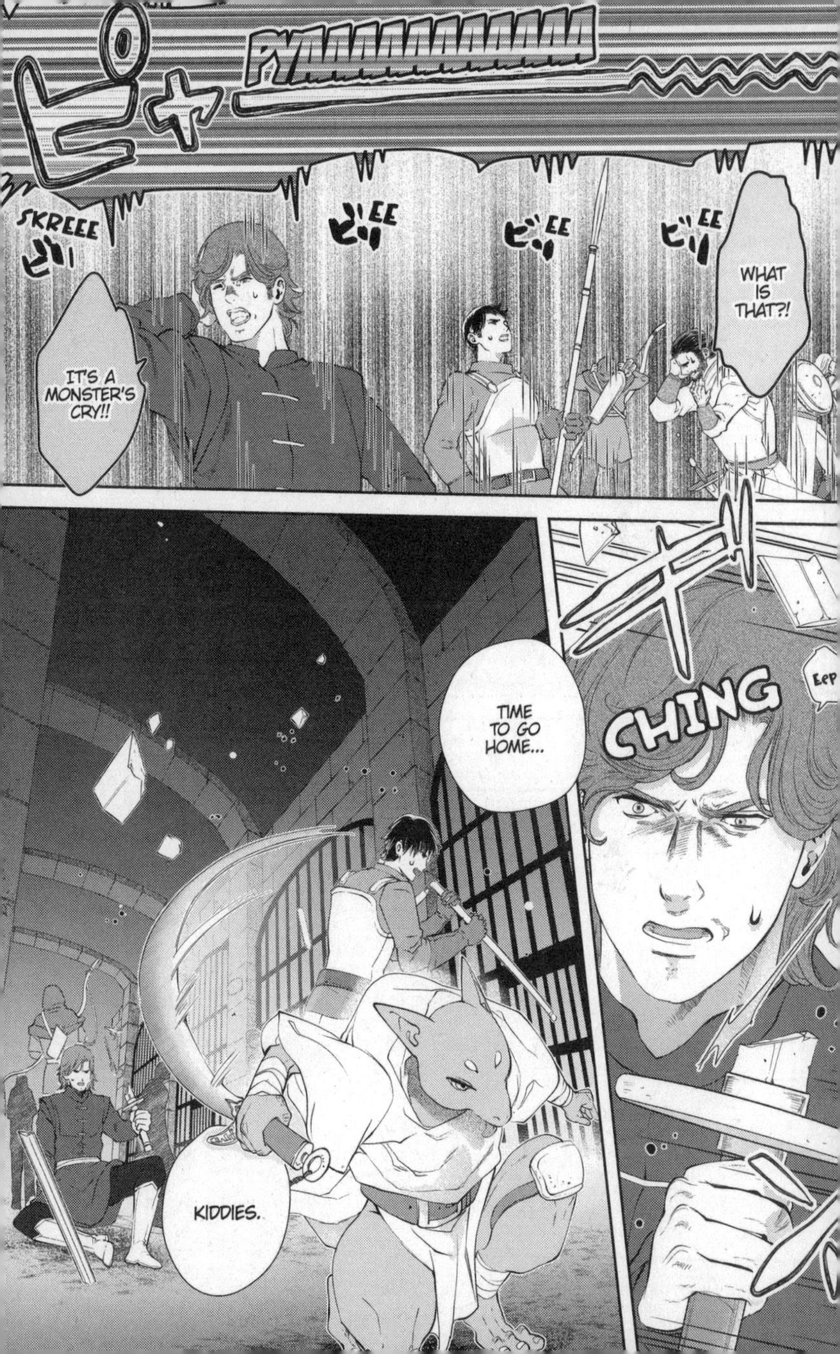
ピャ
PYAAAAAAAAAA
WHAT IS THAT?!
ビッ EE
ビッ EE
ビッ EE
IT'S A MONSTER'S CRY!!
SKREEE ビッ
Eep
CHING
TIME TO GO HOME...
KIDDIES.

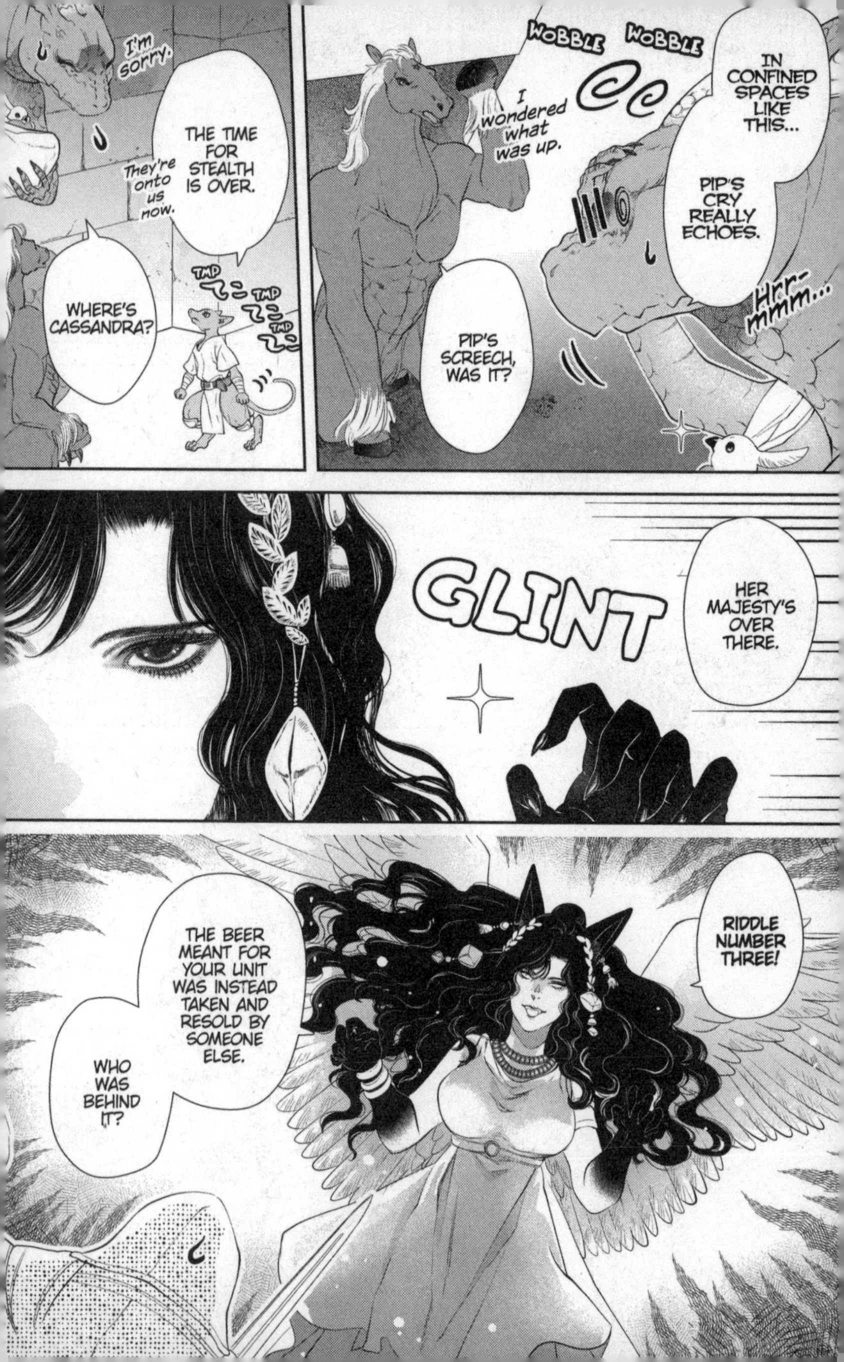
WOBBLE WOBBLE
IN CONFINED SPACES LIKE THIS...
PIP'S CRY REALLY ECHOES.
Hrr-mmm...
I wondered what was up.
PIP'S SCREECH, WAS IT?
I'm sorry.
THE TIME FOR STEALTH IS OVER.
They're onto us now.
TMP TMP TMP
WHERE'S CASSANDRA?
HER MAJESTY'S OVER THERE.
GLINT
RIDDLE NUMBER THREE!
THE BEER MEANT FOR YOUR UNIT WAS INSTEAD TAKEN AND RESOLD BY SOMEONE ELSE.
WHO WAS BEHIND IT?

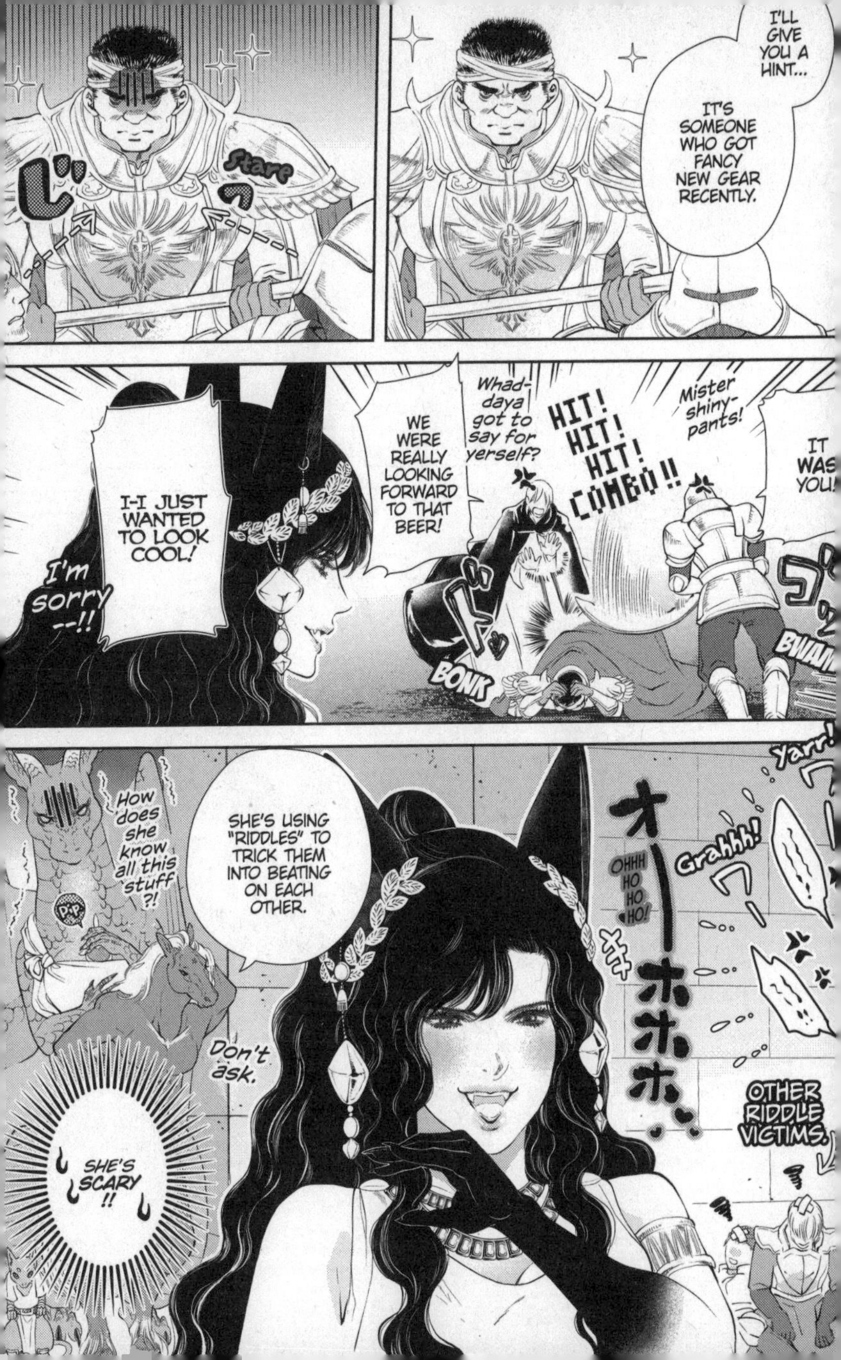
I'LL GIVE YOU A HINT...
IT'S SOMEONE WHO GOT FANCY NEW GEAR RECENTLY.
Stare
IT WAS YOU!
Mister shiny-pants!
BWAM
HIT! HIT! HIT! COMBO!!
Whad-daya got to say for yerself?
WE WERE REALLY LOOKING FORWARD TO THAT BEER!
BONK
I-I JUST WANTED TO LOOK COOL!
I'm sorry--!!
Yarr!
Grahhh!
OTHER RIDDLE VICTIMS.
オーホホホ
OHHH HO HO HO!
SHE'S USING "RIDDLES" TO TRICK THEM INTO BEATING ON EACH OTHER.
How does she know all this stuff?!
Don't ask.
SHE'S SCARY!!

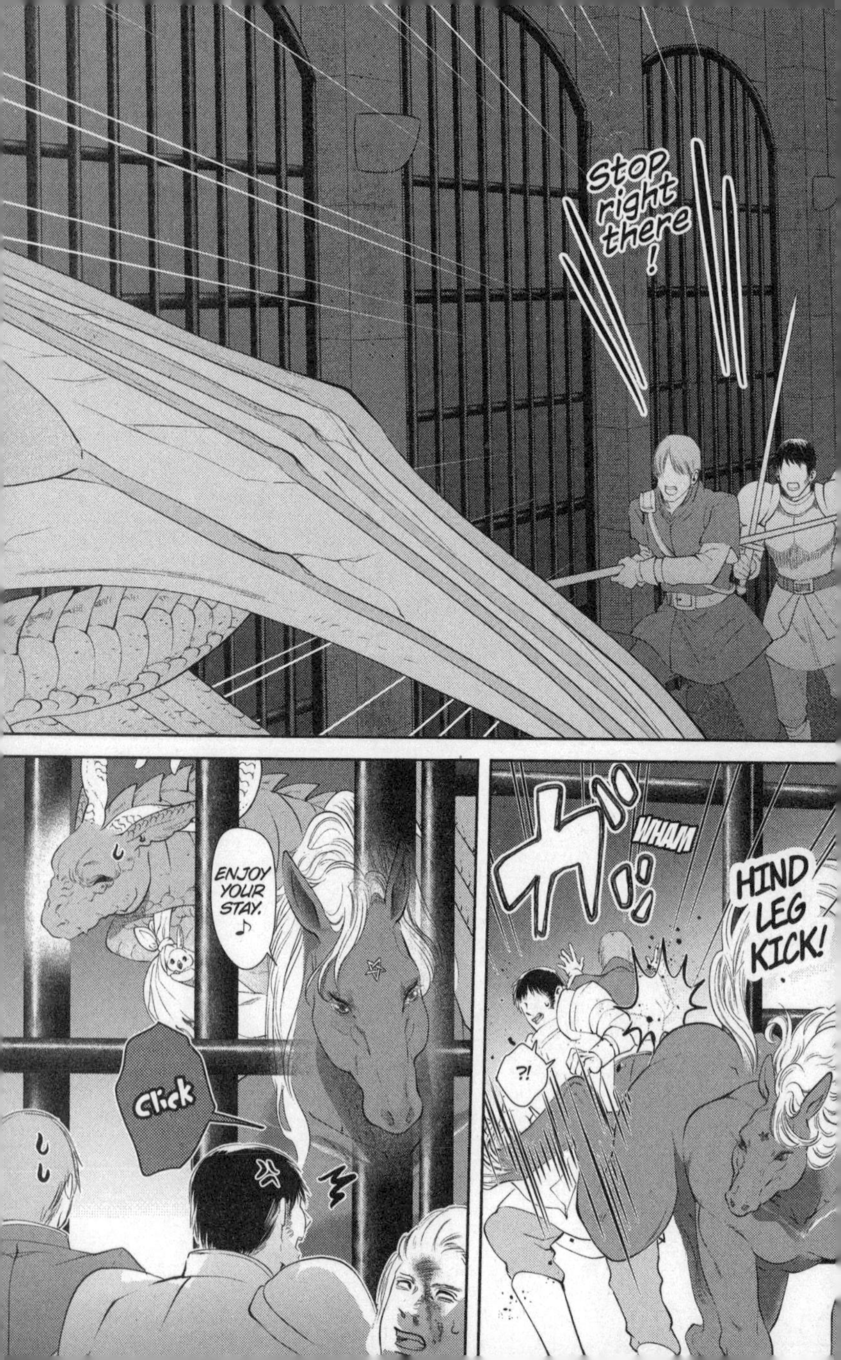
Stop right there!
WHAM
HIND LEG KICK!
?!
ENJOY YOUR STAY. ♪
Click

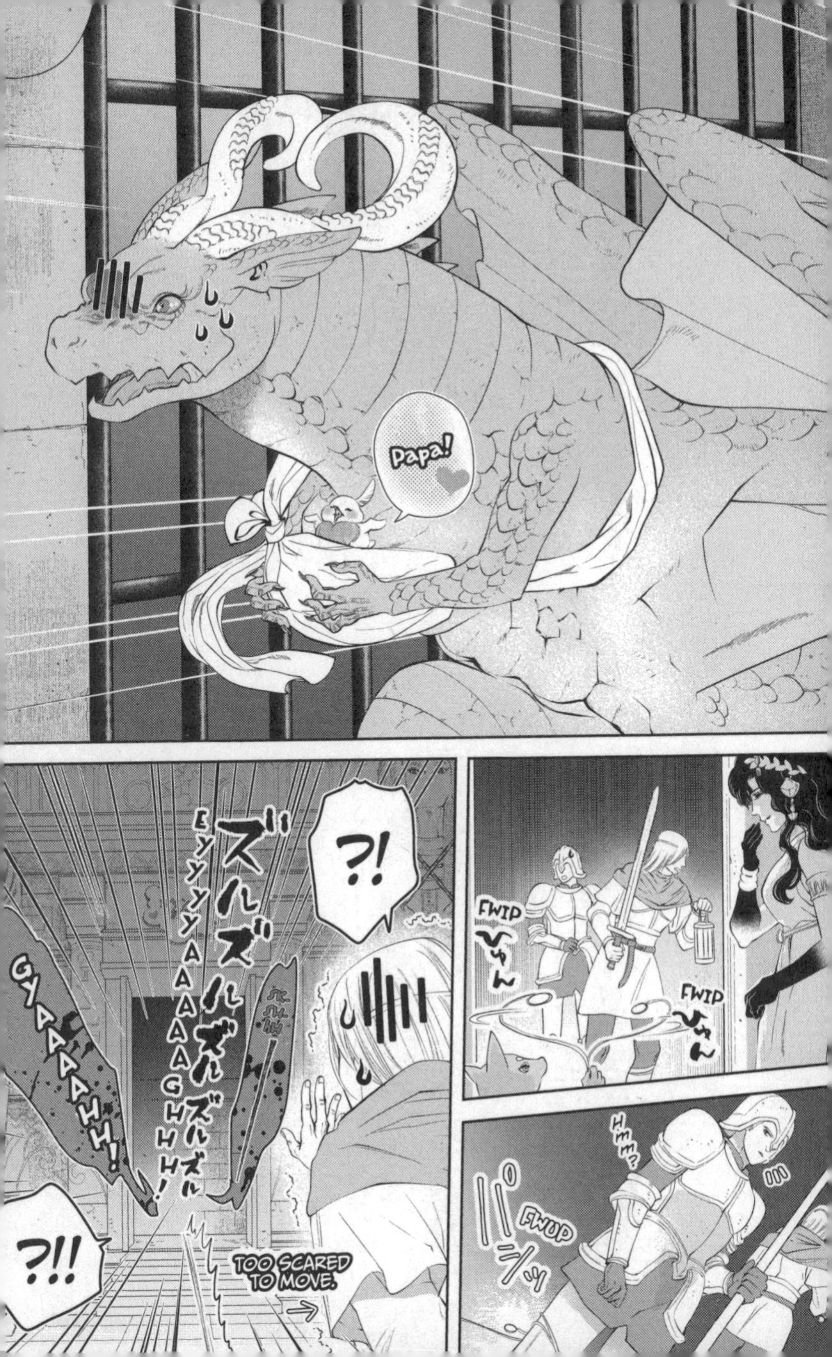

Papa!
FWIP
FWIP
Hmm?
FWUP
?!
EYYYYAAAAAAGHHHH!
SK-SHHH
GYAAAAAHH!
?!!
TOO SCARED TO MOVE.

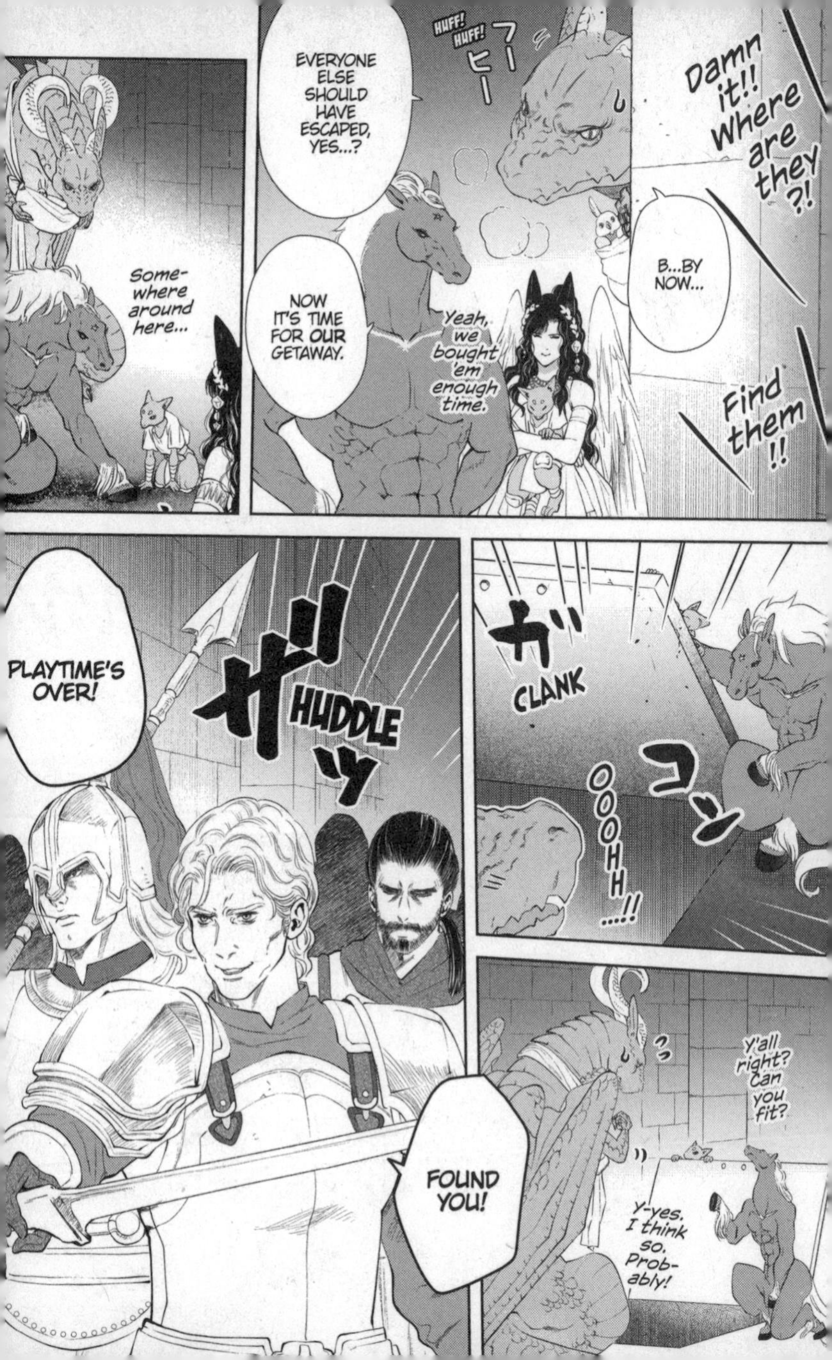
Damn it!! Where are they?!
B...BY NOW...
Find them!!
HUFF! HUFF!
フー ヒー
EVERYONE ELSE SHOULD HAVE ESCAPED, YES...?
NOW IT'S TIME FOR OUR GETAWAY.
Yeah, we bought 'em enough time.
Some-where around here...
ガッ
CLANK
ゴン
OOOHH...!!
Y'all right? Can you fit?
Y-yes. I think so. Probably!
ザッ
HUDDLE
PLAYTIME'S OVER!
FOUND YOU!

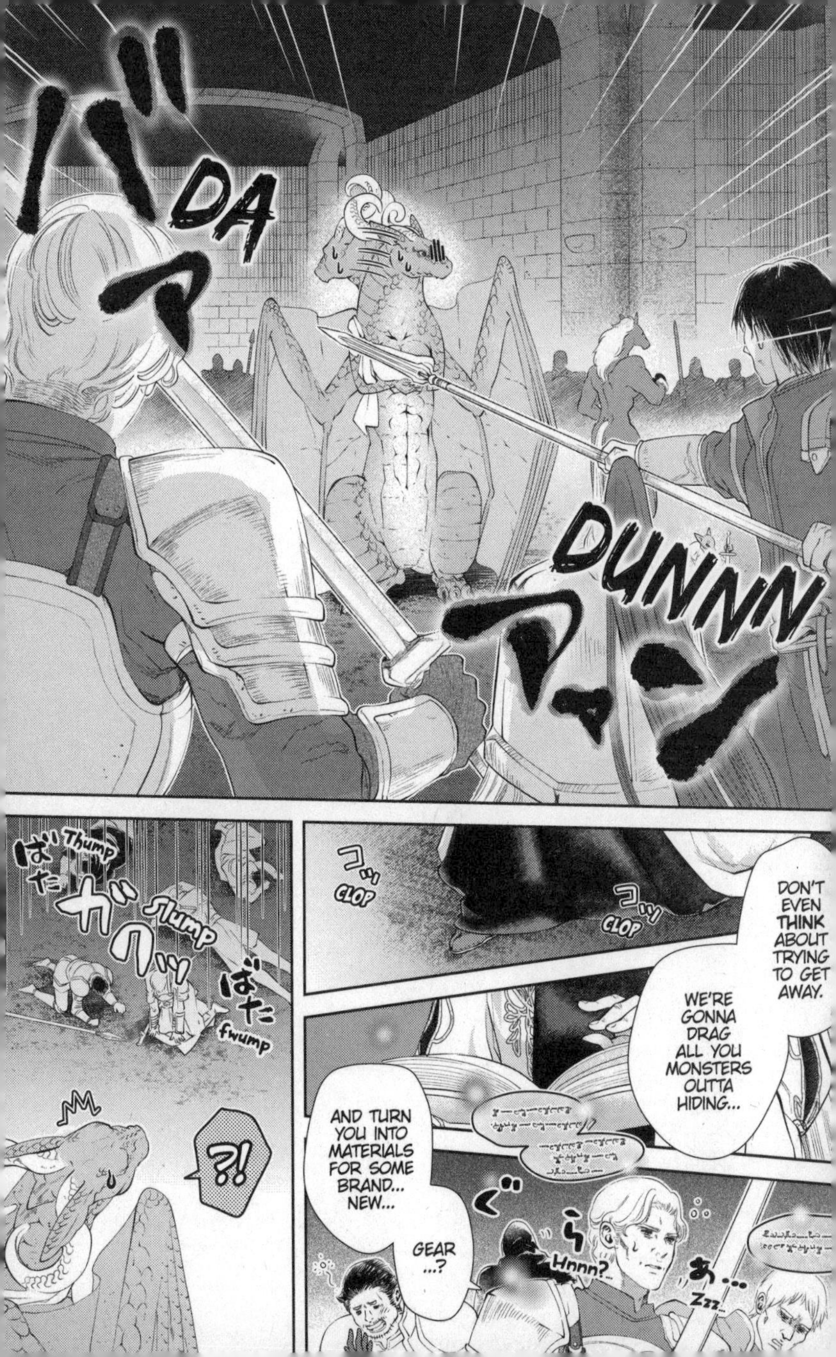
DA
DUNNN
CLOP
CLOP
DON'T EVEN THINK ABOUT TRYING TO GET AWAY.
WE'RE GONNA DRAG ALL YOU MONSTERS OUTTA HIDING...
AND TURN YOU INTO MATERIALS FOR SOME BRAND... NEW...
GEAR ...?
Hnnn?
Zzz...
Thump
Slump
fwump
?!

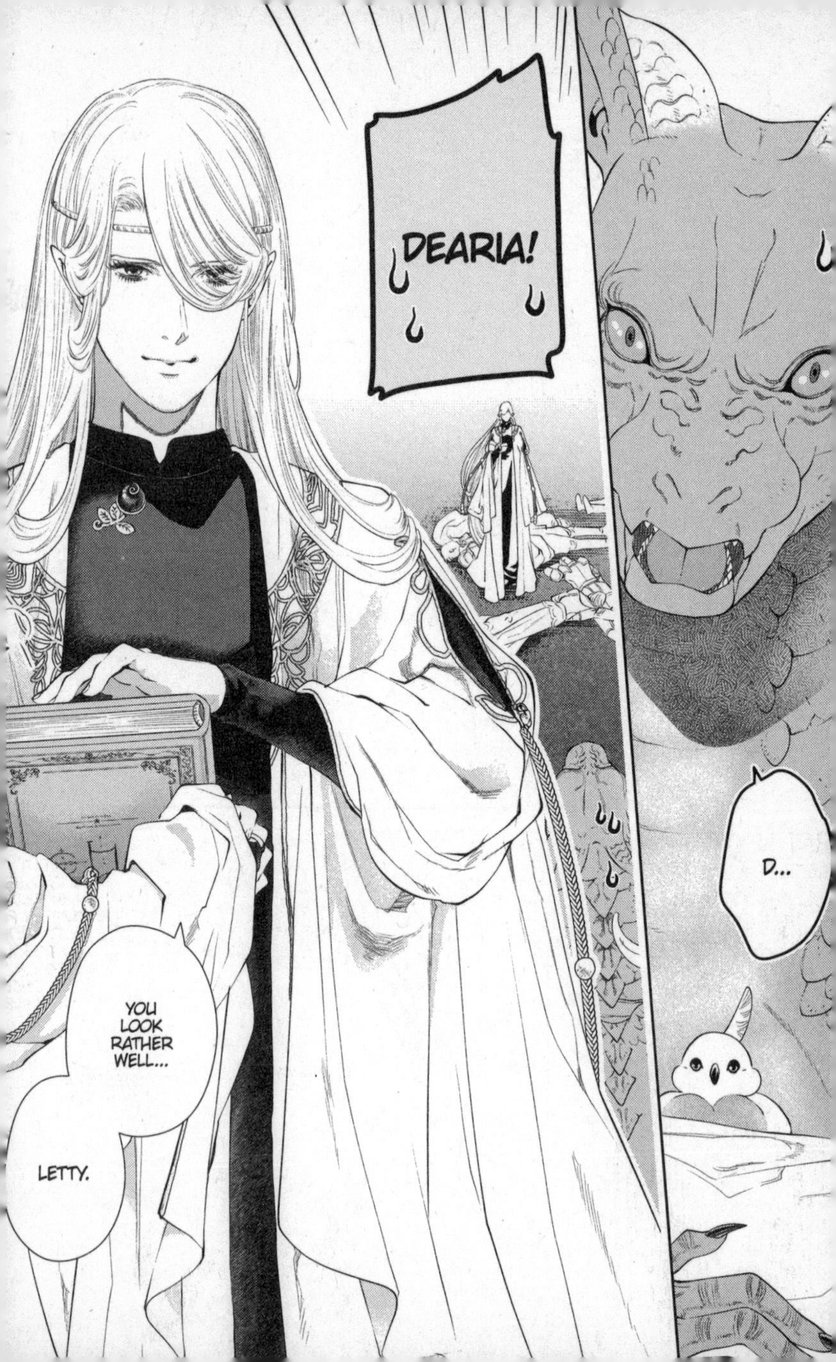
D...
DEARIA!
YOU LOOK RATHER WELL...
LETTY.

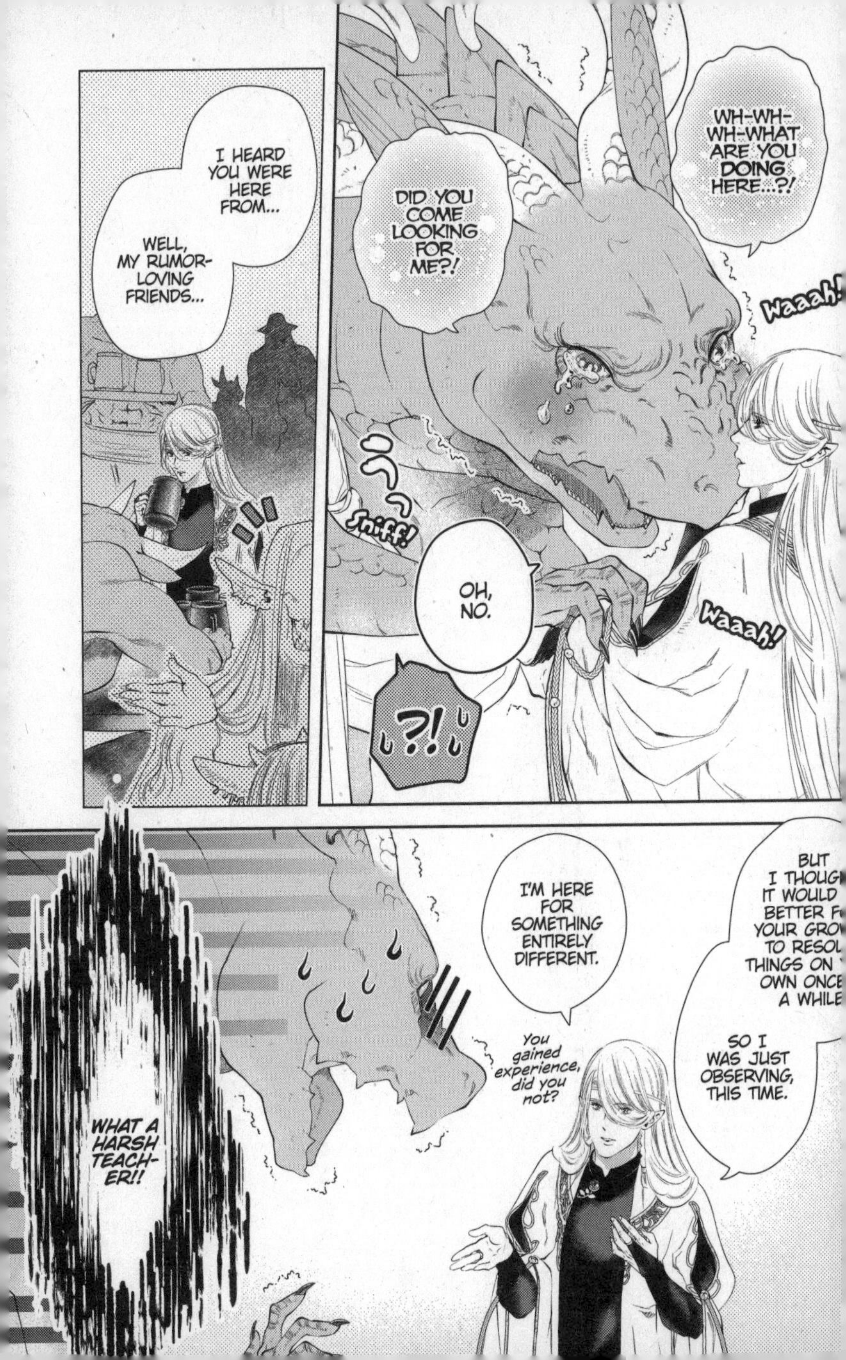

WH-WH-WH-WHAT ARE YOU DOING HERE...?!
DID YOU COME LOOKING FOR ME?!
Waaah!
うっ
Sniff!
OH, NO.
Waaah!
?!
I HEARD YOU WERE HERE FROM...
WELL, MY RUMOR-LOVING FRIENDS...
BUT I THOUG IT WOULD BETTER F YOUR GRO TO RESOL THINGS ON OWN ONCE A WHILE
SO I WAS JUST OBSERVING, THIS TIME.
I'M HERE FOR SOMETHING ENTIRELY DIFFERENT.
You gained experience, did you not?
WHAT A HARSH TEACHER!!

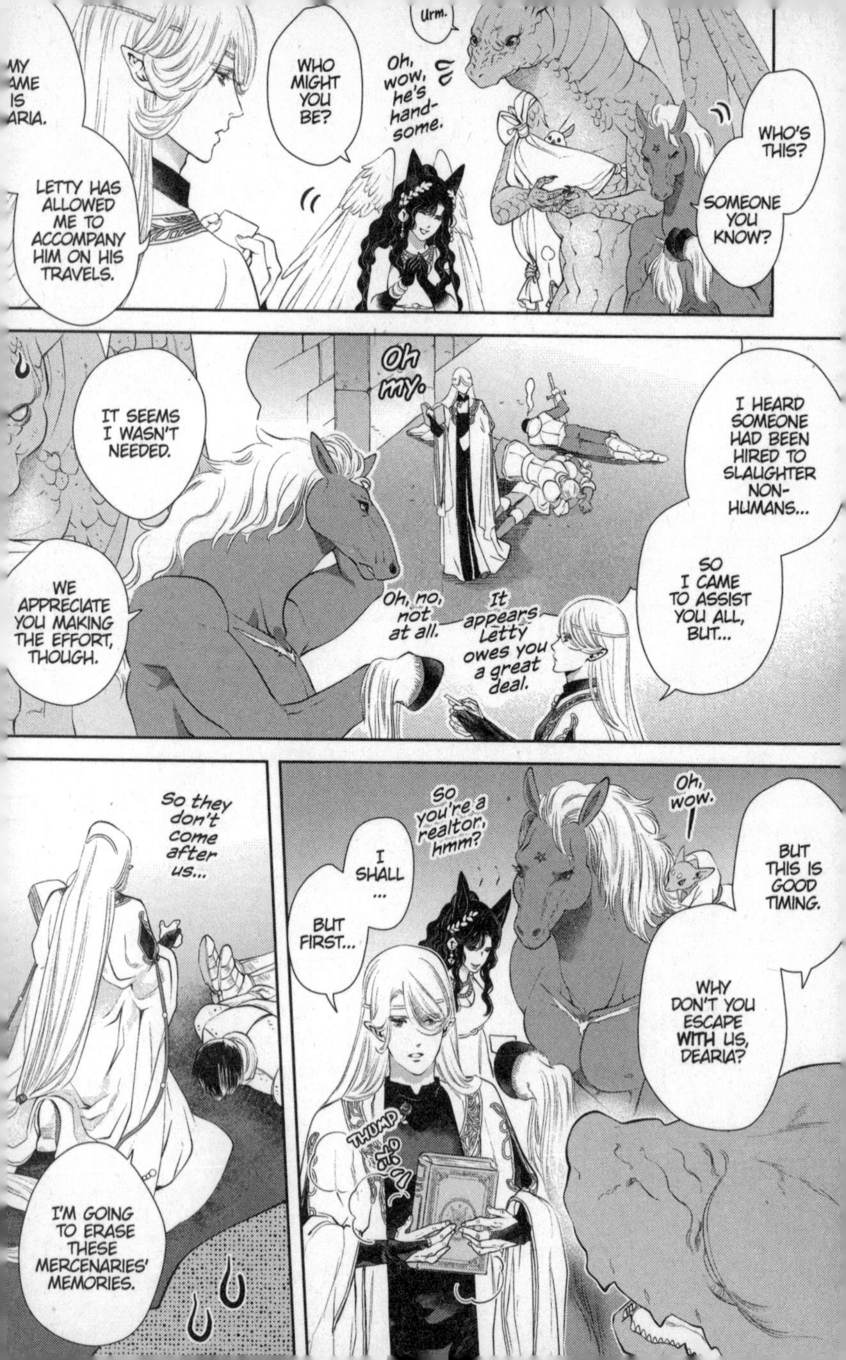
WHO'S THIS?
SOMEONE YOU KNOW?
Urm.
Oh, wow, he's handsome.
WHO MIGHT YOU BE?
MY AME IS ARIA.
LETTY HAS ALLOWED ME TO ACCOMPANY HIM ON HIS TRAVELS.
I HEARD SOMEONE HAD BEEN HIRED TO SLAUGHTER NON-HUMANS...
SO I CAME TO ASSIST YOU ALL, BUT...
Oh my.
It appears Letty owes you a great deal.
Oh, no, not at all.
IT SEEMS I WASN'T NEEDED.
WE APPRECIATE YOU MAKING THE EFFORT, THOUGH.
Oh, wow.
BUT THIS IS GOOD TIMING.
WHY DON'T YOU ESCAPE WITH US, DEARIA?
So you're a realtor, hmm?
I SHALL...
BUT FIRST...
THUMP
So they don't come after us...
I'M GOING TO ERASE THESE MERCENARIES' MEMORIES.

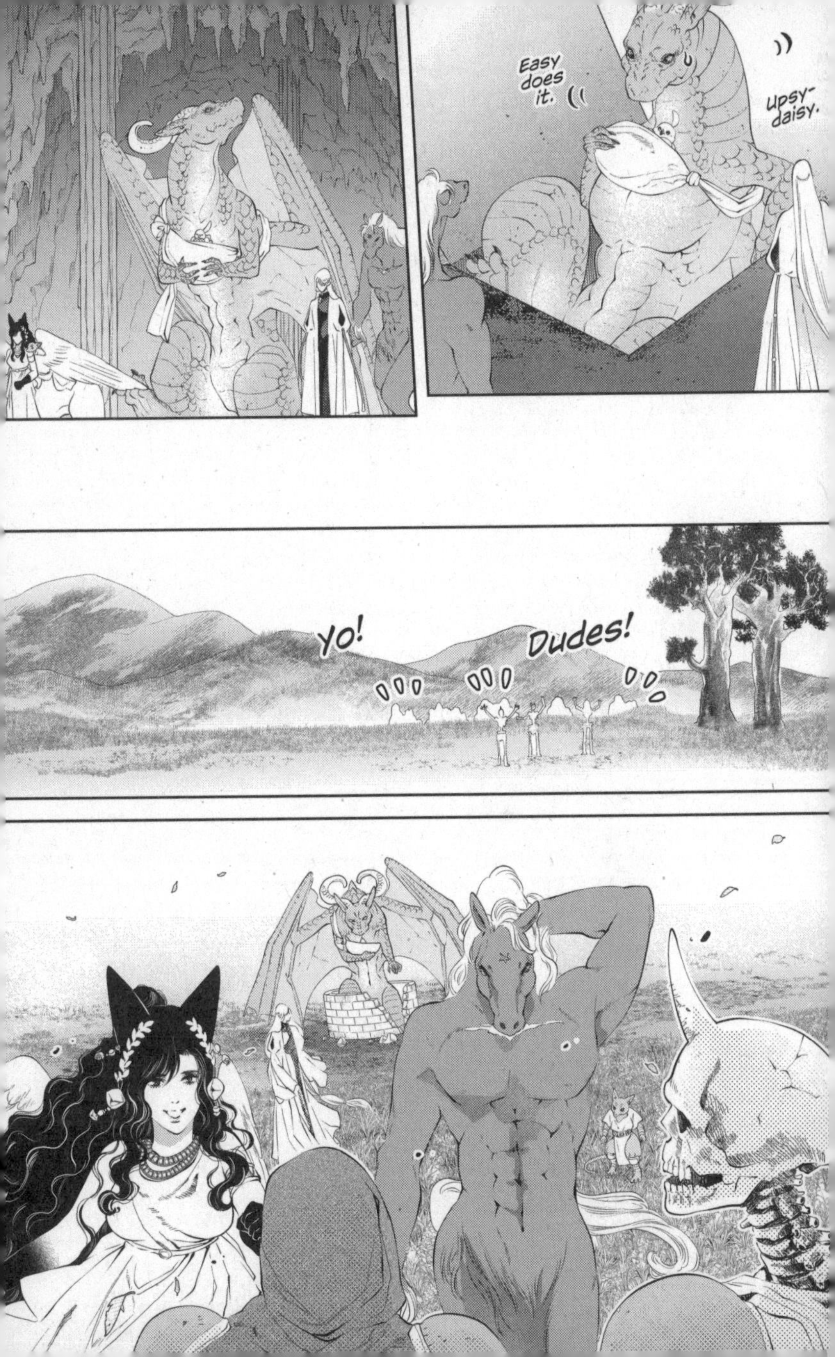
upsy-daisy.
Easy does it.
Dudes!
Yo!

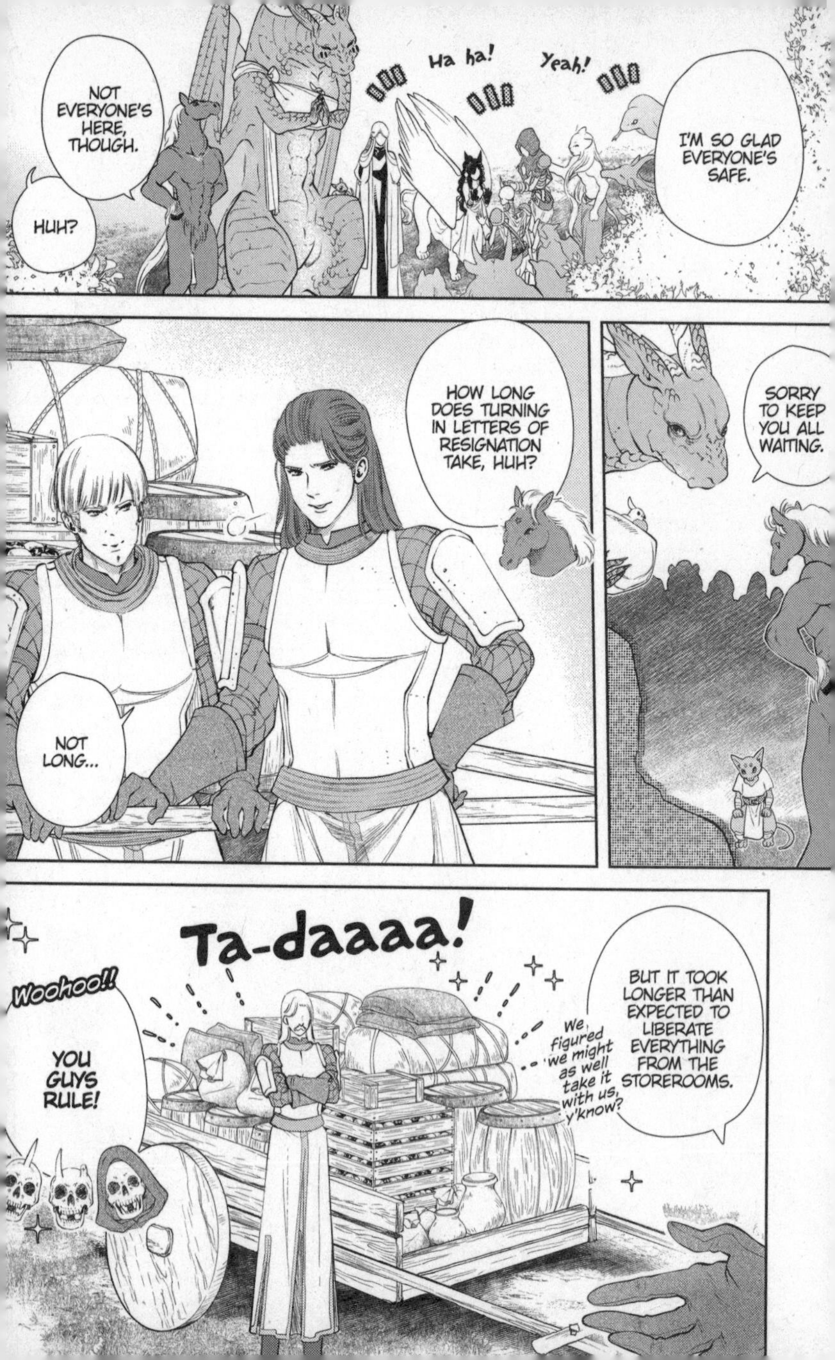
I'M SO GLAD EVERYONE'S SAFE.
Yeah!
Ha ha!
NOT EVERYONE'S HERE, THOUGH.
HUH?
SORRY TO KEEP YOU ALL WAITING.
HOW LONG DOES TURNING IN LETTERS OF RESIGNATION TAKE, HUH?
NOT LONG...
BUT IT TOOK LONGER THAN EXPECTED TO LIBERATE EVERYTHING FROM THE STOREROOMS.
We figured we might as well take it with us, y'know?
Ta-daaaa!
Woohoo!!
YOU GUYS RULE!

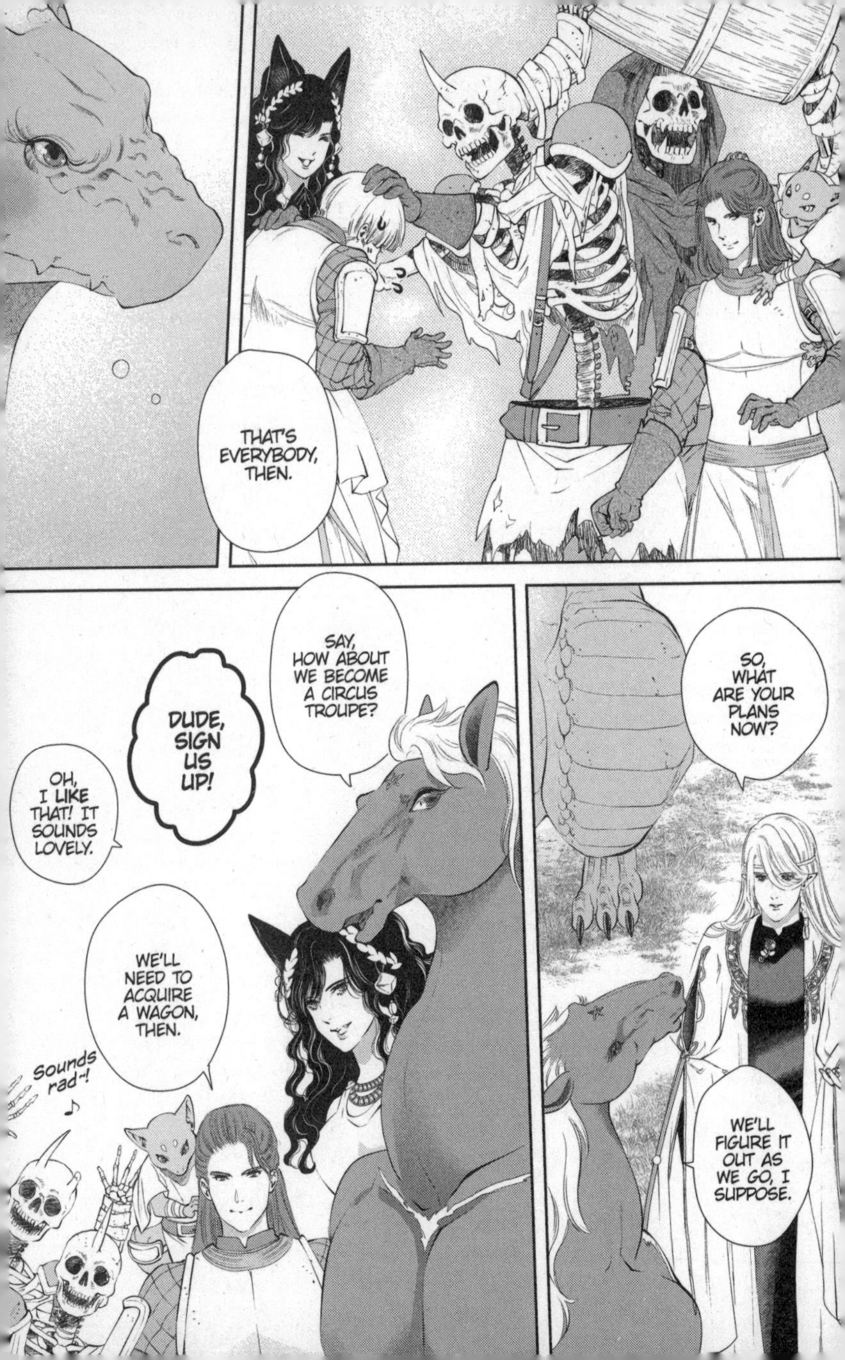
THAT'S EVERYBODY, THEN.
SO, WHAT ARE YOUR PLANS NOW?
WE'LL FIGURE IT OUT AS WE GO, I SUPPOSE.
SAY, HOW ABOUT WE BECOME A CIRCUS TROUPE?
DUDE, SIGN US UP!
OH, I LIKE THAT! IT SOUNDS LOVELY.
WE'LL NEED TO ACQUIRE A WAGON, THEN.
Sounds rad~! ♪

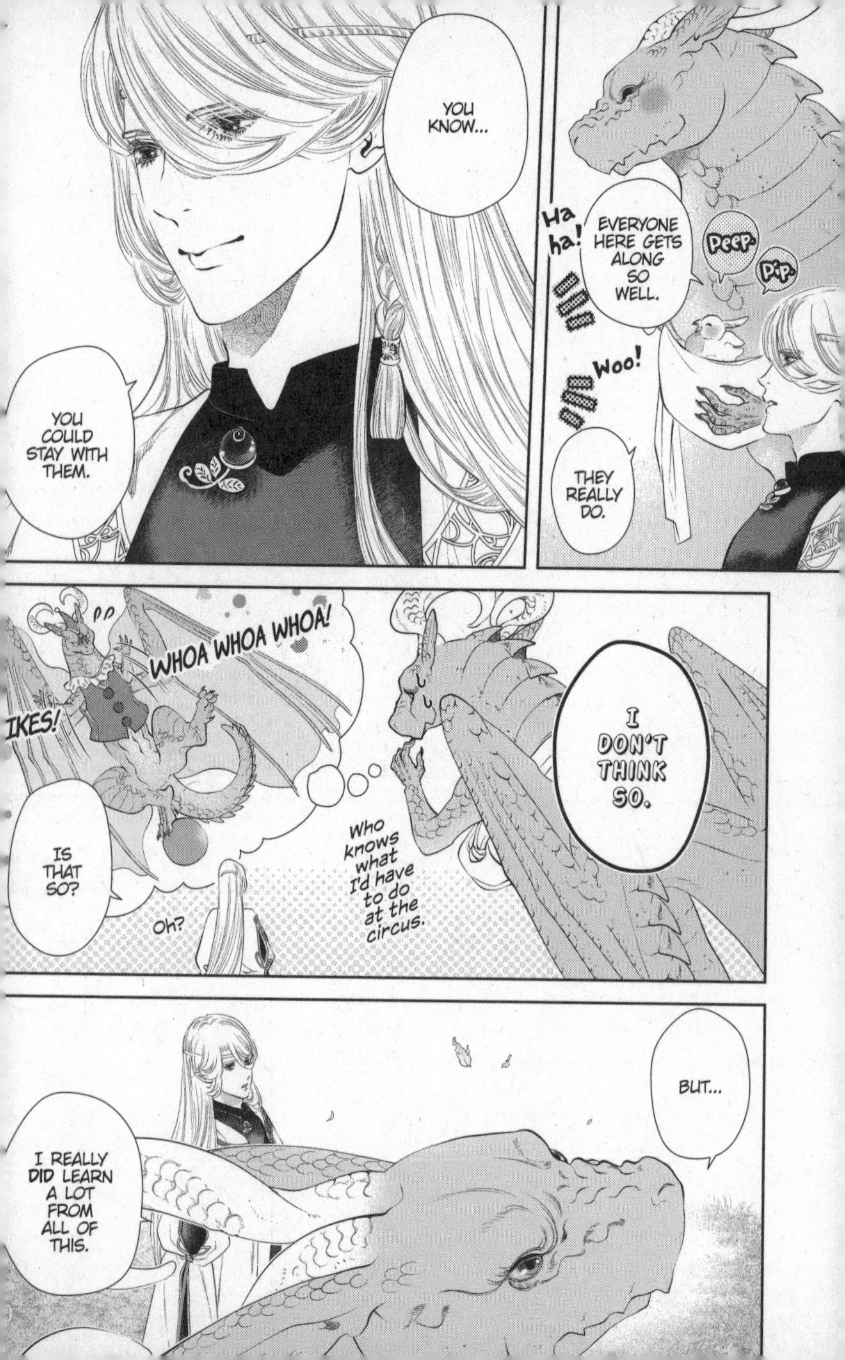

Ha ha!
EVERYONE HERE GETS ALONG SO WELL.
Peep.
Pip.
Woo!
THEY REALLY DO.
YOU KNOW...
YOU COULD STAY WITH THEM.
I DON'T THINK SO.
Who knows what I'd have to do at the circus.
WHOA WHOA WHOA!
IKES!
Oh?
IS THAT SO?
BUT...
I REALLY DID LEARN A LOT FROM ALL OF THIS.

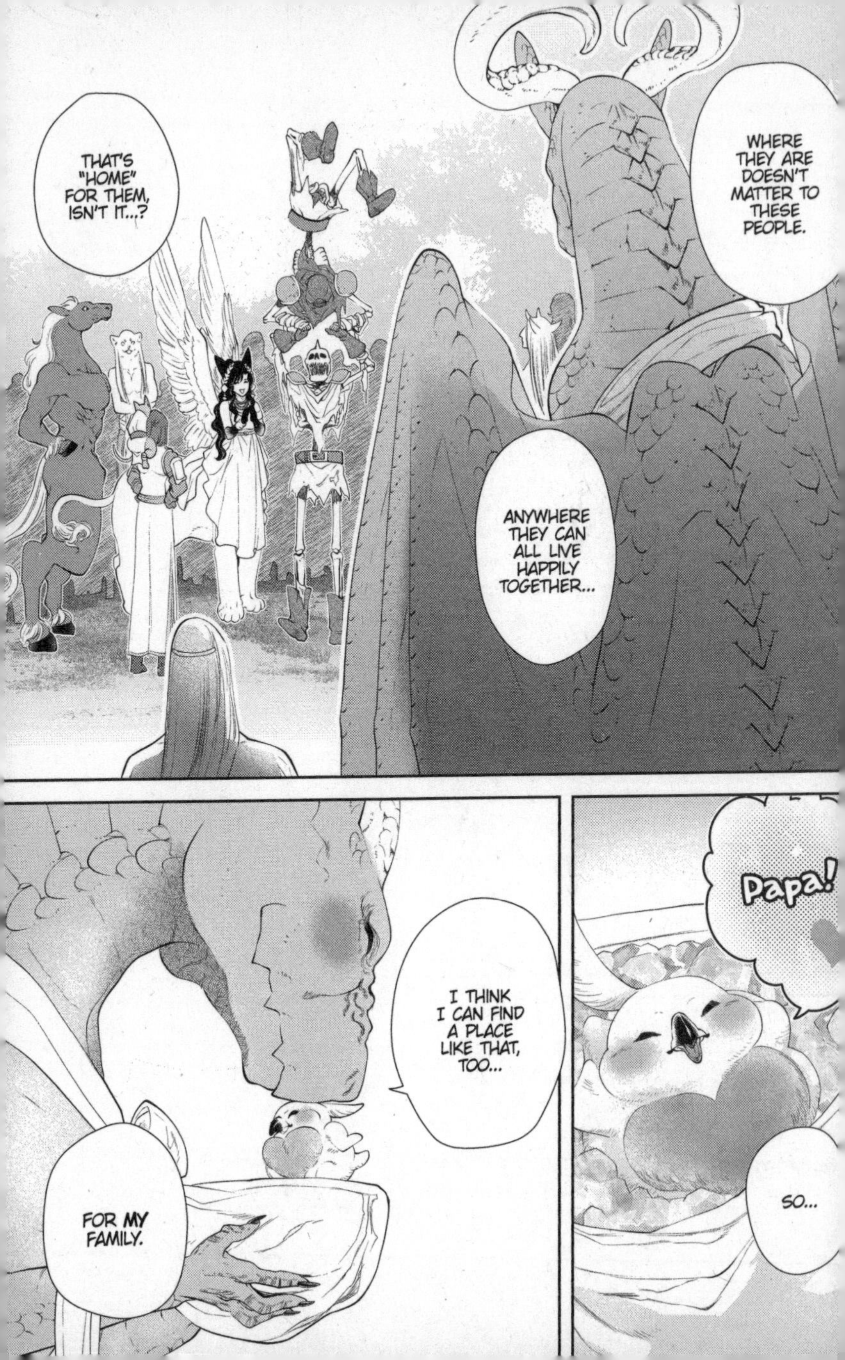
WHERE THEY ARE DOESN'T MATTER TO THESE PEOPLE.
ANYWHERE THEY CAN ALL LIVE HAPPILY TOGETHER...
THAT'S "HOME" FOR THEM, ISN'T IT...?
Papa!
SO...
I THINK I CAN FIND A PLACE LIKE THAT, TOO...
FOR MY FAMILY.

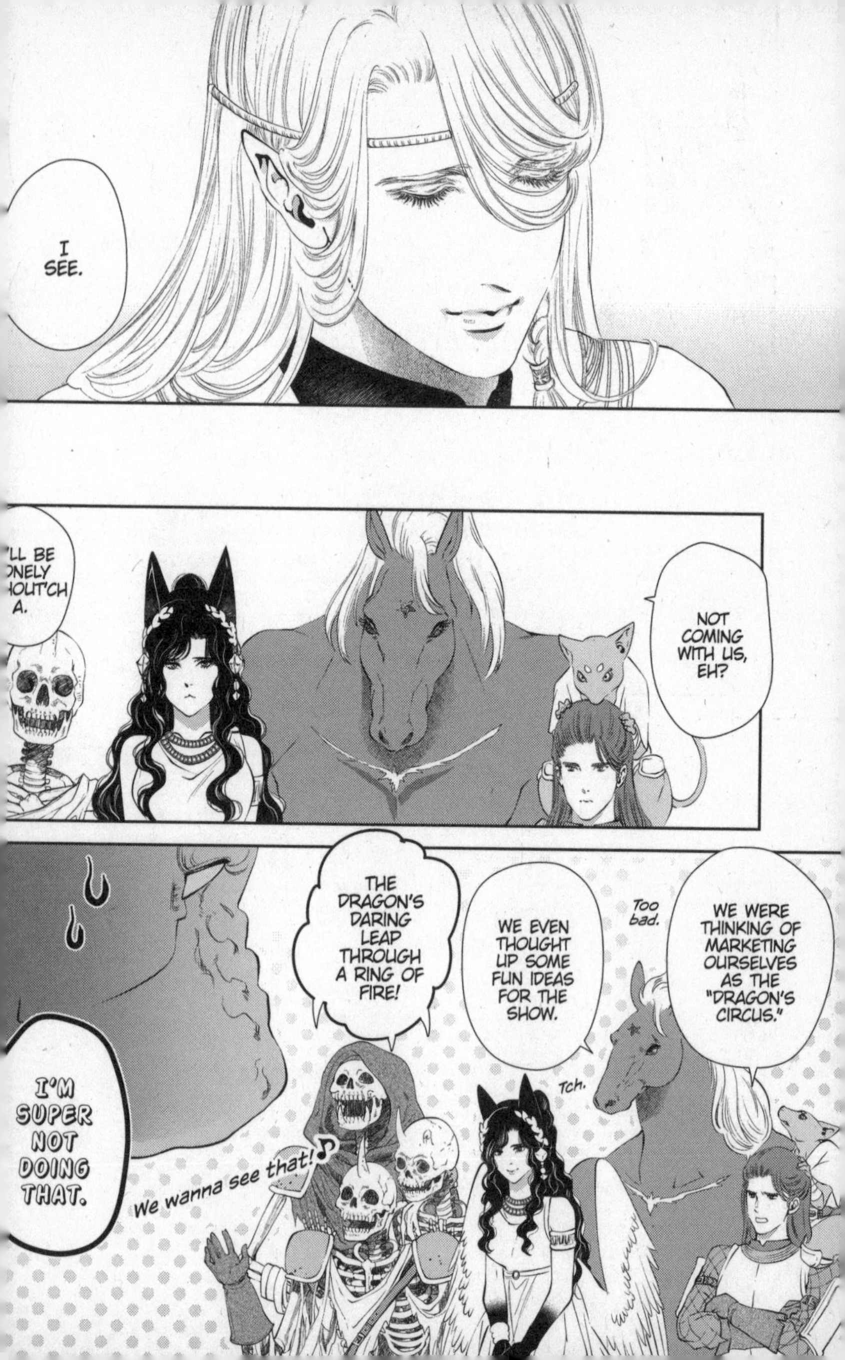
I SEE.
NOT COMING WITH US, EH?
'LL BE ONELY HOUT'CH A.
WE WERE THINKING OF MARKETING OURSELVES AS THE "DRAGON'S CIRCUS."
Too bad.
WE EVEN THOUGHT UP SOME FUN IDEAS FOR THE SHOW.
THE DRAGON'S DARING LEAP THROUGH A RING OF FIRE!
Tch.
We wanna see that!♪
I'M SUPER NOT DOING THAT.

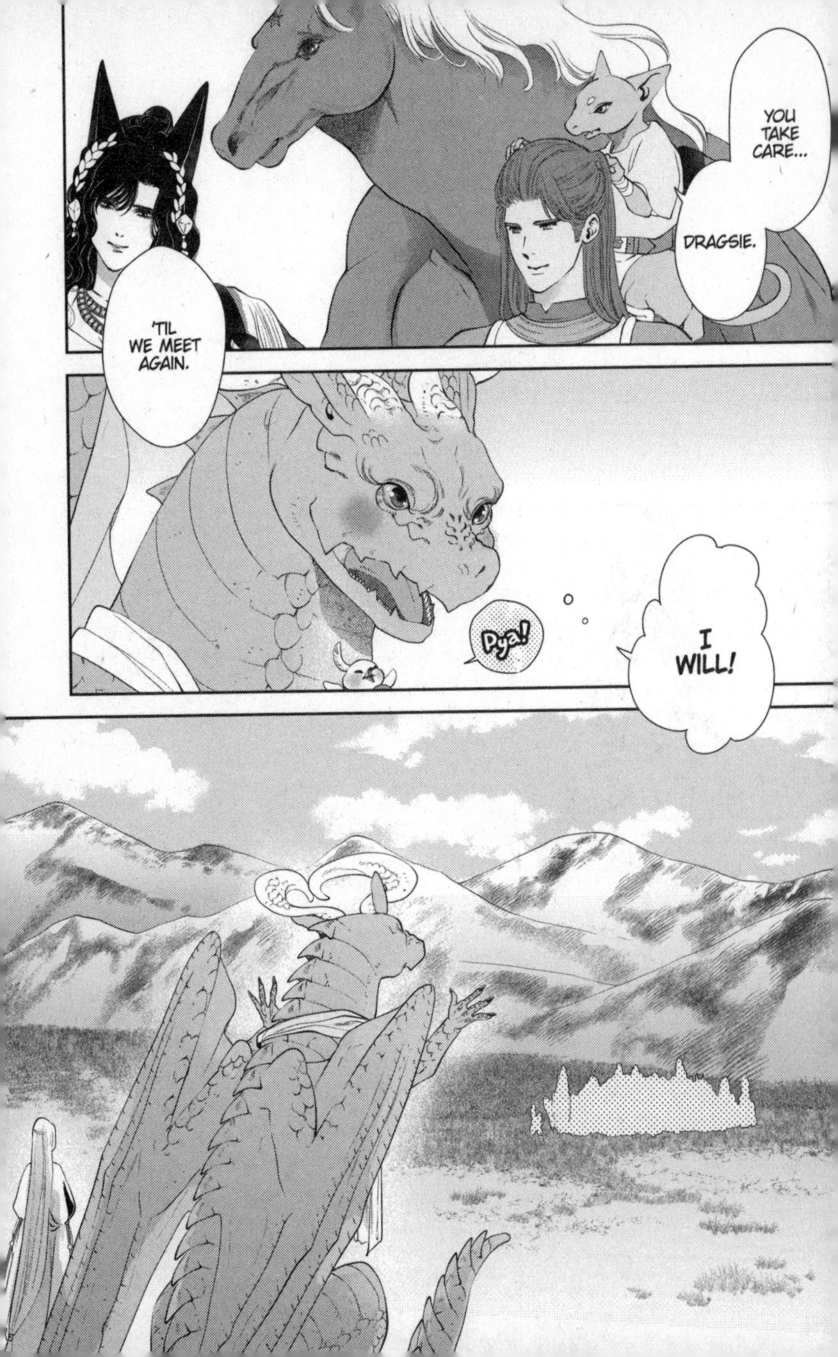
YOU TAKE CARE...
DRAGSIE.
'TIL WE MEET AGAIN.
I WILL!
Pya!

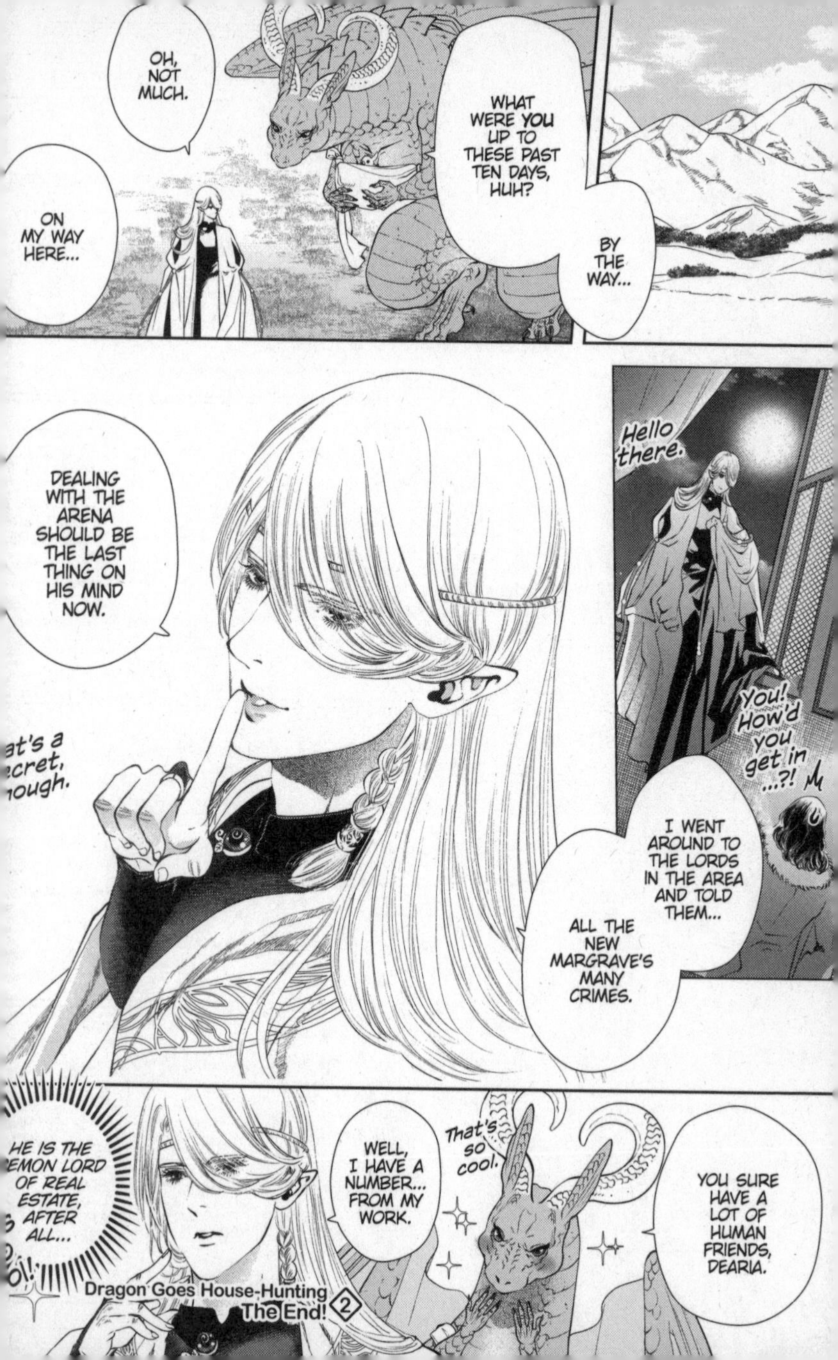
BY THE WAY...
WHAT WERE YOU UP TO THESE PAST TEN DAYS, HUH?
OH, NOT MUCH.
ON MY WAY HERE...
Hello there.
You! How'd you get in ...?!
I WENT AROUND TO THE LORDS IN THE AREA AND TOLD THEM...
ALL THE NEW MARGRAVE'S MANY CRIMES.
DEALING WITH THE ARENA SHOULD BE THE LAST THING ON HIS MIND NOW.
at's a cret, ough.
YOU SURE HAVE A LOT OF HUMAN FRIENDS, DEARIA.
That's so cool.
WELL, I HAVE A NUMBER... FROM MY WORK.
HE IS THE EMON LORD OF REAL ESTATE, AFTER ALL...
Dragon Goes House-Hunting
The End! 2

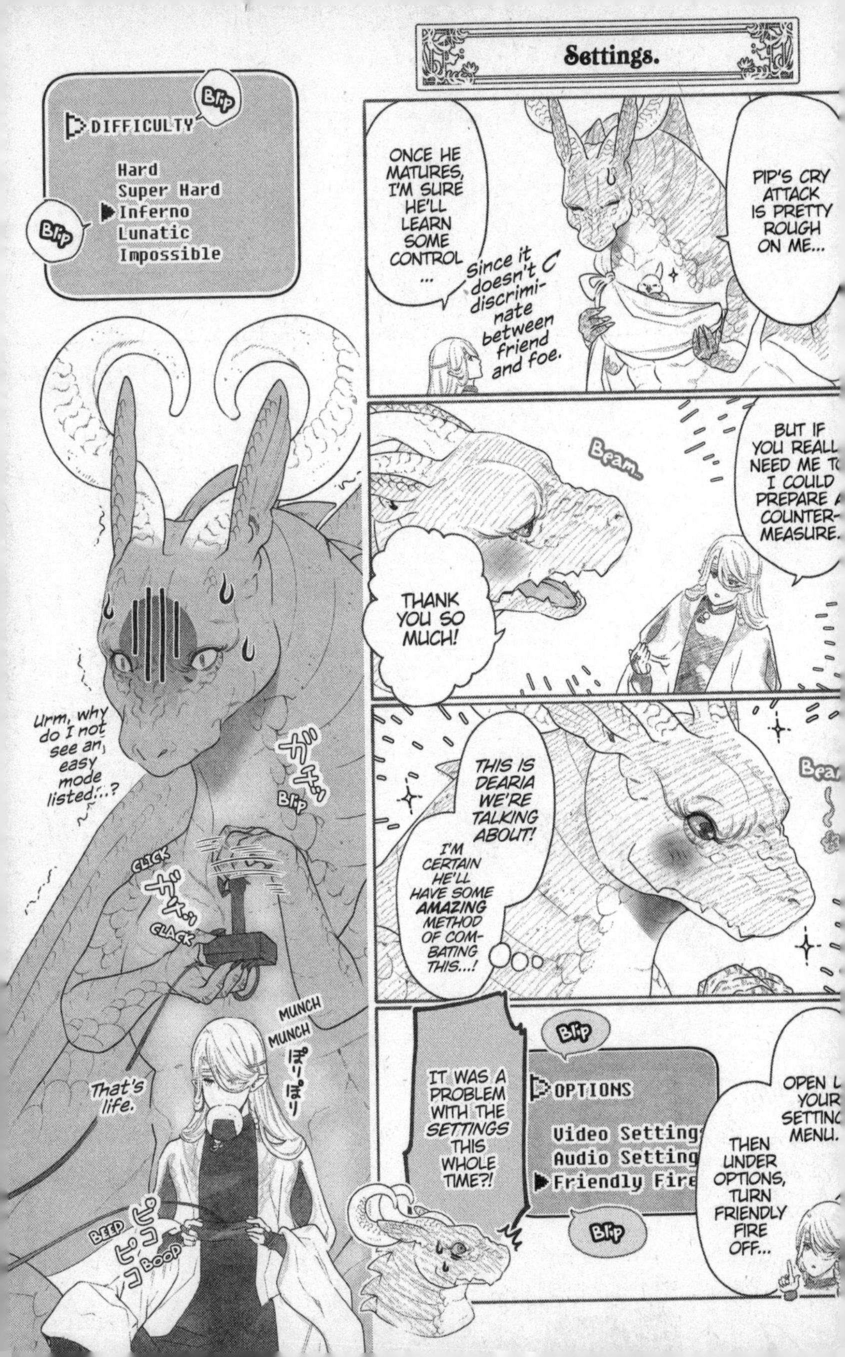
Settings.
PIP'S CRY ATTACK IS PRETTY ROUGH ON ME...
ONCE HE MATURES, I'M SURE HE'LL LEARN SOME CONTROL ...
Since it doesn't discriminate between friend and foe.
BUT IF YOU REALL NEED ME T I COULD PREPARE A COUNTER-MEASURE.
Beam...
THANK YOU SO MUCH!
Bea
THIS IS DEARIA WE'RE TALKING ABOUT!
I'M CERTAIN HE'LL HAVE SOME AMAZING METHOD OF COMBATING THIS...!
OPEN U YOUR SETTIN MENU.
THEN UNDER OPTIONS, TURN FRIENDLY FIRE OFF...
Blip
OPTIONS
Video Setting
Audio Setting
Friendly Fire
Blip
IT WAS A PROBLEM WITH THE SETTINGS THIS WHOLE TIME?!
Blip
DIFFICULTY
Hard
Super Hard
Inferno
Lunatic
Impossible
Blip
Urm, why do I not see an easy mode listed...?
ガチッ
Blip
CLICK
ガチャッ
CLACK
MUNCH MUNCH
ぽりぽり
That's life.
BEEP
ピコピコ
BOOP

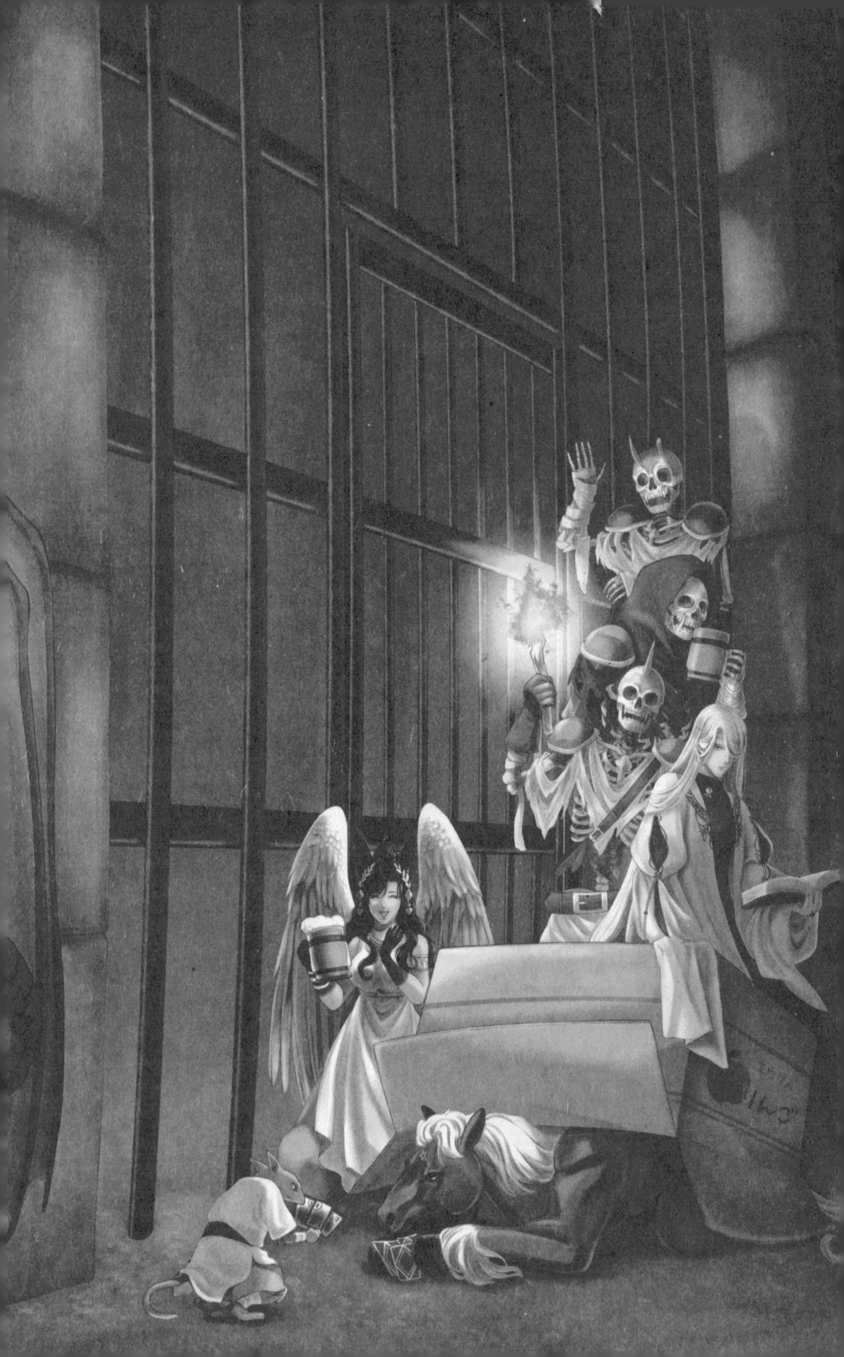

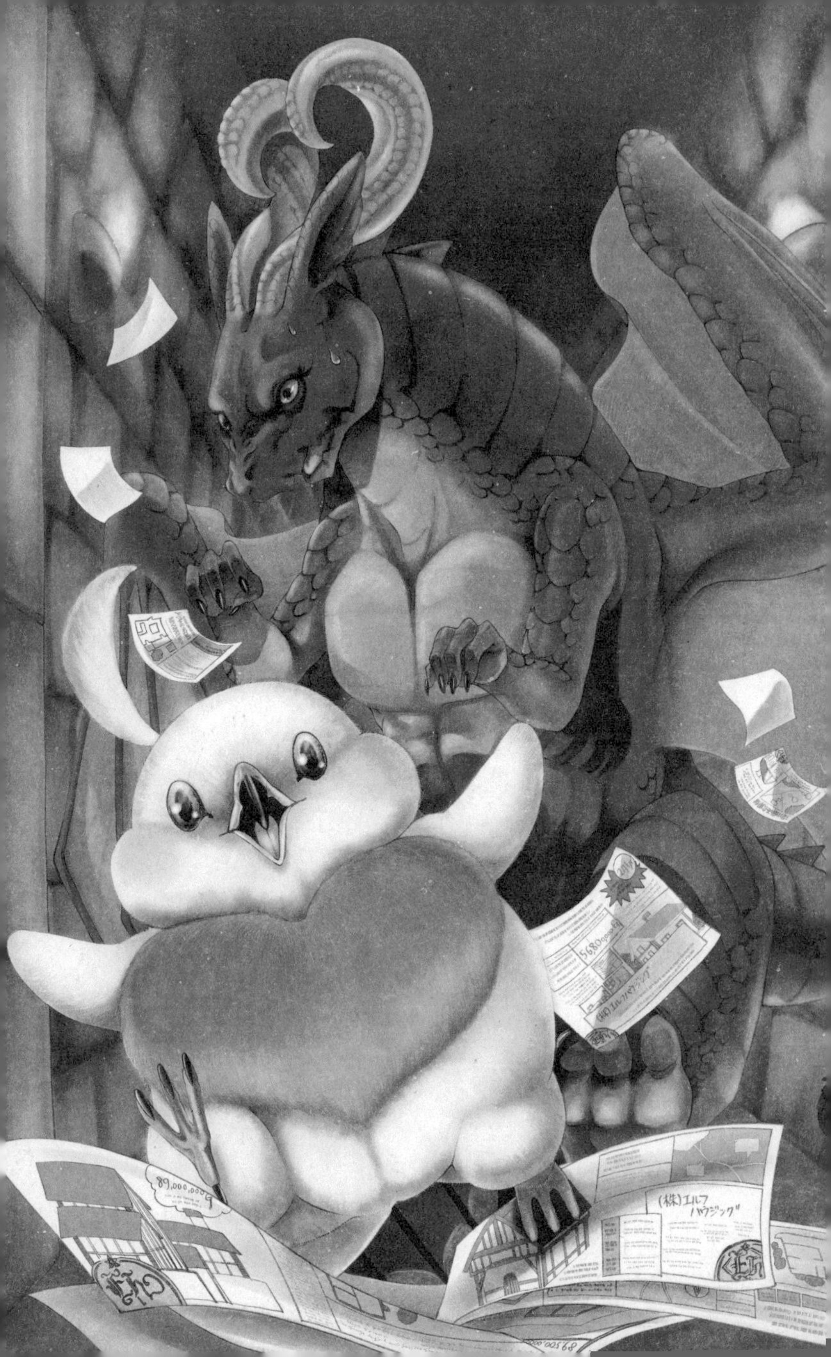
89,000,000
(株)エルフ
ハウジング

Dragon Goes House-Hunting

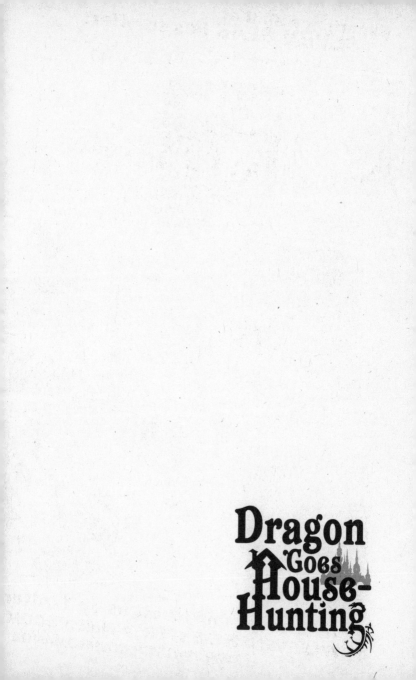

SEVEN SEAS ENTERTAINMENT PRESENTS

VOLUME 2

Dragon Goes House-Hunting

story by **KAWO TANUKI**   art by **CHOCO AYA**

TRANSLATION
Nan Rymer

ADAPTATION
T Campbell

LETTERING
Alexandra Gunawan

COVER DESIGN
KC Fabellon

PROOFREADER
**Danielle King
Shanti Whitesides**

EDITOR
J.P. Sullivan

PRODUCTION ASSISTANT
CK Russell

PRODUCTION MANAGER
Lissa Pattillo

EDITOR-IN-CHIEF
Adam Arnold

PUBLISHER
Jason DeAngelis

DRAGON, IE WO KAU. VOLUME 2
© Kawo Tanuki 2018
© Choco Aya 2018
Originally published in Japan in 2018 by MAG Garden Corporation, Tokyo.
English translation rights arranged through TOHAN CORPORATION, Tokyo.

Seven Seas books may be purchased in bulk for promotional, educational, or
business use. Please contact your local bookseller or the Macmillan Corporate
and Premium Sales Department at 1-800-221-7945, extension 5442, or by
e-mail at MacmillanSpecialMarkets@macmillan.com.

Seven Seas and the Seven Seas logo are trademarks of
Seven Seas Entertainment, LLC. All rights reserved.

ISBN: 978-1-626929-79-1

Printed in Canada

First Printing: March 2019

10 9 8 7 6 5 4 3 2 1

FOLLOW US ONLINE: *www.sevenseasentertainment.com*

READING DIRECTIONS

This book reads from *right to left*, Japanese style.
If this is your first time reading manga, you start
reading from the top right panel on each page and
take it from there. If you get lost, just follow the
numbered diagram here. It may seem backwards at
first, but you'll get the hang of it! Have fun!!

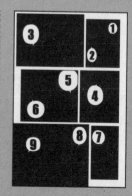